PEARSON EDUCATION
AP* TEST PREP SERIES
AP EUROPEAN HISTORY

FOR

THE WESTERN HERITAGE
Since 1300

10e AP* Edition

Written by:

Matthew Tippens

Prentice Hall

Boston Columbus Indianapolis New York San Francisco Upper Saddle River
Amsterdam Cape Town Dubai London Madrid Milan Munich Paris Montréal Toronto
Delhi Mexico City São Paulo Sydney Hong Kong Seoul Singapore Taipei Tokyo

Prentice Hall
is an imprint of

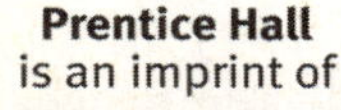

www.PearsonSchool.com/Advanced

ISBN 10: 0-13-136928-8
ISBN 13: 978-0-13-136928-3

CONTENTS

ABOUT YOUR PEARSON AP TEST PREP SERIES*

Pearson is the leading publisher of textbooks worldwide. With operations on every continent, we make it our business to understand the changing needs of students at every level, from kindergarten to college. This gives us a unique insight into what kind of study materials work for students.

We talk to customers every day, soliciting feedback on our books. We think that this makes us especially qualified to offer Pearson AP* Test Prep Series Workbooks tied to some of our best-selling textbooks.

We know that as you study for your AP course, you're preparing along the way for the AP exam. By tying the material in the book directly to AP course goals and exam topics, we help you to focus your time most efficiently. And that's a good thing!

The AP exam is an important milestone in your education. A high score will position you optimally for college acceptance—and possibly will give you college credits that put you a step ahead. Our goal at Pearson is to provide you with the tools you need to excel on the exam … the rest is up to you.

Good luck!

PART I

*INTRODUCTION TO THE AP**
EUROPEAN HISTORY EXAMINATION

This section overviews the advanced placement program, introduces the types of questions you will encounter on the exam, and provides helpful test-taking strategies. It also explains the grading procedure used by the College Board. Finally, a correlation chart is provided that shows where key information commonly tested on the examination is covered in *The Western Heritage*. Review this section carefully before trying the sample items in the following parts.

THE ADVANCED PLACEMENT PROGRAM*

You are probably reading this book for at least a couple of reasons. You may be a student in an Advanced Placement (AP) European History class, and you have questions about how the AP program works. Another reason is probably that you'll be taking an AP European History Examination, and you want to know more about *that*. Well, you've come to the right place. The first part of this book gets you acquainted with the AP European History course and the AP European History Exam. You'll learn helpful details about the different formats—multiple-choice questions and free-response questions—that you'll encounter on the exam. In addition, you'll find dozens of test-taking strategies that will guide you in preparing for and then taking the test. A correlation chart at the end of Part I shows how to use your textbook, *The Western Heritage,* to find the information you'll need to know to score well on the AP European History Exam. By the way, this chart is useful, too, in helping you to identify (and then to disregard) any extraneous material that *won't* be tested. Also in Part I, you'll find information that clarifies the criteria that will be used to evaluate your work on the exam.

The AP program is sponsored by the College Board, a nonprofit organization that oversees college admissions examinations. (The College Board is composed of college and high school teachers and administrators.) The AP program offers thirty-five college-level courses to qualified high school students. If you receive a grade of 3 or higher on an AP exam, you may be eligible for college credit, depending on the policies of the institution you plan to attend. Approximately 3,000 college and universities around the world grant credit to students who have performed well on AP exams. If you are taking several AP courses and if you score well on multiple AP exams, you may even be eligible to enter college as a sophomore. Some institutions grant sophomore status to incoming first-year students who have demonstrated mastery of many AP subjects. In addition, the College Board confers a number of AP Scholar Awards on students who score 3 or higher on three or more AP exams. Additional awards are available to students who receive very high grades on four or five AP exams.

The College Board appoints committees to develop examinations for each of the nineteen subjects in which it administers AP exams. If you're interested in learning more about how the European History Development Committee designs the AP European History Exam, ask your teacher for a copy of *Advanced Placement Course Description: European History.* You can order a copy directly from the College Board, as well.

Why Take an AP Course?

You may be taking one or more AP courses simply because you are thirsty for knowledge. Of course, the fact that colleges look favorably on applicants who have AP courses on their secondary school transcripts is another powerful incentive! Because AP classes usually involve rigorous lessons, a great deal of homework, and many tests, they signal to college admissions officers that AP students are willing to work hard to get the most from their education. Because AP course work is more difficult than average high school work, many admissions officers evaluate AP grades on a kind of curve—if you receive a *B* in an AP class, for example, it might carry the same weight as an *A* in a regular high school class.

Your AP European History course prepares you for many of the skills you will need in college. For example, your teacher may assign research papers and encourage you to use resources outside the scope of your textbook. Some of these resources may be primary sources that permit you to analyze events as a historian would. Other class assignments may require you to write longer-than-usual essays on historical subjects. The AP European History course will challenge you to gather and consider information in new—and sometimes unfamiliar—ways. You can feel good knowing that your ability to use these methods and skills will give you a leg up as you enter college.

Each college or university decides whether or not to grant college credit for an AP course, and each bases this decision on what it considers satisfactory grades on AP exams. Depending on what college you attend and what area of study you pursue, your decision to take the AP European History Exam could end up saving you tuition money. You can contact schools directly to find out their guidelines for accepting AP credits.

Taking an AP Examination

Your AP teacher or school guidance counselor can give you information on how to sign up for an AP exam. Remember, the deadline to sign up and pay the fees for the exam is usually in January, four months before the actual date of the exam in May. If, after taking the exam, you want to have your score report sent to additional schools besides those you named on your registration—or if you want to withhold or cancel your score—you will need to notify the College Board by June 15. Your exam grades will be sent to you by mail in early-mid July. However, for an additional fee, Educational Testing Service (the organization that develops and scores tests for the College Board) will release your score to you over the phone around July 1st. If your school does not administer the AP exam, your teacher or guidance counselor can help you find a nearby school that does. If you continue to have difficulty determining what schools in your region offer the exam, you can always visit the College Board's website (*www.collegeboard.com*) for more information. The cost of the exam frequently changes and can differ depending on the number of exams taken. However, the 2010 cost of a single exam is $86. If you feel that you cannot afford this fee, you may apply to the College Board for a fee reduction based on your financial need.

AP European History: Course Goals

One of the central goals of the AP program in European History is to provide students with a basic narrative of the cultural, economic, political, and social developments in Europe that played a fundamental role in shaping our world. In addition, the College Board's stated goals include helping you to develop:

- an understanding of some of the principal themes in modern European history;
- an ability to analyze historical evidence;
- an ability to analyze and to express historical understanding in writing.

No doubt, AP European History courses vary somewhat from teacher to teacher and from school to school. Yet the focus of your course should reflect these goals, and the instruction you receive will grow out of these basic principles. The European History Development Committee has created a list of major historical themes and has divided them into three distinct groups: intellectual and cultural history, political and diplomatic history, and social and economic history. These themes will be the focus of your AP European History course. Many will be revisited in questions on the AP European History Exam. Here is a list of those themes in their respective historical groupings.

Intellectual and Cultural History
- Changes in religious thought and institutions
- The secularization of learning and culture
- Scientific and technological developments and their consequences
- Major trends in literature and the arts
- Intellectual and cultural developments and their relationship to social values and political events
- Developments in social, economic, and political thought
- Developments in literacy, education, and communication
- The diffusion of new intellectual concepts among different social groups
- Changes in elite and popular culture, such as the development of new attitudes toward religion, family, work, and ritual
- The impact of global expansion on European culture

Political and Diplomatic History
- The rise and functioning of the modern state in its various forms
- Relations between Europe and other parts of the world: colonialism, imperialism, decolonization, and global interdependence
- The evolution of political elites and the development of political parties and ideologies
- The extension and limitation of rights and liberties (personal, civic, economic, and political); majority and minority political persecutions
- The growth and changing forms of nationalism
- Forms of political protest, reform, and revolution
- The relationship between domestic and foreign policies
- Efforts to restrain conflict: treaties, balance-of-power diplomacy, and international organizations
- War and civil conflict: origins, developments, technology, and their consequences

Social and Economic History
- The character of and changes in agricultural production and organization
- The role of urbanization in transforming cultural values and social relationships
- The shift in social structures from hierarchical orders to modern social classes: the changing distribution of wealth and poverty
- The influence of sanitation and health care practices on society: food supply, diet, famine, disease, and their impact
- The development of commercial practices, patterns of mass production and consumption, and their economic and social impact
- Changing definitions of and attitudes toward mainstream and minority groups
- The origins, development, and consequences of industrialization
- Changes in the demographic structure of Europe: their causes and consequences
- Gender roles and their influence on work, social structure, family structure, and interest group formation
- The growth of competition and interdependence in national and world markets
- Private and state roles in economic activity
- The development of racial and ethnic group identities

Using class lectures, assignments, and activities, you can immerse yourself in all three aspects of European history. All of your hard work—including extensive classroom preparation and your own regular practice and study—will pay off in May. This work will be the foundation for your success on the AP European History Exam.

UNDERSTANDING THE AP EUROPEAN HISTORY EXAMINATION

The AP European History Exam incorporates artistic, cartographic, and statistical materials. This cross-disciplinary approach reflects the methods used today in colleges and universities to present historical subject matter.

You're probably aware that in general AP exams are long. In fact, the AP European History Exam takes three hours and five minutes. It consists of a multiple-choice section and a free-response section. You can expect to see diagrams, artwork, cartoons, maps, photographs, and graphs in both sections of the test. At the core of the examination are questions concerning Europe's intellectual, cultural, political, diplomatic, social, and economic history. You should be prepared to demonstrate your awareness of chronology, as well as your understanding of major events and developments in European history from 1450 to the present. Although you should be familiar with elements of the late medieval period that had an impact on events after 1450, you will *not* be asked questions on pre-1450 material.

Section I: Multiple-Choice Questions

The first section of the exam consists of eighty multiple-choice questions designed to test your knowledge of European history from the Renaissance to the present. You will have fifty-five minutes to complete Section I. This portion of the exam is followed by a five- or ten-minute break—the only official break during the examination. The directions for the multiple-choice section of the test are straightforward and similar to the following:

> ***Directions:*** Each of the questions or incomplete statements below is followed by five suggested answers or completions. Select the one that is best in each case and then fill in the corresponding oval on the answer sheet.

Roughly half of the multiple-choice questions cover the period from 1450 to 1815 (see chapters 9–20 in *The Western Heritage*), and the other half cover the period from 1815 to the present (see chapters 20–31). These eighty multiple-choice questions will test your knowledge of European history in the three thematic groupings mentioned earlier—intellectual and cultural history, political and diplomatic history, and social and economic history. The College Board publishes guidelines that tell approximately how many questions from each grouping will be included in the multiple-choice section of the AP European History Exam. You can expect that 20–30% of Section I (16–24 questions) will deal with cultural and intellectual themes; 30–40% of Section I (24–32 questions) will cover political and diplomatic themes; and 30–40% of Section I (24–32 questions) will examine social and economic themes. (Of course, some questions will draw on your knowledge of more than one period or theme.) You may not be familiar with *all* of the material covered on this portion of the test, but you should be acquainted with most of it.

Section I is organized in a fairly consistent way. That is, the eighty multiple-choice questions proceed generally in order of difficulty, with the easiest questions appearing at the beginning of the test and the most difficult questions appearing at the end. Furthermore, questions are arranged in groups of four to seven. The related questions within each grouping are presented roughly in chronological order. However, you may notice abrupt breaks in chronology between one group of questions and the next. Remember, too, that each new group of questions will be more difficult than the previous group.

It will probably not surprise you to read that not all multiple-choice questions are the same. In fact, the AP European History Exam will contain six types of multiple-choice-questions, as listed and described below: identification questions, "NOT/EXCEPT" questions, reading/quotation questions, analysis questions, skill-based questions (including those using maps, graphs, and charts), and illustration-based questions (including those using cartoons, posters, photographs, and images of visual art works).

Identification Questions

About 45% of the questions you will encounter in Section I will ask you to identify a person or event and to connect this person or event to a political, intellectual, or social development. Since these questions tend to be very direct and require little or no historical analysis, you will need to have only a basic understanding of the topic. Here is an example of such a question.

1. The Scientific Revolution
    (A) involved actual warfare between the Church fathers and philosophers
    (B) was characterized by rapid political change
    (C) involved thousands of people laboring in a single laboratory to prove their understanding of the universe to the community
    (D) helped establish a new view of the universe
    (E) brought about the destruction of new social institutions that supported the emerging scientific enterprise

As you think about this question, you should reflect on the fact that the Scientific Revolution effected a gradual change in the way people viewed their universe. This was due to the reappropriation of old knowledge and to the many new discoveries made by a few hundred people in a smattering of European countries. Knowing that the Scientific Revolution was not an actual revolution involving warfare—but rather a transformation in European culture and society brought about by the work of brilliant people who witnessed the establishment of new social organizations to support their enterprises—you can eliminate choices *A, B, C,* and *E.* The correct answer is *D.*

"NOT/EXCEPT" Questions

In about 10% of exam questions, the College Board modifies the format slightly to make identification questions more difficult. In these test items, four answers are correct and only one is incorrect. Throughout this book, these kinds of questions are identified as "NOT/EXCEPT" questions, since they generally contain one of those words. Remember that the test writers aren't really trying to trick you—in fact, they actually signal this type of question by capitalizing the words *not* and *except* to make them more obvious to you. Pay attention to the capitalization of these words in the multiple-choice section of the exam to avoid making a careless mistake. Here is an example of what you might expect to see on the AP European History Exam.

2. Each of the following statements about Diderot's and d'Alembert's 1772 *Encyclopedia* is true EXCEPT
    (A) it was in part a collective plea for freedom of expression.

(B) it survived many attempts to censor it and halt its publication.

(C) it included the most advanced ideas of the time on religion, philosophy, and government.

(D) it included important articles and illustrations on manufacturing, ship construction, and improved agriculture.

(E) it rejected the ideas of the major French *philosophes*.

In a case like this, you may want to underline the word *EXCEPT* in your test booklet to remind yourself that you are looking for the one answer that is *not* true. You may recall that Diderot's *Encyclopedia* was one of the most avant-garde publications of the Enlightenment era, and that it managed many times to avoid censorship and challenges to its publication. Also you may remember that the *Encyclopedia* incorporated advanced ideas on subjects ranging from religion to agriculture and manufacturing, and that it was the collective product of more than 100 authors. These facts allow you to eliminate choices *A, B, C,* and *D,* because these answers contain true information. If you remember that the editors of the *Encyclopedia* solicited (not rejected) entries from the French *philosophes,* you will know immediately that *E* is the correct answer.

Reading/Quotation Questions

Sometimes the AP European History Exam includes quotations and asks you to identify the speaker or author of those words. Less than 10% of questions on the exam are of this type. Usually, these questions are pretty straightforward—after all, you can't be expected to remember *everything* you've ever read. When you encounter a reading/quotation question, keep in mind that the speaker's words may reveal clues to his or her bias or identity. If you can't identify the speaker or author, try to use context clues to arrive at an educated guess. Here is an example.

> "The main thing that now worries Communists and all citizens of this country is the fate of perestroika, the fate of the country, and the role of the Soviet Communist party at the current, probably most crucial, stage of revolutionary transformation."

3. The quotation above is taken from a speech by
   (A) Joseph Stalin
   (B) Mikhail Gorbachev
   (C) Vladimir Lenin
   (D) Leonid Brezhnev
   (E) Fidel Castro

You should have little difficulty identifying the speaker as a Soviet Communist, and this fact allows you to eliminate choice E. Here, the context clue perestroika reveals that the author or speaker cannot be Stalin, Lenin, or Brezhnev, because each of these Soviet leaders preceded the policy of *perestroika* introduced by Gorbachev. So you can eliminate choices *A, C, D,* and *E.* The correct answer is *B.*

Analysis Questions

An analysis question tests not only your broad understanding of historical periods or trends, but also your ability to draw conclusions and to consider the cause-and-effect relationships between events. Knowing how events influence one another can help you to select the correct answer. Approximately 20–30% of multiple-choice questions on the AP European History Exam are analysis questions. Below is an example.

4. Which of the following was a result of the Paris Commune?
   (A) Order was restored to Paris, and, in the process, 20,000 inhabitants were killed.
   (B) The National Assembly reconciled itself with the Communards.
   (C) The Communards gained a foothold in the French government.
   (D) France paid Prussia its indemnity in full.
   (E) A new municipal government came to control Paris.

This is a basic cause-and-effect analysis question that asks you to evaluate each choice to determine its validity. If you recall that the Paris Commune was a short-lived uprising of Paris Communards that was quickly crushed by the French army, you will know that choices *B, C,* and *E* are incorrect. Choice *D* is incorrect because the Prussian settlement was not paid until September, 1873, almost two years after the events of the Paris Commune. *A* is the correct answer.

Skill-Based Questions
Skill-based questions on the AP European History Exam involve maps, charts, or graphs. You can answer these questions by identifying, analyzing, and interpreting the data presented in the chart, map, or graph. Careful study of a graphic—including its title, labels, and key—will yield all the information you need to answer the question. Approximately 10% of questions on the AP European History Exam are skill-based questions.

Illustration-Based Questions
A similar type of multiple-choice question involves your consideration of an illustration, political cartoon, or work of art. In these questions, you are asked to look at an image and to make an assessment or evaluation based on the ideas expressed in that image. You should read this type of question carefully and study the image and its title for any details about the artist that might help you answer the question correctly.

Most of the multiple-choice questions on the AP European History Exam deal with major historical facts and personalities, broad concepts, and historical analysis. You should know also that some subjects are *never* addressed in the exam's multiple-choice questions. For example, you needn't bother studying military history or strategy, because no multiple-choice questions deal directly with those topics. Any questions pertaining to war in Section I of the AP European History Exam concern the larger implications of war—not the specifics of battles themselves. Moreover, you should avoid memorizing esoteric details, since Section I tests how well you know information in a broad context. Certainly it is essential that you understand the main facts about a topic and have a sense of the relevant time frame. However, you will *not* see a question like the following on the AP European History Exam:

5. The French Revolution began in
   (A) 1788
   (B) 1755
   (C) 1801
   (D) 1789
   (E) 1791

You would have no way except rote memorization to deduce that *D* is the correct answer. Don't waste your time and energy memorizing dates or statistics—unless they provide a greater understanding of European history.

Section II: Free-Response Questions

The second portion of the AP European History Examination begins with a compulsory fifteen-minute reading period. This period prepares you for the first free-response question. After the reading period, you will write essays answering a total of three free-response questions.

Part A: The Document-Based Question

In Part A of the exam's free-response section, you will have forty-five minutes to answer a Document-Based Question (DBQ) concerning the material (usually ten to twelve historical documents) that you read during the fifteen-minute reading period. The DBQ gives you an opportunity to use documentary evidence to support your answer to a historical question.

Each of the historical documents is chosen on the basis of the data it conveys about the topic of the DBQ. Moreover, each of the documents provides a slightly different perspective on that topic. The documents assembled for a DBQ include different kinds of primary sources, such as newspaper articles, graphs, maps, political cartoons, speeches, and journal entries. (They will *not* include excerpts from textbooks.) Some documents are "classic" texts that you may know; others will be new to you. You can be assured, however, that all of the documents pertain to historical events and ideas with which you should be familiar. In addition, all of the documents are labeled with source information—often including a year of publication, an author, or a title—that will help you place the document in context.

Most documents are between six and twelve lines long, although some are longer and some are shorter than this. Each and every historical document is important. Don't assume that a short document is less relevant than a long document. Although answering a question based on a large number of documents may seem daunting, you can take comfort in the fact that both the prearranged selection of documents and the brief amount of time given for analysis will actually help you narrow the focus of your response to the question. Remember that there is no single "right" answer to the DBQ. Many approaches and responses are possible, depending entirely on your skill at analyzing the documents and at determining their historical significance. The basic directions to the DBQ will be similar to these:

Directions: The following question is based on the accompanying Documents 1–12. (Some of the documents have been edited for the purpose of this exercise.) Write your answer on the lined pages of the essay booklet.

This question is designed to test your ability to work with historical documents. As you analyze the documents, *take into account both the sources of the document and the authors' points of view*. Write an essay on the following topic that integrates your analysis of the documents. **Do not simply summarize the documents individually.** You may refer to relevant historical facts and developments not mentioned in the documents.

It is imperative that you structure your response so that it clearly answers the Document-Based Question itself. In other words, don't let the array of documents distract you from the point of the actual question. When you first read the DBQ, it may be helpful to break down the question into its basic components. For example, let's suppose the question is: "Discuss the roles played by women during the Industrial Revolution." You might want to write a short summary of this question that breaks it down into essential parts, as shown below.

WHO: women
WHAT: roles
WHEN: the Industrial Revolution

By writing these notes next to the question in your test booklet, you can remind yourself not to stray to topics such as the roles of *men* in the Industrial Revolution, the *eating habits* of women during the Industrial Revolution, or the roles of women during any era *other* than the Industrial Revolution. The DBQ narrows the scope of a topic. So you should use the framework of the question to restrict your thesis and arguments to a distinct period, issue, or group of people.

To give you a sense of what to expect from a DBQ, read through this example. It is taken from the 1999 AP European History Exam released by the College Board. The DBQ reads: "For the period 1861 to 1914, analyze how various Russians perceived the condition of the Russian peasantry and explain how they proposed to change that condition." The question is followed by a paragraph containing relevant historical background information. The twelve documents that appear below the historical background include excerpts from the following sources:

■ A chart from the Russian Ministry of the Interior showing how provinces of Russia were affected by peasant rebellions from 1861–1907;
■ An 1863 petition to Tsar Alexander II in which peasants ask for preservation of their lands;
■ A 1879 journal article by a revolutionary non-Marxist Socialist describing contemporary rural life;
■ An 1885 article by a Russian anarchist describing the injustices done to Russian peasants;
■ A Russian government report on the famine of 1891;
■ Memoirs of a member of the Socialist Revolutionary party detailing her observations of peasants' lives between 1896 and 1903;
■ The short story "Peasants" (1897) by Russian author Anton Chekhov, in which the difficulty of peasant lives is described;
■ A private letter written by the Minister of Finance to Tsar Nicholas II in 1898 urging a new political and social system for peasants;
■ An 1898 police report to the Ministry of the Interior describing peasant attacks against nobles' properties;
■ A 1906 speech by a peasant representative presenting demands to the Russian parliament;
■ A 1906 petition from peasants in a rural province to the Russian parliament requesting that certain rights and laws be granted according to their requests;
■ A graph showing changes in literacy rates in Russia's rural population in 1860 and 1910, as well as in Russia's general population in 1897 and 1914.

This DBQ consists almost entirely of documents that will be unfamiliar to you, yet each one represents a political perspective or point of view that you have studied. In addition, the two graphs offer visual evidence from the period that you can easily interpret. You are probably familiar with the author Anton Chekhov—though you may not have read "Peasants" or know its connection to the subject of Russian peasantry in the late nineteenth and early twentieth centuries. Nevertheless, you will most likely know something of this era from your AP European History course. Even if you don't have a clear recollection of this time period in Russia, you should be able to answer the question, since the DBQ has provided you also with a detailed paragraph of historical background on the topic.

Remember, there is no single correct answer to a Document-Based Question. As long as you support your argument with evidence, you can argue any thesis you like. The strongest responses to a DBQ are those that make extensive use of the documents provided. Look for opportunities to group documents as you refer to them in support of your thesis. Make sure, also, that you take into account (and explain) the bias or point of view of the source of each document. In your response, you can incorporate additional historical information and knowledge that you possess. If you know pertinent information about the era or subject of the DBQ, try to weave it seamlessly into your essay with your other points and arguments.

Part B: Thematic Questions

You will begin working on Part B of Section II as soon as the forty-five-minute DBQ period is over. (Since there is no break between sections, you might want to practice writing longhand for two hours straight, just to condition your hand for this marathon feat!) Now you will be presented with two groups of three thematic essay questions, and you will be asked to choose one question from each group.

Since you are given seventy minutes to complete these two thematic essays, you should expect to spend five minutes planning and thirty minutes writing each response. The thematic questions address a range of historical periods, and the College Board uses different questions each year to ensure that various time periods are covered. Sometimes questions are linked thematically with images of fine art or photography. However, unlike the DBQ, Part B's thematic questions are *not* complemented by documents containing a wealth of historical information. All of the material you include in your essays must come from your pre-existing knowledge of the topic. Because you have less time to prepare and write these essays, they can be dramatically shorter and less comprehensive than your DBQ response. You should articulate a simple, governing thesis and discuss as much relevant information as you can. It's vital to remember your time limitations: seventy minutes is not very much time to choose, outline, and write two entire essays. Don't spend too long writing one essay, or you won't have sufficient time to write the second one.

Most thematic questions treat familiar subjects and allow you to expand upon what you've learned in your AP European History course. Here are two examples of thematic questions.

1. Compare and contrast Locke's and Rousseau's visions of the social contract.
2. Evaluate the political achievements of Queen Elizabeth I.

In these examples, the directives are clear. In the first essay, you will compare and contrast Locke's and Rousseau's conceptions of the social contract. As tempting as it may be to compare and contrast the two philosophers' personalities, nationalities, or strange quirks, you must stick to the subject of their visions of the social contract. Of course, limiting your answer by addressing *exactly* what the question asks will make writing the essay easier for you—and it will help you score a higher grade. In the second thematic question above, you are asked to evaluate (not describe) Queen Elizabeth's political achievements. In other words, you need to identify her achievements and comment on *why* they were achievements. Always take time to determine precisely what is being asked before you formulate a concrete thesis and focus your supporting paragraphs.

GRADING PROCEDURES FOR THE AP EUROPEAN HISTORY EXAMINATION

The raw scores of the AP European History Examination are converted to the following 5-point scale:

5—Extremely Well Qualified
4—Well Qualified
3—Qualified
2—Possibly Qualified
1—No Recommendation

Some colleges give undergraduate course credit to students who achieve scores of 3 or better on AP exams. Other colleges require students to achieve scores of 4 or 5. Remember, if you're considering using your AP European History Exam score for college credit, you should check with individual colleges to find out their specific requirements for credit. Below is a breakdown of how the grading of the AP European History Exam works.

Section I: Multiple-Choice Questions

The multiple-choice section of the exam is worth 50% of your total grade. The raw score of Section I is determined by crediting one point for each correctly-answered question and by deducting one-fourth of one point for each question answered incorrectly. No points are gained or lost for unanswered questions. Consequently, if you are able to eliminate two or more of the five answer choices, statistically it is to your advantage to make an educated guess rather than to leave the answer blank. Naturally it follows that the more answer choices you can eliminate, the better your chance of guessing the right answer.

Section II: Free-Response Questions

The free-response section of the exam is worth 50% of your total grade. Section II is graded by a group of AP European History instructors and professors known as "readers." That is, multiple readers grade each AP European History Examination booklet, assigning scores to individual essays. Each essay receives a score from 0 to 9. (These scores are covered up so that the next reader does not see them.) The raw score for Section II is composed of three separate scores (one for each essay). To determine the final score for Section II, the three free-response scores are weighted as follows:

Part A: The Document-Based Question is worth 45% of the Section II grade.
Part B: The pair of (non-DBQ) Free-Response Questions is worth 55% of the Section II grade.

Readers grade DBQ essays using a method called "core-scoring," which involves assessing how many historical skills you have used in the course of your written response. They assign one point for each historical skill employed in an essay. The scoring scale is from 0 to 9, with 0–6 points representing the coverage of "basic core" skills, and 7–9 points indicating an outstanding use of basic core skills and additional historical skills. In your DBQ response, then, you can earn six points by covering the six basic core skills:

- understanding the basic meaning of documents;
- making use of the majority of documents;

- having an acceptable thesis;
- supporting a thesis with documentary evidence;
- providing analysis of bias in two or three documents;
- demonstrating the ability to group documents.

In order to earn any "expanded core" points, you must first earn all six of the basic core points. You may then earn 0–3 additional points if you excel in more advanced skills, such as:

- incorporating outside knowledge in the essay;
- using every document or almost every document;
- having an analytical and comprehensive thesis;
- discussing bias in a number of documents;
- using documents skillfully as evidence;
- creating additional groupings of documents.

Instructors grade the two non-DBQ free-response questions using the same 0 to 9 scale. However, instead of employing the core-scoring method, they assess students' responses using certain basic criteria. For example, what readers call "stronger essays" (those scored between 6 and 9 points) demonstrate the following qualities with varying degrees of effectiveness:

- has a clear, well-developed thesis;
- is well-organized;
- addresses the terms of the question;
- supports the thesis with specific evidence;
- may contain minor errors.

"Mixed essays" receive a score of 4 or 5, and these essays demonstrate the following qualities with varying degrees of effectiveness:

- contains a thesis, perhaps superficial or simplistic;
- gives an uneven response to the terms of the question—task(s), evidence, content chronology, etc.;
- may contain errors, factual and/or interpretive.

Finally, "weaker essays" (scored 0 to 3) demonstrate the following qualities with varying degrees of effectiveness:

- thesis is confused or absent, or it merely restates the question;
- misconstrues the question or omits major tasks;
- may contain major errors.

TEST-TAKING STRATEGIES FOR THE AP EUROPEAN HISTORY EXAMINATION

Below is a brief list of basic tips and strategies to think about *before* you arrive at the exam site.

- It's a good idea to arrive at the exam site thirty minutes before the start time. This saves you additional worry about arriving late. You should plan your schedule so that you get *two* very good nights of sleep before exam day. On the day of the exam, make sure that you eat good, nutritious meals. These tips may sound corny or obvious, but your body must be in peak form in order for your brain to perform well.
- It's a good idea to have a photo I.D. with you when you arrive at the exam site. (It is essential if you are taking the exam at a school other than your own.) Carrying a driver's license or a student I.D. card will allow you to prove your identity, if anyone needs such proof.
- You should bring at least two pencils for the multiple-choice section, as well as two black or dark blue pens for the free-response section of the exam. Take a moment to make sure that your pencils are labeled #2 and that they have good erasers. After all, the machine that scores Section I of the exam cannot recognize marks made by other types of pencils. Also, it cannot read a correct answer if a previous answer has not been erased completely.
- If possible, it's helpful to have a watch with you at the exam. It's true that most testing rooms will have clocks and that most test administrators will give you periodic reminders of how much time you have remaining. Still, having your own watch makes it easy to keep close track of your own pace. The watch cannot have a calculator or an alarm, however, as these are not permitted in the exam room.
- There are a few other things that are not allowed in the exam room. Do not bring books of any kind, laptop computers, wireless instant-messaging devices, cameras, or portable radios. If you must bring a cellular phone with you, prepare to turn it off and give it to the test proctor until you are finished with your exam.

  Educational Testing Service prohibits the objects listed above in the interest of fairness to all test-takers. Similarly, the test administrators are very clear and very serious about what types of conduct are not allowed during the examination. Below is a list of actions to avoid at all costs, since each is grounds for your immediate dismissal from the exam room.
- Do not consult any outside materials during the three hours and five minutes of the exam period. Remember, the break is technically part of the exam—you are not free to review any materials at that time either.
- Do not speak during the exam, unless you have a question for the test proctor. Raise your hand to get the proctor's attention.
- When you are told to stop working on a section of the exam, you must stop *immediately*.
- Do not open your exam booklet before the test begins.
- Never tear a page out of your test booklet or try to remove the exam from the test room.
- Do not behave disruptively—even if you're distressed about a difficult test question or because you've run out of time. Stay calm and make no unnecessary noise. Remember, too, the worst-case scenario: if you are displeased with your performance on test day, you can always cancel your exam scores.

Section I: Strategies for Multiple-Choice Questions

Having a firm grasp of European history is, of course, the key to your doing well on the AP European History Examination. In addition, being well-informed about the exam itself increases your chances of achieving a high score. Below is a list of strategies that you can use to increase your comfort, your confidence, and your chances of excelling on the multiple-choice section of the exam.

- Pace yourself and keep track of the remaining time as you complete the multiple-choice section of the exam. Remember, you have fifty-five minutes to answer all eighty questions. It's important that you don't get stuck on one question for too long.
- Make a light mark in your test booklet next to any questions you can't answer. Return to them after you reach the end of Section I. Sometimes questions that appear later in the test will refresh your memory of a particular period, and you will be able to answer one of those earlier questions.
- Always read the entire question carefully, and underline key words or ideas. You might wish to double underline words such as *NOT* or *EXCEPT* in that type of multiple-choice question.
- Read each and every one of the answer choices carefully before you make your final selection.
- Trust your first instinct. Since it has been proven statistically that your first choice is more likely to be correct, you should replace it only if you are completely certain that your second choice is correct.
- Use the process of elimination to help you home in on a correct answer. Even if you are quite sure of an answer, cross out the letters of incorrect choices in your test booklet as you eliminate them. This cuts down on distraction and allows you to narrow the remaining choices even further.
- If you are able to eliminate two or more answer choices, it is better to make an educated guess at the correct answer than to leave the answer blank.
- Remember that the multiple-choice section of the AP European History Exam is designed so that easier questions appear at the start of the test. Try to answer the easy questions as quickly as you can without sacrificing care and thoroughness. If you are able to rack up many correct answers at the start of the section, you will conserve time (and mental energy) for the more difficult questions toward the end of the test.
- About a month prior to the test date, you should begin doing drills to prepare for the multiple-choice section of the test. Ask your teacher for copies of old AP European History Exams, and answer the multiple-choice questions. Answer the sample questions in Part II of this book, and take the sample tests in Part III. After you've answered the questions, check your answers and use the answer explanations to determine any content areas that you need to study or review more thoroughly.
- Make yourself completely familiar with the instructions for the multiple-choice questions *before* you take the exam. You'll find the instructions in this book. By knowing the instructions cold, you'll save yourself the time of reading them carefully on the day of the test.
- In the week before the exam, do a comprehensive review of the history you've studied. However, don't dwell on obscure details. Focus on the larger issues that you might confront in the exam. It's a good idea to revisit with your teacher any major themes that you have found confusing or that you feel you don't know as well as you should. You can review using information in the Part I correlation chart and in Part II of this book, as well as in your textbook.

■ Try to grow as familiar as you can with the format of Section I. The more comfortable you
are with the multiple-choice format and with the kinds of questions you'll encounter, the
easier the exam will be. Remember, Part II and Part III of this book provide you with
invaluable practice on the kinds of multiple-choice questions you will encounter on the AP
European History Exam.

In addition to these strategies, be on the lookout for the six types of questions:

■ Identification questions;
■ "NOT/EXCEPT" questions;
■ Reading/quotation questions;
■ Analysis questions;
■ Skill-based questions;
■ Illustration-based questions.

Below you will find an example of each type of multiple-choice question, followed by a
comprehensive analysis of how you should go about approaching similar questions in Section I
of the AP European History Exam.

1. The major force for change in the revolutions of 1848 originated with
    (A) the working class
    (B) the unemployed
    (C) the conservative elite
    (D) the monarchy
    (E) middle-class liberals

In this identification question, you should underline the phrases *major force, revolutions of 1848,*
and *originated with.* When you think back to what you know about 1848—the year of
revolutions across Europe—you should remember that no single factor caused the eruption of
discontent. Throughout the Continent, food shortages had prevailed since 1846, the economy
was depressed, and unemployment was widespread. One of the most important facts about the
revolutions of 1848 is that they were fomented primarily by middle-class political liberals who
were unhappy with working and economic conditions and who wanted increased representation
in government, increased civil liberties, and unrestricted economic life. Answers *A* and *D* can be
eliminated, since the working classes tended to use radical tactics of violence to achieve their
means, and since the monarchy was devastated by the revolutions. Typically, the conservative
elite preferred the *status quo* to the danger or revolution, so answer *C* is not correct. *E* is the
correct answer.

2. Each of the following statements is true of the Fabians EXCEPT
    (A) they hoped to educate the country about the benefits of socialism
    (B) they were interested in collective ownership on the municipal level
    (C) they took their name from Fabius Maximus, the Roman general who used
        avoidance tactics against Hannibal
    (D) their name reflected their gradualist approach to sweeping social reform
    (E) they were Marxist intellectuals

In this "NOT/EXCEPT" question, you should underline the words *true, Fabians,* and *EXCEPT* to remind yourself that you are looking for the single false statement about the Fabians. If you remember the role of Fabians in the context of welfare programs in Britain in the late-nineteenth century, you may remember that Marxism did not make significant progress in Britain. The Fabian Society was Britain's most influential Socialist group, and it was composed of non-Marxist intellectuals. Because all of the other statements about the Fabians are true, *E* is the correct answer.

"Here the question arises; whether it is better to be loved than feared or feared than loved. The answer is that it would be desirable to be both but, since that is difficult, it is much safer to be feared than to be loved, if one must choose."

3. Which of the following is most likely the author of the above passage?
   (A) Michelangelo
   (B) Martin Luther
   (C) Boris Yeltsin
   (D) Niccolò Machiavelli
   (E) Isaac Newton

In this reading/quotation question, you should underline the word *author,* and you may also want to underline the passage "it is much safer to be feared than to be loved." Based on this information, you can eliminate a few of the choices fairly easily. Michelangelo, Martin Luther, and Isaac Newton never held positions of power in which they needed to weigh the benefits of being feared or loved. These choices can quickly be eliminated. If you recall, Niccolò Machiavelli was best known for his treatise *The Prince,* in which he elaborated important personality traits for rulers. Though Boris Yeltsin was a ruler who may have been concerned with being feared or loved, he was not known for such meditations or statements. *D* is the correct answer.

4. Which of the following was an immediate result of the 1949 formation of the North Atlantic Treaty Organization (NATO)?
   (A) Members of NATO were committed to offering assistance in the event of an attack against a member nation.
   (B) The United States was committed to defend allies outside the Western Hemisphere.
   (C) Members of NATO integrated their economies.
   (D) Europe was divided into two unfriendly blocs.
   (E) The Marshall Plan was agreed upon by NATO members.

This analysis question requires you to analyze the results of the formation of NATO. You should underline the words *immediate result, 1949 formation,* and *NATO.* This is not a trick question, yet you must pay close attention to the word *immediate.* In effect, the question is asking you to identify the outcome of the formation of NATO. You should recall that NATO was founded after the creation of the Marshall Plan in 1947. It wasn't until the addition of West Germany, Greece, and Turkey a few years after the initial 1949 formation of NATO (which included Belgium, the Netherlands, Luxembourg, France, Britain, Italy, Portugal, Norway, Denmark, Iceland, Canada, and the United States) that allies outside the Western Hemisphere were incorporated. Thus, choices *B* and *E* can be eliminated. You should also remember that Europe was divided into two blocs *only* after the Eastern alliance COMECON was formed and the Eastern countries' economies were integrated. *A* is the correct answer.

5. The shaded areas on the late-eighteenth century map shown above depict which monarchy's efforts to gain more direct control of the American continents?
   (A) England
   (B) France
   (C) Spain
   (D) Belgium
   (E) Russia

This skill-based question asks you to use your skills to interpret a map. You should underline the words *monarchy's* and *American continents,* and you should note the title of the map, *Viceroyalties in Latin America in 1780.* Once you've determined what the question is asking—which monarchy wanted control of these regions on the American continents—finding the correct answer should be easy. The Spanish Bourbon monarchy sought to establish more direct control of the American continent by introducing more royal officials and by establishing more governmental districts. This Spanish influence remains persistent today in Latin America. *C* is the correct answer.

6. Which of the following best summarizes the point of this poster by the artist Ben Shahn (1898–1969)?
   (A) The poster memorializes the destruction of Lidice, Czechoslovakia, and the Nazis' brutality against the city's citizens.
   (B) The poster suggests that Nazi criminals are anonymous in their crimes.
   (C) The poster insinuates that everyone is a victim of Nazi war crimes.
   (D) The poster attempts to challenge the Nazi regime's policies.
   (E) The poster implies that reports of the destruction of Lidice were exaggerated.

This illustration-based question is straightforward in that it asks you to interpret the meaning of a work of art—in this case, a poster by Ben Shahn. You may want to pay attention to the way in which the poster conveys information, namely through the text on it and the striking image of a man in handcuffs and with a sack over his head. As you consider the question, you will want to underline the words *point* and *summarizes* to help you keep in mind that the poster as a whole reveals a message or has a main idea. As you consider the different answer choices, you should recognize that Shahn's poster does not really challenge the Nazi regime's policies or insinuate that everyone is a victim of Nazi war crimes. Nor does it suggest that the reports of Lidice's destruction were exaggerated. It is clear from the poster that the victims (and not the Nazis) are anonymous—it does not depict a faceless Nazi, but a faceless victim. Thus you can conclude that *A* is the correct answer.

Section II: Strategies for Free-Response Questions
Below is a list of strategies that you can use to increase your chances of excelling on the free-response section of the exam.

- Since you have just two hours and ten minutes to outline and write three essays in the free-response section of the AP European History Exam, you must manage your time carefully.
- Be careful not to stray from the focus of the question being asked. As you read a question, underline any directive words that indicate how you should address and focus the material in your essay. Some of the most frequently used directives on the AP European History Exam

are listed below, along with descriptions of what you need to do in your writing to answer the question.

> *Analyze* (show relationships between events; explain)
> *Assess/Evaluate* (give an opinion of; appraise; discuss advantages and disadvantages)
> *Compare* (address similarities and differences between two or more things)
> *Contrast* (examine to illustrate points of difference or divergence)
> *Defend/Refute* (argue for or against a specific statement or position, using factual support to back up your argument)
> *Describe* (give a detailed account)
> *Discuss* (consider or examine; debate)
> *Explain* (clarify; tell the meaning)
> *To what extent and in what ways* (tell how much and how)

■ As you formulate your thesis, always consider whether or not it will answer the essay question directly.

Part A: The Document-Based Question

The following strategies will help you conceive, organize, and write your response to the DBQ.

■ During the fifteen-minute reading period, begin by reading carefully the DBQ and the historical background provided along with it.

■ Underline key words and make a note of any outside information you might be able to connect to the question or to the historical background material.

■ Then read each of the historical documents in order, reviewing some for more in-depth analysis, and flagging any phrases or words that connect that document to the main theme of the DBQ.

■ Although some documents will be more crucial to an understanding of the topic than others, each document is relevant to the question. Make a mark next to those documents that you feel are the most pertinent and that you will use most extensively to support your argument.

■ Take note of the date of each source and identify the author's position or point-of-view (including any potential bias).

■ If the reading period allows, decide on a thesis statement and plan an outline that will enable you to analyze and interpret as many of the documents as possible into a cohesive essay.

■ Keep in mind that successful DBQ responses incorporate analysis of the majority of documents. However, you do not need to cite every document to get a high score. Specific mention of individual documents should always occur in the context of the overall topic and should help to illustrate or organize arguments made in your essay. In short, documents should *never* be cited or summarized without analysis. One key to your success on the DBQ portion of the exam is a seamless integration of the documents into the body of your essay.

■ Whenever you make use of documents in your DBQ response, ask yourself how they function with respect to your thesis and to the DBQ question itself. It is important also to address any documents that directly refute your thesis. Readers will be as interested to see how you handle material that contradicts your main argument as they will be to see your use of documents that support your thesis.

❑ Remember to refer to individual documents by author name and/or by the document number. If time allows, you may want to write a conclusion to your DBQ essay that reflects on how the documentary evidence illustrates your thesis.

❑ If you have time, try to proofread your essays for any inconsistencies or weaknesses.

Here is an abbreviated version of the kind of DBQ you will encounter on your AP European History Exam. In this sample DBQ, you will have just four historical documents to consider and integrate into your response. A sample analysis of the documents and the manner in which you should proceed to write your essay follows.

1. *To what extent and in what ways did sixteenth-century Spanish attitudes toward the lands and people conquered in the New World affect government policy?*

Background History: The fifteenth century witnessed the beginning of western Europe's expansion into unknown lands. A quest for gold and spices dominated these initial adventures at sea. Christopher Columbus's voyage of 1492 marked the beginning of the Spanish dominance of a vast American territory. Subsequently, Spaniards set up satellite governments in North America and South America, and they recruited and enslaved native Indians to assist them in mining, agriculture, and other endeavors aimed at creating a New World economy to profit Spain.

DOCUMENT 1 Source: Hernán Cortés, Spanish conqueror, second letter to Charles V, 1520.
In the place of these I put images of Our Lady and the Saints, which excited not a little feeling in Montezuma and the inhabitants, who at first remonstrated, declaring that if my proceedings were known throughout the country, the people would rise against me; for they believed that their idols bestowed on them all temporal good, and if they permitted them to be ill-treated, they would be angry and without their gifts, and by this means the people would be deprived of the fruits of the earth and perish with famine. I answered, through the interpreters, that they were deceived in expecting any favors from idols, the work of their own hands, formed of unclean things; and that they must learn there was but one God, the universal Lord of all, who had created the heavens and earth, and all things else, and had made them and us …

DOCUMENT 2 Source: Bartolomé de las Casas (1474–1566), Dominican missionary, "A Brief Account of the Destruction of the Indies," ca. 1542.
That which led the Spaniards to these unsanctified impieties was the desire of Gold, to make themselves suddenly rich … In a word, their covetousness, their ambition, which could not be more in any people under heaven, the riches of the Country, and the patience of the people gave occasion to this their devilish barbarism. For the Spaniards so condemned them … that they used them not like beasts, for that would have been tolerable, but looked upon them as if they had been but the dung and filth of the earth, and so little they regarded the health of their souls, that they suffered this great multitude to die without the least light of Religion …

DOCUMENT 3 Source: "The New Laws of the Indies," laws and ordinances made by Charles V for the government of the Indies and treatment of the Indians, 1542.
As we have ordered provision to be made that from henceforward the Indians in no way be made slaves, including those who until now have been enslaved against all reason and right and contrary to the provisions and instructions thereupon, We ordain and command that the

Audiencias having first summoned the parties to their presence, without any further judicial form, but in a summary way, so that the truth may be ascertained, speedily set the said Indians at liberty unless the persons who hold them for slaves show title why they should hold and possess them legitimately. And in order that in default of persons to solicit the aforesaid, the Indians may not remain in slavery unjustly, We command that the Audiencias appoint persons who may pursue this cause for the Indians and be paid out of the Exchequer fines, provided they be men of trust and diligence.

DOCUMENT 4 Source: Anonymous, "The Gold of the Indies," from the Court of Philip II of Spain, 1559.
[G]reat quantities of gold and silver are no longer found upon the surface of the earth, as they have been in past years; and to penetrate into the bowels of the earth requires greater effort, skill and outlay, and the Spaniards are not willing to do the work themselves, and the natives cannot be forced to do so, because the Emperor has freed them from all obligation of service as soon as they accept the Christian religion. Wherefore it is necessary to acquire negro slaves, who are brought from the coasts of Africa, both within and without the Straits, and these are selling dearer every day, because on account of their natural lack of strength and the change of climate, added to the lack of discretion upon the part of their masters in making them work too hard and giving them too little to eat, they fall sick and the greater part of them die.

This sample DBQ question asks you to consider *how* Spanish attitudes toward lands and peoples in the New World contributed to government policy and *how much* they contributed. By narrowing the focus to Spanish attitudes in the sixteenth century, and by relying on documents exclusively from that period, this question provides you with much of the equipment that you will use in formulating your response.

As you read through each of the documents, pay attention to the author of each work. You should recognize Hernán Cortés, the author of **DOCUMENT 1**, the Spanish conquistador who brutally defeated the Aztecs of Mexico in 1521 and reclaimed the region as New Spain. Here Cortés relates his efforts to convert the Aztecs to Christian worship, and he characterizes their worship of idols as wrong. It is worth noting that Cortés' primary objective in his dealing with the Aztecs was not religious conversion, but the vast quantities of gold held by the Aztec ruler, Montezuma. Cortés and his soldiers brutally conquered the city of Tenochtitlán, killing thousands of Aztecs and asserting Spanish control of the region. Any analysis of this document (and its benevolent but paternalistic attitude toward the Indians) must take into account Cortés's brutality against the Aztecs.

You may be familiar with Bartolomé de las Casas, the author of **DOCUMENT 2**, the Dominican missionary who waged a campaign against the exploitative aspects of conquest in the Americas. You may also recall that the ideas of Las Casas led to new royal regulations of conquest. In this excerpt, you should detect Las Casas' anger at the greed of the Spanish, as well as his frustration at their debasing treatment of the Indians. His emphasis on religion is clear in his condemnation of the Spanish massacre of Indian societies and of the failure to offer Native Americans religious enlightenment.

The third document reflects new royal laws about the treatment of Indians, and it demands their liberty from slavery. The authorship of this officia document from the court of Charles V is unclear, but the sentiments expressed reflect a significant departure from the conditions described by Las Casas (**DOCUMENT 2**) and call for freedom for the Indians under Spanish control.

The fourth document, from the court of Philip II of Spain, alludes to the problem of carrying out some of the labor-intensive mining of gold and silver that has been done in the past by Indians. The author contends that Indians were freed from forced labor as soon as they converted to Christianity, and that African slaves will be necessary to carry out the difficult work. It is worth noting that though the Indians were released from forced servitude, they gained their liberty only by converting to a new faith—hardly the liberty and freedom described in **DOCUMENT 3**.

As you develop a strong thesis that answers the question and enables you to discuss these works in detail, you will want to respond to the "To what extent and in what ways," portion of the question. If you don't know much about this period in history, you can rely on some of the details provided in the documents. You should make use of most of the documents in your response, and you should explain authorial bias whenever you detect it. You should glean the following basic ideas from the documents and keep them in mind as you compose your thesis:

☐　Christianity was important to sixteenth-century Spaniards, many of whom were concerned that the natives in the lands they conquered were not believers.

☐　Natives experienced significant bloodshed and brutality at the hands of the Spanish. Many of the natives were treated by the Spanish as if they were worthless creatures who had no basic rights as human beings.

☐　In the sixteenth century, new laws released natives from enslavement, but these laws were conditional on the natives' conversion to Christianity.

☐　Among the primary motives of sixteenth-century explorers and discoverers was the acquisition of gold and other riches in the New World. This ambition to gain access to more minerals and wealth, coupled with new laws prohibiting native slavery, led Spaniards to seek other unrestricted labor markets, such as those in Africa.

One way to address the question in thesis form would be as follows:

Spanish greed to acquire the riches of the New World at any cost competed with a desire to convert to Christianity the peoples it conquered; the result of these conflicting desires was sixteenth-century legislation that sought to protect the rights of natives but that led ultimately to the exploitation of natives in Africa.

In your first paragraph, you might want to back up your thesis statement by discussing the Spanish quest for riches of the New World. You could cite passages from Bartolomé de Las Casas and from **DOCUMENT 4**, and you could describe the quest of Hernán Cortés to find the gold of the Aztecs. This would be an excellent place in the essay to demonstrate your outside knowledge on the subject, as you could refer to other explorers whose conquests you recall. Using details, you should develop the idea that this quest for wealth led to tremendous exploitation of the natives.

In your second paragraph, you could address the Spanish desire to impart Christian faith in the lands they conquered, and you could cite the Cortés passage. You would want to acknowledge the bias implicit in this document—that is, that Cortés was a brutal conquistador who could liken himself to the Indians and make claims of their being made by the same God, but who could then go on to destroy their civilization. You could also refer to Las Casas' concern that the natives were killed without the benefit of religious enlightenment, and you could allude to the fact (noted in **DOCUMENT 4**) that natives who converted were granted freedom from slavery. You could assert that the campaign of Las Casas and other reformers persuaded

Emperor Charles V that Spanish exploitation of natives was wrong, and that the campaign resulted in the legislation (indicated in **DOCUMENT 3**) that granted natives their freedom from slavery. You might feel that it is worth acknowledging that by 1542, much damage had already been done to these native civilizations, as Columbus had arrived in the New World fully fifty years earlier.

You might close the essay by saying that while Spanish concern for the religious faith of the peoples they conquered was significant, it was overwhelmed by their desire for the wealth of the New World. As **DOCUMENT 4** suggests, though new legislation protected the natives (provided that they agreed to convert—in itself a kind of enslavement, one might argue), it did not compel the Spanish to check their desire to seize the region's riches. The policies of the Spanish government had changed over time as a result of demands from religious organizations seeking human rights assurances, and exploitation of the natives had slowed by the middle of the sixteenth century. However, greedy Spanish colonials sought new labor markets in other continents and displayed a similar disregard for the rights of natives on the African continent.

A response that has a strong thesis statement, develops its ideas clearly, integrates information from most of the documents, identifies and explains any bias demonstrated by those documents, and directly answers the actual Document-Based Question will earn a high score.

Part B: Thematic Questions

The following strategies will help you conceive, organize, and write your response to two thematic questions.

- Read all three questions in each group and note any facts that are relevant to each question. It is best to answer the thematic question for which you have the most information. Decide which question this is. (Sometimes, but not always, this will be a question concerning a subject you have studied extensively in class.)
- As in the DBQ, you should underline key directive words and phrases such as *Analyze, Assess, Evaluate, Compare, Contrast, Defend, Refute, Describe, Discuss, Explain,* and *To what extent and in what ways.*
- Because the time you have to complete these essays is short, you should focus your energy on defending a simple thesis that answers the question and discussing as much relevant historical information as possible.
- Each of your essays should include an introductory paragraph that asserts a thesis, paragraphs that support your argument, and a concluding paragraph that summarizes your argument. As you consider which two thematic questions to answer, think about how you would argue the essay. Do you have a lot to say about the topic? Create a graphic organizer or write an outline to help you organize your ideas.
- Always use concrete historical ideas and examples to substantiate your thesis, and avoid including any information that you are not certain is correct.
- If time allows, proofread both of your essays. Don't worry about crossing out material—readers understand that your responses are first drafts and that you are writing down ideas under the pressure of time. Your answers should be legible, but they do not need to reflect perfect penmanship. Focus your efforts on making the essays strong by backing up your thesis with a clear organization and plenty of historical detail.

Much as in your response to the DBQ, the success of your two thematic essays will depend a great deal on how clearly and extensively you address the question being posed. In Part B of

Section II, of course, you don't have any documents to back up your argument. Thus, it is even more essential that you identify a thesis that responds directly to the thematic question. The structure of your thematic essay depends entirely on your knowledge of a subject. In the introduction of your essay, you should indicate how you will respond to the question. Take a look at an example of such a question below:

To what extent and in what ways did the Reformation alter religious practices and institutions in those lands where it succeeded?

If you opt to answer this question, you should isolate exactly what it is that you must answer. You may want to underline the relevant information in the question to remind yourself of your focus:

To what extent and in what ways did the Reformation alter religious_practices and institutions in those lands where it succeeded?

It will help further to break down the subject into its most essential parts:

WHAT: the Reformation, religious practice and institutions
WHERE: the lands where it succeeded

In some cases, it's a good idea to reword the question in order to cement your understanding of it:

How and *how much* did the Reformation change religious behavior and customs in the regions where it thrived?

In order to answer how much the Reformation changed religious behavior and customs, you need to identify what religious practices and institutions were like prior to the Reformation as well as after the Reformation. As you brainstorm a list of information needed to answer this thematic question, you should make a list of everything you recall about pre-Reformation and post-Reformation religious practices.

Pre-Reformation (late 15th Century)	Post-Reformation (16th Century)
Clergy:	Clergy:
☐ 6–8% of urban population	☐ population falls by 2/3; churches reduced in number by 1/3
☐ exercises political power	☐ punished for crimes in civil courts
☐ legislates, taxes	☐ must pay taxes
☐ unmarried and sworn to celibacy (some have concubines and children)	☐ allowed to marry
Church calendar regulates everyday life; 1/3 of year devoted to religious observance	Religious holidays reduced by 1/3
Monasteries and nunneries powerful institutions	Monasteries and nunneries transformed into hospitals and educational institutions; many nuns and monks pensioned off
Mass and liturgy read entirely in Latin	Worship conducted in vernacular

Images of saints on display, saints' relics are venerated, many religious shrines, indulgence preachers common	Shrines closed down; anyone adoring saints, relics, or images subject to fine; indulgence preachers disappear
Highly decorated churches; many illiterate members "read" ornate windows	In Zwinglian cities, church walls are bare; focus on God's word paramount
Catholic church requires fasts	No required fasts

Once you've determined what you remember about a topic, you should create a thesis that will allow you to use as many facts as possible in your response to the question. In this example, because the student has impressive recall of vast amounts of pre- and post-Reformation information, the thesis can take a strong position on the topic.

> **Sample thesis:** By the end of the sixteenth century in those regions where it flourished, the Reformation witnessed radical changes in religious practices and institutions.

Successive body paragraphs can include accounts of pre- and post-Reformation religious traditions and customs, using the details noted during prewriting.

AP CORRELATION TO *THE WESTERN HERITAGE, AP* Edition*

The following chart is intended for your use as a study device. The left column shows one way to break down into historical eras the time period covered in AP European History courses. The right column includes a detailed breakdown of chapters in your *Western Heritage* textbook where you can learn more about those historical eras. You may want to use this chart throughout the year to review what you've learned. It is also an excellent place to begin your pre-exam review of subjects.

SAMPLE AP COURSE UNITS	CORRELATIONS TO T*HE WESTERN HERITAGE* (AP* Edition, 10th Edition)
Late Middle Ages	**Chapter 9: The Late Middle Ages: Social and Political Breakdown (1300–1453)** □ The Black Death □ The Hundred Years' War and the Rise of National Sentiment □ Ecclesiastical Breakdown and Revival: The Late Medieval Church □ Medieval Russia
Renaissance and Exploration	**Chapter 10: Renaissance and Discovery** □ The Renaissance in Italy (1375–1527) □ Italy's Political Decline: The French Invasions (1494–1527) □ Revival of Monarchy in Northern Europe □ The Northern Renaissance □ Voyages of Discovery and the New Empire in the West and the East
The Reformation	**Chapter 11: The Age of Reformation** □ Society and Religion □ Martin Luther and German Reformation to 1525 □ The Reformation Elsewhere □ Political Consideration of the Lutheran Reformation □ The English Reformation to 1553 □ Catholic Reform and Counter-Reformation □ The Social Significance of the Reformation in Western Europe
Early Modern Society	**Chapter 11: The Age of Reformation** □ Family Life in Early Modern Europe
Religious Wars	**Chapter 12: The Age of Religious Wars** □ Renewed Religious Struggle □ The French Wars of Religion (1562–1598) □ Imperial Spain and the Reign of Philip II (r. 1556–1598) □ England and Spain (1553–1603) □ The Thirty Years' War (1618–1648)
Growth of the State	**Chapter 13: European State Consolidation in the Seventeenth and Eighteenth Centuries** □ The Netherlands: Golden Age to Decline □ Two Models of European Political Development □ Constitutional Crisis and Settlement in Stuart England □ Rise of Absolute Monarchy in France □ Central and Eastern Europe □ Russia Enters the European Political Arena □ The Ottoman Empire

PART II

TOPICAL REVIEW WITH SAMPLE QUESTIONS AND ANSWERS AND EXPLANATIONS

This section is keyed to chapters 9 through 31 in *The Western Heritage*. Chapters 1 to 8 from the textbook are not included, as material prior to 1450 AD is not tested on the AP Exam. Part II overviews important information in bullet form and provides sample questions for every question type. Use these practice questions to arm yourself thoroughly for all kinds of test items you will encounter on the AP exam. Answers and explanations are provided for each question for your further review. Additional review items address additional important topics, for further study or in-class discussion. Answers to these items are not provided in this guide.

CHAPTER 9

The Late Middle Ages: Social and Political Breakdown (1300–1453)

The late Middle Ages was an era marked by major social, religious, and health crises. War, plague, social unrest, and religious schism characterized this era.

The Black Death

The Black Death, also known as the Bubonic Plague, came about as a result of decades of overpopulation, economic depression, famine, and bad health and hygiene in some European regions.

- **The Black Death** was named for the **discoloration of the body.** It is believed to have been introduced by seaborne rats from the **Black Sea** area. By the early fifteenth century, western Europe had lost as much as 40% of its population to the plague.
- Lack of **sophisticated medicine** led to superstitions about the reasons for the plague, including poisonous fumes released during earthquakes and a corruption in the atmosphere. **Jews** were sought as scapegoats for the plague and were persecuted.
- **Popular remedies** against the plague included the use of leeches. **Flagellants** believed that beating themselves until they bled would bring about **divine intervention.**
- **Farm laborers** decreased in numbers, but the number of **skilled artisans** increased dramatically. Peasants rebelled against efforts by governments to limit their wages. Opposition to such legislation spurred the English peasants' revolt of 1381.
- **Cities and skilled industries** prospered from the effects of the plague, which created a need for more expensive goods. The economic power of **trade guilds and artisans** grew.

The Hundred Years' War and the Rise of Nationalist Sentiment

During the late Middle Ages, tremendous violence and political unrest led to the breakdown of European governments. Toward the end of the period, monarchs in England and France began to reassert their power; the Hundred Years' War was the result of their struggle for control.

- **The Hundred Years' War (1337–1453)** began when the English king Edward III claimed his right to the French throne after the death of Charles IV. The territorial proximity of England and France and their quarrel over rights to Flanders exacerbated the dispute.
- **English success** in the war was due to its military superiority and its use of weaponry like the **longbow. French weakness** was due to territorial infighting and a lack of leadership.
- Fighting consisted primarily of sieges and raids. The battles of **Crécy (1346)**, **Poitiers (1356)** and **Agincourt (1415)** were significant victories for the British. **The Peace of Brétigny (1360)** recognized English holdings in France, in exchange for Edward III renouncing his claim to the French throne.

- **Joan of Arc (1412–1431)** a peasant from Domrémy who claimed she heard the voices of God, led the French to victory in the **Battle of Orléans.** Joan served as an inspiration for the French, who eventually defeated the English and won the war. Joan was later burned at the stake at Rouen as a heretic for refusing to recant her beliefs.

Ecclesiastical Breakdown and Revival: The Late Medieval Church

- **Pope Innocent III (r. 1198–1216)** transformed the church into a secular power, creating a papal monarchy with a political mission that included disposing of *benefices* and declaring saints. **Pope Urban IV (r. 1261–1264)** continued the secularization of the church by establishing its own law court, the **Rota Romana,** and by broadening the distribution of *benefices*. The **College of Cardinals** became politicized.
- **Pope Boniface VIII (r. 1294–1303)** refused the English and French efforts to tax the clergy, and issued a bull, *Clericis laicos,* which forbade taxation of the clergy without papal approval. Boniface was forced to make a concession to Philip the Fair of France, but the dispute led the two into further debates. In 1302, Boniface issued the bull *Unam Sanctum,* which declared that temporal authority was subject to the power of the church. Pope Clement V moved the papacy to **Avignon,** to avoid the French king and Rome. The time in Avignon was called the **"Babylonian Captivity,"** in an allusion to the biblical bondage of the Israelites.
- **Pope John XXII (r. 1316–1334)** tried to restore the papacy to Rome. **William of Ockham** and **Marsilius of Padua** protested papal power. **John Wycliffe** and **John Huss** led popular lay movements **the Lollards** and **the Hussites** that protested the rights of the papacy.
- **The Great Schism (1378–1417)** occurred when **Pope Clement VII,** a cousin of the French king, was elected by a council of cardinals just five months after they had elected an Italian archbishop, **Pope Urban VI. Two papal courts** now claimed the right to power.
- **Cardinals deposed both popes** and elected a new pope, **Alexander V.** For a time, there were three popes who claimed spiritual authority.
- The **Conciliar Movement,** an effort to control regulate the actions of the pope by councils, grew during this time. In 1414, the council of Constance met. In a document known as the **Sacrosancta,** the council recognized the **Roman pope Gregory XII,** and one pope ruled.

Medieval Russia

Prince Vladimir of Kiev (972–1015) chose Greek Orthodoxy as the religion of Russia.

- **Kiev** was a cultural center that rivaled Constantinople. Three cultural groups —the **Great Russians,** the **White Russians,** and the **Little Russians (Ukrainians)** —developed. Russia's hierarchical social structure divided freemen (clergy, army officers, *boyars,* townspeople, and peasants) from slaves. Debtors made up an intermediate group.
- **Mongols,** led by **Ghengis Khan,** ruled Russia in 1223, and Russian cities became parts of the Mongol empire until their liberation by **Grand Duke Dimitri** and **Ivan the Great.**

For Additional Review

Compare the experiences of peasants and artisans in the aftermath of the Bubonic Plague.

1. The population decline of the fourteenth century led many English landowners to
   (A) experiment with deep furrow planting to allow for longer planting seasons.
   (B) seek greener pastures in the New World.
   (C) switch from traditional farming to sheep raising.
   (D) turn to planting more stable cash crops like turnips and corn.
   (E) sell their lands and move to urban areas.

2. All of the following are true of the Black Death EXCEPT
   (A) It is believed to have been carried to Europe by seaborne rats.
   (B) It caused discoloration in its victims.
   (C) It was highly contagious.
   (D) It could be cured by flagellation.
   (E) It probably came to Europe from the Black Sea area.

3. English strength in the Hundred Years' War was due in part to its
   (A) superior naval warfare.
   (B) use of the longbow.
   (C) ability to fight primarily on its own lands.
   (D) secret allies among the French privileged classes.
   (E) superior armor.

4. The church during the Late Middle Ages is best characterized as
   (A) growing increasingly focused on secular matters.
   (B) growing increasingly focused on spiritual matters.
   (C) enjoying harmonious relationships with European monarchs.
   (D) enjoying popular support.
   (E) enjoying an improved relationship with local dioceses.

5. *Unam Sanctum* expressed which of the following views?
   (A) Temporal power was subject to the spiritual power of the church.
   (B) The power of the church was subject to the power of the monarch.
   (C) Only one pope could serve as the head of the church.
   (D) The Conciliar Movement was unjust.
   (E) Joan of Arc was a heretic.

6. The Avignon Papacy was established by which of the following popes?
   (A) Pope Boniface VIII (r. 1294–1303)
   (B) Pope Innocent III (r. 1198–1216)
   (C) Pope Urban IV (r. 1261–1264)
   (D) Pope Celestine V (r. 1294)
   (E) Pope Clement V (r. 1305–1314)

7. All of the following figures opposed the growing papal authority EXCEPT
   (A) John Huss.
   (B) John Wycliffe.
   (C) William of Ockham.
   (D) Marsilius of Padua.
   (E) Bernard Saisset.

8. To what period of church history does the "Babylonian Captivity" refer?
   (A) the Great Schism
   (B) the period of two popes
   (C) the period of three popes
   (D) the Conciliar Movement era
   (E) the Avignon papacy

9. What faith did Prince Vladimir of Kiev (972–1015) adopt in Russia?
   (A) Islam
   (B) Catholicism
   (C) Judaism
   (D) Greek Orthodox Christianity
   (E) Buddhism

10. Which of the following best describes Joan of Arc's role in the French victory at Orléans?
   (A) Joan of Arc led the military attack against the English.
   (B) Joan of Arc served as the inspiration to the French military.
   (C) Joan of Arc was a military advisor to King Charles VII.
   (D) Joan of Arc helped confuse the English forces during the battle.
   (E) Joan of Arc helped determine military strategy for the battle.

How did Europeans respond to the plague that struck Europe in 1347? What does their response tell us about their understanding of disease and its spread?

DOCUMENT 1 Source: A procession of flagellants at Tournai in Flanders in 1349.

DOCUMENT 2 Source: Spread of the Black Death.

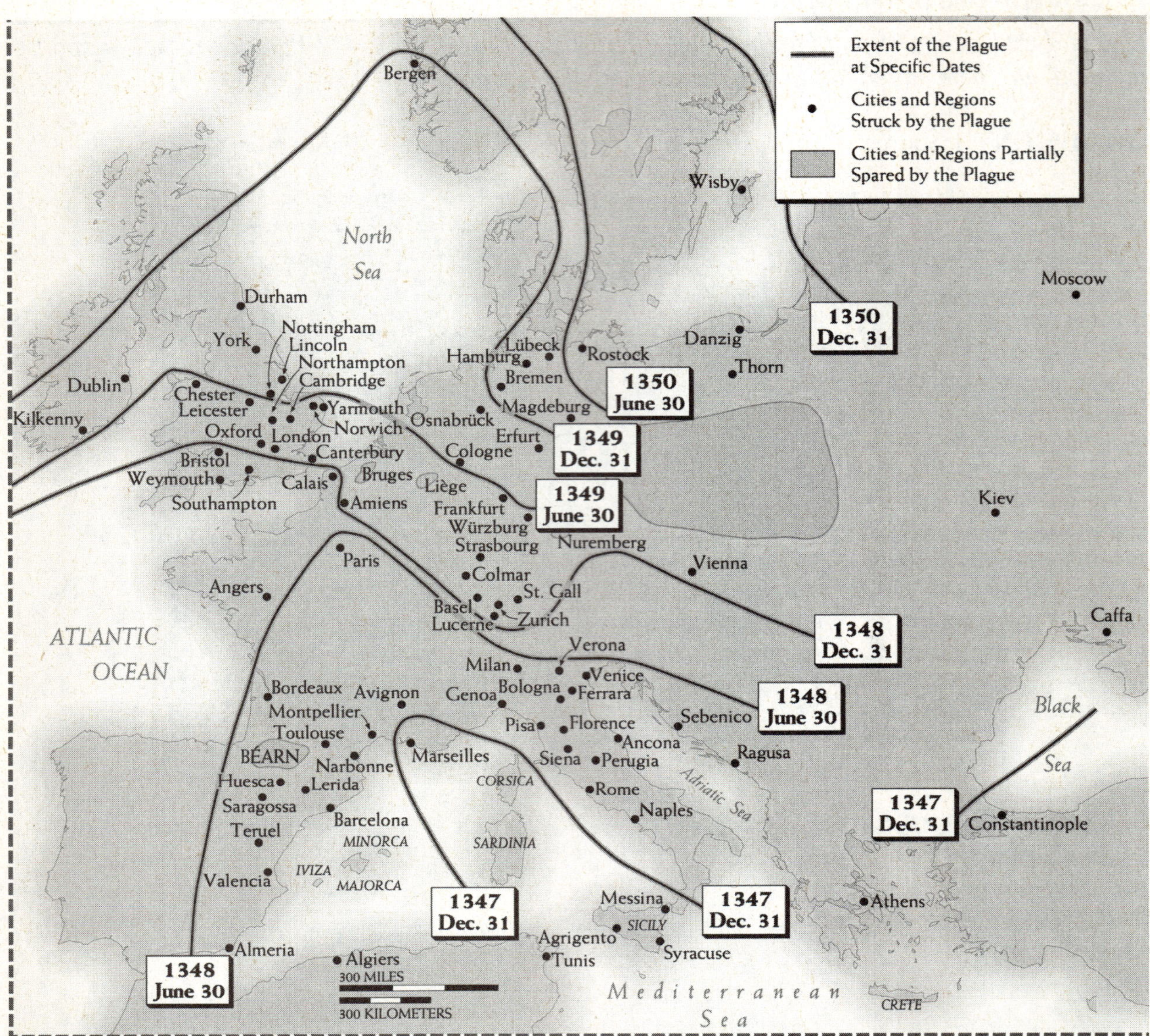

Map 9–1 **SPREAD OF THE BLACK DEATH** Apparently introduced by seaborne rats from Black Sea areas where plague-infested rodents had long been known, the Black Death brought huge human, social, and economic consequences. One of the lower estimates of Europeans dying is 25 million. The map charts the plague's spread in the mid-fourteenth century. Generally following trade routes, the plague reached Scandinavia by 1350, and some believe it then went on to Iceland and even Greenland. Areas off the main trade routes were largely spared.

DOCUMENT 3 Source: Giovanni Boccaccio, poet and humanist, describes the ravages of the Black Death, The Decameron

In Florence, despite all that human wisdom and forethought could devise to avert it, even as the cleansing of the city from many impurities by officials appointed for the purpose, the refusal of entrance to all sick folk, and the adoption of many precautions for the preservation of health; despite also humble supplications to God, and often repeated both in public procession and otherwise by the devout; towards the beginning of the spring of the said year [1348] the doleful effects of the pestilence began to be horribly apparent by the symptoms that [appeared] as if miraculous.

Which maladies seemed to set entirely at naught both the art of the physician and the virtues of physic; indeed, whether it was that the disorder was of a nature to defy such treatment, or that the physicians were at fault…and, being in ignorance of its source, failed to apply the proper remedies; in either case,…almost all died within three days of the appearance of the said symptoms.

DOCUMENT 4 A caricature of physicians. [Image: Kagan, page 261]

A caricature of physicians (early sixteenth century). A physician carries a uroscope (for collecting and examining urine); discolored urine signaled an immediate need for bleeding. The physician/surgeon wears surgical shoes and his assistant carries a flail—a comment on the risks of medical services.   Hacker Art Books Inc.

DOCUMENT 5 Source: Robert of Avesbury, reporting on a procession of flagellants through the streets of London in 1349.

About Michaelmas 1349 over six hundred men came to London from Flanders, mostly of Zeeland and Holland origin. Sometimes at St. Paul's and sometimes at other points in the city they made two daily public appearances wearing cloths from the thighs to the ankles, but otherwise stripped bare. Each wore a cap marked with a red cross in front and behind. Each had in his right hand a scourge with three tails.   Each tail had a knot and through the middle of it there were sometimes sharp nails fixed. They marched naked in a file one behind the other and whipped themselves with these scourges on their naked and bleeding bodies. Four of them would chant in their native tongue and another four would chant in response like a litany. Thrice they would all cast themselves on the ground in this sort of procession, stretching out their hands like the arms of the cross. The singing would go on and, the one who was in the rear of those thus prostrate acting first, each of them in turn would step over the others and give one stroke with his scourge to the man lying under him. This went on from the first to the last until each of them had observed the ritual to the full tale of those on the ground. Then each put on his customary garments and always wearing their caps and carrying their whips in their hands they retired to their lodgings. It is said that every night they performed the same Penance.

Free-Response Question

Discuss the pre-existing conditions that contributed to the health crisis of the Black Death during the late Middle Ages.

ANSWERS AND EXPLANATIONS

Multiple-Choice Questions

- **1. (C) is correct.** To recoup their losses, some landowners converted arable land to sheep pasture, substituting more profitable wool production for labor-intensive grains.
- **2. (D) is correct.** Flagellation was not a cure for the Black Death; rather it was the behavior of religious fanatics and extremists who believed that by making themselves bleed, they would summon divine intervention and God would rescue them from their illness. This behavior did not result in a cure of the Black Death.
- **3. (B) is correct**. English strength in the Hundred Years' War was due in part to the use of the longbow, a weapon that enabled the English to fire six arrows a minute with a force sufficient to penetrate an inch of wood or the armor of a knight at 200 yards.
- **4. (A) is correct.** The church during the Late Middle Ages was growing increasingly focused on consolidating its political powers and handling secular matters. This condition weakened its spiritual authority and pitted it against monarchs and congregants, who felt that it was asserting too much control over everyday affairs.

☐ **5. (A) is correct.** *Unam Sanctum* expressed the view of Pope Boniface VIII (and, by extension, the Catholic church) that the temporal power of monarchs and rulers was ultimately beneath the spiritual power of the church as represented in the leadership of the Pope. This papal bull was Boniface's defensive response to Philip the Fair's relentless antipapal campaign.

☐ **6. (E) is correct.** The Avignon Papacy was established by Pope Clement V, who moved the papal court to Avignon to land that belonged to the pope. Clement made it his permanent residence to escape the pressure of Philip the Fair and to leave a Rome that had been divided by the confrontation between Boniface and Philip after the *Unam Sanctum* bull.

☐ **7. (E) is correct.** Bernard Saisset, was Pope Boniface's Parisian legate and the Bishop of Parmiers. He was also a powerful secular lord who angered Philip the Fair and wound up being accused of heresy and treason. Boniface demanded Saisset's release and acclaimed him as a defender of clerical political independence in France.

☐ **8. (E) is correct.** The "Babylonian Captivity" is a reference to the Avignon Papacy—specifically to the isolation of the papacy in remote Avignon. The expression alludes to the biblical experience of the Israelites.

☐ **9. (D) is correct.** Prince Vladimir of Kiev received delegations of Roman Catholics, Muslims, Jews, and Greek Orthodox Christians, all of whom hoped to see Russia embrace their faith. Vladimir chose Greek Orthodoxy, closely aligning the Russian region with its neighbors in the Byzantine empire.

☐ **10. (B) is correct.** Joan of Arc was a visionary whose impeccable sense of timing enabled the French to defeat the English at the Battle of Orléans. Joan of Arc served as a source of inspiration and gave confidence to the French military.

Document-Based Question

How did Europeans respond to the plague that struck Europe in 1347? What does their response tell us about their understanding of disease and its spread?

Convincing essays might note:

☐ The terrifying rapidity with which the plague spread throughout Europe and the consequences of that rapidity for Europeans practical and psychological response to the pandemic (See **Documents 2** and **3**)

☐ The tendency of the plague to follow trade routes and of groups like the flagellants to do the same (See **Documents 1, 2**, and **5**)

☐ The diversity of the response to the plague, a response that included public policy, medical, and religious components (See Documents **1, 3, 4**, and **5**)

☐ The relationship between the diverse responses and the implied causes of the plague (See Documents **1, 3, 4**, and **5**)

Free-Response Question

Discuss the pre-existing conditions that contributed to the health crisis of the Black Death during the late Middle Ages.

The Black Death did not appear out of nowhere in the 1340s. In fact, there were numerous conditions that existed in the late Middle Ages that made Europe a fantastic breeding ground for the Black Death.

The largely agrarian workforce had increased the food supply and the amount of arable land, and these developments had stimulated the population growth. Europe doubled its population between 1000 and 1300. At the same time, modest advances in science and trade had encouraged the growth of cities. Around 1300, the population explosion began to exceed the rate of food production, and unemployment and famine became common occurrences for many Europeans. Crop failures in the early fourteenth-century exacerbated the inadequate food supply, and many towns experienced tremendous suffering and loss of life. A lack of understanding about good hygiene made people more vulnerable to illness and infection. By the 1340s, most Europeans had been weakened by decades of overpopulation, famine, and illness generally.

The Black Death, which appeared in Europe in the mid-fourteenth century and spread rapidly, was facilitated by these conditions. Rats spread the disease quickly into various areas on major trade routes. Already undernourished and in bad health, Europeans were especially susceptible to Bubonic Plague, which was transmitted by rat or human-borne fleas. The plague passed quickly from one victim to another—often through germs spread by sneezing and coughing. Because medical technology and hygiene during the late Middle Ages were not sophisticated, physicians did not realize that quarantining plague victims and exterminating rodents could help slow the spread of the disease.

CHAPTER 10

Renaissance and Discovery

The Renaissance era in European history is associated with Italy because its major city-states were venues for some of the most significant events of the period. Italy's strategic location at the crossroads of the East and the West and its profitable Eurasian trade enabled the country to prosper during the late Middle Ages. Italian rulers and merchants served as patrons to the arts, government, and education, and this patronage led to an unprecedented cultural Renaissance, or rebirth.

The Renaissance in Italy (1375–1527)

The three major city-states in Italy during the Renaissance were Florence, Milan, and Venice.

- **The Treaty of Lodi (1454–1455)** was a fragile alliance between the city-states of Naples, Milan, and Florence, and their rivals, Venice and the Papal States.
- **Cosimo dé Medici (1389–1464)** was a wealthy Florentine who manipulated elections and influenced the local council, the *Signoria,* in his uncontested control of the city. His grandson, **Lorenzo the Magnificent (1449–1492)** ruled Florence with a totalitarian regime from 1478–1492. The later Florentine ruler, **Piero dé Medici,** allied with Naples against Milan in 1494, and he was exiled after handing Pisa and other Florentine possessions over to Charles VIII of France.
- **The Visconti family** came to rule Milan in 1278, and the **Sforza family** took over in 1450. Both ruled without constitutional restraint or political competition. A Sforza, **Ludovico il Moro** appealed to French in 1494 for aid against Naples and its allies, an appeal that resulted in France's acquisition of Florence.
- In response to the takeover of Florence by Charles VIII of France, in 1495 Ferdinand of Aragon created the **League of Venice,** a counter-alliance designed to protect Venice, Milan, the Papal States, and Emperor Maximilian I from France.
- **Girolamo Savonarola (1452–1498),** a radical Dominican monk, convinced a mob of Florentines to exile Piero dé Medici and claimed that France's victory was divine justice. Savonarola ruled Florence until his imprisonment and execution in 1498.
- **Venice** was an exception to the trend of despotic rule. It was ruled by a **merchant oligarchy,** a 300-member senate, and a judicial council.

Humanism

The growth of Humanism, the study and appropriation of the ideals expressed in Latin and Greek classics and other works of antiquity, played an important role in the Italian Renaissance. Humanists were innovative educators who believed in the importance of well-rounded education and in the noble ideals expressed by **Baldassare Castiglione (1478–1529)** in his ***Book of the Courtier.***

- Humanists espoused a program of study that included rhetoric, politics, moral philosophy, poetry, history, and that embraced classical and biblical sources. In Florence, the **Florentine Platonic Academy** arose under the patronage of Cosimo dé Medici to enable humanists to devote their attention to Plato and the Neoplatonists.

- Scholars consider **Francesco Petrarch (1304–1374)** the "father of humanism." Other important works and authors of the era include *The Divine Comedy* by **Dante Alighieri (1265–1321)** and *The Decameron* by **Giovanni Boccaccio (1313–1375).**
- In art, new techniques like *chiaroscuro* and **linear perspective** were perfected and implemented by Renaissance artists of extraordinary talent, including **Michelangelo Buonarroti (1475–1564)**, **Leonardo da Vinci (1452–1519)**, and **Raphael (1483–1520)**.

The Northern Renaissance

Northern humanism was stimulated by the learning imported by students returning to the Netherlands from Italy, and the movement was spread further by the effects of the French invasions of Italy.

- Northern humanism was supported by the **Brothers of the Common Life,** a lay religious movement based in the Netherlands. Northern humanists often had more diverse social backgrounds and were more interested in religious reform than were their Italian counterparts. They were able also to convey their educational ideals to more people as a result of **Johann Gutenberg**'s invention of printing with movable type in 1450.
- **Desiderius Erasmus (1466?–1536)**, the most famous northern humanist, tried in his writings to unite the classical ideal of civic virtue with Christian ideals. His works embraced anticlerical views and satirized religious superstition. He produced a Greek edition of the New Testament (1516), and then a Latin translation of the Greek edition.
- The English humanist **Thomas More (1478–1535)** is best known for *Utopia,* a critique of society that envisioned an imaginary society based on tolerance and communal property.

Voyages of Discovery and the New Empire in the West

Primarily economic motives led western European countries to the exploration of faraway lands. A quest for gold and spices led European explorers to Africa and India.

- Explorers such as **Christopher Columbus (1451–1506)**, **Amerigo Vespucci (1451–1512)**, **Ferdinand Magellan (1480–1521)**, and **Henry the Navigator (1394–1460)** sought to conquer unknown worlds and bring riches and supplies back to Europe.
- The effects of discoveries on the culture and history of conquered peoples frequently involved exploitation and, in some cases, complete destruction.

For Additional Review

Compare the northern Renaissance with the Italian Renaissance in terms of scholarly, literary, and artistic production.

1. Which of the following is NOT an attribute of Renaissance humanism?
    (A) It ignored the contributions of religion.
    (B) It celebrated worldly achievements.
    (C) It was based on solid scholarly methods.
    (D) It emphasized man's potential.
    (E) The contributions of Petrarch.

2. For the most part, Italian city-states during the Renaissance
    (A) were governed by democratically-elected bodies.
    (B) were dominated by despotic rule.
    (C) worked in cooperation with neighboring city-states.
    (D) were characterized by extreme poverty.
    (E) were characterized by central organization.

3. Which of the following figures in Italian history is most responsible for the French invasion of Italy in 1495?
    (A) Girolamo Savonarola
    (B) Cosimo dé Medici
    (C) Ludovico il Moro
    (D) Cesare Borgia
    (E) Lucrezia Borgia

4. The works of art created by Renaissance artists
    (A) did not represent a departure from the works of medieval artists.
    (B) tended to be less secular in subject than works by medieval artists.
    (C) incorporated new techniques of *chiaroscuro* and linear perspective.
    (D) tended to be less multi-dimensional than works by Byzantine and Gothic counterparts.
    (E) were generally more abstract than works by medieval artists.

5. All of the following views might have been expressed by Erasmus EXCEPT
    (A) *philosophia Christi.*
    (B) "where there is smoke, there is fire."
    (C) doctrine and disputation are as important to faith as are piety and Christian practice.
    (D) ancient Christian sources should be available in their original versions.
    (E) "leave no stone unturned."

6. Which of the following books examines Renaissance court life and conduct?
    (A) Castiglione's *Courtier*
    (B) Machiavelli's *Prince*
    (C) Boccaccio's *Decameron*
    (D) Erasmus's *Adages*
    (E) More's *Utopia*

7. Which of the following developments stimulated the spread of humanism in Northern Europe?
   (A) the publication of Erasmus's *Adages*
   (B) the creation of the Vulgate
   (C) artistic patronage in Renaissance Italy
   (D) the collapse of humanism in Italy
   (E) the French invasions of Italy

8. Thomas More's *Utopia* is best described as
   (A) a critique of contemporary society.
   (B) a series of sonnets to a woman named Laura.
   (C) a book of proverbs.
   (D) a book of dialogues.
   (E) an epic poem about an imaginary land.

9. Which of the following conditions was most responsible for the extraordinary cultural developments that occurred in Italy during the Renaissance?
   (A) a lack of European conflicts
   (B) a unified country
   (C) a lack of conflicts among city-states
   (D) an abundance of wealth
   (E) politically conservative, despotic rulers

10. The phase of European discovery and exploration that occurred during the Renaissance was prompted mainly by the quest for
   (A) gold and spices.
   (B) silver and gold.
   (C) slaves and horses.
   (D) antiquities and gold.
   (E) slaves and Christian converts.

How did fifteenth and sixteenth-century Europeans see the inhabitants of the New World? How did knowledge of New World peoples shape European's vision of themselves?

DOCUMENT A Source: Martin Behaim's map of the world, the basis for Columbus's assumptions about global geography.

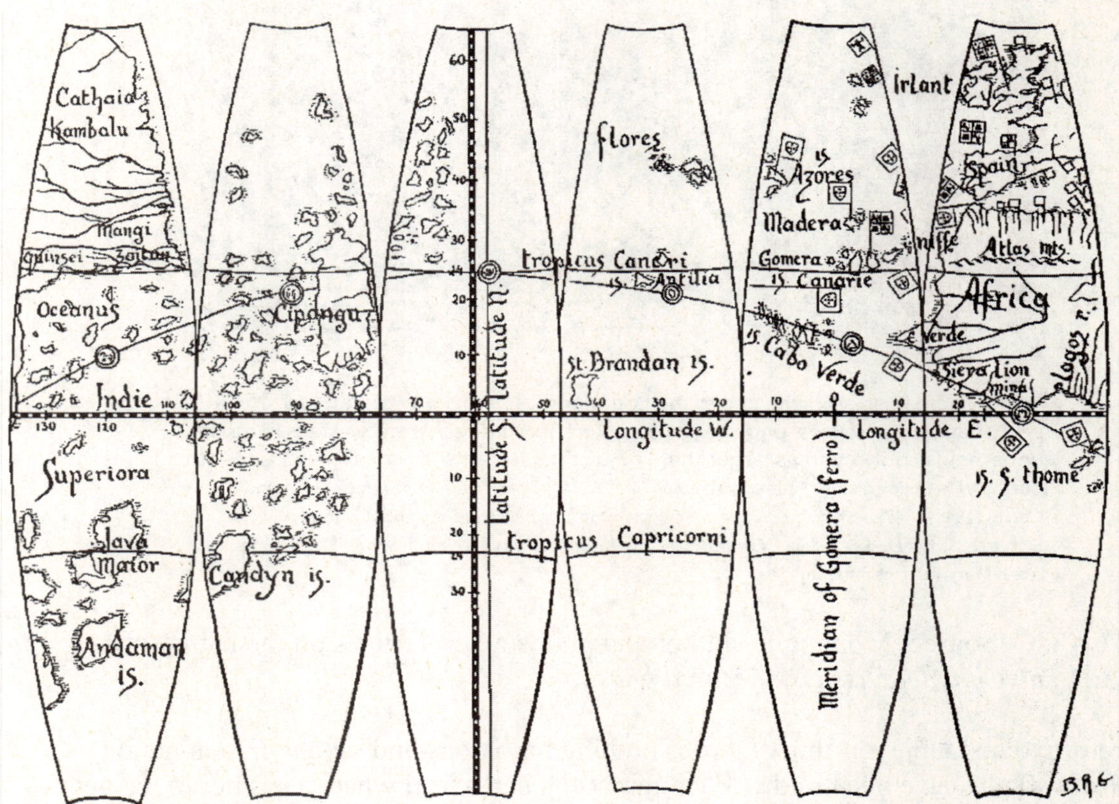

What Columbus knew of the world in 1492 was contained in this map by the Nuremberg geographer Martin Behaim, creator of the first spherical globe of the earth. The ocean section of Behaim's globe is reproduced here. Departing the Canary Islands (in the second section from the right), Columbus expected his first major landfall to be Japan (Cipangu, in the second section from the left). When he landed at San Salvador, he thought he was on the outer island of Japan. Thus, when he arrived in Cuba, he thought he was in Japan.   From Admiral of the Ocean Sea by Samuel Eliot Morison. Copyright © 1942 by Samuel Eliot Morison; Copyright © renewed 1970 by Samuel Eliot Morison. By permission of Little, Brown and Company, (Inc.)

Armored Spanish soldiers, under the command of Pedro de Alvarado (d. 1541)
and bearing crossbows, engage unprotected and crudely armed Aztecs, who are
nonetheless portrayed as larger than life by Spanish artist Diego Duran (sixteenth
century).   Codex Duran: Pedro de Alvarado (c. 1485–1541), companion-at-arms of Hernando
Cortés (1845–1547) besieged by Aztec warriors (vellum) by Diego Duran (16th Century), Codex
Duran, Historia De Las Indias (16th century). Biblioteca Nacional, Madrid, Spain. The Bridgeman
Art Library International Ltd.

DOCUMENT C Source: Montaigne, author and philosopher, reflects on the nature of
"barbarism," *The Complete Essays of Montaigne*.

Now, to return to my subject, I think there is nothing barbarous and savage in that nation
[Brazil], from what I have been told….Each man calls barbarism whatever is not in his own
practice; for indeed it seems we have no other test of truth and reason than the example and
pattern of the opinions and customs of the country we live in. There [we] always [find] the
perfect religion, the perfect government, the perfect and accomplished manners in all things.
Those [foreign] people are wild, just as we call the fruits that Nature has produced by herself and
in her normal course; where really it is those that we have changed artificially and led astray
from the common order that we should call wild. The former retain alive and vigorous their
genuine virtues and proprieties, which we debased the latter by adapting them to gratify our
corrupted taste….It is not reasonable that [our human] art should win the place of honor over our
great and powerful mother nature.

DOCUMENT D Source: Christopher Columbus, describing his first voyage to the New World.

The people of this island and of all the other islands which I have found and of which I have information, all go naked, men and women, as their mothers bore them….They have no iron or steel or weapons, nor are the fitted to use them. This is not because they are not well built and of handsome stature, but because they are very marvelously timorous….They refuse nothing that they possess, if it be asked of them; on the contrary, they invite any one to share it and display as much love as if they would give their hearts….They do not hold any creed nor are they idolaters; but they all believe that power and good are in the heavens and were very firmly convinced that I, with these ships and men, came from the heavens.

DOCUMENT E Source: Dominican friar Bartholomew De Las Casas describes the inhabitants of the New World.

God has created all these numberless people to be quite the simplest, without malice or duplicity, most obedient, most faithful to their natural lord, and to the Christians, whom they serve; the most humble, most patient, most peaceful, and calm, without strife nor tumults; not wrangling, nor querulous, as free from uproar, hate and desire of revenge, as any in the world….

They are likewise of a clean, unspoiled, and vivacious intellect, very capable, and receptive to every good doctrine; most prompt to accept our Holy Catholic Faith, to be endowed with virtuous customs; and they have as little difficulty with such things as any people created by God in the world.

Free-Response Question

Discuss the impact of the invention of the printing press on the northern Renaissance.

ANSWERS AND EXPLANATIONS

Multiple-Choice Questions

☐ **1. (A) is correct.** Renaissance Europe, especially after the fourteenth century, was characterized by growing national consciousness and political centralization, an urban economy based on organized commerce and capitalism, and growing lay and secular control of thought and culture, including religion.

☐ **2. (B) is correct.** There were five major city-states in Italy during the Renaissance: the duchy of Milan, the republics of Florence and Venice, the Papal States, and the kingdom of Naples. Competition for political power in the city-states was so intense during this period that the most of the city-states had devolved into despotism. Venice was the exception to this rule because it was ruled by a merchant oligarchy. These wealthy city-states were rich in trade and did much of the banking for the rest of Europe, but they were constantly at war with each other and were autonomous.

3. **(C) is the correct.** Ludovico il Moro asked the French to aid him when Milan was challenged by Italian city-state rivals Naples, Florence, and the Borgia Pope Alexander VI. Charles VIII responded with an invasion of Florence and Naples. When Piero dé Medici tried to appease Charles VIII, Girolamo Savonarola helped agitate the Florentines, and they exiled Piero. Louis XII, Charles's successor, eventually invaded Milan in 1499. Ludovico il Moro spent his last years in a French prison.

4. **(C) is correct.** Renaissance artists implemented *chiaroscuro,* a kind of shading that replicated the natural play of light and dark, and *linear perspective,* an adjustment of the size of figures in works to create in viewers a feeling of continuity with the painting. Renaissance artwork represented a significant departure from the works of medieval artists, and was—on the whole—more secular, more multi-dimensional, and less abstract than medieval works.

5. **(C) is correct.** Erasmus described his own beliefs with the phrase *philosophia Christi,* which meant that his piety involved imitating Christ. He was most offended by Scholastics and Lutherans who allowed doctrine and differences of opinion to overshadow the basics of Christian piety and practice. The adages "where there is smoke, there is fire" and "leave no stone unturned" are from Erasmus's *Adages.* Like his fellow Humanists, Erasmus believed in the primacy of ancient Christian sources; he edited the works of the Church fathers and offered a Greek edition of the New Testament in 1516.

6. **(A) is correct.** Baldassare Castiglione's *Courtier* was basically an instruction book in behavior for those in the court at Urbino. It encouraged knowledge of many ancient languages and history, athletic prowess, and military skill, and it emphasized a high moral character governed by courtesy.

7. **(E) is correct.** The French invasions of Italy made possible the spread of Italian learning to France. Italian humanism helped bring about educational and religious reform in France. Guillaume Budé and Jacques Lefèvre d'Étaples were the leaders of French humanism. Erasmus's *Adages* did not dramatically advance the cause of Northern humanism. The Vulgate had been used by Christian Europe for over a thousand years; artistic patronage in Renaissance Italy did not have any dramatic effect on Northern humanism; and the collapse of humanism in Italy came at a later point in time—by then Humanism in Northern Europe was well under way.

8. **(A) is correct.** Thomas More's *Utopia* was his vision of an ideal society in which people were treated equally and were tolerant of one another, and property was communal.

9. **(D) is correct.** The vast wealth of Italian city-states was responsible for the cultural flowering of the Italian Renaissance. Italian rulers and benefactors had tremendous fortunes to spend on luxuries like great artwork, scholarly pursuits, and writing; on the patronage of sculptors and painters like Michelangelo and Leonardo da Vinci; and on enabling writers to focus their efforts of poetry and prose.

10. **(A) is correct.** While there was demand for slaves and Christian converts, the primary motives for the exploration and discovery during the Renaissance were economic. Explorers were looking to gain access to African gold and West Indian spices, highly-coveted European commodities.

Document-Based Question

How did fifteenth and sixteenth-century Europeans see the inhabitants of the New World? How did knowledge of New World peoples shape European's vision of themselves?

Convincing essays might note:
- The tendency of Europeans to identify the New World and its peoples with "nature" (See **DOCUMENTS C, D,** and **E**)
- The way in which ideas about the inhabitants of the New World are connected to each author's self-image (See **DOCUMENTS B, C, D,** and **E**)
- The diversity of responses to the peoples of the New World (See **DOCUMENTS B, C, D,** and **E**)
- The tendency of European authors to see the inhabitants of the New World through the lens of preconceived ideas (See **DOCUMENTS A, B, C, D**, and **E**)

Free-Response Question

Discuss the impact of the invention of the printing press on the northern Renaissance.

The invention of the printing press by Johann Gutenberg around 1450 had a tremendous impact on the northern Renaissance. Gutenberg invented printing with movable type in the German city of Mainz, which was then the center of printing in western Europe. This invention, coming as it did in a German city, enhanced the ability of northern humanists like Erasmus to get their works into publication, to expand their readership, and to spread their ideas across the rest of Europe.

By 1400, as a result of an expansion of schools and universities during the Middle Ages, a larger population of literate lay readers existed. The development of the printing press in 1450 put books and pamphlets containing the ideas of northern humanists into the hands of those readers. Following Gutenberg's invention, books were produced more rapidly, were more affordable, and were enjoyed by scholarly and lay readers alike. By 1500, printing presses were operating in more than sixty cities in Germany alone, and 200 cities internationally. Many of the popular books at this time included books of piety and religion, calendars, and "how to" books on child rearing, animal husbandry, and agriculture. In addition, clergymen were able to mass-produce indulgences and religious tracts.

Erasmus' far-reaching influence is an index of the impact of the invention of the printing press on the northern Renaissance. In his *Colloquies* and *Adages,* Erasmus transmitted his anticlerical views and critiques of popular religious superstition to many loyal Catholics readers throughout Europe who were seeking church reforms in the period before the Reformation. Erasmus' Greek New Testament and Latin translation reached Martin Luther, who relied on those translations in preparing his own German edition of the New Testament.

The printing press made possible the more rapid and more widespread dissemination of ideas. As the new ideas of the Renaissance emerged, they were carried through the printed word to various cities and rural areas alike. The importance of the invention of the printing press to the spread of northern Renaissance thought cannot be overestimated.

CHAPTER 11

The Age of Reformation

The Protestant Reformation was a reaction against the traditions, policies, dogma, and abuses of the Catholic Church. Those who opposed the church were called **Protestants** for the various protests they waged. These protests altered the religious unity of Europe, brought about religious wars, and resulted in the fragmentation of the Christian faith into many different denominations.

The Protestant Reformation

Some of the issues that led to this religious shift away from the Catholic Church include:

- **The Great Schism:** Two different popes **(Clement VII and Urban VI)** claimed authority over the Catholic Church; this conflict was not resolved until the **Council of Constance in 1414,** and the overall result was the weakening of church unity
- **Sales of indulgences, nepotism, simony:** These everyday aspects of Catholic life angered Protestants, who believed that they were not scripturally sound
- **Clerical immorality and absenteeism:** Protestants were alienated by these conditions
- **Humanism:** The rise of scholarship during the Renaissance, and humanists' interest in returning to classical texts made study of and access to the Bible of great importance

Protestant Leaders

- **Martin Luther (1483–1546)** was a German theologian who was discontented with the medieval Christian teachings that God required perfect righteousness for salvation. Luther argued on behalf of **"justification by faith alone"** whereby grace was given freely to those who believed in Jesus Christ. In 1517, Luther famously attacked the Catholic system of indulgences promoted by preachers like **John Tetzel,** when he posted his **Ninety-five Theses** on the door of Castle Church in Wittenberg. Condemned to heresy in 1520, Luther was protected by friends who hid him in a castle, where he translated the New Testament into German, using Erasmus's Greek text and Latin translation.
- **Ulrich Zwingli (1484–1531)** headed the Reformation in Switzerland. He was opposed to the sale of indulgences and to religious superstition. Zwingli successfully petitioned for the **end to clerical celibacy** and the **clerical right to marry,** which was adopted by all Protestant groups. Zwingli believed that anything that lacked literal support in Scripture was not to be believed. He questioned traditional behaviors like fasting, adoration of saints, pilgrimages, and other sacraments. His beliefs translated into a regime of harsh discipline in Zurich, and made Switzerland an example of puritanical Protestantism. Zwingli and Luther disagreed in the famous **Marburg Colloquy** (1529) over the presence of Christ's body in the **Eucharist.**
- **John Calvin (1509–1564)** was the leader of the Calvinists, who believed in divine **predestination** or the concept of **"the elect"** and the individual's duty to reform society according to God's plan. Calvin's *Institutes of Christian Religion* is a theological statement of the Protestant faith. Calvin believed in the unity of church and state, and he stressed the **sovereignty of God** over all creation. He led a theocracy in Geneva.

The English Reformation

Protestant ideas did not take hold in England until the sixteenth century. Important figures are listed below.

- **Martin Bucer,** a Strasbourg reformer who influenced Calvin, was forced into exile during the Augsburg Interim and helped to draft the religious texts of the English Reformation.
- **William Tyndale (1492–1536)** translated the New Testament into English in 1524–1525, and it began to circulate in England in 1526.
- **Cardinal Thomas Wolsey (1475–1540)** and **Sir Thomas More (1478–1535)**, chief ministers to King Henry VIII, guided the royal response to English Protestantism.
- **Henry VIII (r. 1509–1547)**, married to Catherine of Aragon, who did not produce an heir; in order to divorce her and then to marry Anne Boleyn, he converted himself (and the rest of England) to Anglicanism.
- **Thomas Cranmer (1489–1556)** and **Thomas Cromwell (1485–1540)**, Lutheran sympathizers who helped Henry VIII declare himself supreme ruler over English affairs, which enabled him to take charge of the Church of England and put an end to Catholic interference with his policies.
- **Edward VI (r. 1547–1553)**, Henry's son, presided over the flourishing of Protestantism in England. Oversaw all vestiges of Catholicism removed from churches and English life.

The Counter-Reformation

Important figures, documents, and groups of the Counter-Reformation are listed below.

- **The Society of Jesus,** the new order of Jesuits, was one of the most influential Counter-Reformation groups, organized by **Ignatius of Loyola** in the 1530s. Loyola's ***Spiritual Exercises*** embodied a program of spiritual disciplines that encouraged believers to transform their spiritual selves through discipline and practice.
- **The Council of Trent,** the result of an effort by Emperor Charles V to force Pope Paul to reassert church doctrine, met from 1545–1563, and was attended predominantly by Italians. The council made reforms in internal Church affairs (including restricting the selling of church offices and religious relics), strengthened the authority of local bishops, and subjected them to new rules requiring them to reside in their dioceses and be visible and accessible to their congregations.

For Additional Review

Consider what family life was like in early modern Europe during the Reformation. Focus on marriage, family size, birth control, education, and childcare.

" … To praise sacramental confession and the reception of the Most Holy
Sacrament once a year, and much better once a month, and better still every
week …"

" … To praise the relics of the saints … [and] the stations, pilgrimages,
indulgences, jubilees, Crusade indulgences, and the lighting of candles
in the churches …"

1. The spiritual "to do" list shown above was most likely written by which of the following?
   (A) Ulrich Zwingli
   (B) Martin Luther
   (C) John Calvin
   (D) Ignatius of Loyola
   (E) Thomas Bucer

2. A main tenet of the Anabaptists was
   (A) infant baptism being required of its adherents.
   (B) the Eucharist representing the symbolic presence of Christ.
   (C) "justification by faith alone."
   (D) adult baptism being essential to an acceptance of one's faith.
   (E) salvation through predestination.

3. The Peace of Augsburg
   (A) made permanent the division between Catholicism and Lutherans in Germany.
   (B) recognized Anabaptism as a legal form of Christian worship.
   (C) resulted in a surge of Catholic converts.
   (D) recognized Calvinism as a legal form of worship.
   (E) led to the weakening of the Calvinist sect.

4. Which of the following was NOT a major tenet in Luther's religious views?
   (A) God can be approached solely through good works.
   (B) Faith comes through study of the Word of God.
   (C) Justification by faith alone.
   (D) The equality of all believers in God's eyes.
   (E) Luther attacked the sale of indulgences.

5. Which of the following resulted from Martin Luther's nailing his list of ninety-five theses to
   the door of the Castle Church at Wittenberg?
   (A) German peasants decided to stage their revolt in solidarity with Luther's ideas.
   (B) Martin Luther was imprisoned and exiled a few days later.
   (C) Luther became famous overnight, and German officials began official proceedings
       against him.
   (D) John Calvin assumed the role of chief Protestant leader and rallied believers to Luther's
       aid.
   (E) Pope Leo X excommunicated Luther.

6. Which of the following is NOT a reason for the princes' support of Luther?
    (A) Lutheran support for the power of civil authorities.
    (B) Their religious convictions.
    (C) The command of the Holy Roman Emperor.
    (D) The need to protect their revenues from Church taxation.
    (E) The *Babylonian Captivity of the Church*.

7. The chief disagreement between Luther and Zwingli at the Marburg Colloquy involved
    (A) whether or not Protestants and Catholics should be allowed to marry.
    (B) the question of the Christ's physical presence in the Eucharist.
    (C) whether traditions such as fasting, pilgrimages, and worship of saints were acceptable to
        Protestants.
    (D) the role of celibacy among Protestant clergy.
    (E) whether or not the German New Testament or the Vulgate should be used in Protestant
        houses of worship.

8. Which of the following authored *The Book of Common Prayer?*
    (A) Martin Luther
    (B) Thomas Cranmer
    (C) Thomas Cromwell
    (D) Edward VI
    (E) St. Ignatius of Loyola

9. Henry VIII's transition from Catholic ruler to head of the Church of England came about as a
    result of
    (A) pressure from the English Protestant faction that a ruler must represent the faith of his or
        her subjects.
    (B) an uprising within the Catholic Church that effectively excommunicated Henry for
        various heresies.
    (C) his conversion following his marriage to Anne Boleyn.
    (D) the influence of his daughter, Mary I.
    (E) his desire to annul his marriage with Catherine of Aragon and to wed Anne Boleyn.

10. Followers of John Calvin believed that
    (A) every Christian believer was predestined for salvation.
    (B) salvation could come by faith alone.
    (C) society required a complete moral transformation.
    (D) women's rights were less important than men's rights.
    (E) "the elect" were eternally damned.

Defend or refute the following statement: The Protestant Reformation was a unified movement of dissent against the Catholic Church.

Historical Background: The Protestant Reformation officially began with Martin Luther's posting his "Ninety-five Theses" on the door of Castle Church in Wittenberg in 1517, but discontent with the dogma and policies of the Catholic Church had begun long before that. Luther's act dramatized the internal division in the western church. As this powerful religious movement spread throughout northern Europe, Protestant reformers challenged many aspects of the Catholic Church and traditional religion that they found troublesome and not scripturally sound. These leaders, including Martin Luther, John Calvin, Ulrich Zwingli, and others, sought to worship as Christians in a church free from papal influence and clerical corruption.

DOCUMENT 1   Source: The Apostles' Creed, official statement of faith for Catholic Church, ca. 1200.

I believe in God, the Father Almighty, the Creator of heaven and earth, and in Jesus Christ, His only Son, our Lord:
Who was conceived of the Holy Spirit, born of the Virgin Mary, suffered under Pontius Pilate, was crucified, died, and was buried.
He descended into hell.
The third day He arose again from the dead.
He ascended into heaven and sits at the right hand of God the Father Almighty, whence He shall come to judge the living and the dead.
I believe in the Holy Spirit, the holy Catholic Church, the communion of saints, the forgiveness of sins, the resurrection of the body, and life everlasting. Amen.

DOCUMENT 2   Source: Anonymous, caricature of indulgence preacher John Tetzel, 1517. The last lines of the jingle read: "As soon as gold in the basin rings, right then the soul to Heaven springs."

A contemporary caricature depicts John Tetzel, the famous indulgence preacher. The last lines of the jingle read, "As soon as gold in the basin rings, right then the soul to Heaven springs." It was Tetzel's preaching that spurred Luther to publish his ninety-five theses.   Courtesy Stiftung Lutherge-denkstaten in Sachsen-Anhalt/Lutherhalle, Wittenberg

DOCUMENT 3   Source: Martin Luther, German theologian, letter to Albert of Mainz, October 31, 1517

Finally, works of piety and love are infinitely better than indulgences, and yet these are not preached with such ceremony or such zeal; nay, for the sake of preaching the indulgences they are kept quiet, though it is the first and the sole duty of all bishops that the people should learn the Gospel and the love of Christ, for Christ never taught that indulgences should be preached. How great then is the horror, how great the peril of a bishop, if he permits the Gospel to be kept quiet, and nothing but the noise of indulgences to be spread among his people! Will not Christ say to them, "straining at a gnat and swallowing a camel"? In addition to this, Most Reverend Father in the Lord, it is said in the Instruction to the Commissaries which is issued under your name, Most Reverend Father (doubtless without your knowledge and consent), that one of the chief graces of indulgence is that inestimable gift of God by which man is reconciled to God, and all the penalties of purgatory are destroyed. Again, it is said that contrition is not necessary in those who purchase souls [out of purgatory] or buy confessionalia.

DOCUMENT 4   Source: Martin Luther, "Ninety-five Theses," document posted on door of Castle Church, Wittenberg, 1517.

32. Those who believe that they can be certain of their salvation because they have indulgence letters will be eternally damned, together with their teachers.
33. Men must especially be on guard against those who say that the pope's pardons are that inestimable gift of God by which man is reconciled to him.
34. For the graces of indulgences are concerned only with the penalties of sacramental satisfaction established by man.
35. They who teach that contrition is not necessary on the part of those who intend to buy souls out of purgatory or to buy confessional privileges preach unchristian doctrine.
36. Any truly repentant Christian has a right to full remission of penalty and guilt, even without indulgence letters.
37. Any true Christian, whether living or dead, participates in all the blessings of Christ and the church; and this is granted him by God, even without indulgence letters.

DOCUMENT 5   Source: "Parody of the Apostles Creed," ca. 1520.

I believe in the Pope, binder and looser in heaven, earth, and hell,
and in Simony, his only son our lord,
Who was conceived by the canon law
and born of the Romish church.
Under his power truth suffered,
was crucified, dead and buried,
and through the ban descended to hell,
rose again through the gospel and Paul
and was brought to Charles,
sitting at his right hand,
who in future is to rule over spiritual and worldly things.
I believe in canon law,
in the Romish church,
in the destruction of faith and of the communion of saints,
in indulgences both for the remission of guilt and penalty in purgatory,
in the resurrection of the flesh in an Epicurean life,
because given to us by the Holy Father, the Pope. Amen.

DOCUMENT 6   Source: Martin Luther, letter to his wife, October 4, 1529.

Grace and peace in Christ! Dear Käthie—Our friendly conference at Marburg is almost ended, and we have agreed upon nearly all points, except that our opponents maintain that only bread and wine are present in the sacrament, although admitting Christ's spiritual presence in the elements. Today, Landgrave is making every effort to unite us, or at least to make us consider each other brethren and members of Christ's body.

DOCUMENT 7   Source: Martin Luther, *Against Catholicism,* 1535.

If the pope were the head of the Christian Church, then the Church were a monster with two heads, seeing that St. Paul says that Christ is her head. The pope may well be, and is, the head of the false Church. Where the linnet is, there is also the cuckoo, for he thinks his song a thousand times better than the linnet's. Even thus, the pope places himself in the Church, and so that his song may be heard, overcrowds the Church. The cuckoo is good for something, in that its appearance gives tidings that summer is at hand; so the pope serves to show us that the last day of judgment approaches. There are many that think I am too fierce against popedom; on the contrary, I complain that I am, alas! too mild; I wish I could breathe out lightning against pope and popedom, and that every word were a thunderbolt.

DOCUMENT 8   Source: John Calvin, Protestant reformer, *Institutes of the Christian Religion,* 1536.

The covenant of life not being equally preached to all, and among those to whom it is preached not always finding the same reception, this diversity discovers the wonderful depth of the Divine judgment. Nor is it to be doubted that this variety also follows, subject to the decision of God's eternal election. If it be evidently the result of the Divine will, that salvation is freely offered to some, and others are prevented from attaining it—this immediately gives rise to important and difficult questions, which are incapable of any other explication, than by the establishment of pious minds in what ought to be received concerning election and predestination—a question, in the opinion of many, full of perplexity; for they consider nothing more unreasonable, than that, of the common mass of mankind, some should be predestinated to salvation, and others to destruction.

DOCUMENT 9   Source: Philip Melanchthon, German humanist and religious scholar, *Of the Power and Primacy of the Pope,* 1537.

On this account our consciences are sufficiently excused; for the errors of the kingdom of the Pope are manifest. And Scripture with its entire voice exclaims that these errors are a teaching of demons and of Antichrist. The idolatry in the profanation of the masses is manifest, which, besides other faults are shamelessly applied to most shameful gain. The doctrine of repentance has been utterly corrupted by the Pope and his adherents. For they teach that sins are remitted because of the worth of our works. Then they bid us doubt whether the remission takes place. They nowhere teach that sins are remitted freely for Christ's sake, and that by this faith we obtain remission of sins.

Thus they obscure the glory of Christ, and deprive consciences of firm consolation, and abolish true divine services, namely, the exercises of faith struggling with despair concerning the promise of the Gospel. They have obscured the doctrine concerning sin, and have invented a tradition concerning the enumeration of offenses, producing many errors and despair.

They have devised, in addition, satisfactions, whereby they have also obscured the benefit of Christ. From these, indulgences have been born, which are pure lies, fabricated for the sake of gain. Then, how many abuses and what horrible idolatry the invocation of saints has produced! What shameful acts have arisen from the tradition concerning celibacy!

DOCUMENT 10   Source: The Forty-two Articles of 1553, issued in England during the reign of Edward VI.

XII. Works before Justification

Works done before the Grace of Christ, and the inspiration of his Spirit, are not pleasant to God, for as much as they spring not of Faith in Jesus Christ; neither do they make Men meet to receive Grace, or (as the School Authors say) deserve Grace of Congruity; yea rather for that they are not done as God hath willed and commanded them to be done, we doubt not but they have the nature of Sin.

Free-Response Question

Compare and contrast the policies of the Catholic Church in Europe before and after the Council of Trent.

ANSWERS AND EXPLANATIONS

Multiple-Choice Questions

☐   **1. (D) is correct.** The references to relics, pilgrimages, indulgences, and jubilees indicate that this author is Catholic. Only Ignatius of Loyola fits this category. This passage comes from his *Spiritual Exercises.*

☐   **2. (D) is correct.** Anabaptists rejected infant baptism, and they maintained that adult baptism was required because it was more respectful of adult freedom to choose one's faith and it was consistent with adult baptism in the Bible. "Justification by faith alone" was a tenet of Lutherans. The concept of predestination was a feature of Calvinism. Zwinglians believed in the symbolic presence of Christ in the Eucharist.

☐   **3. (A) is correct.** The Peace of Augsburg effectively ratified the division between Catholics and Lutherans in Germany by recognizing that rulers of lands could determine the religion of their lands. Lutherans were allowed to retain all church lands seized before 1552. The Peace of Augsburg did not recognize or extend any benefits to Anabaptists or Calvinists. Following the Peace of Augsburg, Calvinists organized national revolutions throughout northern Europe.

☐   **4. (A) is correct.** The issue was not whether good works should be done, but how those works should be regarded. It was unbiblical, Luther argued, to treat works as contributing to one's eternal salvation, something only an almighty God could bestow.

☐   **5. (C) is correct.** Martin Luther achieved fame after October 31, 1517, when he nailed his list of ninety-five complaints against the Catholic Church to the Castle Church door. The boldness of his act prompted official proceedings against him. In October of 1518 he was called before the general of the Dominican order of Augsburg. He was not imprisoned. While he was eventually excommunicated by Pope Leo X, this did not occur until 1521, some four years later, and it was as much a result of Luther's challenging the infallibility of the pope in a 1519 debate with the Ingolstadt professor John Eck. German peasants did not stage their revolt until 1525. John Calvin did not rise to the head of the Protestant Reformation or assist Luther during his time as *persona non grata* with the Catholic Church; he was just 8 years old the year that Luther posted his famous theses.

□ **6. (C) is correct.** In April 1521, Luther presented his views before the Diet of Worms, over which the newly elected Emperor Charles V presided. Ordered to recant, Luther declared that to do so would be to act against Scripture, reason, and his conscience. On May 26, 1521, he was placed under the imperial ban, which made him an "outlaw" to secular as well as religious authority. For his own protection, friends disguised and hid him in Wartburg Castle at the instruction of Elector Frederick.

□ **7. (B) is correct.** The chief disagreement between Luther and Zwingli at the Marburg Colloquy involved their theological interpretation of the Eucharist, and whether or not Christ was actually physically present in the bread that represented his body, and the wine that represented his blood. Luther believed that Christ was physically present, and Zwingli was adamant that Christ was only symbolically present. The two men were unable to resolve their disagreement.

□ **8. (B) is correct**. Thomas Cranmer authored *The Book of Common Prayer,* and the Act of Uniformity imposed it in all English churches in 1549 under Edward VI.

□ **9. (E) is correct.** Henry VIII desperately wanted to divorce his wife, Catherine of Aragon, who had been unable to conceive an heir, and to marry one of her ladies-in-waiting, Anne Boleyn. Because his marriage to Catherine had required special papal dispensation and had lasted 18 years, Henry was not in a good position to be granted an annulment. Henry's advisers, Thomas Cranmer and Thomas Cromwell, both Lutheran sympathizers, realized that the chances of Henry's receiving a papal annulment were not likely, and they helped him declare himself supreme in religious and domestic affairs, thus establishing the Protestant Church of England.

□ **10. (C) is correct.** Calvinists were motivated by a desire to transform the morality of their society. They believed that only certain Christians—namely Calvinists—were predestined for salvation and that only those who were predestined and sought actively to perform every action according to God's law were "the elect," or God's chosen one. Lutherans believed that salvation was possible through faith alone. Calvinists had a reputation for protecting women from abusive men. For this reason, Geneva was called a "woman's paradise."

Document-Based Question

Defend or refute the following statement: The Protestant Reformation was a unified movement of dissent against the Catholic Church.

The Protestant Reformation grew into a powerful movement of dissent against the Catholic Church, despite the fact that it was made up of several distinct branches of revolt. Leaders such as Martin Luther, John Calvin, and Ulrich Zwingli agreed on a criticism of Catholicism for financial corruption and for perpetuating superstitions that were not grounded in scripture. Yet these men differed—sometimes sharply—in their religious beliefs and in their ambitions. Consequently, as the Reformation spread across Germany and Switzerland and then into much of northern Europe, it gave rise to a variety of Protestant churches, each with its own defining characteristics.

The Protestant Reformation was jump-started by Martin Luther's posting of his "Ninety-five Theses" on the door of the Castle Church in Wittenberg in 1517. The force and certainty of this brazen physical act is echoed in Luther's voice as he assails the corruption and ignorance that he believes informs every level of the Catholic Church (**DOCUMENT 4**). Luther injects special fury into his condemnation of the Catholic Church's abuse of indulgences, or remissions of the temporal penalties imposed by priests on penitents for their sins. In fact, indulgences were regularly issued for small payments of cash, and they were used to remit not only the sins that the laity might commit in the future, but also the sins their dead relatives might be committing continually in purgatory. One of the most notorious abusers of the sale of indulgences was John Tetzel. The caricature of Tetzel (**DOCUMENT 2**) uses both a visual image and verbal sarcasm to suggest the extent of this preacher's moral corruption. By contrast, Luther believed that any truly repentant Christian could seek remission of guilt without a letter of indulgence. Luther amplified his objection to the detrimental effect of indulgences in a letter to Albert of Mainz (**DOCUMENT 3**). There he criticizes bishops for spending so much time encouraging Catholics to purchase grace that the bishops have little time left to preach the gospel and lead parishioners to a deeper engagement with God. Philip Melanchthon, an ally of Luther's, carries this argument one step further in *Of the Power and Primacy of the Pope.* Melanchthon condemns the pope and other Catholic leaders, and he uses words such as *demons* and *Antichrist* to suggest that the selling of indulgences is actually satanic.

While most Protestant reformers felt as Martin Luther did about the problem of indulgences, they took up other issues also in their dissent against the teachings of the Catholic Church. For instance, as Ulrich Zwingli brought Protestantism to Switzerland, he argued not only against the use of indulgences but also against the propagation of religious superstitions. Like Luther, Zwingli opposed clerical celibacy and proposed the right of clergy to marry—an idea that was later accepted among all Protestants. Zwingli differed from Luther on one crucial aspect of Protestant dogma—the presence of Christ in the Eucharist. This difference of agreement came to a head at the Colloquy of Marburg, which Philip of Hesse had arranged in order to unite Swiss and German Protestants into a single alliance. Zwingli believed that Christ's presence in the Eucharist was symbolic. As Luther made clear in a letter to his wife, he and his followers believed that Christ was present in the Eucharist bodily (**DOCUMENT 6**). Neither leader was willing to compromise; as a result, the Protestant movement remained divided over this issue.

Most Protestants agreed that the power of the pope in the Catholic Church was not justified in the scriptures. Luther voiced this concern in his work *Against Catholicism,* in which he argued provocatively that—in claiming to be the head of the church—the pope effectively was unseating no less than Christ (**DOCUMENT 7**). His contempt is underscored by his use of animal imagery to describe the church ("a monster") and the pope ("the cuckoo"). Luther answers critics of his ferocity by stating his wish that he had the power to discipline, if not kill, the pope with "lightning." Of course, not all critics of the central role of the pope in the Catholic Church used a tone of unbridled fury. The Protestant reformers' distaste is conveyed humorously in the 1520 parody of the Apostles' Creed (**DOCUMENT 5**), which ridicules the Catholic Church for its papal abuses by adapting the format of the actual Apostles' Creed (**DOCUMENT 1**). This brilliant and savage parody illustrates the deep anger Protestants felt toward what they perceived as the Catholic Church's many abuses of the sacredness of the Christian faith.

Though Luther and Zwingli could not agree on all aspects of their Protestant agendas, they shared a basic moderation in their aims. In contrast, an in response to discontent with Luther and Zwingli, various radical movements developed during the Protestant Reformation. These included the Anabaptist Movement, which Zwingli and Luther (together with Catholics) sought to suppress, and other groups, like the Spiritualists and Antitrinitarians. These diverse groups held beliefs that were incompatible with those of more moderate Protestants. Each group tended to focus more on its own emergence as a religious movement than on opposing the Catholic Church.

John Calvin brought the Protestant movement to Geneva, and by the second half of the sixteenth century Calvinism had replaced Lutheranism as the major Protestant force in Europe. Calvin believed that individual souls were pre-destined to be elected (or not elected) by God for salvation (**DOCUMENT 8**). This focus differed dramatically from Lutheranism, and shifted the focus of the Protestant Reformation toward self-discipline and personal morality and away from opposition to the Catholic Church.

The Protestant Reformation contained a variety of sometimes contentious religious leaders and systems. Despite the presence of divergent theories and practices, the Protestant Reformation developed into an impressive movement of dissent that lessened the power and reach of the Catholic Church dramatically.

Reader's Comments on Sample Student DBQ Essay

☐ The essay has a clear thesis that is substantiated with documentary evidence
☐ The student makes use of most of the documents
☐ The student groups relevant documents and analyzes the points of view of their authors
☐ The essay has an impressive grasp of the major issues faced by Protestant Reformers
☐ The student makes excellent use of outside information

Possible student score: 7-8

Free-Response Question

Compare and contrast the policies of the Catholic Church in Europe before and after the Council of Trent.

The Council of Trent was a turning point in the policies of the Catholic Church. The Catholic Church called the Council of Trent in 1545—at the behest of Emperor Charles V—to deal with the success of the Protestant Reformation and to reassert church doctrine. Pope Paul appointed a commission aimed at reform, headed by Caspar Contarini, a leading liberal theologian and a critic of the church's fiscal policies. Prior to the Council of Trent, the Catholic Church had experienced many instances of internal corruption. Some of the Catholic Church policies that most angered the Reformation opposition included simony, absenteeism, immorality, nepotism, clerical ignorance, and the sale of indulgences. In response to these perceived shortcomings, the Council of Trent made numerous reforms that addressed and attempted to solve these issues.

Simony, or the practice of selling church offices to the highest bidder, was a common Catholic Church practice before Trent. The Council of Trent took steps to curtail the selling of church offices and other religious goods. In addition, the Council addressed the absenteeism that had outraged many Protestants, as it required bishops who resided in Rome to move to their appointed offices within their dioceses. Trent also strengthened the authority of local bishops, allowing them to oversee and maintain religious practices in their dioceses. Clerical immorality in the era prior to Trent typically involved church leaders' violating laws of celibacy and seeking worldly entertainments. Trent cracked down on such behavior by requiring the clergy to maintain strict celibacy. To limit instances of nepotism (which had been prevalent before the Council of Trent), clergy were required to be better educated and were instructed to award positions on merit rather than on personal or political connections. Despite the best efforts of the council, not all goals were accomplished completely or satisfactorily. For instance, both nepotism and clerical ignorance remained despite having been reduced greatly. The council upheld the policy of selling indulgences—a Catholic Church policy that fueled the fury of Protestants.

The Council of Trent did make sweeping changes and reforms that addressed some of the issues of internal corruption, but it by no means did away with all of the conditions that remained objectionable to Protestant and Catholic reformers.

CHAPTER 12

The Age of Religious Wars

In this era, religious conflict between Protestants and Catholics and dynastic rivalries fueled wars.

The French Wars of Religion (1562–1598)

- French Protestants, or **Huguenots,** were under surveillance in France as early as 1520, when Lutheran ideas began to circulate in Paris. Huguenot persecution was essentially a policy under **Henry II**, and it continued until **Henry IV (Henry of Navarre)** took the throne in 1589.
- **Catherine de Médicis,** who served as regent for Charles IX, sought allies among the Protestant factions. In 1562, she issued the **January Edict,** which granted Protestants freedom to worship publicly outside towns and to hold synods.
- In March of 1562, a duke from the powerful Guise family led a massacre on the Huguenots, starting the French Wars of religion. In the series of wars that followed, Huguenots and their Protestant allies fought against the Guise faction. Catherine of Médicis aligned herself with the Guises, and plotted against Coligny, the leader of the Huguenots. Catherine supported the 1572 **St. Bartholomew's Day Massacre,** in which 3,000 Huguenots were killed. Within three days, 20,000 Huguenots had been executed.
  - **The Peace of Beaulieu,** led by Henry III in May, 1576, granted Huguenots almost complete religious and civil freedom, but within seven months, the Catholic League forced Henry to back down from these liberties. After Henry III's murder, the Protestant Henry IV (Henry of Navarre) rose to the throne, converted to Catholicism, and proclaimed a formal religious settlement with the Protestants. Called the **Edict of Nantes** and made on April 13, 1598, this proclamation recognized and sanctioned Huguenots' rights within France. It granted them freedom of worship, right of assembly, and a series of other liberties.

Imperial Spain and the Reign of Philip II (r. 1556–1598)

Philip II of Spain was the extremely powerful Catholic ruler of Habsburg lands of Bohemia, Austria, and Hungary, as well as Castile, in Spain.

- Spain dominated the Mediterranean in the **Battle of Lepanto,** in which the Turkish fleet was brutally put down. Under **Philip II,** Spain annexed Portugal and gained access to their empires in Africa, India, and the Americas.
- Philip did not see similar success in his attempts to conquer the **Netherlands.** When Cardinal Granvelle attempted to institute ecclesiastical reform in the Netherlands, **William of Orange** and the Count of Egmont led the resistance. Egmont was executed, and the resistance was put down by the Duke of Alba, but the Dutch continued their campaign against Spanish governance.

- In 1576, Catholic and Protestant provinces came together in opposition to Spain in what is known as the **Pacification of Ghent.** True peace with Spain was not achieved until 1609, when the **Twelve Years' Truce** gave the northern provinces independence. Full recognition was finalized in the **Peace of Westphalia** in 1648.

England and Spain (1553–1603)

The Catholic Mary Tudor (Mary I) ascended the English throne after challenging the right of Protestant Lady Jane Grey. Mary brought sweeping change to England, restoring the Catholicism of Henry VIII and executing the Protestants Thomas Cranmer, Hugh Latimer, and John Hooper.

- Mary's half-sister, **Elizabeth I,** was her successor following a **1559 Act of Supremacy** that undid much of the anti-Protestant legislation Mary had enacted. The act asserted Elizabeth's right as "supreme governor" over spiritual and secular affairs. Elizabeth strove to maintain a middle ground by not granting too much control to Catholics or Protestants.
- Facing a real threat from Spain, England allied with France in 1571. At this time, explorers Francis Drake and John Hawkins were preying on Spanish ships. Elizabeth's decision to execute **Mary Stuart, Queen of Scots,** an ardent Catholic and French royal with a legitimate heir to the Scottish throne, aroused Catholic anger.
    - Philip II of Spain ordered his Armada to prepare for war with England. This battle resulted in a complete victory for England and encouraged European Protestants.

The Thirty Years' War (1618–1648)

The Thirty Years' War was a complicated series of battles in four phases—**Bohemian (1618–1625), Danish (1625–1629), Swedish (1630–1635),** and the **Swedish-French (1635–1648)**—between countries with radically opposed political and religious agendas.

- In the **Bohemian Period,** Calvinists demanded more freedom from Catholic Habsburg ruler Ferdinand. Protestant nobility responded to Ferdinand's revocation of religious rights by throwing two of his regents out a window in the **"defenestration of Prague."**
- In the **Danish Period,** King Christian IV of Denmark, tried to bring Protestantism to Germany and was forced to retreat by Maximilian. In 1629, Ferdinand outlawed Calvinism by issuing the **Edict of Restitution.**
- In the **Swedish Period,** military tactics of King Gustavus Adolphus of Sweden helped Protestants win the battle at Breitenfeld. The Swedes refused to join the **Peace of Prague Agreement**—a compromise between German Protestant states and Ferdinand.
- The **Swedish-French Period,** the final phase of the Thirty Years' War, involved French, Swedish, and Spanish soldiers wreaking havoc in Germany. At this most destructive point in the war, religious issues became secondary to political ones.
- **The Treaty of Westphalia of 1648** stopped Ferdinand's Edict of Restitution and recognized Calvinists. The independence of the Swiss Confederacy and provinces of Holland was proclaimed. German princes were acknowledged as the supreme rulers over their principalities. The treaty broadened the legal status of Protestantism in the realm, but it perpetuated Germany's internal division and political weakness.

For Additional Review

Analyze the achievements and disappointments of the Thirty Years' War.

1. In 1588 King Henry III of France ordered the murder of
   (A) Henry of Navarre
   (B) the duc d' Anjou
   (C) the duc de Conde
   (D) two prominent members of the Guise family
   (E) Henry II

2. The "Defenestration of Prague" was a response to which monarch's policies?
   (A) Elizabeth I
   (B) Mary Stuart
   (C) Ferdinand, Archduke of Styria
   (D) Philip II
   (E) Mary Tudor

3. The defeat of the Spanish Armada resulted in all of the following EXCEPT
   (A) a stunning victory for England.
   (B) encouragement for Catholics across Europe.
   (C) Philip II's death.
   (D) the destruction of one third of Spain's ships.
   (E) the end of Spanish naval victories.

"It is apparent that there is a mutual obligation between the king and the officers of a kingdom; that the government of the kingdom is not in the hands of the king in its entirety, but only the sovereign degree; and that there are definite conditions on either side."

4. The above quotation comes from a work by which of the following figures?
   (A) Queen Elizabeth I
   (B) Catherine de Médicis
   (C) Sir William Cecil
   (D) Theodore Beza
   (E) Philip II

5. Which of the following was NOT a phase of the Thirty Years' War?
   (A) The Swedish-French Period
   (B) The Danish Period
   (C) The Bohemian Period
   (D) The Swedish Period
   (E) The French-Netherlandish Period

6. Between 1618 and 1648, the Thirty Years' War involved
   (A) virtually every major European land.
   (B) primarily nations in southern Europe.
   (C) only religious factions in the British Isles.
   (D) only the 360 political entities that comprised Germany.
   (E) only nations south of Denmark.

7. The January Edict
    (A) abolished Calvinism in France.
    (B) granted Protestants in France the freedom to worship outside towns and to hold synods.
    (C) forbade French Protestants from holding synods.
    (D) resulted in the deaths of over 20,000 Huguenots.
    (E) was issued by Henry III.

8. Which of the following was responsible for restoring England to the Catholicism of Henry VIII?
    (A) Mary Tudor
    (B) Mary Stuart
    (C) Elizabeth I
    (D) Sir Francis Walsingham
    (E) Hugh Latimer

9. All of the following were elements of the Treaty of Westphalia of 1648 EXCEPT
    (A) it rescinded Ferdinand's Edict of Restitution.
    (B) it reasserted the religious settlement of the Peace of Augsburg.
    (C) it recognized Calvinists.
    (D) it elevated Sweden to the rank of an elector state.
    (E) it proclaimed the independence of the Swiss Confederacy and the United Provinces of Holland.

10. The Act of Supremacy that passed Parliament in 1559
    (A) repealed Mary Tudor's anti-Protestant legislation and asserted Elizabeth's right as supreme governor over spiritual and secular affairs.
    (B) mandated a revised version of the second *Book of Common Prayer*.
    (C) enabled Elizabeth I to declare war on Spain.
    (D) required Elizabeth to deal cautiously with Protestants.
    (E) resulted in England and France signing a mutual defense pact.

What were the limits of Henry IV of France's willingness to embrace religious toleration? How were his views shaped by the events of decades leading up to the Edict of Nantes (1598)?

Document A Source: The Massacre of worshiping Protestants at Vassay, France (March 1, 1562).

Document B Source: Theodore Beza, Protestant pamphleteer, defends the right to resist tyranny, *Three Treatises by Hotman, Beza, and Mornay.*

We must now speak of the third class of subjects, which though admittedly subject to the sovereign in a certain respect, is, in another respect, and in cases of necessity the protector of the rights of the sovereignty itself, and is established to hold the sovereign to his duty, and even, if need be, to constrain and punish him….The people is prior to all the magistrates, and does not exist for them, but they for it….Whenever law and equity prevailed, nations neither created nor accepted kings except under definite conditions. From this it follows that when kings flagrantly violate these terms, these who have the power to give them their authority have no less power to deprive them of it.

Document C Source: Henry IV recognizes Huguenot religious freedom, *The Edict of Nantes* (April 13, 1598).

Art. I. Firstly, that the memory of everything done on both sides...shall remain extinct and suppressed, as if it were something which had never occurred….
Art. II. We forbid all our subjects...to attack, be hostile to, injure or provoke each other in revenge for the past….

Art. III. We ordain that the Catholic, Apostolic, and Roman religion shall be restored and reestablished in all places…where its practice has been interrupted….

Art. VI. And we permit those of the so-called Reformed religion to live and dwell in all towns and districts of this our kingdom…provided that they conduct themselves in other respects to the provisions of our present Edict….

Art. XXI. Books dealing with the matters of the aforesaid so-called Reformed religion shall not be printed and sold publicly….

Free-Response Question

Analyze some of the existing conditions that led to the Thirty Years' War.

ANSWERS AND EXPLANATIONS

Multiple-Choice Questions

☐ **1. (D) is correct.** Forced by his weakened position into unkingly guerilla tactics, and also emboldened by the news of the English victory over the Spanish Armada in 1588, Henry had both the duke and the cardinal Guise assassinated.

☐ **2. (C) is correct.** The "Defenestration of Prague" was a literal tossing out a window two of Ferdinand's regents in May 1618. The Protestant nobility in Prague was responding to Ferdinand's revocation of religious freedoms of Bohemian Protestants.

☐ **3. (B) is correct.** The defeat of the Spanish Armada did not encourage Catholics across Europe because Spain was defeated so dramatically by the English. It did boost the morale of Protestants around the world. Spain continued to win impressive victories into the 1590s, but the Armada did mark the end of Spanish invincibility.

☐ **4. (D) is correct.** Theodore Beza was famous for *On the Rights of Magistrates Over Their Subjects,* a work that justifies the rights of lower authorities to overthrow tyrannical rulers. Queen Elizabeth I and Sir William Cecil (her adviser) could not be the authors of this passage, because they were constantly asserting Elizabeth's right over all aspects of her kingdom. Philip II would also be an unlikely candidate for authorship, because he attempted to dominate his subjects. Catherine de Médicis is also not the correct choice; she would have been in favor of a monarchy that could not be challenged.

☐ **5. (E) is correct.** The French-Netherlandish Period was not one of the four phase of the Thirty Years' War. Those were (in order) the Bohemian Period, the Danish Period, the Swedish Period, and the Swedish-French Period.

☐ **6. (A) is correct.** As various conflicts multiplied, virtually every major European land became involved in the Thirty Years' War.

☐ **7. (B) is correct.** The January Edict was Catherine de Médicis's response to the growing Protestant minority. It granted Protestants the freedom to worship publicly outside towns and to hold synods. The Saint Bartholomew's Day Massacre resulted in the deaths of over 20,000 Huguenots.

☐ **8. (A) is correct.** Mary Tudor married Philip II of Spain, one of the most overtly Catholic leaders of the age. Under her domestic policies, Parliament repealed the Protestant statutes of Edward VI and reverted to the Catholic practice of her father, Henry VIII. Hugh Latimer was one of the respected Protestant leaders who was executed by Mary. Mary Stuart, Queen of Scotland, was Catholic, but she did not exert her beliefs on the Protestant majority in her realm. Sir Francis Walsingham advised Queen Elizabeth on various plots against her life, including one in which Mary Stuart was complicit.

☐ **9. (D) is correct.** The Treaty of Westphalia did not elevate Sweden to the rank of elector state. Using the process of elimination, you should know that the Treaty of Westphalia *did* rescind Ferdinand's Edict of Restitution, recognize Calvinism, reassert the settlement at Augsburg, and proclaim the independence of the Swiss Confederacy and the United Provinces of Holland. It also elevated Bavaria to the rank of an elector state.

☐ **10. (A) is correct.** In 1559, an Act of Supremacy passed Parliament, revoking all of Mary Tudor's anti-Protestant legislation and declaring Elizabeth's right as "supreme governor" over religious and secular affairs. The Act of Uniformity mandated the revised version of the second *Book of Common Prayer*.

Document-Based Question

What were the limits of Henry IV of France's willingness to embrace religious toleration? How were his views shaped by the events of decades leading up to the Edict of Nantes (1598)?

Convincing essays might note:

☐ Henry IV's awareness of the cycle of violence created by sectarian conflict in France (See Documents A and C)

☐ The argument Beza makes for the use of force against a monarch and Henry IV's willingness to compromise (See Documents B and C)

☐ Henry IV's determination to prohibit provocative action (See Document C)

☐ Henry IV's unwillingness to grant equal status to Protestantism, signaled by the phrase "so-called Reformed religion," and his insistence that it be contained to specific areas in his realm where it was already dominant (See Document C)

Free-Response Question

Analyze some of the existing conditions that led to the Thirty Years' War.

The Thirty Years' War was the outgrowth of major religious and political differences that had been brewing throughout Europe for many years. Major religious conflicts of the era broke out between Catholics and Protestants, as well as among various Protestant churches.

As a result of the Peace of Augsburg, which attempted to freeze the land holdings of Lutherans and Catholics, a series of land disputes arose between Lutherans and Catholics. In addition, Catholic rulers sought to have returned to the Catholic Church any Catholic property that had been won by Protestant communities as a result of religious conversions. Lutherans tended to ignore these efforts by Catholic leaders, and this behavior led to increased hostility between the two groups.

Lutherans and Calvinists also experienced religious strife at this time. A series of warring factions within German universities was the outgrowth of this strife. Lutherans came to fear and distrust Calvinists after the latter had gained power in Geneva and become allied with England, France, and the Netherlands. Differences of religious opinion and theory about the presence of Christ in the Eucharist further divided Lutherans and Calvinists.

Another major religious conflict involved the Jesuits. The Jesuits dominated in Bavaria, where Catholic ideas and the goals of the Counter-Reformation were upheld. The Jesuits sought to defend their control against the Protestant alliance with the Catholic League. The Jesuits formed an army and set the stage for political conflict over religious differences.

Other political differences that came into play at this period included Germany's politically fragmented status. Germany at this time consisted of numerous autonomous political entities, many of which were distinct from neighboring communities. This lack of centralized government in Germany made it difficult for any consensus; some German princes made outside alliances with leaders of foreign nations; and a general sense of disorganization and lack of unity characterized the German political system in the years prior to the Thirty Years' War.

CHAPTER 13

European State Consolidation in the Seventeenth and Eighteenth Centuries

In the seventeenth century, England and France moved in different political directions—one toward a constitutional form of government, and the other toward monarchy rule.

The Netherlands: Golden Age to Decline

- **The United Provinces of the Netherlands** were the only new state to appear in Europe during the early modern period. A formal republic, the Netherlands central government exercised its authority through **cooperation with the provinces.** Dutch life was marked by **religious toleration** and an economic prosperity that derived from the country's extensive trade and overseas commercial empires and its urban consolidation. The highly advanced **Dutch capital system** financed economic life throughout Europe.

Two Models of European Political Development

- **Monarchy:** England's monarchs' efforts to get new sources of income threatened the country's political and economic stability. In France, Louis XIV made the French nobility dependent upon his patronage, but he allowed the *Parlement* of Paris to oversee his royal decrees and regional *parlements* to administer local taxation.
- **Religion:** In England, the Protestant religious movement of Puritanism opposed the Stuart monarchy and sought to limit its powers. In France, Louis XIV, with the support of Roman Catholics, crushed the Protestant dissident movement to create religious unity.
- **Government:** The English system of a representative Parliament remained ingrained in the political culture, even if it was not the strong institution it would become by the end of the seventeenth century. Parliamentary government in England involved nobility and large landowners trying to limit the power of the monarch to interfere on a local level. The French nobility preferred to support Louis XIV and to benefit from his patronage. In France, the Estates General was not an institutional base for political reform.

Constitutional Crisis and Settlement in Stuart England

- **King James I** was an outsider, a Scot who advocated **the divine right of kings.** James angered many of his subjects by his decision to maintain and augment Anglican episcopacy. He enforced a series of levies on his subjects—new custom duties known as *impositions* that were unpopular with Parliament. In 1620, **Puritan separatists** left England and founded the **Plymouth Colony** in Cape Cod Bay in North America. Another group left a few years later and founded the **Massachusetts Bay Colony.**
- **Charles I** forced more unpopular levies and taxes on the English people, and stationed troops en route to war with Spain in private homes. Parliament forced Charles to agree to the

Petition of Right, a document that required the monarch to gain consent of Parliament before levying taxes or quartering soldiers in private homes. In 1629, when Parliament declared that Charles's levying of taxes without consent was an act of treason.

- In 1641, Parliament presented Charles with the **Grand Remonstrance,** a summary of grievances. Charles invaded Parliament with his soldiers, and Parliament began to raise an army of its own, bringing about the civil war (1642–1646) of England. **Oliver Cromwell (1599–1658)** led the reorganized parliamentary army, known as the **New Model Army** into victory against Charles I's forces. England became a Puritan republic from 1649 until 1660, led by the military dictator Cromwell, who ruled as **"Lord Protector"** until his death in 1658. By then the exiled Charles II was permitted to return and to bring peaceful rule back to England.

- **Charles II**'s rule is known as the **Stuart Restoration** because it brought England back to the conditions of the 1640s, when an Anglican Church was at the fore of religion, and the monarch had little or no responsibility to call Parliament.

- **James II** renewed fears of a Catholic England by openly appointing Catholics to high positions in the court and in the army. In 1689, after James fled to France in the face of William of Orange's superior army, William and Mary were declared the new monarchs of England. This bloodless accession was known as the **Glorious Revolution,** and the subsequent **Bill of Rights** that William and Mary recognized limited the powers of the monarchy, prohibited Roman Catholics from occupying the throne, and guaranteed the role of Parliament in government.

Rise of Absolute Monarchy in France

- **Louis XIV ("The Sun King")** successfully suppressed discontent among the nobility and landowners through absolute monarchy and strict Catholic rule. His motto was **"one king, one law, one faith,"** and he sought glory for France in an aggressive series of foreign wars. Louis XIV was helped early in his reign by **Cardinal Mazarin,** who continued Richelieu's policy of centralization of government.

- Louis XIV was a master of propaganda and the cultivation of his public image. He believed himself to have a **divine right** to his royal authority and was contented to be unbound by the rules of princes and parliaments. He is famous for his alleged outburst, **"L état c'est moi"** ("I am the state").

- Louis XIV's palace court and permanent residence at **Versailles** were symbolic of his majesty. Louis supported religious conformity and helped to suppress the rise of the **Jansenists,** a group of Catholics opposed to the influence of Jesuits on Catholic theology. During Louis XIV's reign, France was superior to other European countries in its administrative bureaucracy, military, and national unity. **Jean-Baptiste Colbert,** controller general of finances, helped Louis XIV consolidate France's wealth and create an economic base for funding wars. Colbert's close government control of the economy (known as **mercantilism)** aimed to maximize exports and internal stores of bullion.

- In 1685, Louis revoked the **Edict of Nantes,** which resulted in the immediate closure of Protestant churches and schools, the expulsion of Protestant ministers, the forced conversion of the laity, and the voluntary emigration of more than a quarter million French people, who joined resistance to France throughout the world.

Central and Eastern Europe

Central and eastern Europe were less economically advanced than their western European rivals, and their economies were more agrarian than maritime in nature.

- **Charles XII** of Sweden came to the throne and led a strong campaign against the Russians in the Great Northern War (1700–1721), but was ultimately defeated. He exhausted Swedish military and economic resources and lost a section of the Baltic coast.
- **The Ottoman Empire** was overextended by the end of the seventeenth century, and its economy was dependent on the loyalty of local rulers in far-flung provinces. Russia began to extend its territory into the Ottoman Empire, and the Turks made a treaty with the Habsburgs and surrendered their control of revenues from Hungary, Transylvania, Croatia, and Slavonia.
- **King John Sobieski (r. 1674–1696)** struggled against a nobility that refused to submit to authority. Poland couldn't collect taxes or build an army without unity in the legislative body.
- The **Austrian Habsburgs** consolidated their political power in the modern Czech Republic, Slovakia, Moravia, Silesia, Hungary, Croatia, and Transylvania. In the early eighteenth century, the Habsburgs received the former Spanish Netherlands, Lombardy, and the kingdom of Naples. These inherited territories faced problems of **Magyar resistance** in Hungary.
- The **Hohenzollerns of Brandenburg-Prussia** acquired a collection of land holdings and transformed them into a single unit. **Frederick William (r. 1640–1688)** forged these disparate areas by breaking up nobles' estates and organizing a royal bureaucracy. Known as **the Great Elector,** Frederick imposed taxes to build up a strong military, members of which took an oath of loyalty to him. Frederick I (the Great Elector's son) built palaces, patronized the arts, and eventually was rewarded for putting his army at the disposal of the Habsburg Holy Roman Emperor with the title of King of Prussia. Frederick I's son, Frederick William I, was a disciple of military discipline, and he built up the size of his army to more than 80,000 in 1740. The army became a great symbol of Prussian power.

Russia Enters the European Political Arena

- The reign of Ivan the Terrible ended with a period of anarchy known as the **Time of Troubles.**
- In 1613, Michael Romanov was elected tsar by Russian nobles. This dynasty would rule Russia until 1917. In 1682, **Peter the Great** ascended the Russian throne as co-ruler with his half-brother, Ivan V. They rose to power under the *strelsy,* the guards of the Moscow garrison. Peter ruled personally, navigating between the jealousy of the *boyars* (nobles) and the greed of the *strelsy.* Peter's determination to **westernize Russia** had five main goals: controlling the *boyars* and *strelsy,* gaining secular control of the church, reorganizing governmental administration, growing the economy, and building a major army and navy.

The Ottoman Empire

- Throughout the sixteenth and seventeenth centuries, Europeans found themselves in frequent conflict with the Ottoman Empire.
- The Ottoman Empire was the dominant political power in the Muslim world after 1516. The Ottomans extended far more religious toleration to their subjects than existed anywhere in

Europe. Islamic religious authorities played an important role in Ottoman political, legal, and administrative life.

■ Military defeats, combined with European advances, put an end to Ottoman expansion. Despite these defeats, the empire remained inward looking, sure of its superiority to the European West.

For Additional Review

Consider the legacy that Louis XIV left France.

Multiple-Choice Questions

1. Jansenists
   (A) were a group of Catholics disenchanted with the influence of the Jesuit order.
   (B) were a minority Protestant sect in France that supported the goals of the Huguenots.
   (C) were recognized by Louis XIV as having the same rights as other religious groups in France.
   (D) were a group of Catholics most closely aligned with the Jesuit order that sought recognition from Louis XIV.
   (E) were supporters of Louis XIV's foreign policy in the Americas.

2. The Glorious Revolution in England involved the accession of
   (A) James II.
   (B) James I.
   (C) William and Mary.
   (D) Charles I.
   (E) Charles II.

3. Puritans began to leave England *en masse* during the rule of which of the following?
   (A) James II
   (B) James I
   (C) Charles I
   (D) Charles II
   (E) Oliver Cromwell

4. The Grand Remonstrance
   (A) was Charles I's address to Parliament requesting that it repeal its declaration of war.
   (B) was Parliament's summary of grievances against Charles I.
   (C) was Oliver Cromwell's defense of his behavior during the English civil war.
   (D) was Louis XIV's declaration of his supreme rule over France.
   (E) resulted in the expulsion of over quarter of a million of French Protestants.

5. The Triple Alliance that formed in 1667 as a result of Louis XIV's military aggression consisted of
   (A) England, Germany, and Sweden.
   (B) Holland, Sweden, and Belgium.
   (C) Switzerland, Sweden and Belgium.
   (D) England, Switzerland, and Holland.
   (E) Sweden, England, and Holland.

6. "L'état c'est moi" ["I am the state"] is the infamous phrase of which of the following French figures?
(A) Louis XIII
(B) Catherine de Médicis
(C) Henry IV
(D) Louis XIV
(E) Cardinal Richelieu

7. The series of laws passed by Parliament between 1661 and 1665 known as the Clarendon Code stipulated all of the following EXCEPT
(A) Roman Catholics being excluded from Parliament.
(B) strict adherence to the *Book of Common Prayer*.
(C) penalties being imposed for attending Anglican worship services.
(D) Presbyterians being excluded from Parliament.
(E) Independents being excluded from Parliament.

8. The *strelsy* played a role in which Russian ruler's ascension to the throne?
(A) Michael Romanov
(B) Ivan the Terrible
(C) Peter the Great
(D) Alexis I
(E) Theodore III

9. The Dutch Golden Age was characterized by all of the following EXCEPT
(A) urban prosperity.
(B) an active Baltic grain trade.
(C) agricultural diversification.
(D) reliance on overseas trade to support a vast domestic shipbuilding industry.
(E) religious intolerance.

10. The Mississippi Bubble
(A) was an argument between France and the Netherlands over rights to the French colony of Louisiana.
(B) was a financial scandal in France involving the Mississippi Company.
(C) was a disputed region of the Mississippi River.
(D) involved speculative investments in Mississippi real estate.
(E) resulted in the wide popularity of John Law and the duke of Orléans.

Document-Based Question

In Louis XIV's view, what were the qualities of an effective monarch? In his opinion, what were the main obstacles to absolute rule?

Document A Source: Cardinal Richelieu, offering advice to Louis XIV predecessor, Louis XIII, "On the Nobility."

It is a very common fault on the part of those born into the nobility to use violence against the common people to whom God seems to have given arms for earning a living rather than for defending themselves. It is very important to stop such disorders by a constant sternness which will make the weakest of yours, although disarmed, as secure in the shelter of your laws as those who are armed.

The nobility had demonstrated, in the recent war, that it inherited the virtue of its ancestors; it is now necessary to discipline the nobles so that they may preserve their former reputation and usefully serve the state. Men who are injurious to the public are not useful to the state; it is certain that nobility which does not serve in war is not only useless, but a burden to the state, and can be compared to a body which supports a paralyzed arm….

As gentry they merit being well treated when they do well, but it is necessary to be severe with them when they fail to do the things their birth binds them to do….

VERSAILLES

LOUIS XIV CONSTRUCTED his great palace at Versailles, as painted here in 1668 by Pierre Patel the Elder (1605–1676), to demonstrate the new centralized power he sought to embody in the French monarchy.

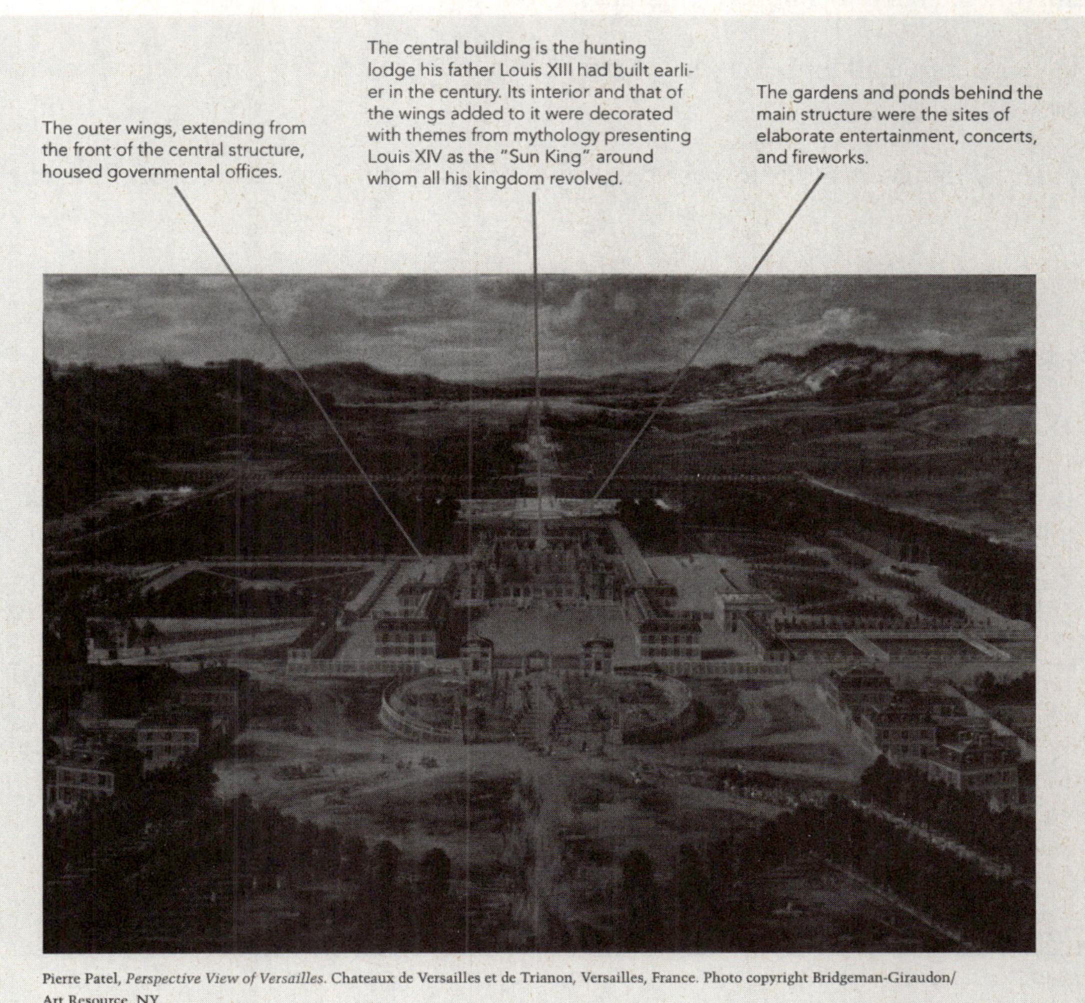

Pierre Patel, *Perspective View of Versailles*. Chateaux de Versailles et de Trianon, Versailles, France. Photo copyright Bridgeman-Giraudon/ Art Resource, NY

Document C Source: Louis XIV revokes the Edict of Nantes, *Church and State Through the Centuries*.

Art. 1. We desire…that all the temples of the people of the aforesaid so-called Reformed religion….be demolished forthwith.

Art. 2. We forbid our subjects of the so-called Reformed religion to assemble any more for public worship of the above-mentioned religion….

Art. 3. We likewise forbid all lords, of whatever rank they may be, to carry out heretical services in houses and fiefs….

Art. 4. We order all ministers of the aforesaid so-called Reformed religion…to depart from our kingdom….

Art. 10. The members of the so-called Reformed religion, while awaiting God's pleasure to enlighten them…can live in the towns and districts of our kingdom….on condition…that they do not make public profession of [their religion].

Document D Source: Louis XIV, *Memoires for the Instruction of the Dauphin*.

But kings must learn not to permit their servants to become to powerful….I am not saying that we should not for our own interest and grandeur wish that our greatness is shared by those in our good graces, but we must carefully guard against their excess. My advice to guarantee this consists of three principle observations. The first is that you must know your affairs completely, because a king who does not know them is always dependent on those who serve him….The second, that you divide your confidence among many, so that each of those you have entrusted will check the elevation of his rival, ensuring that the jealousy of one will bridle the ambition of the other. And the third, that even though you admit a small number of persons into your secret affairs or into your casual conversations, never permit anyone to imagine that they have the power to speak as they please….

Free-Response Question

Describe the experience of Huguenots in seventeenth-century France.

Multiple-Choice Questions

☐ **1. (A) is correct.** Jansenism arose as a response within the Catholic church to the theology and political clout of the Jesuit order. Jansenists particularly opposed Jesuit teachings about free will and believed that original sin so corrupted human beings that their only hope at salvation was divine grace. Louis XIV purged the Jansenists by banning their religion and shutting down their community at Port-Royal.

☐ **2. (C) is correct.** The Glorious Revolution in England involved the accession of William and Mary to the throne. James II fled to France and the protection of Louis XIV, an act that enabled Parliament to declare the throne vacant and then to appoint William and Mary to the throne.

☐ **3. (B) is correct.** Puritans under James I had hoped that James's Protestant upbringing and experience with the Scottish Presbyterian church would help their efforts to advance the English Reformation. James had decided, as had Elizabeth before him, that he was not going to accommodate Puritan demands, but he went a bit further and offended Puritans with his more liberal attitudes on religious observance.

☐ **4. (B) is correct.** Issued on December 1, 1641, the Grand Remonstrance was a summary consisting of more than 200 articles and detailing Parliamentary grievances against the crown during the rule of Charles I.

☐ **5. (E) is correct.** The Triple Alliance that formed in 1667 as a result of Louis XIV's military aggression in Flanders and the Franche-Comté consisted of Sweden, England and the United Provinces of Holland.

☐ **6. (D) is correct.** "L'état c'est moi" ["I am the state"] is a phrase ascribed to Louis XIV, and is consistent with his absolute monarchy and political and cultural embodiment of total power and authority.

☐ **7. (C) is correct.** The laws that comprised the Clarendon Code were intolerant of Catholics, Presbyterians, and Independents, but they wholeheartedly supported Anglican religious practice. The authors of the code were ultraroyalist Anglicans who designed laws that imposed penalties for attending *non*-Anglican worship services.

☐ **8. (C) is correct.** The *strelsy* supported the ascension of Peter the Great (and his sickly brother Ivan V) to the position of Russian tsar. The *boyars* supported the ascension of Michael Romanov and his two successors, Alexis I and Theodore III.

☐ **9. (E) is correct.** The Dutch Golden Age was an era of religious tolerance. The Calvinist Reformed Church was the official national church, but a significant number of Protestant and Roman Catholics lived in the Netherlands and did not belong to it. In addition, the country was a haven for Jews who had emigrated from lands that were intolerant of their religious faith.

☐ **10. (B) is correct.** The Mississippi Bubble was a financial scandal involving the duke of Orléans and John Law, both gamblers. The duke asked Law to oversee the management of France's finances, and Law proceeded to establish a bank in France that issued paper money. He then set up a monopoly company that had exclusive trading privileges with the French colony of Louisiana. When investors traded in their stocks for paper money and demanded an exchange in gold for their cash, the bank could not back up the paper money with bullion, and Law's scheme fell through, causing a mass panic in France.

Document-Based Question

In Louis XIV's view, what were the qualities of an effective monarch? In his opinion, what were the main obstacles to absolute rule?

Convincing essays might note:

- The stress placed on controlling the nobility and directing their energies to the service of the state (See Documents A, B, and C)
- The emphasis on the king's central role as the sole arbiter of justice (See Documents B and C)
- Possible explanations for Louis XIV's insistence on uniformity of public religious practice (See Document D)
- The notion that the king embodies the state and that all subjects must serve the state, and thus, the king (See Document A, B, C, D)

Free-Response Question

Describe the experience of Huguenots in seventeenth-century France.

Huguenots in seventeenth-century France suffered as a result of the policies of Louis XIV. French Catholic persecution of Huguenots had been halted somewhat in the sixteenth century by the Edict of Nantes, in which Huguenots were granted certain political and religious rights. However, following the Peace of Nijmwegen, Louis XIV began a massive campaign against the French Huguenots that attempted to solidify France and to eliminate Protestant believers (who were dissenting from the official Catholicism of the realm).

As a result of Louis XIV's efforts, Huguenots were forced out of public life, banned from government offices, excluded from more desirable professions (such as medicine), and forbidden from other professions—for instance, printing—that would enable them to make their objections known. Louis used various methods to try to convince Huguenots to convert to Catholicism, including subsidies and selective taxation. In 1681, he forced his troops into Huguenot towns, in an effort to coerce them to give up their Protestant views. Huguenots suffered during this time from a lack of civil rights and brutal repression.

Louis further infringed on the rights of the Huguenots by revoking the Edict of Nantes, which Henry IV had brokered in 1598. As a result of this revocation, Protestant churches and schools were shut down, all Protestant ministers were exiled, and those Huguenots that refused to convert to Catholicism were forced into slavery. In some cases, Protestant children were re-baptized by Catholic priests against the wishes of their parents.

During this period, the lives of Huguenots were filled with turmoil and uncertainty. Many thousands of Huguenots fled to other countries where they were allowed to practice and observe their Protestant faith. All in all, a quarter of a million French Huguenots emigrated rather than be forced to abide by Catholic policies and the persecution of Louis XIV. Some of those who did not emigrate became part of an underground resistance to the policies of Louis XIV.

CHAPTER 14

New Directions in Thought and Culture in the Sixteenth and Seventeenth Centuries

This period saw a total transformation in the scientific understanding of the universe—a transformation that affected all aspects of daily life, including other branches of scientific thought, philosophy, and faith.

The Scientific Revolution

- The **Scientific Revolution** was not a unified event, but rather a gradual movement that involved around a few hundred brilliant scientists laboring independently over many years in different countries. This "new" science, and especially the many significant discoveries in the field of **astronomy,** captured the public's imagination and enabled scientific discovery and knowledge to gain cultural authority.
- **Nicholas Copernicus (1473–1543)** is famous for questioning the geocentric view of the universe sponsored by Ptolemy (in which the Earth was believed to be at the center of the universe). In his work *On the Revolutions of Heavenly Spheres,* Copernicus argued on behalf of a heliocentric view of the universe.
- **Tycho Brahe (1546–1601)** spent much of his life advocating a geocentric view of the universe, but he made more extensive observations of the planets than any of his predecessors. Brahe's assistant, **Johannes Kepler (1571–1630),** used Brahe's research findings to advance a heliocentric view and demonstrate that **planets orbited around the sun in an elliptical fashion** in his book *The New Astronomy* (1609).
- **Galileo Galilei (1564–1642)** was one of the first astronomers to view the sky with the **telescope.** He popularized a Copernican interpretation of the heavens using the empirical, rational evidence that he found in his research.
- **Isaac Newton (1642–1727),** an English scientist, published his famous *Principia Mathematica* in 1687 In it he asserted (and proved mathematically) that planets and other physical objects moved through mutual attraction, or **gravity.**

Philosophy Responds to Changing Science

The revolution in scientific thought extended to the philosophy of the era, which came to see the world in terms of its mechanical principles.

- The image of God as a **divine watchmaker** came into vogue at this time, and a new emphasis on mathematics and a mechanical understanding of nature pervaded all fields.
- **Francis Bacon (1561–1626)** urged his peers to continue their search for the truth in the natural world. In his *Novum Organum* and *The Advancement of Learning,* Bacon attacked the belief that everything had already been discovered, and he encouraged experiment.

- **René Descartes (1596–1650)** developed a scientific method that relied on deduction more than it did on empirical study and induction. In his 1637 *Discourse on Method*, Descartes endorsed the idea that all thought should be founded on a mathematical model, and he rejected outright any thought not postulated on reason.
- **Thomas Hobbes (1588–1679)** was supportive of the scientific movement and befriended Descartes and Galileo. Hobbes's *Leviathan* (1651) portrays human beings as materialistic, egotistical and hedonistic. Hobbes believed human beings were at war with others and themselves. He felt that rulers should have no limits on their power.
- **John Locke (1632–1704)** was critical of Hobbes's views of absolutism and helped lay a foundation for European traditions of liberal political philosophy. In his *First Treatise of Government,* Locke rejected the idea of absolute government based on the concept of a patriarchal model of fathers ruling over a family. In his *Second Treatise of Government,* Locke argued for a government that was both accountable for and alert to the needs of the government. He believed that human beings were creatures of basically good will that entered into a social contract to preserve their existing liberties and rights.

The New Science and Religious Faith

- **Galileo** angered the Catholic Church because he interpreted scripture in accord with the new science. For his disobedience, Galileo was put on trial and forced to live under house arrest.
- **Blaise Pascal (1623–1662)** was a French mathematician who saw religion as separate from reason and science; he believed that religion required a "leap of faith." He allied himself with the **Jansenists.** Pascal's famous **wager** with the skeptics was that it was better to believe that God exists and stake everything on his benevolence than not to do so.
- Faith in a **rational God** was an element in the English approach to the new science. Scientific advances came to be interpreted as a fulfillment of God's plan for mankind.

Continuing Superstition

- From 1400 to 1700, an estimated 70,000–100,000 people were sentenced to death for magic and witchcraft. Growing religious and political tensions of the age made use of theology that portrayed demons and the Devil as powerful. **Cunning folk** were believed to possess special powers. Over time, these abilities came into conflict with the sacred rituals of the Christian church, like the sacraments, and the exorcism of demons. The Church declared that only its priests could possess legitimate magical abilities and that those who practiced magic outside the church were infernally inspired.

For Additional Review

Consider the participation of women in the Scientific Revolution.

Multiple-Choice Questions

1. Which of the following is the seventeenth-century philosopher who anticipated liberal political philosophy in Europe and America?
   (A) Thomas Hobbes
   (B) René Descartes
   (C) John Locke
   (D) Blaise Pascal
   (E) Francis Bacon

2. Which field of scientific inquiry was most influential in persuading Europeans of the importance of natural knowledge?
   (A) Chemistry
   (B) Medicine
   (C) Astrology
   (D) Physics
   (E) Astronomy

3. Which of the following was a new kind of institution that played an important role in supporting the "new" science?
   (A) the university
   (B) the laboratory
   (C) the scientific society
   (D) the hospital
   (E) the observatory

4. Cunning folk were
   (A) scientists who predicted astronomical events using mathematical techniques
   (B) local healers who purported to use magic to aid their societies
   (C) witches and warlocks
   (D) the philosophers who opposed the "new" science
   (E) artisans and assistants who shared their special techniques with scientists

5. All of the following made important contributions to the "new" science EXCEPT
   (A) Galileo Galilei.
   (B) Tycho Brahe.
   (C) Nicolaus Copernicus.
   (D) Johannes Kepler.
   (E) Jacob Sprenger.

6. What was Johannes Kepler's contribution to the Scientific Revolution?
   (A) The discovery of Pluto
   (B) The earth-centered cosmos
   (C) The discussion of Jupiter's moons
   (D) The elliptical orbits of the planets
   (E) the theory of gravity

7. Between 1400 and 1700, between 70,000 and 100,000 people were sentenced to death for
    (A) practicing astronomy.
    (B) following a philosophy based on empirical study and induction.
    (C) professing that religion was separate from reason and science.
    (D) posing as priests.
    (E) using magic or witchcraft.

8. The view of the universe developed by Copernicus involved
    (A) a geocentric design, with planets orbiting in epicycles.
    (B) a heliocentric design, with planets orbiting in ellipses.
    (C) a heliocentric design, with planets orbiting in epicycles.
    (D) a geocentric design, with planets orbiting in ellipses.
    (E) the moon and sun orbiting around the Earth, and the planets orbiting around the sun.

9. Which of the following statements is consistent with the thought of Blaise Pascal?
    (A) Religion can be proved by scientific inquiry.
    (B) A leap of faith is required in matters of religion.
    (C) Belief in God cannot improve one's life.
    (D) In their hearts, human beings are free of sin.
    (E) Reason is sufficient to explain the problems of human nature.

10. Which of the following was put on trial for his investigations of the order of the universe?
    (A) Francis Bacon
    (B) Isaac Newton
    (C) Galileo Galilei
    (D) Tycho Brahe
    (E) Johannes Kepler

Based on the following documents, how would you characterize Galileo's attitude toward religious and classical authorities? In his view, what was the relationship between science and theology and between science and classical scholarship?

Document A Source: 1543 map of the heavens based on the writings of Nicholas Copernicus.

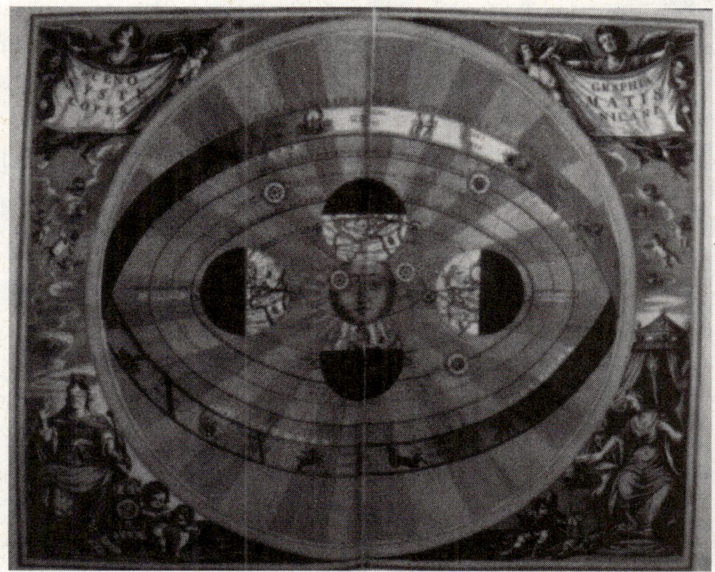

This 1543 map of the heavens based on the writings of Nicholas Copernicus shows the earth and the other planets moving about the sun. Until well into the 1600s, however, astronomers continued to debate whether the sun revolved around the earth.
British Library, London, UK/Bridgeman Art Library

Document B Source: Copernicus ascribes movement to the earth, *The Copernican Revolution.*

I pondered long upon this uncertainty of mathematical tradition in establishing the motions of the system of spheres. At last I began to chafe that philosophers could by no means agree on any one certain theory of the mechanism of the Universe, wrought for us by a supremely good and orderly Creator....I therefore took pains to read again the works of all the philosophers on whom I could lay hand to seek out whether any of them had ever supposed that the motions of the spheres were other than those demanded by the [Ptolemaic] mathematical schools. I found first in Cicero that Hicetas had realized that the Earth moved. Afterwards I found in Plutarch that certain others held the like opinion....

Document C Source: Galileo discusses the relationship of science to the Bible, *Discoveries and Opinions of Galileo*.

…I think in the first place it is very pious to say and prudent to affirm that the holy Bible can never speak untruth – whenever its true meaning is understood. But I believe nobody will deny that it is often very abstruse, and may say things which are quite different from what is bare words signify….

From this I do not mean to infer that we need not have an extraordinary esteem for the passages of holy Scripture. On the contrary, having arrived at any certainties in physics, we ought to utilize these as the most appropriate aids in the true exposition of the Bible….I should judge the authority of the Bible was designed to persuade men of those articles and propositions which, surpassing all human reasoning, could not be made credible by science, or by any other means than through the mouth of the Holy Spirit….

But I do not feel obliged to believe that the same God who has endowed us with senses, reason, and intellect has intended us to forgo their use….

Document D Source: Galileo rejects Aristotle, *Discoveries and Opinions of Galileo*.

….There remain in opposition to my work some stern defenders of every minute of the Peripatetics. So far as I can see, there education consisted in being nourished from infancy on the opinion that philosophizing is and can be nothing but to make a comprehensive survey of the texts of Aristotle, that from divers passages they may quickly collect and throw together a great number of solutions to any proposed problem. They wish never to raise their eyes from those pages – as if this great book of the universe had been written to be read by nobody but Aristotle, and his eyes had been destined to see for all posterity….

Free-Response Question

Compare and contrast the political views of John Locke and Thomas Hobbes.

ANSWERS AND EXPLANATIONS

Multiple-Choice Questions

☐ **1. (C) is correct.** John Locke was an ardent critic of absolutism who rejected the patriarchal political model of a father ruling over a family. He argued that government should be both responsible and responsive to the needs of the governed, which laid the groundwork for the liberal political philosophy that took root much later in Europe and America.

☐ **2. (E) is correct.** The amazing advances in astronomy—particularly those of Galileo, Copernicus, Brahe, Kepler, and Newton in determining the relation of the earth to the sun and to the other planets shocked the world of sixteenth- and seventeenth-century Europe, which had come to believe that there was nothing left to discover. These discoveries were unsettling, and they upset the Church and other sources of authority in the era, but they also whetted society's appetite for further discovery and scientific investigation.

☐ **3. (C) is correct.** The advent of scientific societies and academies was an outgrowth of the need for debate and experimentation in the "new" science. While universities lent their support to many of the scientists, some of them were slow to assimilate the advances made by new discoveries. The societies served as important places where like-minded innovators could share their discoveries in a climate receptive to change.

☐ **4. (B) is correct.** Cunning folk were local people in villages who claimed to have special healing or magical powers. Their neighbors often turned to them in times of calamity or trouble, and the cunning folk served as psychologists, midwives, or impromptu physicians. Very often, these cunning folk tended to be people in need of security and influence, such as elderly and unmarried women.

☐ **5. (E) is correct.** Jacob Sprenger was a co-author with Heinrich Krämer of the misogynistic *The Hammer of Witches.* He did not contribute in any way to the advancement of the "new" science; rather he perpetuated some of the superstitions about women and witchcraft that had persisted for generations.

☐ **6. (D) is correct.** Based on the mathematical relationships that emerged from his study of Brahe's observations, Kepler set forth the first astronomical model that actually portrayed motion—that is, the path of the planets—and those orbits were elliptical, not circular.

☐ **7. (E) is correct.** Between 1400 and 1700, between 70,000 and 100,000 people suspected of using magic and witchcraft were put to death. Witch hunts and panics erupted in nearly every western European land.

☐ **8. (C) is correct.** Copernicus rejected an Earth-centered universe and advanced his idea of a heliocentric universe. He modified Ptolemy's idea of planetary motion by advancing the notion of planets moving in smaller epicycles (a condition that was later disproved by Kepler).

☐ **9. (B) is correct.** Blaise Pascal believed that religion could not be explained by science or reason. He was a devoted Christian, and a Jansenist, who believed that human beings were born with original sin. He felt that the only way that humans could believe in the existence of God was through blind faith.

☐ **10. (C) is correct.** Galileo was put on trial for asserting the Copernican world view in his publication *Dialogue on the Two Chief World Systems* (1632). Pope Urban VIII, who had permitted Galileo to expand on the Copernican system in his work, was offended by the way in which Galileo mocked the views of Urban and others. Pope Urban ordered an investigation to see if Galileo had disobeyed the mandate of 1616 (which censored Copernican views). Galileo was found guilty and condemned to house arrest.

Document-Based Question

Based on the following documents, how would you characterize Galileo's attitude toward religious and classical authorities? In his view, what was the relationship between science and theology and between science and classical scholarship?

Convincing essays might note:
- Differences between Galileo and Copernicus's approach to ancient authorities (See Documents A, B, and D)
- Galileo's insistence on the primacy of reason and personal experience in the explanation of natural phenomenon (See Documents C and D)
- Galileo's willingness to challenge received truths (See Documents A, B and D)
- Galileo's confidence in his ability to judge the proper use of received authorities (See Documents C and D)

Free-Response Question

Compare and contrast the political views of John Locke and Thomas Hobbes.

Both Thomas Hobbes and John Locke were influenced by the growing importance of science and by the experimental attitudes that were in vogue in their native England. Yet the two men differed more than they agreed about political theory. The main political differences between John Locke and Thomas Hobbes involved their views of the proper form of government: Hobbes advocated for absolutism, whereas John Locke was in favor of a more moderate liberty.

Hobbes believed that mankind was inherently quarrelsome and prone to conflict. He contended that the dangers of anarchy and tyranny were ever-present, and in his view only an absolute monarch could protect men from destroying themselves. Hobbes thought that men entered into a social contract to surrender freedom to an absolute ruler, in exchange for the maintenance of law and order. In this scenario, the subject could never rebel and the monarch was entitled to use any force necessary to quell rebellion. Hobbes's ideas were never much in favor among Europeans, and he was overshadowed by his peer, John Locke.

Unlike Hobbes, John Locke articulated his belief in man's essential goodness. In his *Two Treatises on Government,* Locke set out various ideas underlying his theory of government, known as the Social Contract, in which people enter into a social agreement to establish a government with limited powers. Locke's idea of "the consent of the governed" gave the people the right to rebel if they felt that their rights were being violated by their government. Locke's ideas were extremely popular and formed the basis of the ideas in the American *Declaration of Independence.*

Clearly, Thomas Hobbes and John Locke held sharply opposed views of how the roles and responsibilities of government and of citizens.

CHAPTER 15

Society and Economy under the Old Regime in the Eighteenth Century

The period known as the *ancien régime,* or the Old Regime, usually refers to the various political and social relationships and situation prior to the French Revolution of 1789. During this time both nobles and peasants called for the return to traditional rights, and society was fairly hierarchical.

The Aristocracy

- **Aristocrats** represented a mere 5% of the population but controlled the majority of land, as well as social, economic, and political power. As monarchs' powers expanded, European aristocrats used existing governmental institutions to **limit the power of the monarchy.**
- In England, **game laws** gave aristocratic landowners the exclusive legal rights from 1671 to 1831 to hunt. The English aristocracy owned one-fourth of all arable land and consisted of about 400 families, many of whom controlled the **House of Lords and the House of Commons.**
- In France, the nobility consisted of **military officers, bureaucrats,** or other individuals who paid for it. French nobles fell into two groups: those who held court at Versailles, and those who did not.
- In eastern Europe, the nobility had more rights over peasants. Polish aristocrats exerted total control over serfs. In Austria and Hungary, nobles were exempt from taxation. In countries like Hungary and Poland, nobles were the only ones with political representation. In Prussia, nobles had authority over serfs. In Russia, nobles became determined to resist compulsory state service. In the **1785 Charter of the Nobility,** Catherine the Great defined the legal rights of nobles and their families in exchange for the nobility's voluntary service of state.

The Land and Its Tillers

- Over three-quarters of all Europeans lived in the country in the eighteenth century; many of them were peasants who were quite poor and lived through subsistence agriculture.
- In Great Britain, farmers had legal rights of English citizens, but the courts were run by landowners. French peasants had to pay feudal dues and were responsible for a certain amount of forced labor, known as *corvée.*
- In Prussia and Austria, landlords exercised almost complete control over serfs. The condition of serfs in Russia was worst; serfs had no legal rights and were effectively slaves. Russia experienced numerous peasant revolts between 1762 and 1769, a period culminating in Pugachev's Rebellion between 1773 and 1775. Southeastern European peasants were free, but only because of a scarcity of labor. Balkan peasants eventually became dependent on their Ottoman Empire landlords because they sought protection from them from bandits and rebels.

Family Structures and Family Economy

- **Households** in northwestern Europe often consisted of a married couple, children through their teens, and servants (people who were hired under contract to work for the head of the household in exchange for room, board, and wages). Households were **small,** usually no more than five or six people. Mortality was high, and no more than two generations lived together under one roof. Most children eventually married and formed their own household—a phenomenon known as *neolocalism.* The marriage age was in the mid-twenties for men and women.
- In Eastern Europe, the marriage age was much earlier, usually before the age of 20. Wives were often older than their husbands. Russian households often consisted of as many as 3 or 4 generations living together in one house.

The Revolution in Agriculture

- The movement to improve agricultural production began in the Netherlands, where farmers built dikes, expanded land, and experimented with new crops. English landlords popularized these Dutch innovations. **Jethro Tull** financed the experiments of others and conducted his own, including permitting land to be cultivated for longer period without having to be left fallow. **Robert Bakewell** pioneered new methods of animal breeding. **Charles Townsend** learned how to use fertilizer and instituted crop rotation. By the second half of the seventeenth century, the **enclosure method** replaced the open-field method of farming. Enclosures commercialized agriculture, maximizing the profits of the landowner.

The Industrial Revolution of the Eighteenth Century

- The second half of the eighteenth century witnessed the industrialization of the European economy, which made possible the production of more goods and services than ever before. New machinery was invented that enabled this industrialization, including the **spinning jenny, the water frame,** and **the steam engine. Iron production** during this era was essential to the manufacturing of machinery. The Industrial Revolution forced women into cottage industries and resulted in the workplaces of men and women becoming more separate.

The Growth of Cities

- Between 1650 and 1700, cities that grew most in population were capitals and ports; the urban Industrial Revolution, overseas trade, and governmental bureaucracy came to control European economies. New cities began to emerge in the middle of the eighteenth century; improved agricultural production enabled the growth of nearby urban centers that gave farmers access to consumer goods. Social divisions were marked between the upper classes, middle class, artisans, and peasants.

The Jewish Population: The Age of the Ghetto

- The **majority of Jews** lived in **Eastern Europe,** with the Netherlands being a notable exception. The Jewish population was concentrated in Lithuania, Poland, and the Ukraine. Catherine the Great was intolerant of the Jewish population in Russia and discouraged their settlement there. Jews were often victims of intolerance in the countries where they settled.

For Additional Review

Consider how popular consumption was affected by the Industrial Revolution and the shift of populations to urban centers.

Multiple-Choice Questions

1. Which of the following is the best definition of *neolocalism?*
   (A) the forced movement of serfs in eighteenth-century societies from landowner to landowner
   (B) the alternation of crops as an agricultural practice
   (C) the habit of adult children marrying and forming family units of their own
   (D) the efforts on the part of nobles to suppress serf's rights
   (E) the attempts by Jews to establish new communities in the ghettos of eighteenth-century Europe

2. As a result of the Industrial Revolution, women's opportunities in the work force
   (A) became more restricted and tended to gravitate toward cottage industries and menial labor.
   (B) became dramatically improved and tended to involve skilled work.
   (C) did not change significantly.
   (D) tended to involve higher-paying positions.
   (E) shifted toward the jobs traditionally held by men.

3. All of the following were innovations during the Industrial Revolution EXCEPT
   (A) the steam engine.
   (B) the spinning jenny.
   (C) the manufacture of high-quality iron.
   (D) the water frame.
   (E) the manufacture of steel.

4. The *corvée*
   (A) was a tax assigned exclusively to French nobles that required them to pay their serf's feudal dues.
   (B) was involuntary forced labor imposed on French peasants.
   (C) was a special, annual tax exemption granted to French nobles.
   (D) was a tool that improved the annual plowing of soil intended for agricultural use.
   (E) was the annual tax increase levied against nobles in France.

5. From 1671 to 1831, the English game laws
   (A) gave people of lower classes equal access to game animals.
   (B) provided landless nobles with the opportunity to hunt game animals.
   (C) gave needy peasants the right to hunt game on the properties belonging to landowners.
   (D) gave members of Parliament the exclusive right to hung game animals.
   (E) gave English landowners the exclusive right to hunt game animals.

6. All of the following facts are true of the eighteenth-century enclosure method of farming EXCEPT
    (A) enclosures were intended to use land more rationally.
    (B) enclosures were aimed at gaining greater commercial profits.
    (C) enclosures brought turmoil to the social life of the countryside.
    (D) enclosures increased food production.
    (E) enclosures aided independent farmers, who relied on common pasturage.

7. During the Old Regime, European Jews
    (A) were permitted equal access to social and economic opportunities in western European countries.
    (B) were separated from non-Jews in districts called ghettos.
    (C) were pro-monarchy.
    (D) were living primarily in western Europe.
    (E) enjoyed the rights and privileges of other subjects.

8. Which of the following regions saw the most dramatic population growth between 1600 and 1750?
    (A) capitals and medieval industrial cities
    (B) medieval industrial cities and landlocked trading centers
    (C) landlocked trading centers and capitals
    (D) ports and capitals
    (E) ports and medieval industrial cities

9. The Old Regime *(ancien régime)* refers to the period
    (A) after the Industrial Revolution.
    (B) prior to the Industrial Revolution.
    (C) prior to 1789.
    (D) prior to the Agricultural Revolution.
    (E) after 1800.

10. Sumptuary laws
    (A) required people of different classes to distinguish themselves by their dress.
    (B) required landowners to provide peasants with an annual supply of food.
    (C) were the rules that governed servants in the houses of landowners.
    (D) were anti-competitive measures that restricted artisans from free trade.
    (E) dictated that landowners had exclusive access to game.

Document-Based Question

What role did women play in the eighteenth-century economy? Do you agree or disagree with the assertion that eighteenth-century women were limited to the domestic sphere?

Document A Source: Francis Wheatly's painting "Morning."

Document B Source: An eighteenth-century French dress and hat shop.

Consumption of all forms of consumer goods increased greatly in the eighteenth century. This engraving illustrates a shop, probably in Paris. Here women, working apparently for a woman manager, are making dresses and hats to meet the demands of the fashion trade. As the document on page 000 demonstrates, some women writers urged more such employment opportunities for women. Bildarchiv Preussischer Kulturbesitz

Document C Source: J.B.S. Chardin's painting "The Washerwoman."

In the eighteenth century washing linen clothing by hand was a major task of women servants. J. B. S. Chardin, *The Washerwoman*. Nationalmuseum med Prins Eugens Waldemarsudde. Photo: The National Museum of Fine Arts

Document D Source: Priscilla Wakefield demands more occupations for women, *Reflections on the Present Condition of the Female Sex*.

Another heavy discouragement to the industry of women is the inequality of the reward of their labor, compared with that of men; an injustice which pervades every species of employment performed by both sexes.

In employments which depend on bodily strength, the distinction is just; for it cannot be pretended that the generality of women can earn as much as men, when the produce of their labor is the result of corporeal exertion; but it is a subject of great regret, that this inequality should prevail even where an equal share of skill and application is exerted.

Besides these employments which are commonly performed by women, and those already shown to be suitable for such persons as are above the condition of hard labor, there are some professions and trades customarily in the hands of men, which might be conveniently exercised by either sex.

Free-Response Question

Describe some of the ways in which the Industrial Revolution transformed the workplace for women.

ANSWERS AND EXPLANATIONS

Multiple-Choice Questions

1. **(C) is correct.** Neolocalism is the practice of moving away from home and creating a new family unit. During the eighteenth century, neolocalism was the most common form of household creation. When young men and women who had left home for work married and established their own independent household, neolocalism occurred.

2. **(A) is correct.** The transformation of the industrial opportunities available to women in the eighteenth century diminished the role and importance of those women already in the work force. Many working women were displaced from jobs because of the increased mechanization caused by the Industrial Revolution. Some women were forced into cottage industries that brought reduced income and involved more menial skills. Many others became domestic servants, because the job creation in the new, industrial economy was not geared toward women.

3. **(E) is correct.** The manufacture of steel was a development of during the Second Industrial Revolution. In the 1850s, the English engineer Henry Bessemer discovered a new process for manufacturing steel cheaply in large quantities. The steam engine, developed by Thomas Newcomen and improved by James Watt, the water frame, invented by Richard Arkwright, the spinning jenny, invented by James Hargreaves, and the manufacture of high-quality iron, helped by Henry Cort's puddling process, were all developments during the first Industrial Revolution (in the eighteenth century).

4. **(B) is correct.** The *corvée* was forced labor on public works, and this labor usually fell to the peasants. The French aristocracy and nobles were exempt from such requirements.

5. **(E) is correct.** From 1671 to 1831, the English game laws gave English landowners the exclusive right to hunt game animals. By law, only persons who owned a certain amount of property were permitted to hunt these animals. Wealthy city merchants, people renting land, and the poor were generally excluded from this right. The prohibitions led to rampant poaching.

6. **(E) is correct.** Enclosures were blights for independent farmers, because they forced them off the land they tilled. Because independent farmers did not own the land they farmed, they lost the common pasturage that they needed to survive.

7. **(B) is correct.** During the Old Regime, European Jews were segregated from non-Jews in urban districts known as ghettos. These communities were separate from areas of the city where non-Jews lived, and they were characterized by a lack of services and were often located in the least-desirable areas of the city.

8. **(D) is correct.** Capitals and ports saw the greatest growth of population between 1600 and 1750. This growth is explained by the increased reliance on overseas shipping for local economies, and the growing importance of centralized governments with their attendant bureaucracies. These industries involved significant job creation, which drew people to them.

9. **(C) is correct.** The Old Regime *(ancien régime)* refers to the period prior to 1789. The phrase is used to describe the attitudes and relationships that characterized a way of life prior to the French Revolution.

10. **(A) is correct.** Sumptuary laws were hierarchical rules about what clothes people from different classes were allowed to wear. Such laws forbade peoples in particular occupations or classes from wearing clothes worn by their social superiors. These laws, while highly ineffective and difficult to enforce, sought to make the social hierarchy visible.

Document-Based Question

What role did women play in the eighteenth-century economy? Do you agree or disagree with the assertion that eighteenth-century women were limited to the domestic sphere?

Convincing essays might note:

- The significance of depictions of women engaged in work (See Documents A, B, and C)
- Wakefield's assumption that women were working and her argument that they could do more (See Document D)
- The implied place of women in the eighteenth-century consumer society (See Documents B and D)
- The relationship between social class and women's occupations (See Documents A, B, C and D)

Free-Response Question

Describe some of the ways in which the Industrial Revolution transformed the workplace for women.

Women were dramatically affected by the Industrial Revolution, since the Industrial Revolution displaced many women from their jobs. The increased mechanization that the Industrial Revolution brought to many industries was the cause of the loss of many jobs for women. In most cases, women were deemed too fragile or not capable of handling large machines, and typically men were assigned to machinery in factory settings. Those women who were able to enter the factory labor force tended to be assigned jobs that were more menial than the jobs they had performed prior to the Industrial Revolution.

Some women were unable to find jobs as a result of the advances of the Industrial Revolution, and these women were forced to turn to cottage industries—producing goods from their homes—to make a living. Cottage industries usually involved piece-work and other crafts, such as sewing or stitching, which brought in less income than did the jobs women held prior to the Industrial Revolution. As the workplace for females shifted away from the factory and into the home, some women became domestic servants in the homes of others to make ends meet. During the nineteenth century, domestic servitude was the largest area of employment for women. However, even work in cottage industries and in other people's homes sometimes wasn't enough. As a result, some women who were desperate for a steady income turned to other kinds of higher-paid, but more risky pursuits, such as various types of criminal activity.

Prior to the Industrial Revolution, men's and women's workplaces tended to be one and the same. As a result of the sweeping changes caused by improved technology and mechanization, however, the workplaces of men and women became increasingly distinct. Women had fewer career and professional opportunities as a result of the Industrial Revolution, and women generally became associated with domestic concerns rather than with the marketplace and the industrial world.

CHAPTER 16

The Transatlantic Economy, Trade Wars, and Colonial Rebellion

Mercantile Empires

- **The Treaty of Utrecht (1713)** established the boundaries of empire until the 1750s.
- **Mercantilism** was the economic theory behind the system of acquiring colonies, and it entailed governments heavily regulating trade and commerce in hope of increasing national wealth. During this period, the economic well-being of the home country was the primary concern; colonies provided markets and resources for the industries of the home country, which would help administer and defend the colony. Home countries and colonies had navigation laws, tariffs, and bounties to encourage production and to prohibit trade with other neighboring countries or colonies controlled by other empires.
- **The West Indies** and the **Indian subcontinent** were great sources of rivalry among European powers, because they had resources that appealed to many of these powers.

The Spanish Colonial System

- Spanish control of the Americas was subject to few limitations. Colonial political structures existed to buoy Spanish commercial interests. Spain used the *flota* system to control supplies and bullion that went to and from its colonies. Trade outside the *flota* was forbidden.
- The Spanish throne saw the Spanish Habsburgs were replaced by the **French Bourbons,** which led to some increased royal involvement and administrative changes in the Spanish colonies. **Charles III (r. 1759–1788)** abolished some of the Spanish monopolies, opened more South American ports to trade and commerce, and attempted to increase tax collection and end corruption. He introduced the *intendent* into the Spanish empire. These reforms stimulated the Spanish economy and brought the empire more fully under Spanish control.

Black African Slavery, the Plantation System, and the Atlantic Economy

- **Slave labor** became a fundamental aspect of empire building. Labor shortages led Europeans settling in the New World to exploit Native Americans, but disease killed many of them, so Europeans turned to the labor of imported African slaves. Slave markets in central West Africa, Sierra Leone, the Gold Coast, and other areas were sources for slaves.
- Slavery exploded in Brazil and in the Caribbean, thanks to the **cultivation of sugar** on **plantations** and the growing consumer demand for the product. High rates of mortality led to the constant need for a fresh influx of slaves.

Mid–Eighteenth-Century Wars

- Spain and England disagreed over British rights to the Spanish market in the West Indies, and during a 1731 coastal patrol of an English vessel, Spaniards cut off the ear of an English captain named Robert Jenkins. **The War of Jenkins's Ear** began in 1739, when Robert Walpole responded to pressure to stop Spanish intervention in trade.
- In December of 1740, Frederick II of Prussia seized Silesia, an Austrian province belonging to the Habsburg Dynasty. Cardinal Fleury, minister to Louis XV, supported the Prussian aggression against Austria. This move threatened Britain, which wanted the Low Countries to remain in possession of Austria rather than France. In 1744, the British-French conflict expanded beyond Europe as France supported Spain against Britain in the Americas. **The War of the Austrian Succession** ended in a stalemate in 1748.
- **The Diplomatic Revolution of 1756** involved a series of alliances that set the stage for larger European conflict. Britain and Prussia signed the **Convention of Westminster,** an alliance aimed at preventing the entry of foreign troops into Germany. Britain aligned itself with the enemy of its former ally, Austria. Austria and France allied, with the goal of crushing Prussia.
- **The Seven Years' War (1756–1763)** began with Frederick II's invasion of Saxony, which led to France, Austria, Sweden, Russia, and smaller German states agreeing to destroy Prussia. Prussia and Russia made peace, and Frederick II held off Austria and France. **William Pitt** used the continental wars to leverage England's position in America. Pitt used an unprecedented number of soldiers in the American colonies, India, and Canada to dominate against the French in every theater of battle and to gain English possessions.
- In **The Treaty of Paris of 1763,** Britain received all of Canada, the Ohio River Valley, and the eastern half of the Mississippi River Valley. Britain returned Pondicherry and Chandernagore in India and the West Indian islands of Guadeloupe and Martinique to the French. Great Britain emerged a world power as a result of its international efforts. A quest to pay the war debt had consequences in the British colonies of North America.

The American Revolution and Europe

- The revolt of British colonies in North America was a reaction to perceived unfairness in revenue collection. The British wanted the colonies to pay for their protection and administration. The **1764 Sugar Act** and the **Stamp Act of 1765** were rejected as unfair by the American colonists, who argued that they were not represented in the Parliament.
- In March 1770, the **Boston Massacre** occurred, further inflaming colonists against Britain. The famous **Boston Tea Party** episode of 1773 escalated the conflict. By April 1775, battles between colonials and British regiments had begun at Lexington and Concord.
- A colonial army and navy were established, and in 1776, the **Continental Congress** opened American ports to trade with all nations. On July 4, 1776, the Continental Congress adopted the **Declaration of American Independence.** The American Revolutionary War continued until 1781, when George Washington defeated Lord Cornwallis at Yorktown.
- France and Spain came to the aid of the colonies. **The 1783 Treaty of Paris** concluded the conflict, and the American colonies established their independence. The American Revolution had a broad impact on Continental views of government and established the idea of a government based on popular consent rather than on divine law or monarchy.

Analyze how William Pitt's strategy in the French West Indies and India led to England's acquisition of America.

Multiple-Choice Questions

1. All of the following were boundaries established by the 1713 Treaty of Utrecht EXCEPT
   (A) Spain controlled all of mainland South America, except Brazil.
   (B) Britain controlled the colonies on the North Atlantic seaboard, Nova Scotia, Newfoundland, Jamaica, and Barbados.
   (C) France controlled the Saint Lawrence River valley, and the Ohio and Mississippi River valleys.
   (D) France controlled Java, in present-day Indonesia.
   (E) Spain controlled Florida, Mexico, California, and southwestern North America.

2. American colonists objected to both the Sugar and Stamp Acts because
   (A) they felt that they didn't use sugar or stamps more than their English counterparts.
   (B) they believed that as colonists, they deserved privileges not granted to people dwelling in England.
   (C) they were upset that these taxes were set by a Parliament that did not include colonists in its body, and they feared loss of control over their colonial government.
   (D) they felt that these taxes were astound ingly high and would put an undue burden on the colonies.
   (E) they were displeased with these luxuries being taxed and felt that other imports should be taxed instead.

3. The War of Jenkins's Ear arose
   (A) over pressures put on Parliament to relieve Spanish intervention in West Indies trade.
   (B) over a peninsula in the West Indies that a British man, Jenkins, claimed belonged to him.
   (C) as a result of the king of Prussia's acquisition of Silesia.
   (D) as the result of an alliance between Britain and Spain about how to handle conflicts in the West Indies.
   (E) as a response to limited natural resources in the West Indies.

4. Which of the following is true of African slaves in the Americas in the eighteenth century?
   (A) The number of African slaves in the Americas declined significantly during this time.
   (B) The number of African slaves in the Americas increased dramatically during this time.
   (C) The number of African slaves in the Americas at this time was not significant.
   (D) The number of African slaves in the Americas did not change during this time.
   (E) The number of African slaves in the eighteenth century was not known in comparison to numbers in earlier centuries.

5. The commercial vessels used by the Spanish to control imports and exports to and from their colonies were called
   (A) audiencias.
   (B) corregidores.
   (C) asientos.
   (D) factories.
   (E) flotas.

6. The major eighteenth-century mercantile rivalries concerned
   (A) England, Spain, and France.
   (B) France, the Netherlands, and Spain.
   (C) Spain, England, and the Netherlands.
   (D) England, the Netherlands, and France.
   (E) Portugal, Spain, and England.

7. According to the map showing part of North America above, what is the most accurate way of describing the American colonies?
   (A) They lay west of the Mississippi River.
   (B) They were contiguous with all five of the Great Lakes.
   (C) They lay along the Atlantic seaboard.
   (D) They bordered territory controlled by Spain.
   (E) They gave Great Britain access to the St. Lawrence River.

8. William Pitt's strategy for winning North America for England involved
   (A) a policy of peaceful negotiation with France.
   (B) economic sanctions against the French.
   (C) bartering land that was strategically significant to the French to gain territories.
   (D) sending vast numbers of soldiers to battle the French in the Saint Lawrence Valley and the Great Lakes Basin.
   (E) compensating the French financially for North American colonies.

9. Which agricultural crop was responsible for the explosion of eighteenth-century slavery in the Caribbean and Brazil?
   (A) corn
   (B) sugar
   (C) wheat
   (D) coffee
   (E) rubber

10. The Boston Massacre involved the killing of
    (A) British troops by American colonists.
    (B) five American colonial citizens by British troops.
    (C) Lord North, who put the Intolerable Acts into place.
    (D) a series of animals imported by the British for consumption in the American colonies.
    (E) John Boston, the leader of colonial resistance by British troops.

To what extent was the War of the American Revolution a European conflict?

Historical Background: European involvement in the colonies of North America had been a source of conflict for some time. French and English settlers had long coveted the various river valleys of the region, but William Pitt's strategic use of military forces enabled Britain to gain control of the North American colonies. When Britain attempted to exert greater control over the colonies in the form of a series of tariffs and taxes, the colonists rebelled against their imperial benefactors. The American Revolution and the colonies' independence followed. The American colonies sought French assistance in their battles against the British, further arousing European resentments and hostilities.

DOCUMENT 1 Source: John Locke, English philosopher, *Two Treatises on Civil Government,* 1690.

The reason men enter into society is to protect their property. And the reason they choose a government is to make laws to guard that property.... Certainly society does not want to give the government the power to destroy the very property which it was chosen to protect. Therefore, whenever government tries to take away and destroy the property of the people, or reduce the people to slavery, it puts itself in a state of war with the people. The people are freed from any further obedience to that government … and have the right to establish a new government.

DOCUMENT 2 Source: British Parliamentary document, *Stamp Act, an Act Applying Certain Stamp Duties in the American Colonies,* March 22, 1765.

Whereas by an act made in the last session of parliament, several duties were granted, continued, and appropriated, toward defraying the expenses of defending, protecting, and securing the British colonies and plantations in America … we, your Majesty's most dutiful and loyal subjects, the commons of Great Britain … have therefore resolved to give and grant unto your Majesty the several rates and duties herein…. For every skin or piece of vellum or parchment, or sheet or piece of paper, on which shall be engrossed, written or printed, any declaration, plea, replication, rejoinder, demurrer, or other pleading, or any copy thereof, in any court of law within the British colonies and plantations in America, a stamp duty of three pence….

DOCUMENT 3 Source: Transcript of "The Stamp Act Congress," from *Journal of the First Congress of the American Colonies,* 1765.

… IV. That the people of these colonies are not, and cannot, be represented in the House of Commons in Great Britain.
V. That the only representatives of the people of these colonies are persons chosen therein by themselves, and that no taxes ever have been, or can be constitutionally imposed on them, but by their respective legislatures….

DOCUMENT 4 Source: William Pitt (the Elder), British statesman, *Speech by William Pitt in the House of Commons Opposing Parliament's Right to Tax the American Colonies,* January 16, 1766.

There is an idea in some, that the colonies are virtually represented in the house. I would fain know by whom an American is represented here? Is he represented by any knight of the shire, in any county in this kingdom? Would to God that respectable representation was augmented to a greater number! Or will you tell him that he is represented by any representative of a borough—a borough, which, perhaps, its own representatives never saw. This is what is called the rotten part of the constitution. It cannot continue a century. If it does not drop, it must be amputated. The ideal of a virtual representation of America in this house is the most contemptible idea that ever entered into the head of a man. It does not deserve a serious refutation.

DOCUMENT 5 Source: Thomas Jefferson, American president, an account of points made at the June 8, 1776, meeting in Congress, prior to the publication of the *Declaration of Independence,* from Jefferson's *Autobiography* (1821).

That the present campaign may be unsuccessful, & therefore we had better propose an alliance while our affairs wear a hopeful aspect:

That to await the event of this campaign will certainly work delay, because during this summer France may assist us effectually by cutting off those supplies of provisions from England & Ireland on which the enemy's armies here are to depend; or by setting in motion the great power they have collected in the West Indies, & calling our enemy to the defense of the possessions they have there:

That it would be idle to lose time in settling the terms of alliance, till we had first determined we would enter into alliance:

And that the only misfortune is that we did not enter into alliance with France six months sooner, as besides opening their ports for the vent of our last year's produce, they might have marched an army into Germany and prevented the petty princes there from selling their unhappy subjects to subdue us.

DOCUMENT 6 Source: Thomas Paine, Political theorist, *The American Crisis,* December 23, 1776.

Britain, with an army to enforce her tyranny, has declared that she has a right (not only to TAX) but "to BIND us in ALL CASES WHATSOEVER," and if being bound in that manner, is not slavery, then is there not such a thing as slavery upon earth. Even the expression is impious; for so unlimited a power can belong only to God.

DOCUMENT 7 Source: *Treaty of Alliance with France* between the American colonial government and Louis XVI of France, February 6, 1778.

ART. 1. If war should break out between France and Great Britain during the continuance of the present war between the United States and England, His Majesty and the said United States shall make it a common cause and aid each other mutually with their good offices, their counsels, and their forces, according to the exigence of conjunctures, as becomes good and faithful allies.

DOCUMENT 8 Source: *Articles 2 and 3 of the Treaty of Amity and Commerce between the United States and France,* February 6, 1778.

ART. 2.nd The most Christian King, and the United States engage mutually not to grant any particular Favor to other Nations in respect of Commerce and Navigation, which shall not immediately become common to the other Party, who shall enjoy the same Favor freely…
ART. 3.d The Subjects of the most Christian King shall pay in the Port Havens, Roads, Countries Islands, Cities or Towns, of the United States or any of them, no other or greater Duties or Imposts of what Nature soever they may be, or by what Name soever called, than those which the Nations most favoured are or shall be obliged to pay; and they shall enjoy all the Rights, Liberties, Privileges, Immunities and Exemptions in Trade, Navigation and Commerce, whether in passing from one Port in the said States to another, or in going to and from the same, from and to any Part of the World, which the said Nations do or shall enjoy.

DOCUMENT 9 Source: Treaty between Great Britain and the United States of America, signed at Paris and ending the War of the American Revolution, September 3, 1783.

ART. 1 His Britannic Majesty acknowledges the said United States. viz. New Hampshire, Massachusetts Bay, Rhode Island, and Providence Plantations, Connecticut, New York, New Jersey, Pennsylvania Delaware, Maryland, Virginia, North Carolina, South Carolina, and Georgia, to be free, sovereign, and independent States; that he treats with them as such, and for himself, his heirs, and successors, relinquishes all claims to the Government, propriety and territorial rights of the same, and every part thereof.

DOCUMENT 10 Source: Exchange of notes between Benjamin Franklin, American statesman and diplomat, and Gravier de Vergennes, French statesman, referring to *Articles 2 and 3 of the Treaty of Amity and Commerce between the United States and France,* September 1784.

Sir: I have the Honour to transmit to your Excellency by Order of Congress a Resolution of theirs, dated the 11th of May last, which is in the Words following, Viz, Resolved,

"That Doctor Franklin be instructed to express to the Court of France the constant Desire of Congress to meet their Wishes; That these States are about to form a general System of Commerce by Treaties with other Nations: That at this Time they cannot foresee what Claim might be given to those Nations by the explanatory Propositions from the Count de Vergennes on the **2d & 3d** Articles of our Treaty of Amity & Commerce with His most Christian Majesty; but that he may be assured it will be our constant Care to place no People on more advantageous Ground than the Subjects of his Majesty."
With great Respect I am. Sir, Your Excellency's, most obedient and most humble Servant. VERSAILLES, 9th September, 1784. Benjamin Franklin
Sir: I have received the letter which you did me the honor to write me the third instant. You there declare in the name of Congress that the United States will be careful not to treat any other nation, in matters of commerce, more advantageously than the French nation. This declaration, founded on the treaty of the 6th February, 1778, has been very agreeable to the King; and you, Sir, can assure Congress that the United States shall constantly experience a perfect reciprocity in France. I have the honor to be, etc., GRAVIER DE VERGENNES

Discuss how slavery was linked to the economies of Europe, the Americas, and Africa.

ANSWERS AND EXPLANATIONS

Multiple-Choice Questions

- **1. (D) is correct.** Java was controlled by the Netherlands, not France. The Treaty of Utrecht established the boundaries of empire during the first half of the century. Spain controlled all of mainland South America, except for Brazil, which was ruled by Portugal. In North America, Spain ruled Florida, Mexico, California, and the Southwest. Spain also governed Central America and the islands of Cuba, Puerto Rico, and half of Hispaniola. The British Empire included the New England colonies on the North Atlantic coast, Nova Scotia, Newfoundland, Jamaica, and Barbados, plus some trading stations in India. The French controlled the Saint Lawrence River valley and the Ohio and Mississippi River valleys. They also ruled Saint Domingue (Hispaniola), Guadeloupe, and Martinique. The Dutch controlled Surinam, trading stations in Ceylon and Bengal, and trade with Java in what is now Indonesia.

- **2. (C) is correct.** American colonists objected to both the Sugar and Stamp acts, because they believed that it was unjust that they were being subjected to taxes set by a governing body in England that did not represent their interests. Colonists argued that they alone had the right to tax themselves.

- **3. (A) is correct.** The War of Jenkins's Ear arose between the British and the Spanish when an English captain, Robert Jenkins, got involved in a fight with some Spaniards who boarded his ship to determine whether or not he had contraband that violated the Spanish monopoly on trade in the region. Jenkins carried his severed ear back to England and appeared before the British Parliament in 1738, showing his ear as an example of Spanish brutality toward British merchants in the West Indies. Sir Robert Walpole, British prime minister, came under political pressure to strike back at the Spanish.

- **4. (B) is correct.** The number of African slaves in the Americas increased vastly during the eighteenth century, with the majority arriving in the Caribbean or Brazil, where the sugar crop was most in need of their labor.

- **5. (E) is correct.** Spain had a complicated system of trade and bullion fleets administered from Seville, in Southern Spain. These vessels helped Spain maintain its monopoly. Each year, a fleet of commercial vessels, called *la flota,* escorted by warships, carried goods from Spain to a few ports in the Americas. The ships would then return to Spain, loaded with gold or silver bullion.

- **6. (A) is correct.** The major eighteenth-century mercantile rivalries concerned the Spanish, the French, and the British.

- **7. (C) is correct.** The thirteen colonies lay along the Atlantic seaboard, east of the Mississippi River and south and east of the St. Lawrence River. The colonies were contiguous with only two of the Great Lakes, and territory occupied by Native Americans separated the colonies from the Spanish territory west of the Mississippi.

■ **8. (D) is correct.** William Pitt's strategy for winning North America for England involved a series of brilliant administrative decisions that helped Britain gain North America. Pitt sent more than 40,000 troops against the French in Canada, and these British troops were able to defeat the French easily because of the corrupt military administration, lack of resources, and divided military and political commands of the French.

■ **9. (B) is correct.** The sugar crop was responsible for the explosion of eighteenth-century slavery in the Caribbean and Brazil. By the close of the seventeenth century, the Caribbean islands were the world center for the production of sugar and the primary supplier for the ever-growing consumer demand for the product. The opening of new areas of cultivation required additional slaves during this time.

■ **10. (B) is correct.** The Boston Massacre involved the killing of five colonial citizens by British troops. The crisis occurred when the ministry of Charles Townsend sent over its own customs agents to administer the Stamp and Sugar acts. The British troops that had been sent along to protect the customs agents got involved in an incident with colonists, and the troops shot the colonists.

Document-Based Question

To what extent was the War of the American Revolution a European conflict?

The War of the American Revolution was not an isolated event on the American continent, but rather it was an event of international consequence that directly involved European powers, especially Great Britain and France. The American colonists made opportunistic use of the existing rivalry between France and Great Britain in waging their revolution. The colonists capitalized on the tension between these two European powers (which had flared up between 1756 and 1763 during the Seven Years' War) and took advantage of their ever-growing distrust of one another. In addition, the American Revolution was stimulated in part by the Enlightenment ideas promulgated by the philosophers and writers of England and France.

The immediate spur to the War of the American Revolution was conflict relating to revenue collection. After the end of the Seven Years' War, Britain needed to recover lost revenue, so it sought income from the American colonists for the protection and administration of their colonies. To many American colonists, this domestic taxation seemed grossly unfair, because it involved taxation from a legislative body that did not have any colonists among its members. The sentiments of John Locke, a British philosopher who had advanced many of the ideas of the Enlightenment reform in his work *Two Treatises on Civil Government,* were consonant with the colonists' views. Locke's condemnation of a government's seeking to control and destroy people's property ends with his conclusion that such actions constitute an act of war against citizens (**DOCUMENT 1**). Some seventy-five years later, many of the American colonists echoed their European forebear as they protested British efforts to tax them.

The British Parliament sought additional revenue in the Sugar Act in 1764, and in the Stamp Act of 1765. These acts were particularly egregious to the colonists, who felt that Britain was forcing them to abide by laws that they had not themselves approved. Among the many stipulations in the Stamp Act of 1765, colonists were not allowed to submit any petitions to courts of law in the American colonies without paying a three-pence tax (**DOCUMENT 2**). The American colonists' response to the English Stamp Act involved the organization of the Stamp Act Congress in 1765, in which they issued their official complaint that the Stamp Act had been imposed upon them by a body that did not include "representatives of the people of these colonies" (**DOCUMENT 3**). This idea was fairly radical for its time, and it stemmed largely from the views of Enlightenment thinkers who, in the tradition of John Locke, believed that individuals should be liberated from the bonds of government. In addition, the colonists conceived of the English Revolution of 1688 as having established some of their fundamental political liberties, and they believed that the various taxes imposed by George III and the British Parliament were inconsistent with those freedoms.

Not all English members of Parliament felt that Britain should exclude the American colonies from representation. William Pitt, who had served as the military genius behind the British victory and gain of the American colonies in the Seven Years' War, claimed that such a condition was "the rotten part of the constitution" and encouraged that American representation in Parliament be increased (**DOCUMENT 4**). This sentiment differed dramatically from American colonists, who did not seek to be incorporated into Parliament as much as they wished to have their own autonomous rule over their colonies. Thomas Paine's *The American Crisis,* along with his publication *Common Sense,* endorsed the view that the American colonies should escape "slavery" by splitting away from their British oppressors (**DOCUMENT 6**).

The rising tensions between Britain and the American colonies were not restricted to a simple dispute between an imperial power and its colonial protectorate. Rather they extended to France, a country that had supported the American colonies during the Seven Years' War and that would come to its aid in its fight against Great Britain. The American colonies made a series of treaties with France that were designed to be mutually beneficial. Thomas Jefferson, in his account of June 1776 discussions in the American Congress, acknowledged the serious political calculations that went into the alliance with France, including the possibility that France could incite Great Britain to defend itself in the West Indies (**DOCUMENT 5**). By bringing another European power into the War of the American Revolution, the American colonists redistributed political and military weight in what had been a delicate political balance.

For its part, France had suffered a depleted economy after its defeat in the Seven Years' War and so was eager to establish a relationship with the American colonies that could improve its economic situation and further hurt its enemy, Great Britain. In the Treaty of Alliance and the Treaty of Amity and Commerce—both signed on February 6, 1778—France effectively secured its special privileges and access in the American colonies (**DOCUMENT 8**) in exchange for agreeing to ally with the American colonies against Britain in the event of another French and British conflict (**DOCUMENT 7**). The Francophile Benjamin Franklin was instrumental in helping to assure the French of their special status with the American colonies; this Franco-American alliance effectively turned what had been a purely colonial conflict into a conflict of European proportion (**DOCUMENT 10**).

The American colonists' perspective on taxation at the hands of their British overseers was informed by Enlightenment theories developed by Europeans like John Locke and others. The Americans' political alliance with France enabled them to squeeze Great Britain further, as it forced the British to confront the possibility of another conflict with another European power for control of the colonies. In the end, Great Britain granted the American colonies the right "to be free, sovereign, and independent States" in the Treaty of Paris in 1783 (**DOCUMENT 9**). It is ironic that this treaty was signed in Paris, since the French played an important role in turning this colonial revolution into a conflict with European dimensions.

Reader's Comments on Sample Student DBQ Essay

- The essay has a clear, well-developed thesis
- The student makes use of all of the documents
- The essay analyzes the documents—taking into consideration the point of view of the authors—and groups documents appropriately
- The student includes additional information that is relevant
- The essay effectively considers the extent to which European powers played a role in the American War of Independence

Possible student score: 8-9

Free-Response Question

Discuss how slavery was linked to the economies of Europe, the Americas, and Africa.

As more European countries became invested in the resources and markets of the Americas, they found that they needed laborers to help them harvest labor-intensive crops like sugarcane. Many Europeans tried initially to impress Native Americans into servitude, but many of them perished as a result of diseases they contracted by coming into contact with the Europeans.

Slave labor became a fundamental aspect of European conquest in the Americas around the sixteenth century. The plantation economies that the Spanish and the Portuguese established in South America—and later in the British colonies in North America—required massive numbers of laborers. This need for labor led to negotiations between Europe and Africa, as Europeans in the Americas sought to acquire more slaves for their growing colonies. The Portuguese had begun to import African slaves to the Iberian Peninsula in the mid-fifteenth century, after the Ottoman Empire had banned the importation of white slaves from regions under its control.

Existing slave markets in central West Africa and elsewhere facilitated European slave traders' quest for labor. As the West Indies and parts of Brazil became more developed, the need for slaves increased. Colonial trade reflected the dependence on slaves from Africa, as European goods (frequently guns) were shipped to Africa and traded for slaves. These slaves were then taken to the West Indies or Brazil and traded there for sugar and other products destined to be shipped back to consumers in Europe. Slaves became a commodity in this kind of transatlantic economy. Without slaves, the European economies could not trade for products they desperately desired, such as tobacco, cotton, and sugar.

CHAPTER 17

The Age of Enlightenment: Eighteenth-Century Thought

The eighteenth-century sentiment that economic and political reforms were possible was a novel conviction that was fostered by people and ideas of the Enlightenment.

- The intellectuals, writers, and critics who championed this reform in the emerging print culture were known as ***philosophes.*** The *philosophes* were interested in greater freedoms and liberties, and they sought rational improvement on many levels of society.

Formative Influences on the Enlightenment

- **Isaac Newton's** determining the role of **gravitation** in the relationship between objects enabled other Europeans to realize that much remained to be discovered. His use of empirical support for general laws became an important feature of Enlightenment thought.
- **John Locke's** view of **psychology**—that all humans begin life as a *tabula rasa,* or blank page—gave Enlightenment thinkers grounds for arguing that the human condition could be improved by modifying the surrounding social and political environment.
- **Britain's domestic stability,** religious toleration, freedom of the press, small army, unregulated domestic life, and the political sovereignty of Parliament all suggested to Enlightenment thinkers that absolutist monarchy might not be the best path.
- **Louis XIV's** heavy taxation, absolute monarchy, religious persecution, and large standing army were perceived by *philosophes* as obstacles to reform. **Voltaire** suggested reforms in his book, *Letters on the English,* that he believed could improve French life, modeling his theories on the English system. In *Candide* he attacked war and religious persecution.
- The emergence of a **print culture** during the Enlightenment helped spread the ideas of *philosophes* like Voltaire. The public became more literate during this era, a process that enabled these printed materials to be more influential in shifting public opinion.

The *Encyclopedia*

- Assembled by **Denis Diderot** and **Jean le Rond d'Alembert,** the *Encyclopedia* was a major undertaking by Enlightenment thinkers. The book was the product of writing by more than 100 authors, and it survived many attempts at censorship. It included the most advanced ideas of the day, secularized learning and was, in part, a plea for freedom of expression.

The Enlightenment and Religion

- Many *philosophes* were critical of Christianity. Voltaire's famous slogan **"Crush the Infamous Thing,"** summed up their general attitude. *Philosophes* felt that Christianity focused attention on the world to come to the detriment of the present condition. *Philosophes* also objected to the power structure of the old regime, which gave special rights to clergy.

- **Deism,** or the belief that religion and reason could be combined, was popular among some of the *philosophes,* who believed that God must be rational and religion should be so as well. Deists believed that God existed and could be empirically justified in the study of nature.

The Enlightenment and Society

- The *philosophes* were concerned with the application of laws of reason to the social condition. The Italian *philosophe,* Cesare Beccaria (1738–1794) attacked torture and capital punishment in his work *On Crimes and Punishments,* and he used critical analysis to address the problem of making punishments just and effective.
- Many *philosophes* believed that economic policy could be reformed in a way that was consistent with the operation of natural laws. These reformers, known as **physiocrats,** believed that mercantilist policies hampered the expansion of trade. Their leaders included François Quesnay and Pierre Dupont de Nemours.
- The English economist **Adam Smith** believed that economic liberty was the foundation for a natural economic system, and he urged that the mercantilist system of England be abolished. Smith believed that individuals should be able to pursue their own economic interests, and he is widely credited with the founder of *laissez-faire* economic thought and policy. Smith's four-stage theory of human social and economic development enabled Europeans to see themselves dwelling at the highest level of achievement, which served as a major justification for their economic and imperial domination of the world.

Political Thought of the *Philosophes*

- In his 1748 book, *Spirit of the Laws,* **Baron de Montesquieu** held up the British constitution as an example of the wisest model for regulating the power of government. A political conservative, Montesquieu championed the aristocracy in improving French political regime.
- In *The Social Contract* (1762), **Jean-Jacques Rousseau** envisioned a society in which each individual could maintain personal freedom while participating as a loyal member in a larger community. He saw human beings as enmeshed in social relationships, and he believed that loyalty to the community should be encouraged.

Women in the Thought and Practice of the Enlightenment

- Women helped promote the careers of *philosophes* by giving them access to their social and political contacts and providing a forum for them to circulate their ideas. Louis XV's mistress, the marquise de Pompadour, helped the *Encyclopedia* overcome censorship efforts. Madame de Tencin promoted Montesquieu's *Spirit of the Laws* by purchasing it and circulating it among friends. The *philosophes* were by no means ardent feminists; Mary Wollstonecraft addressed their shortcomings and critiqued Rousseau in *A Vindication of the Rights of Woman,* in 1792.

Enlightened Absolutism

- The phrase, "enlightened absolutism," refers to the phenomenon (observed during the last third of the eighteenth century) of several European rulers' embrace of the reforms set out by the *philosophes.* Monarchs most closely associated with this phenomenon included **Frederick II of Prussia, Joseph II of Austria,** and **Catherine II of Russia.** These monarchs pushed for innovations that would increase their revenue.

Consider the contributions to Enlightenment thought of Baruch Spinoza and Moses Mendelsohn.

Multiple-Choice Questions

1. "Crush the Infamous Thing!" was a phrase of Voltaire's that referred to
   (A) the monarchy.
   (B) the Prussians.
   (C) the Church.
   (D) the *philosophes*.
   (E) the *parlements*.

2. Women contributed to the cause of *philosophes* in all of the following ways EXCEPT
   (A) authoring pieces in the *Encyclopedia*.
   (B) holding salons.
   (C) buying their works and circulating them.
   (D) blocking the circulation of works that attacked the *philosophes*.
   (E) introducing them to people who could protect and fund them.

3. All of the following were important influences on the Enlightenment EXCEPT
   (A) English political and economic stability.
   (B) consolidation of a print culture.
   (C) a Ptolemaic worldview.
   (D) the need for economic reform in France after the rule of Louis XIV.
   (E) ideas of Newton and Locke.

4. The phrase "enlightened absolutism" refers to which of the following?
   (A) the view held privately by many *philosophes* that absolutism was not really a bad kind of government
   (B) absolutism that was characterized by greater access to the monarch
   (C) absolutism that occurred after the Enlightenment
   (D) a late-eighteenth-century phenomenon whereby European rulers embraced the reforms of the *philosophes*
   (E) absolutism that the *philosophes* endorsed because of prevailing social or political conditions

5. The government of which of the following countries was a model to Enlightenment thinkers?
   (A) Spain
   (B) Germany
   (C) Prussia
   (D) Britain
   (E) Austria

6. Which of the following authors envisioned a society in which individuals maintained their
   personal freedoms while participating as loyal members of the community at large?
   (A) Baruch Spinoza
   (B) Adam Smith
   (C) Jean-Jacques Rousseau
   (D) Voltaire
   (E) Baron de Montesquieu

7. The economic policy of *laissez-faire*
   (A) argues that all must contribute to the good of the society in order for it to remain
       economically viable.
   (B) sets out a series of governmental controls over individual economic pursuits.
   (C) contends that individuals should be allowed to pursue their own economic interests.
   (D) focuses on regulation on the local level to shape economic growth.
   (E) argues that strict economic controls should serve as the basis for the economic system.

8. The image of God as a divine watchmaker is associated with
   (A) Catholics.
   (B) Deists.
   (C) Huguenots.
   (D) Jews.
   (E) Lutherans.

9. The *philosophes* of the Enlightenment were
   (A) invariably associated with religious professions.
   (B) mainly philosophers.
   (C) exclusively politicians.
   (D) primarily writers and critics.
   (E) often scientists and inventors.

10. The view of human personality as *tabula rasa* is usually associated with which of the
    following thinkers?
    (A) Rousseau
    (B) Voltaire
    (C) Locke
    (D) Montesquieu
    (E) Diderot

Evaluate the political, social, and cultural reforms Enlightenment thinkers sought in eighteenth century European society.

Historical Background: During the eighteenth century, new convictions began to spread about the possibility for wide economic change and social reform. These attitudes grew over time, and the movement that stimulated such ideas became known as the Enlightenment. The leading figures of the Enlightenment were inspired by the fruits of the Scientific Revolution, and they believed in the power of rational criticism to challenge the intellectual authority of traditional institutions and the Church.

DOCUMENT 1   Source: John Locke, English philosopher, excerpt from *An Essay Concerning Human Understanding*, 1690.

Let us then suppose the mind to be, as we say, white paper void of all characters, without any ideas. Whence comes it to be furnished? Whence comes it by that vast store which the busy and boundless fancy of man has painted on it with an almost endless variety? Whence has it all the materials of reason and knowledge? To this I answer, from experience; in that all our knowledge is founded, and from that it ultimately derives itself. Our observation, employed either about external sensible objects, or about the internal operations of our minds perceived and reflected on by ourselves, is that which supplies our understanding with all the materials of thinking. These two are the foundations of knowledge, from whence all the ideas we have, or can naturally have, do spring.

DOCUMENT 2   Source: Alexander Pope, English poet and satirist, excerpt from *An Essay on Man*, 1733.

Know then thyself, presume not God to scan;
The proper study of mankind is Man.
Placed on this isthmus of a middle state,
A being darkly wise, and rudely great:
With too much knowledge for the skeptic side,
With too much weakness for the Stoic pride,
He hangs between; in doubt to act, or rest,
In doubt to deem himself a god, or beast;
In doubt his mind or body to prefer;
Born but to die, and reasoning but to err;
Alike in ignorance, his reason such,
Whether he thinks too little, or too much;
Chaos of thought and passion, all confused;
Still by himself abused, or disabused;
Created half to rise, and half to fall;
Great lord of all things, yet a prey to all;
Sole judge of truth, in endless error hurled
The glory, jest, and riddle of the world!

DOCUMENT 3   Source: Baron de Montesquieu, French political philosopher, *The Spirit of Laws*, 1748.

Democratic and aristocratic states are not in their own nature free. Political liberty is to be found only in moderate governments; and even in these it is not always found. It is there only when there is no abuse of power. But constant experience shows us that every man invested with power is apt to abuse it, and to carry his authority as far as it will go …

To prevent this abuse, it is necessary from the very nature of things that power should be a check to power …

In every government there are three sorts of power: the legislative, the executive in respect to things dependent on the law of nations; and the executive in regard to matters that depend on the civil law [the realm of the judiciary]…

When the legislative and the executive powers are united in the same person, or in the same body of magistrates, there can be no liberty; because apprehensions may arise, lest the same monarchy or senate should enact tyrannical laws, to execute them in a tyrannical manner.

Again, there is no liberty, if the judiciary power be not separated from the legislative and executive. Were it joined with the legislative, the life and liberty of the subject would be exposed to arbitrary control; for the judge would be then the legislator. Were it joined to the executive power, the judge might behave with violence and oppression.

DOCUMENT 4   Source: Jean-Jacques Rousseau, French philosopher, excerpt from the novel *Émile or On Education*, 1762.

Once it is demonstrated that man and woman are not and ought not be constituted in the same way in either character or temperament, it follows that they ought not to have the same education. In following nature's directions, man and woman ought to act in concert, but they ought not to do the same things. The goal of their labors is common, but their labors themselves are different, and consequently so are the tastes directing them.…

The good constitution of children initially depends on that of their mothers. The first education of men depends on the care of women. Men's morals, their passions, their tastes, their pleasures, their very happiness also depend on women. Thus the whole education of women ought to relate to men. To please men, to be useful to them, to make herself loved and honored by them, to raise them when young, to care for them when grown, to counsel them, to console them, to make their lives agreeable and sweet—these are the duties of women at all times, and they ought to be taught from childhood. So long as one does not return to this principle, one will deviate from the goal, and all the precepts taught to women will be of no use for their happiness or for ours.

DOCUMENT 5   Source: François Marie Arouet de Voltaire, French author, *Philosophical Dictionary*, 1764

Fanaticism is to superstition what delirium is to fever and rage to anger. The man visited by ecstasies and visions, who takes dreams for realities and his fancies for prophecies, is an enthusiast; the man who supports his madness with murder is a fanatic …

The most detestable example of fanaticism was that of the burghers of Paris who on St. Bartholomew's Night [1572] went about assassinating and butchering all their fellow citizens who did not go to mass, throwing them out of windows, cutting them in pieces.

Once fanaticism has corrupted a mind, the malady is almost incurable …

The only remedy for this epidemic malady is the philosophical spirit which, spread gradually, at last tames men's habits and prevents the disease from starting; for once the disease has made any progress, one must flee and wait for the air to clear itself. Laws and religion are not strong enough against the spiritual pest; religion, far from being healthy food for infected brains, turns to poison in them …

Even the law is impotent against these attacks of rage; it is like reading a court decree to a raving maniac. These fellows are certain that the Holy Spirit with which they are filled is above the law, that their enthusiasm is the only law they must obey.

What can we say to a man who tells you that he would rather obey God than men, and that therefore he is sure to go to heaven for butchering you?

DOCUMENT 6   Source: Jean le Rond d'Alembert, French philosopher and editor, *Preliminary Discourse to the Encyclopedia of Diderot*, 1772.

The mechanical arts depend on manual operation and are enslaved, if I may be permitted the term, to a species of routine, and so are left to those men whom prejudice places within the lowest classes. Poverty has driven these men to apply themselves to such work more often than taste or native genius drew them towards it, and for this reason these arts have come to be despised, so much does poverty darken what accompanies it. On the other hand, the free operations of the intellect are the lot of those who think themselves to be the most favored of nature. Nevertheless, the advantage which the liberal arts have over the mechanical, because the former demands hard, intellectual work and requires difficulty to excel, is sufficiently compensated by the far greater usefulness the latter arts for the most part provide for us. It is this very utility which forced these arts to be reduced to merely mechanical operations, so that a greater number of men could practice them. But society, in justly respecting the great geniuses which have enlightened it, need not on that account vilify the hands of those who serve it. The discovery of the compass is no less advantageous to the human race than the explanation of the properties of the compass needle is to physics. Finally, considering in itself the distinction we are discussing, how many of the so-called scholars are there for whom science is, in reality, only a mechanical art? And what is the real difference between a head filled with facts without any order, any usefulness or any connections, and the instinct of an artisan reduced to a mechanical operation?

DOCUMENT 7   Source: Immanuel Kant, German philosopher, excerpt from 'Was ist Aufklärung?' ("What is Enlightenment?"), 1783.

If the question is put in the form: are we living in an enlightened age?, then the answer is no, but we are indubitably living in an age of enlightenment. As things now stand in the main, we have a long way to go before men may be fit to employ their own reason in matters of religion confidently and justly without the guidance of another. But there is manifest evidence that a field has been opened up to them where they may freely use that faculty, and that the obstacles to universal enlightenment or the emergence of mankind from its self-imposed minority are gradually diminishing, and in that sense this is an age of enlightenment.

DOCUMENT 8   Source: List of grievances from the Third Estate of the French city of Dourdan (Dourdan Cahiers de Doléances), delivered to Versailles, 1789.

The order of the third estates of the City … of Dourdan … supplicates [the king] to accept the grievances, complaints, and remonstrances which it is permitted to bring to the foot of the throne, and to see therein only the expression of its zeal and the homage of its obedience.

   It wishes:

1. That his subjects of the third estate, equal by such status to all other citizens, present themselves before the common father without other distinction which might degrade them.…

3. That no citizen lose his liberty except according to law: that, consequently, no one be arrested by virtue of special orders, or, if imperative circumstances necessitate such orders, that the prisoner be handed over to regular courts of justice within forty-eight hours at the latest.

12. That every tax, direct or indirect, be granted only for a limited time, and that every collection beyond such term be regarded as peculation, and punished as such.…

16. That such tax be borne equally, without distinction, by all classes of citizens and by all kinds of property, even feudal … rights.

17. That the tax substituted for the *corvée* be borne by all classes of citizens equally and without distinction. That said tax, at present beyond the capacity of those who pay it and the needs to which it is destined, be reduced by at least one-half.

DOCUMENT 9   Source: Mary Wollstonecraft, British author, excerpt from *A Vindication of the Rights of Women*, 1792.

… Rousseau declares that a woman should never, for a moment, feel herself independent, that she should be governed by fear to exercise her natural cunning, and made a coquettish slave in order to render her a more alluring object of desire, a sweeter companion to man, whenever he chooses to relax himself. He carries the arguments, which he pretends to draw from the indications of nature, still further, and insinuates that truth and fortitude, the cornerstones of all human virtue, should be cultivated with certain restrictions, because, with respect to the female character, obedience is the grand lesson which ought to be impressed with unrelenting rigour.

   What nonsense! When will a great man arise with sufficient strength of mind to put away the fumes which pride and sensuality have thus spread over the subject! If women are by nature inferior to men, their virtues must be the same in quality, if not in degree, or virtue is a relative idea; consequently, their conduct should be founded on the same principles, and have the same aim.

   Connected with man as daughters, wives, and mothers, their moral character may be estimated by their manner of fulfilling those simple duties; but the end, the grand end of their exertions should be to unfold their own faculties and acquire the dignity of conscious virtue.…

   … I … will venture to assert, that till women are more rationally educated, the progress of human virtue and improvement in knowledge must receive continual checks.…

DOCUMENT 10   Source: Thomas Munck, historian, T*he Enlightenment: A Comparative Social History 1721–1794.*

Average annual output of new and reprinted works in English (books, pamphlets and smaller items) in key cities of the British Isles

	LONDON	DUBLIN	EDINBURGH	GLASGOW
1710–1719	1,705	114	160	12
1720–1729	1,378	162	144	11
1730–1739	1,446	160	147	12
1740–1749	1,345	157	214	41
1750–1759	1,567	216	201	65
1760–1769	1,693	209	379	58
1770–1779	2,038	195	249	55
1780–1789	2,434	247	207	53
1790–1795	3,472	374	316	90
Mid-century population in the thousands	675	90	57	24

Free-Response Question

Discuss the attitudes of Enlightenment thinkers toward organized religion.

ANSWERS AND EXPLANATIONS

Multiple-Choice Questions

- **1. (C) is correct.** "Crush the Infamous Thing!" was a phrase of Voltaire's that referred to the Church.
- **2. (A) is correct.** Women contributed to the cause of *philosophes* in all of the following ways *except* authoring pieces in the *Encyclopedia*. The editors, Diderot and d'Alembert, recruited men exclusively as contributors.
- **3. (C) is correct.** By the time of the Enlightenment, the Ptolemaic worldview (a geocentric view of the universe) had been disproved by Copernicus and Galileo. The Newtonian view of the universe (one in which all objects were subject to the laws of gravitation) and Locke's conception of the human personality as a *tabula rasa,* played great roles in shaping Enlightenment thought about reason and knowledge.
- **4. (D) is correct.** The phrase "enlightened absolutism" refers to the phenomenon of European rulers embracing many of the reforms espoused by the *philosophes*. The monarchs most closely associated with this are Frederick II of Prussia, Joseph II of Austria, and Catherine II of Russia.

■ **5. (D) is correct.** In his *Spirit of the Laws,* Baron de Montesquieu argued that the British constitution was the best model for regulating the power of government. The domestic stability of Great Britain after the Restoration of the monarchy and the religious tolerance, financial prosperity, and freedom of speech were also aspects of British culture that Enlightenment thinkers admired.

■ **6. (C) is correct.** Jean-Jacques Rousseau's *Social Contract* advanced the idea that independently, human beings can achieve very little without a relationship to the larger community. Rousseau contended that a perfect society was one in which individuals could maintain their personal freedoms but behave as loyal members of the community at large.

■ **7. (C) is correct.** The economic policy of *laissez-faire* favors a limited role for the government in economic life and encourages individuals to pursue their own economic interests.

■ **8. (B) is correct.** Deism was a movement that began during the Enlightenment and that was led by believers who maintained that religion and reason could be integrated. The image of God as a divine watchmaker is associated with deists, many of whom felt that God was responsible for creating human nature; they believed that after He set in motion human nature, then He left it to run on its own.

■ **9. (D) is correct.** The *philosophes* of the Enlightenment were primarily writers and critics. Many were intellectuals who were not identified as philosophers or politicians but who were interested in issues of philosophy and politics. On the whole, *philosophes* were antagonistic toward traditional religion, which they felt impeded progress in their society.

■ **10. (C) is correct.** The view of human personality as *tabula rasa* is usually associated with John Locke, who advanced this idea in his work *An Essay Concerning Human Understanding* in 1690. Locke believed that personality emerged as a product of sensations experienced by the individual during the course of his or her life. Enlightenment thinkers seized this theory and expanded it to allow for the reform and modification of their society.

Document-Based Question

Evaluate the political, social, and cultural reforms Enlightenment thinkers sought in eighteenth-century European society.

Enlightenment thinkers, known as *philosophes*, helped to inject social, political, and cultural change into traditional European institutions and traditional European ways of life. Their ability to effect sweeping changes on their society was hugely important in shaping the cultures, governments, and politics of these countries in future years. Many of these changes can be traced back to some of the works of these early Enlightenment figures. The intellectual climate of Europe at this time also contributed dramatically to the reception of these new and, in some cases, radical ideas.

One of the most important characteristics of this period was the increasing rate of literacy and the increased production and manufacturing of reading material. Europe's population was more literate than ever before, and its citizens were debating ideas that they encountered in various publications including newspaper and books. As the chart in **DOCUMENT 10** demonstrates, in England, the average annual output of new and reprinted works continued its ascent through the eighteenth century. It seems safe to conclude that more Europeans were buying, reading, and exploring worlds in literature that were previously unknown to them. This emergence of a print culture was significant to the success of the reforms instituted by Enlightenment thinkers.

Two of the major intellectual figures of the Enlightenment whose work profoundly influenced reformers were Isaac Newton and John Locke. (Newton had explained the law of gravitation, and Locke had articulated a vision of a government committed to individual liberty.) Locke explained human psychology in terms of experience in his work *An Essay Concerning Human Understanding,* in which he developed the idea of the human mind as a blank sheet that could gain definition and shape only with experience (**DOCUMENT 1**). Locke's famous vision of humans as a *tabula rasa* was compelling to Enlightenment reformers, who interpreted his idea as evidence that human personality is changeable and could be altered by modifying the surrounding environment.

One of the first major Enlightenment works to emerge and dramatically alter the course of the social and political landscape in Europe was the massive *Encyclopedia* edited by D'Alembert and Diderot. The *Encyclopedia,* which had survived attempts at censorship and suppression, represented a towering achievement for the hundreds of *philosophe* authors whose works were anthologized in it. It included some of the most advanced ideas of the age on subjects ranging from mechanical arts to animal husbandry. Embedded in these works were revolutionary ideas and philosophical musings that questioned the *status quo,* such as d'Alembert's analysis of how economics, political power, and perceptions of native intelligence inter-relate in contemporary French society (**DOCUMENT 6**). The *Encyclopedia* secularized learning and ignored the Christian tradition, preferring to focus on the application of reason over the Christian model of ethics.

Many Enlightenment thinkers were reacting against the autocratic monarchies that characterized their governments. Locke's thinking drove this reform. In his 1748 *Spirit of the Laws,* Montesquieu advocated a balance of power, and endorsed a division of the government into the legislative, the executive, and the judicial branches (**DOCUMENT 3**). Montesquieu held up the example of the British constitution as the proper way to regulate a government. While some of his ideas took root in governments (Montesquieu's division of powers was adopted in the U.S. Constitution) by 1789, many of the political grievances in France reflected a frustration with the lack of democratic opportunities for citizens. As the *Cahiers de Doléances* of 1789 reveals, the Third Estate was frustrated with its unequal status in the French government (**DOCUMENT 8**). The thinking of the Enlightenment was certainly responsible, in some sense, for pushing the French into the Revolution.

Enlightenment thinkers were notoriously opposed to the influence of the Church. Voltaire, whose famous *"Crush the Infamous Thing"* remark reflects a general distrust of the church and Christianity, develops these ideas in his *Philosophical Dictionary* of 1764. In his withering critique of the Catholic measures against French Protestants, Voltaire reveals his contempt for religious fanaticism (**DOCUMENT 5**). Like Voltaire, Alexander Pope was drawn to the use of reason and to the focus on rational life and empirical experience, rather than the mystical aspects of religion, to understand his society (**DOCUMENT 2**).

Enlightenment thinkers supported changes in education, and were fairly progressive in their attitudes toward children's need to learn. Jean-Jacques Rousseau, while a progressive in some respects, did not believe that women and men were equally suited to education (**DOCUMENT 4**). His view became popular around this time, but not among more enlightened Enlightenment feminists, such as Mary Wollstonecraft, who took umbrage with Rousseau's view of women (**DOCUMENT 9**). Wollstonecraft's spirited defense of women, in her *A Vindication of the Rights of Women* effectively pokes holes in Rousseau's arguments and reveals their weaknesses. Wollstonecraft was a proto-feminist, whose views continue to influence contemporary thinking about the roles of men and women.

Enlightenment thinkers strove to push their society beyond the boundaries of the *status quo*. They sought to escape the confines of religious tradition, to incorporate some of the empirical forces brought to bear during the Scientific Revolution on other areas of everyday life. This period was a time of major change, much of which came about as a result of these fearless *philosophes*, pioneers of new ways of thinking who were unafraid to expose their views to their society.

Reader's Comments on Sample Student DBQ Essay

- The essay has a clear, well-developed thesis that is reinforced by the use of the documents
- The student makes use of most of the documents
- The essay groups documents appropriately and pays attention to the significance of authorship
- The outside information is pertinent to the essay and helps to unify the use of the documents
- The essay grasps the interrelated issues faced by the Enlightenment *philosophes*, making connections among the Scientific Revolution, the religious crises, education reform, and governmental reform
- The essay shows time consciousness
- The student displays an impressive amount of erudition and a breadth of knowledge on the subject and uses the documents to great advantage

Possible student score: 8-9

Free-Response Question

Discuss the attitudes of Enlightenment thinkers toward organized religion.

Many Enlightenment thinkers were extremely critical or skeptical of the benefits of organized religion. One of the most vocal critics of the period was Voltaire, who's "Crush the Infamous Thing" reverberated among his fellow *philosophes*. Many Enlightenment thinkers found the Church's strength and dominance an obstacle to many of the social reforms that they were trying to achieve. The Church, with its faith in miracles and things "seen and unseen," was diametrically opposed to the rationality advanced by the *philosophes*. Roman Catholicism especially bore the brunt of Enlightenment critique.

Enlightenment thinkers disapproved of the Church's insistence on the depravity of man, which they felt denied the possibility for human improvement on earth. This latter idea, of course, was a hallmark of intellectual developments of the period, including some of the improvements made by scientific study and empirical inquiry. In addition, the *philosophes* resented the power of the Church to dictate political and social affairs in their countries. In some cases, they were expressing their discontent with the intolerance and bigotry promoted by Church policies.

All organized religion was not repellent to the Enlightenment *philosophes*. During this period, the religious faith *Deism* was established. Deism, which stressed the existence of a God that could be empirically justified and was tolerant and founded on reason, was appealing to many of the *philosophes*. What they objected to in organized religion, after all, was fanaticism and intolerance. The Enlightenment thinkers' call for tolerance—and their critical attitudes toward most organized religions—was based on the simple idea that human relationships should not be treated as less valuable than religion itself.

CHAPTER 18

The French Revolution

The Crisis of the French Monarchy

- The French monarchy emerged from the Seven Years' War defeated and in debt; support of the American Revolution further endangered its financial stability. **Louis XV** and **Louis XVI** were unable to solve taxation disputes with the *parlements.*
- **Jacques Necker** issued a report blaming the aristocratic government for France's financial troubles. In 1786, **Charles Alexandre de Calonne** proposed new taxes, like the *gabelle,* on salt, and a new tax on landowners, regardless of status. An Assembly of Notables met with Calonne and claimed they had no authority to consent to new taxes; only the **Estates General** had that right. In 1788, Louis XVI agreed to convene the Estates General in 1789.

The Revolution of 1789

- The Estates General consisted of the **First Estate** (the clergy), the **Second Estate** (the nobility), and the **Third Estate** (wealthy members of the professional middle class). The organization of the Estates General was a source of initial debate. After the calling of the Estates General, new conflicts between aristocrats and the bourgeoisie emerged.
- The **Cahiers de Doléances** were lists of grievances presented to the monarch. The Third Estate petitioned the king for equality of rights among the king's subjects. After a standoff, the Third Estate invited the clergy and nobles to join them in creating a new legislative body. On June 17, the body declared itself the National Assembly. Members pledged their loyalty in the **Tennis Court Oath** and renamed their group the **National Constituent Assembly.**
- On July 14, more than 800 Parisians stormed the **Bastille** in search of weapons for the citizen militia they had formed in response to the presence of royal troops in the city and their frustrations with Louis XVI. The crowd stormed the fortress, released prisoners, and killed troops as well as the governor.
- The **"Great Fear"** that swept the countryside was driven by peasants who felt that they were reclaiming what was rightfully theirs but what had been lost to aristocrats over time.
- In August of 1789, the Assembly set forth the **Declaration of the Rights of Man and Citizen,** a document that claimed that all men were "born and remain free and equal in rights." Louis XVI was forced by a group of women to return from Versailles to Paris.

The Reconstruction of France

- The National Constituent Assembly declared that only **"active citizens"**—men paying annual taxes equal to three days of local labor were allowed to vote for electors, who, in turn, voted for members of the legislature. Women could not vote or hold office. This law transferred power from aristocratic wealth to anyone with accumulated land or property.
- In local and judicial administration, eighty-three *departements* replaced ancient provinces.
- The National Constituent Assembly suppressed guilds, liberated the grain trade, and established the **metric system.**

- The Roman Catholic church was reconstructed by the Assembly into a branch of the secular state by the issuance of the **Civil Constitution of the Clergy**.
- Disgruntled aristocrats known as *émigrés* left France and resettled in areas near the French border where they plotted counterrevolution.

A Second Revolution

- A group of deputies from the Third Estate, called **Jacobins,** pressed for more radical reform. In the Legislative Assembly, a group of Jacobins known as **Girondists** ordered the émigrés to return or suffer loss of property and demanded that clergy that had refused to take the oath to support the Civil Constitution do so or lose their state pensions. Louis XVI vetoed both acts.
- In August of 1792, a Parisian crowd invaded the Tuileries Palace and forced Louis XVI and Marie Antoinette to take refuge in the Legislative Assembly. Louis effectively lost his power, which was now in the hands of the **Paris Commune,** a committee of representatives from wards of Paris. During the **September Massacres,** the Paris Commune murdered about 1,200 people in jails, many of whom were aristocrats or priests. Following these acts, the Convention, a new assembly, declared France a **republic**. In December of 1792, Louis XVI was executed; one month later, France was at war with England, Holland, Spain, and Prussia.

Europe at War with the Revolution

- **Edmund Burke,** a British statesman and Irish-born writer, condemned the Revolution for its extreme measures in *Reflections on the Revolution in France* (1790). Other European leaders, like **William Pitt** in England, and rulers in Prussia, Russia, discouraged popular uprisings.

The Reign of Terror

- War brought new challenges for the Republic of France. The revolutionary government established a series of committees to protect its new creation. **The Committee of General Security** and the **Committee of Public Safety** were created to carry out executive duties of the government. A *levée en masse* or military conscription for all males in the population was mobilized to defend the country. This citizen army led to **The Reign of Terror,** a period marked by quasi-judicial executions from autumn 1793 to mid-summer 1794. The Christian calendar, with its religious holidays, was replaced by a secular calendar, and other places of worship were "de-Christianized."
- Executions were increasingly arbitrary, with *sans-culottes* **revolutionaries** serving as victims as well as persecutors. Marie Antoinette and other members of the royal family were the first victims. **Maximilien Robespierre,** a powerful member of the Committee for Public Safety, who established the **"Cult of the Supreme Being,"** a civic religion modeled after the views of Rousseau, had encouraged the execution of key republican political figures, including his Committee colleague **Jacques Danton.** Robespierre was also executed during this period. The Reign of Terror claimed more than 25,000 victims.

The Thermidorian Reaction

- The Thermidorian Reaction involved political reconstruction, and abandoned the Constitution of 1793. In its place, the Convention issued the **Constitution of the Year III,** which provided for a legislature of two houses. The upper body, or Council of Elders, consisted of men over 40 who were husbands or widowers. The lower Council of Five

Hundred consisted of men of at least 30 years old who were either married or single. The executive body was a 5-person Directory, chosen by the Elders from a list submitted by the Council of Five Hundred.

For Additional Review

Consider the *sans-culottes* and their role in the politics of this era.

Multiple-Choice Questions

1. The proposed *gabelle* of Charles de Calonne was a tax on
   (A) sugar.
   (B) salt.
   (C) newspapers.
   (D) marriage.
   (E) land.

2. Which of the following forced Louis XVI and Marie Antoinette to return to Paris from Versailles?
   (A) a destructive fire set by the *sans-culottes*
   (B) an assassination attempt
   (C) an angry mob of Parisian women
   (D) the Paris *Parlement*
   (E) the fall of the Bastille

3. During the French Revolution, *émigrés* were
   (A) foreigners who wanted to join the *sans culottes* in the Revolution.
   (B) immigrants from the French colonies who sought political refuge in France.
   (C) aristocrats who relocated on the French border and tried to stimulate a counter-revolution.
   (D) members of the Jacobin group.
   (E) women who were denied admission to the Convention.

4. According to the rules of the French Constitution of 1791, "active citizens" were defined as
   (A) married men, with property and family.
   (B) men who paid annual taxes equal to three days of labor wages.
   (C) men who were landowners and had servants or employees under their care.
   (D) women and men who paid their taxes and could demonstrate an income.
   (E) men who could prove their aristocratic or noble status.

5. Following the end of the Reign of Terror, the Jacobins
   (A) were summarily executed.
   (B) took control of the Republic.
   (C) were imprisoned.
   (D) were made to conform their political views to the more moderate views of the Thermidorians.
   (E) were exiled.

6. The result of the Tennis Court Oath was the formation of the
   (A) *sans-culottes*
   (B) National Assembly.
   (C) Third Estate.
   (D) Estates General.
   (E) Second Estate.

7. Which of the following groupings represents the membership of the First, Second, and Third
   estates, respectively?
   (A) clergy; nobility; commercial and professional middle class
   (B) nobility; clergy; commercial and professional middle class
   (C) commercial and professional middle class; nobility; clergy
   (D) commercial and professional middle class; clergy; nobility
   (E) clergy; commercial and professional middle class; nobility

8. The Declaration of the Rights of Man and Citizen was modeled after the
   (A) American colonies' *Declaration of Independence*.
   (B) Magna Carta.
   (C) Declaration of Rights adopted by Virginia.
   (D) Tennis Court Oath.
   (E) American colonies' 1787 constitution.

9. The founder of the civic religion, the Cult of the Supreme Being, was
   (A) Montesquieu.
   (B) Danton.
   (C) Robespierre.
   (D) Louis XVI.
   (E) Marie Antoinette.

10. The Civil Constitution of the Clergy, issued in 1790,
    (A) prohibited the clergy from public worship.
    (B) transformed the Roman Catholic church into a branch of the French state.
    (C) encouraged members of the clergy to organize their own diocese borders and to handle
        administrative aspects of the Church independently from the government.
    (D) was positively received by the French church, which welcomed the change.
    (E) was designed to increase the number of bishoprics in the country.

Analyze the political and social forces that helped bring about the Paris Commune of 1871, as well as those that led to its downfall.

Historical Background: The Prussian occupation of Paris that followed the end of the Franco-Prussian War angered many Parisians, who felt that their suffering during the Prussian siege was ignored by the National Government in its negotiation of this occupation in the Frankfurt Treaty. Increasingly, Parisians and residents of the French provinces experienced political divisions. A group of Parisians elected a new municipal government, called the Paris Commune, which was formally proclaimed on March 28, 1871. The Commune was suppressed by the army of the National Assembly on May 28, 1871, after a violent battle that resulted in many deaths and that devastated the Parisian infrastructure.

DOCUMENT 1   Source: The First Proclamation of the Government, September 5, 1870

Frenchmen!
The people have disavowed a Chamber which hesitated to save the country when in danger. It had demanded a Republic. The friends of its representatives are not in power but in peril. The Republic has vanquished the invasion of 1792. The Republic is proclaimed! The Revolution is accomplished in the name of right and public safety. Citizens! Watch over the army confided to you. Tomorrow you will be, with the army, avengers of the country.

DOCUMENT 2   Source: *Journal Officiel de la République Française,* editorial, March 21, 1871

The proletariat, faced with a constant threat to its rights, a total denial of all its legitimate aspirations, along with the imminent destruction of the country and of all its hopes, has realized that it is its imperative duty and absolute right to take its destiny in its own hands by seizing political power.

DOCUMENT 3   Source: Edmond de Goncourt, French writer, *Journal,* March 28, 1871

In the events taking place the newspapers see only a question of decentralization. Decentralization, indeed! What is happening is very simply the conquest of France by the workers and the enslavement under their despotism of the nobles, the middle lass, and the peasants. The government is leaving the hands of those who have, to go into the hands of those who have not, going from those who have a material interest in conservation of society to those who are completely unconcerned about order, stability, or conservation. Is it possible that in the great law underlying changes here on earth the workers are for modern societies what the Barbarians were for ancient societies, convulsive agents of dissolution and destruction?

DOCUMENT 4   Source: Proclamation of the Paris Commune, March 28, 1871

The Commune is the foundation of all political states, exactly as the family is the embryo of human society. It must have autonomy; that is to say, self-administration and self-government, agreeing with its particular genius, traditions, and wants; preserving, in its political, moral, national, and special groups its entire liberty, its own character, and its complete sovereignty, like a citizen of a free town.

DOCUMENT 5   Source: Charles Delescluze, Paris Commune's delegate of war, proclamation at news of entry of Versailles troops, May 22, 1871

Enough of militarism! No more staff officers bespangled and glided along every seam! Make way for the people, for fighters, for bare arms! The hour for revolutionary warfare has struck. The people know nothing of intricate maneuvers; but when they have a gun in their hand, paving stones underfoot, they have no fear of all the strategies of the monarchical school. To arms! Citizens, to arms! It is now a matter, as you know, of either winning or falling into the hands of the reactionaries and clericals of Versailles, of those wretches who have deliberately handed France over to the Prussians, and who are making us pay the ransom for their treachery.

DOCUMENT 6   Source: Appeal by Central Committee of the National Guard to soldiers of Versailles, May 23, 1871

Soldiers of the Versailles Army,
We are family men. We are fighting so that our children will never have to bend, as you must, under military despotism. One day you will have children too. If you fire on the people today your sons will condemn you, as we condemn the soldiers who massacred the people in June 1848 and December 1851. Two months ago, on 18 March, your brothers of the Paris Army, bitterly resentful of the cowards who had betrayed France, fraternized with the people. We urge you to follow their example. Soldiers, our sons and our brothers, listen to these words and let your conscience decide: *When the orders are immoral, disobedience is a duty.*

DOCUMENT 7   Source: Madame Cornélie Morisot to her daughter, Berthe Morisot (French impressionist painter), May 25, 1871

Paris on fire! This is beyond any description … Throughout the day the wind kept blowing in charred papers; some of them were still legible. A vast column of smoke covered Paris, and at night a luminous red cloud, horrible to behold, made it all look like a volcanic eruption. There were continual explosions and detonations; we were spared nothing. They say the insurrection is crushed; but the shooting has not yet stopped…. Latest official dispatch: the insurrection is now driven back to a very small part of Paris, the Tuileries is reduced to ashes, the Louvre survives, the part of the Finance ministry building fronting on the Rue de Rivoli is on fire, the Cour des Comptes is burned down, twelve thousand prisoners, Paris strewn with dead.

DOCUMENT 8   Source: Marshal MacMahon, French military leader, proclamation of return to order and end of Paris Commune, May 28, 1871

French Republic—Inhabitants of Paris:
The French Army has come to your rescue.
Paris has been delivered.
At four o'clock our soldiers took over the last rebel positions.
At last the fighting is over; order, work, and security will reign once more.

DOCUMENT 9   Source: Sketch, Paris during Prussian siege of 1871

DOCUMENT 10   Source: Vladimir Lenin, Russian Communist leader, speech, "Lessons of the Commune," March 18, 1908

But despite all its mistakes the Commune was a superb example of the great proletarian movement of the nineteenth century. Marx set a high value on the historic significance of the Commune—if, during the treacherous attempt by the Versailles gang to seize the arms of the Paris proletariat, the workers had allowed themselves to be disarmed without a fight, the disastrous effect of the demoralization that this weakness would have caused in the proletarian movement, would have been far, far greater than the losses suffered by the working class in the battle to defend its arms. The sacrifices of the Commune, heavy as they were, are made up for by its significance for the general struggle of the proletariat: it stilled the Socialist movement throughout Europe, it demonstrated the strength of civil war, it dispelled patriotic illusions, and it destroyed the naïve belief in any efforts of the bourgeoisie for common national aims. The Commune taught the European proletariat to pose concretely the tasks of the Socialist revolution.

Free-Response Question

To what extent was the Third Estate responsible for altering the course of the French government?

ANSWERS AND EXPLANATIONS

Multiple-Choice Questions

☐ **1. (B) is correct.** The proposed *gabelle* of Charles de Calonne was a tax on salt.

☐ **2. (C) is correct.** Louis XVI and Marie Antoinette were confronted on October 5 at Versailles by a crowd of as many as 7,000 armed Parisian women demanding more bread. The women intimidated the king, and he agreed to sanction the decrees of the assembly. The women demanded that Louis and his family return to Paris, and on October 6, he followed the crowd into the city.

☐ **3. (C) is correct.** During the French Revolution, *émigrés* were aristocrats who left France when it became clear that the rights they'd enjoyed under *ancien régime* policies were disappearing. Many settled on the French border and sought to foment counterrevolution.

☐ **4. (B) is correct.** According to the rules of the French Constitution of 1791, "active citizens" were defined as men who paid annual taxes equal to three days of labor wages. Women were not permitted to vote in the French Constitution of 1791. Active citizens were permitted to vote to choose electors, who, in turn, could vote for members of the legislature.

☐ **5. (A) is correct.** Following the end of the Reign of Terror, Jacobins were attacked and murdered. This period, known as the "white terror," involved summary executions of former terrorists who had been involved in the Reign of Terror. Jacobins were killed without remorse.

☐ **6. (B) is correct**. The result of the Tennis Court Oath was the formation of the National Assembly, which renamed itself the National Constituent Assembly.

☐ **7. (A) is correct.** The Estates General consisted of the First Estate (the clergy), the Second Estate (the nobility), and the Third Estate (wealthy members of the professional middle class).

☐ **8. (C) is correct.** The Declaration of the Rights of Man and Citizen was modeled after the Declaration of Rights adopted by Virginia in 1776.

☐ **9. (C) is correct.** The founder of the civic religion, the Cult of the Supreme Being was Robespierre.

☐ **10. (B) is correct.** The Civil Constitution of the Clergy issued in 1790 effectively eliminated the religious component of the Roman Catholic church and annexed the institution as a secular branch of the French state. In addition, it reduced the number of bishoprics from 135 to 83, brought the borders of the dioceses into conformity with the newly formed *departments,* provided for the election of priests and clergy, whose salaries were paid by the state. This passage of this law created great animosity between the French church and state.

Document-Based Question

Analyze the political and social forces that helped bring about the Paris Commune of 1871, as well as those that led to its downfall.

The Paris Commune was officially formed on March 28, 1871 when a group of Parisians elected a new municipal government that was intended to administer the citizens of Paris separately from the rest of France. In the official proclamation of its creation, the Paris Commune imagined itself as an autonomous governmental organization and used the simile "like a citizen in a free town" to describe its role (**DOCUMENT 4**). There were numerous issues that brought the Paris Commune into being, but its desire for "self-administration and self-government" were high on the list. The unrest caused to the social order by the Paris Commune assisted in its downfall.

Members of the Paris Commune were, by and large, disgruntled citizens who had endured the Prussian siege during the Franco-Prussian War and were angered by the decision of monarchists in the National Assembly to permit the Prussians to remain in Paris until France paid off its war indemnity. The Prussian siege had been extraordinarily difficult for Parisians, who suffered food shortages and were forced to coexist with the enemy. The image in **DOCUMENT 9** shows that the privations and shortages experienced by Parisians included the butchering of cats and dogs for meat. The Prussian presence did not affect French citizens who lived in the provinces and outside of Paris as extremely. The Paris Commune was in part a reaction against politicians who seemed ignorant of the experiences of Parisians.

France was still in the initial stages of a republic when the war with Prussia began. The Second Empire came to an end with the capture of Napoleon III at the Battle of Sedan in 1870. Shortly thereafter, the Third Republic was proclaimed, declaring "The Revolution is accomplished in the name of right and public safety," but what followed was the disaster of the Franco-Prussian conflict and the civil war brought on by the Paris Commune (**DOCUMENT 1**). The participants in the Paris Commune were radicals and socialists of all kinds. Because they represented an extreme element in French society, they were feared by the monarchist government of the Nationalist Assembly headed by Adolphe Thiers. Lenin and Marx and their adherents believed in the Paris Commune as a genuine example of socialism, and Lenin praised it as "a superb example of the great proletarian movement of the nineteenth century" (**DOCUMENT 10**). The Commune was never genuinely a proletarian government; it counted petty bourgeois members among its members.

Needless to say, these agitators for social reform were not welcomed by many members of the upper- and middle-classes, who believed that these extremists were anarchists rather than reformists. Edmond de Goncourt hints at this in his journal entry of March 28, 1871, the day of the proclamation of the Commune, and he equates the Communards with "Barbarians" (**DOCUMENT 3**). Similarly, in her letter to her daughter, the Impressionist painter Berthe Morisot, Cornélie Morisot focuses her attention on the destruction wrought by the Paris Commune rather than its political agenda or the reforms it sought to achieve (**DOCUMENT 7**). The Paris Commune did not have a broad support among upper class members of French society, who saw it as a threat to their way of life.

The threat of the Paris Commune to the French way of life assisted in its downfall. Even as publications like the *Journal Officiel de la République Française* were arguing for the "imperative duty and absolute right" of the Commune to "take its destiny in its own hands by seizing political power," the monarchist forces at the National Assembly were gaining moral support from the provinces and from the upper and middle-classes. The Commune sought to win over converts by inveighing against the betrayal of the National Assembly: "It is now a matter, as you know, of either winning or falling into the hands of the reactionaries and clericals of Versailles, of those wretches who have deliberately handed France over to the Prussians," in an unusual reversal—calling the members of the National Assembly the "reactionaries" (**DOCUMENT 5**). The Commune also sought to persuade the soldiers of Versailles to betray the French government and to come over to their side (**DOCUMENT 6**). But ultimately, the National Assembly triumphed over the Commune's National Guard and restored Paris as a French city. In his declaration of the return to order, Marshal MacMahon promises "At last the fighting is over; order, work, and security will reign once more." The profound need for order and security in French society after the trauma of the Prussian occupation and the uncertain beginnings of the Third Republic helped to quash the Paris Commune.

Reader's Comments on Sample Student DBQ Essay

- The essay has a clear, well-developed thesis that is reinforced by the use of the documents.
- The student makes use of all of the documents.
- The essay groups documents appropriately and recognizes authorial bias.
- The outside information, while not abundant, is relevant to the essay.
- The essay offers a fairly nuanced consideration of the different political forces of the era during the Paris Commune.
- The essay shows time consciousness.
- The essay treats the forces that led to the Commune in greater detail than those that led to its downfall.

Possible student score: 7-8

Free-Response Question

To what extent was the Third Estate responsible for altering the course of the French government?

The Third Estate played a significant role in altering the course of the French government. The Third Estate's very public disagreement with the aristocracy in 1788 on the organization of the Estates General brought these issues to the surface. The Third Estate refused to submit to a status of third-class citizenship, as it were, and demanded in its *cahier de doléance* to the King that they receive equal opportunities to vote. On June 1, 1789, the Third Estate invited members of the First and Second estates (clergy and nobles, respectively) to join them and organize a new legislative body.

This occasion was significant because it transformed the political arena in France. Shortly after this initial meeting, the National Assembly was created. Its members took an oath to sit until they could provide France with a new constitution. This oath, known as the Tennis Court Oath, and an influx of clergy and nobles who subsequently joined the National Assembly, resulted in the body's getting formal recognition from the king. The king was forced to ask the First and Second estates to meet with the new National Assembly for the purposes of voting. As a result, a new government was created, in which voting occurred by head instead of by privileged order.

These changes were dramatic, and they set the stage for further changes in the French government. The Third Estate had effectively remade the French government by protesting policies and traditions that its representatives found unacceptable and unfair. The French government was forced to respond to the demands of the Third Estate because it had a critical mass of supporters. It is entirely possible that without the determination of the Third Estate to assert its rights to Louis XVI, the French government might have remained stratified by class. The Third Estate's presence in the National Assembly (later known as the National Constituent Assembly) involved a new composition of members who came from all classes of society and who shared goals for the reform of France. This radical political move effectively began the revolution against government in France that would continue in one way or another over the course of the French Revolution.

CHAPTER 19

The Age of Napoleon and the Triumph of Romanticism

The Rise of Napoleon Bonaparte

- **Napoleon Bonaparte (1769–1821)** rose to power in the aftermath of the Thermidorian Reaction by defending the new regime on October 5, 1795 against a rebellion.
- In November of 1799 Napoleon overthrew the Directory through a *coup d'état,* issued the Constitution of Year VIII, which effectively established him as ruler, and formed a new government: **the Consulate.**

The Consulate in France (1799–1804)

- The Consulate was composed of three Consuls, but Napoleon retained all of the power as First Consul. His constitution was overwhelmingly approved in a **plebiscite.**
- Bonaparte quickly made peace with France's enemies, restored peace and order at home, requiring loyalty from those he employed from every political faction. He was also ruthless and efficient in suppressing opposition. Napoleon made peace with the Catholic church in the **Concordat of 1801**. In 1802, a plebiscite ratified Napoleon as consul for life, and Napoleon began the codification of French law by producing the Civil Code of 1804—also known as the **Napoleonic Code.**

Napoleon's Empire (1804–1814)

- In 1804, Napoleon crowned himself **Napoleon I**. He proceeded to conquer much of Europe in a series of military campaigns that transformed the map of the continent.
- Citizen loyalty and a *levée en masse* gave Napoleon virtually limitless resources of soldiers to wage war. Napoleon sent an army to restore the rebellious colony of Haiti to French rule.
- **William Pitt the Younger** formed the **Third Coalition,** persuading Austria and Russia to move against French aggression in Germany. In 1805, the British defeated Napoleon's navy at the Battle of Trafalgar, which ended to Napoleon's plans to invade the British isles.
- In his greatest victory, Napoleon defeated Austrian and Russian forces at Austerlitz in 1805. The subsequent treaty with Austria gave Napoleon major concessions and recognized him as king of Italy. In 1806, Napoleon organized the **Confederation of the Rhine,** enabling the dissolution of the Holy Roman Empire.

European Response to the Empire

- The Napoleonic Code was established in the territories that French forces had conquered, and Enlightenment attitudes of liberalism and nationalism spread to nations throughout Europe.
- When Napoleon deposed the Spanish Bourbons and put his brother on the throne, a rebellion broke out, which began a guerilla war that was consummated when British and Spanish forces under the Duke of Wellington drove the French out.
- Napoleon resolved to invade Russia after Alexander I withdrew from the Continental System in 1812, which prohibited trade with Britain. Napoleon had superior manpower, but the

Russians burned crops and villages, destroying all food and supplies as they retreated. Napoleon captured Moscow, but ordered his army to retreat; many of his soldiers perished during this ill-fated attempt at domination. Napoleon **abdicated** his throne in 1814 and was exiled to **Elba,** an island off the Italian coast.

The Congress of Vienna and the European Settlement
- **The Congress of Vienna** took more than a year to conclude, and England, Prussia, Russia, and Austria dominated the discussions. All the powers agreed that France should not be allowed to dominate Europe again. However, to pacify France, the leaders restored the French Bourbon monarchy and worked out a boundary settlement that was not overly punitive.
- Napoleon returned from exile and was restored to power for 100 days before the Duke of Wellington defeated him at the **Battle of Waterloo.** Thereafter, Napoleon lived on Saint Helena. The **Quadruple Alliance** among England, Austria, Prussia, and Russia was renewed. The purpose of the alliance was to serve as a coalition for peace and to maintain the balance of power, while suppressing revolutionary ideas of nationalism.

The Romantic Movement
- **Romanticism** was a reaction against much of the thought of the Enlightenment. Romantic writers rejected the ideas of the *philosophes* and sought to interpret nature in terms of their experience with it and reaction to it, rather than through mechanical terms or categories.
- Romanticism elevated the role of the individual and the importance of individual cultures. A new spirit of nationalism developed across Europe, partly in reaction to the new importance placed on individual feeling and experience.
- Many Romantics believed in the **supremacy of the imagination** for perceiving nature and the world, and they were drawn to the medieval Christianity and spiritual mysteries of all kinds, believing that religion and their beliefs were compatible. **Methodism,** a faith that stressed inward, heartfelt religion was founded by **John Wesley** in England.
- Some of the intellectuals affiliated with the Romantic movement were influenced by the work of **Jean-Jacques Rousseau.** Rousseau's *Émile* focuses on the importance of letting children grow and learn by trial and error. This concept of human development appealed to Romantics who believed that people should grow in accord with their individual natures.
- **Immanuel Kant's** works of philosophy endorsed his belief in human freedom, immortality, and existence in God. Many Romantics believed his work refuted the rational focus of the Enlightenment, which negated the importance of imagination and feeling.

Romantic Literature
- Romantic authors wrote works that did not conform to classical rules and made use of the imagination. This kind of literature was represented by **Victor Hugo** in France, and **Goethe** and **Schlegel** in Germany. English Romantics tended to be absorbed by the idea of the imagination, how it was affected by nature, and the mystical elements of experience. **William Blake, Samuel Taylor Coleridge, William Wordsworth,** and **Lord Byron** are some of the most important English Romantics.

Consider what reforms the Napoleonic Code made to French society.

Multiple-Choice Questions

1. Napoleon Bonaparte gained power of France through
   (A) a plebiscite.
   (B) a coup d'état.
   (C) an election.
   (D) an act of war.
   (E) a treaty.

2. All of the following were figures of Romanticism EXCEPT
   (A) William Blake.
   (B) Johann Wolfgang von Goethe.
   (C) Friedrich Schlegel.
   (D) Samuel Taylor Coleridge.
   (E) Jean Racine.

3. Romantics placed a premium of importance on
   (A) the intellect.
   (B) the body.
   (C) the afterlife.
   (D) the imagination.
   (E) marital life.

4. Bonaparte's 1805 military victory at Austerlitz resulted in
   (A) the defeat of the Holy Roman Empire.
   (B) his being recognized as the king of Italy.
   (C) a battle with Britain.
   (D) few concessions from Austria.
   (E) a secret alliance between Napoleon and William Pitt the Younger.

5. Napoleon divorced his wife, Empress Josephine, because
   (A) she was unfaithful to him.
   (B) she was unable to bear him a child.
   (C) she was active in resisting his efforts to gain more land for France.
   (D) she was a political handicap to his rule.
   (E) he believed that she was plotting against his life.

6. The Quadruple Alliance included all of the following European powers EXCEPT
   (A) Britain.
   (B) Austria.
   (C) Russia.
   (D) Prussia.
   (E) Italy.

7. Which of the following religions developed in Europe during the Romantic era?
    (A) Deism
    (B) Unitarianism
    (C) Presbyterianism
    (D) Methodism
    (E) Mormonism

8. The Concordat of 1801
    (A) elevated the symbolic importance of the Catholic church in France.
    (B) declared Catholicism the religion of most French citizens.
    (C) effectively prohibited Catholic worship in France.
    (D) pleased Napoleon's anticlerical supporters.
    (E) granted the Catholic church greater power independent of the French state.

9. Napoleon's "Continental System" aimed at
    (A) defeating other European powers and incorporating them into the French empire.
    (B) establishing members of his family as rulers of European countries defeated by France.
    (C) free trade within the French empire.
    (D) cutting off all British trade with the Continent.
    (E) establishing peace with Britain.

10. The famous German Romantic figure who authored *Faust* was
    (A) Friedrich Schlegel.
    (B) Immanuel Kant.
    (C) Johann Wolfgang von Goethe.
    (D) Friedrich Schiller.
    (E) Johann Gottfried Herder.

Document-Based Question

What do the documents below tell us about the Romantic's views of nature and history? What about religion?

Document A Source: Madame de Staël describes the new Romantic literature of Germany, *Concerning Germany*.

The literature of romance is alone capable of further improvement, because, being rooted in our own soil, that alone can continue to grow and acquire fresh life: it expresses our religion; it recalls our history; its origin is ancient, although not of classical antiquity….

   The new school maintains the same system in the fine arts as in literature, and affirms that Christianity is the source of all modern genius; the writers of this school also characterize, in a new manner, all than in Gothic architecture agrees with the religious sentiments of Christians. It does not follow however, from this, that the moderns can and ought to construct Gothic churches;…it is only of consequence to us, in the present silence of genius, to lay aside the contempt which has been thrown on all the conceptions of the middle ages.

Document B Source: John Constable's *Salisbury Cathedral*.

John Constable's *Salisbury Cathedral from the Meadows* displays the appeal of Romantic art to both medieval monuments and the sublime power of nature. John Constable (1776–1837), *Salisbury Cathedral from the Meadows*, 1831. Oil on canvas, 151.8 × 189.9. © The National Gallery, London

Document C Source: Caspar David Frieddrich's *The Polar Sea.*

Caspar David Friedrich's *The Polar Sea* illustrated the power of nature to diminish the creations of humankind as seen in the wrecked ship on the right of the painting.   Kunsthalle, Hamburg, Germany/A.K.G., Berlin/SuperStock

Document D Source: Joseph Turner's *Rain, Steam, and Speed.*

Joseph Mallord William Turner's *Rain, Steam, and Speed—The Great Western Railway* captured the tensions many Europeans felt between their natural environment and the new technology of the industrial age.   Joseph Mallord William Turner, 1775–1851, *Rain, Steam, and Speed—The Great Western Railway* 1844. Oil on canvas, 90.8 × 121.9. © The National Gallery, London

Document E Source: Chateaubriand on "Gothic churches."

Although "Everything ought to be put in its place" is a trivial truth which carries force by its constant repetition, nevertheless without accepting it one cannot, after all, have anything perfect. The Greeks would not have appreciated an Egyptian temple at Athens any more than the Egyptians would a Greek temple at Memphis. The two buildings in exchanging place would have lost their main beauty, that is to say their relationship with the institutions and practices of the people. We can apply the same reflection to old Christian edifices. It is pertinent to remark that, even in this century of unbelief, poets and novelists, by a natural return to the customs of our ancestors, like to introduce…Gothic temples into their fictions; so great is the charm of memories linked with religion and the history of our country. Nations do not discard their ancient customs as people do their old clothes.

Free-Response Question

Using examples from the works of at least two English Romantics, describe the philosophy of the Romantic movement in literature.

ANSWERS AND EXPLANATIONS

Multiple-Choice Questions

☐ **1. (B) is correct.** Napoleon Bonaparte gained power of the French government through a coup d'état in which legislators of the Directory were driven out of power.

☐ **2. (E) is correct.** Jean Racine was a seventeenth-century classical dramatist, whose work was criticized by Henri Beyle, a French Romantic who was the first to declare his affiliation with the Romantic movement.

☐ **3. (D) is correct.** Romantics placed a premium on the imagination, and the English Romantics in particular believed that the artist's imagination was God at work in the mind. They discarded the Enlightenment focus on the intellect in favor of imagination or intuition.

☐ **4. (B) is correct.** Bonaparte's 1805 military victory at Austerlitz resulted in his being named king of Italy.

☐ **5. (B) is correct.** Napoleon divorced his wife, Empress Josephine, because she had not borne him a child by age forty-five, and he wanted to secure an heir for his rapidly growing empire.

☐ **6. (E) is correct.** Italy was not one of the four members of the Quadruple Alliance.

☐ **7. (D) is correct.** John Wesley founded the Methodist church during the Romantic period. It originated as a revolt against Deism and rationalism and focused on inward, heartfelt religion rather than the rational focus of Enlightenment faith. Presbyterianism and Unitarianism existed prior to the Romantic movement; Mormonism was founded in America.

☐ **8. (B) is correct.** The Concordat of 1801 weakened the role of the Catholic Church in France, even as it declared Catholicism to be the religion of most French citizens. Napoleon's anticlerical supporters were distressed that Napoleon brokered a deal with Pope Pius VII, but the Concordat did not really grant the pope or the Catholic Church any religious dominance in France, which is what the pope had wanted.

9. **(D) is correct.** Napoleon's "Continental System" aimed at destroying the British economy by cutting off their access to trade with the European continent. Napoleon hoped to cripple their domestic stability and force unrest that would help drive them from the war.

10. **(C) is correct.** Goethe was the author of *Faust,* his greatest masterpiece—a long dramatic poem that was critical of previous Romantic writers and that addressed the spiritual problems Europeans would encounter if the traditional moral values of Christianity were discarded.

Document-Based Question

What do the documents below tell us about the Romantic's views of nature and history? What about religion?

Convincing essays might note:

- The passion and drama of Romantic depictions of nature (See Documents C and D)
- The emphasis on Christianity's central place in European identity (See Documents A, B and E)
- The celebration of the medieval at the expense of the classical (See Documents A, B, and E)
- The connection made between the history, religion, and essence of a national people (See Documents A and E)
- The emphasis on authentic and natural feeling and emotion (See documents A, B, C, D, and E)

Free-Response Question

Using examples from the works of at least two English Romantics, describe the philosophy of the Romantic movement in literature.

The English Romantic writers contended that poetry was an outcropping of the imaginative and creative forces within the individual. Poetry was linked with the divine, and some English Romantics believed that the artist's imagination was literal proof of God at work in man. Because poetry transmuted divine inspiration into language, the Romantics considered it to be one of the most rarefied of intellectual and imaginative pursuits.

Two of the most important English poets of the Romantic era were William Blake and William Wordsworth. These authors differed significantly in their creative output. William Blake was drawn to the mystical—authoring poetic epics that described imaginary worlds in a prophetic, dream-like vision. Blake's Romanticism is perhaps best known in his *Songs of Innocence* and *Songs of Experience,* two collections of short poems that depict the world in a pre-fallen state and in a corrupt state respectively. For Blake, the opposing forces of innocence and experience were reflected in the natural world as well as inside the human soul.

For William Wordsworth, who endorsed an entirely new way of writing poetry as a reaction against the rationalism and wit of the eighteenth-century verse, Romanticism was an expression of the poet's immersion in nature. Wordsworth's *Prelude* offers considerations of some of the political events of the era filtered through an individual sensibility and an appreciation of the fleeting beauty of the everyday. Wordsworth's writing is more grounded in the real world than is Blake's; it is characterized by an appreciation of the innocence of childhood and of the precious quality of creative inspiration.

Works by both of these authors embody some of the qualities of Romantic literature, as they stress natural beauty and divine inspiration, and maintain a belief in the importance of imagination in the artist.

The Conservative Order and the Challenges of Reform (1815–1832)

Nationalism was the most powerful political ideology of nineteenth- and twentieth-century European affairs.

The Challenges of Nationalism and Liberalism

- Early nineteenth-century nationalists opposed the **Congress of Vienna** because it did not allow for individual representation of ethnic groups, but rather upheld monarchies and dynasties in its redistribution of land. Many issues of **nationalism** arose during this era.
- Nineteenth-century European conservatives defined as *liberal* anything or anyone that challenged their own political, social, or religious values. Nineteenth-century liberals were influenced by Enlightenment writers and the French Revolution, and they sought to gain legal equality, religious toleration, and freedom of speech. Many liberals had economic goals of being able to enrich themselves without governmental interference. The economic ideas of **Adam Smith** were popular among economic liberals.

Conservative Governments: The Domestic Political Order

- **Nineteenth-century conservatism** was dominated by **monarchies, landed aristocracies, and established churches** that united over their resistant to change of the social order. These groups cooperated to slow the progress of nationalism and liberalism.
- **Austrian Prince Metternich** embodied conservatism more than any other nineteenth-century statesman. Metternich feared that recognizing minority rights would destroy his empire.
- **Frederick III of Prussia** reneged on his pledge to create constitutional government, and resisted aspirations by German nationalists to dissolve the conservative order.
- Students in the southern German states **Baden, Bavaria** and **Württemberg** reacted against the lack of popular sovereignty and formed *Burschenschaften,* or student associations, to address their goal of a unified Germany.
- In England, the Tory ministry of **Lord Liverpool** focused on the issues of land owners and the elite rather than on the average citizens. Unruly meetings of reformers resulted in Parliament's passage of the **Coercion Act of March 1817,** which suspended the rights of *habeas corpus* and discouraged free speech. By 1819, a liberal crowd gathered in Manchester at Saint Peter's Fields, and when the militia moved into the audience, it set off a mass panic. Eleven people were killed, many more were injured; the event is known as the **Peterloo Massacre.** Parliament went on to pass laws called the **Six Acts,** which were designed at intimidating agitators and limiting their free speech.
- A Bourbon restoration in France brought **Louis XVIII** to the throne after Napoleon's abdication. He issued a constitution known as the **Charter** that gave the monarch greater control over government leaders, maintained the Declaration of the Rights of Man and

Citizen, and did not challenge the property rights of lands confiscated from aristocrats and the church. Louis XVIII's moderate Charter angered royalists who carried out attacks against Napoleon's allies. In 1820, the assassination of the duke of Berri gave royalists an excuse to persecute liberal politicians. Louis XVIII responded with more repressive measures that gave royalists and conservatives greater power.

The Conservative International Order

- After the Congress of Vienna, the major European powers met informally to discuss their differences in what was known as the **Concert of Europe.** This system functioned well for the first few years, until 1820, when the Bourbon Ferdinand VII of Spain violated his promise to govern according to a written constitution. At this time, revolution occurred in Naples. Metternich was especially concerned about the events in Italy, because it threatened to spread to Austria. The other powers were divided on the proper course of action.
- Metternich sought the help of Prussia and Russia, and unofficial groups from Britain and France assisted in suppressing the revolution. They issued the **Protocol of Troppau,** which stated that stable governments could intervene in countries experiencing revolution to help restore order. All of the interventions that occurred through the congress system sought to maintain the international order achieved at the Congress of Vienna.
- Other **movements for independence**—such as that of the Greek Revolution of 1821 and the 1830 fight for Serbian independence—demonstrated the growing issues of nationalism and liberalism coming into conflict with conservatism. Wars of independence in Latin America included efforts by Haiti, Brazil, and the present day lands of Venezuela, Mexico, Paraguay, Uruguay, and Argentina to shed their colonial ties to Europe and gain their sovereignty.

The Conservative Order Shaken in Europe

- Political discontent spread to Europe in the mid–1820s. In Russia, Russian officers who had fought Napoleon were exposed to ideas of the Enlightenment, and they developed reformist sympathies. Two secret societies, the **Northern Society** and the **Southern Society** united forces in 1825 to carry out a coup d'état in 1826. When the Russian army was required to swear its allegiance to the new Tsar Nicholas, the Moscow regiment refused, and Nicholas had the artillery attack them. This so-called **Decembrist Revolt** came to symbolize to Russian liberals the oppressive conditions of life under the tsars. Nicholas reasserted his conservative authority when Poland nationalists agitated for change.
- In France in 1830, Charles X was the new king, and he favored aristocrats and ultra-royalists. He restored the rule of **primogeniture,** supported the Catholic church, and gave special rights to the descendants of émigrés. Liberals gained enough seats in the Chamber of Deputies in 1827 to override some of Charles's new laws. When this happened again after the elections of 1830, Charles attempted a royalist seizure of power of the Chamber of Deputies. Parisians responded by staging massive protests and Charles X turned troops against them before departing in August for exile. The **July Monarchy** as Louis Philippe's ascension was called, focused on his role as a king of the French people.

For Additional Review

Analyze the basic differences between nationalism, conservatism, and liberalism as these ideologies were expressed in the early-nineteenth-century Europe.

1. The Charter developed by Louis XVIII
   (A) provided for a hereditary monarchy and a bicameral legislature.
   (B) ensured equal rights for peasants, landowners, and bourgeois.
   (C) granted all rights to the ultraroyalists, angering the liberals.
   (D) granted all rights to the liberals, infuriating the ultra royalists.
   (E) did not allow for religious toleration.

2. The "Irish problem" in the early nineteenth century involved
   (A) religious differences between Irish citizens.
   (B) Irish nationalists wanting independence from Britain.
   (C) the terrible famine that afflicted Ireland.
   (D) Britain's refusal to allow Ireland to elect members to the British Parliament.
   (E) the racism the Irish experienced when they emigrated to Britain.

3. Which of the following was NOT a member of the Quadruple Alliance?
   (A) Britian.
   (B) Russia
   (C) Poland.
   (D) Prussia
   (E) Austria

4. The *Burschenschaften* in Baden, Bavaria, and Württemberg were
   (A) ultraroyalists.
   (B) aides to Metternich.
   (C) a minority ethnic group seeking political recognition and sovereignty.
   (D) student associations.
   (E) a council of representatives from different ethnic factions.

5. Nationalists generally contended that
   (A) legitimate monarchies should provide the basis for political unity.
   (B) ethnic boundaries should be distinct from political boundaries.
   (C) ethnic boundaries and political boundaries should coincide.
   (D) official versions of language should come from the government rather than from
       inhabitants.
   (E) multinational states were preferable to single ethnic kingdoms.

6. The Protocol of Troppau
   (A) permitted Russia and Prussia to build up their armies.
   (B) advocated intervention in Italian affairs.
   (C) dismantled the Concert of Europe.
   (D) permitted stable governments' interven tion into countries experiencing revolution for the
       purpose of restoring order.
   (E) required countries experiencing revolution to temporarily concede their authority to allied
       European powers.

7. The liberation of Argentina was achieved by
   (A) the armies of Simon Bolívar.
   (B) the armies of José de San Martín.
   (C) the Buenos Aires *junta*.
   (D) the Buenos Aires *peninsulares*.
   (E) the armies of Bernardo O'Higgins.

8. Which of the following rulers embodied the most extreme form of nineteenth-century autocracy?
   (A) Alexander I
   (B) Nicholas I
   (C) Louis XVIII
   (D) William IV
   (E) Milos

9. In the immediate postwar years, Metternich's policy toward Germany endeavored to
   (A) unify the German Confederation.
   (B) restore the Holy Roman Empire.
   (C) prevent any movement toward constitu tionalism in the German Confederation.
   (D) oppose the monarchy of William III.
   (E) recognize the political rights and aspirations of the various ethnic groups involved.

10. All of the following statements are true of Charles X's rule of France EXCEPT
   (A) he sympathized with ultra royalists.
   (B) he was successful in destroying the Chamber of Deputies.
   (C) he restored the rule of primogeniture to France.
   (D) he was supportive the Catholic church's role in France.
   (E) he gave special rights to descendants of émigrés.

Document-Based Question

What did supporters of the Great Reform Bill of 1832 hope it would accomplish? What did opponents of the bill fear would be its result?

Document A Source: Engène Delacroix's, *Liberty Leading the People*, a symbolic representation of the 1830 Revolution in France.

Document B Source: Thomas Macaulay, a member of the House of Commons, defends the Great Reform Bill, *Hansard's Parliamentary Debates*.

[The principle of the ministers] is plain, rational and consistent. It is this – to admit the middle class to a large and direct share in the Representation, without any violent shock to the institutions of our country….I hold it to be clearly expedient, that in a country like this, the right of suffrage should depend on a pecuniary qualification. Every argument…which would induce me to oppose Universal Suffrage, induces me to support the measure which is now before us. I oppose Universal Suffrage, because I think it would produce a destructive revolution. I support this measure because I am sure it is our best security against revolution….

Document C Source: Thomas Macaulay, a member of the House of Commons, satirizes radical politicians.

For rows and revolutions;
There's no receipt like pike and drum
For crazy constitutions.
Close, close the shop! Break, break the loom!
Desert your hearths and furrows,
And throng in arms to seal the doom
Of England's rotten boroughs….

The peer shall dangle from the gate,
The bishop from his steeple,
Till all recanting, own, the State
Means nothing but the People.

Document D Source: John Cam Hobhouse recalls Lord John Russell's speech in which the Great Reform Bill was outlined, *Recollections of a Long Life* (1910).

Lord John Russell began his speech at six o'clock. Never shall I forget the astonishment of my neighbors as he developed his plan. Indeed, all the House of Commons seemed perfectly astounded; and when he read the long list of the boroughs to be either wholly or partially disfranchised there was a sort of wild ironical laughter. Baring Wall, turning to me, said, "They are mad! They are mad!" and others made use of similar exclamations - all but Sir Robert Peel; he looked serious and angry, as if he had discovered that the Ministers, by the boldness of their measure, had secured the support of the country. Burdett and I agreed there was very chance of the measure being carried, and that a revolution would be the consequence.

Document E Source: Thomas Creevey, "Letter to Miss Old on the passing of the Reform Act," (June 5, 1832).

Thank God! I was in at the death of this Conservative plot, and the triumph of the Bill! This is the third great event of my life at which I have been present, and in each of which I have been to a certain extent mixed up - the battle of Waterloo, the battle of Queen Caroline, and the battle of Earl Grey and the English nation for the Reform Bill.

Free-Response Question

Describe the achievements of the Great Reform Bill of 1832.

ANSWERS AND EXPLANATIONS

Multiple-Choice Questions

☐ **1. (A) is correct.** The Charter developed by Louis XVIII was the constitution of the French restoration. It allowed for hereditary monarchy and a bicameral legislature, gave the monarch greater control over government leaders, maintained the Declaration of the Rights of Man and Citizen, and did not challenge the property rights of lands confiscated from aristocrats and the church.

☐ **2. (B) is correct.** The "Irish problem" in the early nineteenth century related to the question of Irish sovereignty and independence from Britain. England had brought Ireland under direct rule in 1800 and had allowed the Irish to elect members to the British Parliament in Westminster, but Irish nationalists wanted larger measures of self-government. The famous potato famine in Ireland occurred decades later.

☐ **3. (C) is correct.** The Quadruple Alliance consisted of Russia, Austria, Prussia, and Britain.

☐ **4. (D) is correct.** The *Burschenschaften* in Baden, Bavaria, and Württemberg were student associations that served multiple functions, including supporting political agendas like the unification of Germany. These clubs were often anti-Semitic.

☐ **5. (C) is correct.** Nationalists generally contended that nations are composed of people who share a common language and common customs, and that they should be administered by a government that has those same shared things in common. Nationalists supported the idea that ethnic boundaries should be national, or political, boundaries.

☐ **6. (D) is correct.** The Protocol of Troppau was a declaration issued by Austria, Prussia, and Russia that said that stable governments could intervene to restore order in countries in the throes of revolution.

☐ **7. (C) is correct.** The liberation of Argentina was achieved by the Creole *juntas,* or political committees. In 1810, the *junta* in Buenos Aires dismissed Spanish authority and sent forces into Paraguay and Uruguay to help liberate them from Spanish domination. Though the armies were defeated, Spanish control was lost in these areas as well.

☐ **8. (B) is correct.** Nicholas I came to symbolize the most extreme form of nineteenth-century autocracy: he was unwilling to change the status quo and turned his back on all reforms that would improve the social conditions for serfs and peasants in Russia. Censorship and secret police were common during his rule.

☐ **9. (C) is correct.** Metternich epitomized conservatism, and his policy toward Germany and other states seeking national recognition, in the immediate postwar years, was to prevent any movement toward constitutionalism. Metternich rejected constitutionalism in a political memoir he wrote for the monarchs and ministers who assembled in post-war conferences to stanch the spread of revolution.

☐ **10. (B) is correct.** Charles X was not successful in his attempt to destroy the Chamber of Deputies. While he was able to stage a royal coup d'état that dissolved the Chamber of Deputies (which had recently been filled with liberals in a landslide election), Charles X was not able to push through all of his royalist reforms. He abdicated and was exiled in England; thereafter, the Chamber of Deputies named a new ministry filled with constitutional monarchists.

Document-Based Question

What did supporters of the Great Reform Bill of 1832 hope it would accomplish? What did opponents of the bill fear would be its result?

Convincing essays might note:
- The fear of revolution expressed by both supporters and opponents of the bill (See Documents A, B, C and D)
- The desire of reformers to "save" the nation (See Documents A, B, C and E)
- The opposition of supporters of the middle class to a more inclusive notion of the "people" (See Documents A and B)
- The unwillingness of conservatives to compromise (See Document D)

Free-Response Question

Describe the achievements of the Great Reform Bill of 1832.

The Great Reform Bill of 1832 was not a triumph for liberalism or democracy, but rather it was a triumph for moderate reform. It dramatically enlarged the English electorate, increasing the number of voters by about 50%. But it also maintained a property qualification for voters, which meant that it still retained some of the restrictions of previous eras. Women were not enfranchised by the Great Reform Bill, and some working-class members even *lost* the right to vote.

The Reform Bill did succeed in allowing a wider variety of property to have representation in the House of Commons. The reform bill also gave some property owners (especially those in British manufacturing cities) who had been previously unrepresented the opportunity to make their voices heard. The act helped align economic interests with political institutions, and this transformation led the way to similar reforms in other areas, including the church and municipal government, in later years.

People who had previously been denied access to the political forum were now given the ability to participate in the legislative process. By this transformation of its political system, Great Britain was able to avoid the kind of revolution that was sweeping through other governments.

CHAPTER 21

Economic Advance and Social Unrest (1830–1850)

Toward an Industrial Society

- Through its **textile industry,** Britain achieved economic stability that led to its dominance in the world in the nineteenth century.
- As industrialization spread, the population of Europe continued to grow, and **more people chose to live in cities.** Migration from the countryside put new pressures on urban infrastructure: poor harvests from 1845 to 1847 caused massive emigration to cities.
- The explosion of **railway building** in the 1830s and 1840s and the improvement of canals and roads made transportation to urban centers easier and increased industrialization.

The Labor Force

The nineteenth-century workforce was extremely varied; conditions differed from country to country and decade to decade.

- Artisans and factory workers alike underwent a process of **proletarianization,** whereby they entered into a wage economy and gradually lost significant ownership in the means of production. This process occurred rapidly wherever the factory system existed.
- The economic security of factory workers was often better than that of urban artisans. By the nineteenth century, it became more difficult for artisans to exercise control over their trades; European liberals disapproved of and **banned labor and guild organizations.**
- Some workshops began the practice known in France as *confection,* which involved the production of goods in standard sizes and styles rather than by special orders, in order to compete with larger establishments or machine production.
- In 1836, William Lovett and other radical London artisans formed the **London Working Men's Association,** and in 1838 they demanded six specific reforms in a Charter: universal male suffrage, annual election of the House of Commons, the secret ballot, equal electoral districts, abolition of property qualifications for members of the House of Commons, and payment of salaries to members of the House of Commons. **Chartism,** as this movement was called, failed as a national faction, but many of the **Six Points** were enacted into law.

Family Structures and the Industrial Revolution

- Prior to the Industrial Revolution, home life and economic life occurred in the same place; thereafter, these worlds were increasingly distinct. Factory wages for skilled adult males enabled some families to rely solely on the male breadwinner's income. As machines became less complex and required fewer skilled operators, more women and children maintained them, earning reduced salaries compared to their adult male counterparts.
- As more husbands were able to support their families on one salary, more wives came to be associated with domestic duties, such as housekeeping, food preparation, and **cottage industries.** By the 1820s, more **unmarried women** became employed in **factories,** tending machines that required little skilled labor. These women were young, single, or widowed.

- The **English Factory Act of 1833** prohibited the **employment of children** under the age of nine, limited the workday for children, and required that children receive two hours of daily education at the factory owner's expense. The wage economy meant that families were not spending as much time together as they had before.

Problems of Crime and Order

- Cities became associated with crime as the Industrial Revolution continued.
- Propertied members of society strove to improve the crime situation during this time via prison reform and better systems of police. Professional police forces helped an orderly European society emerge.

Classical Economics

- Most economists followed the *laissez-faire* thought of Adam Smith's *Wealth of Nations,* and encouraged most economic decisions being made through the mechanism of the marketplace. They emphasized thrift, competition, and personal industry, all of which appealed to the middle class.
- **Thomas Malthus (1766–1834)** published his *Essay on the Principle of Population,* in which he argued that population would eventually outstrip food supply. He encouraged chastity and discouraged the raising of families. **David Ricardo (1772–1823)** argued his theory of "the iron law of wages" based on Malthus's principles that if wages were raised, more children would be produced, which would cause wages to fall and working people to produce fewer children, which would then cause wages to rise, in a continuous cycle.

Early Socialism

- Early Socialists were in favor of the new productive capacity of industrialism. A group of writers known as the **utopian Socialists** questioned the structures and values of the existing capitalistic framework. Other important forms of socialism, including **Saint-Simonianism, Owenism, Fourierism, Anarchism,** and **Marxism** developed during this period.

1848: Year of Revolutions

- A series of **liberal and nationalist revolutions** exploded across the Continent in 1848. Political liberals were the chief advocates of reforms. In France, a "Second Republic" emerged with Napoleon's nephew, Louis Napoleon Bonaparte, at the helm. In 1851, he seized power and became Emperor in 1852, returning France to a dictatorship. The Habsburg lands saw unrest and revolts in Hungary and Austria. Czech nationalists rebelled and the Pan-Slavic Congress—which consisted of Poles, Ruthenians, Czechs, Slovaks, Croats, Slovenes, and Serbs—called for national equality of Slavs and protested the repression of all Slavic peoples. Other revolts in Italy and Germany were suppressed, the liberal era ended, and the European middle class ceased to be revolutionary.

For Additional Review

Consider the various forms of nineteenth-century prison reform.

1. The French practice of *confection* refers to
   (A) the production of custom-made goods in factories that hired artisans.
   (B) the production of custom-made goods by artisans as a means of competing with the mass production of factories.
   (C) the proliferation of small businesses in factory towns.
   (D) an excess production of goods to anticipate demand.
   (E) the production of goods in standard sizes.

2. Police forces in the early eighteenth century were
   (A) staffed by community volunteers.
   (B) politically appointed.
   (C) paid and professionally trained.
   (D) a special branch of the local government.
   (E) funded by local aristocrats concerned with falling property values.

3. Jeremy Bentham's utilitarianism
   (A) promoted the view that population grew geometrically while food supplies grew arithmetically..
   (B) demanded workers' cooperatives be created in place of a market economy.
   (C) argued for human happiness through the "greatest happiness of the greatest number.".
   (D) asserted that wages would stabilize at the subsistence level.
   (E) stated that class identity should be associated with the means of production.

4. *The Condition of the Working Class in England* was written by
   (A) Adam Smith.
   (B) Friedrich Engels.
   (C) Karl Marx.
   (D) David Ricardo.
   (E) Thomas Malthus.

5. In 1849 the crown of the new Germany created at the Frankfurt Parliament was offered to which European ruler?
   (A) Lajos Kossuth
   (B) Frederick William IV of Prussia
   (C) Friedrich Herder
   (D) Franz Josef I of Austria
   (E) Louis Napoleon

6. After the passage of the English Factory Act in 1833
   (A) there was a marked decrease in productivity.
   (B) more children were exploited in the workplace.
   (C) many British working class laborers demanded shorter workdays for adults.
   (D) the workday for adults and older teenagers was shortened.
   (E) working-class parents became more involved in the education of their children.

7. The largest group of employed women in France in the mid-eighteenth century worked
   (A) in factories.
   (B) as prostitutes.
   (C) in cottage industries.
   (D) on the land.
   (E) as urban artisans.

8. The "Second Republic" in France was headed by
   (A) Charles X.
   (B) Louis Napoleon Bonaparte.
   (C) Louis XVIII.
   (D) Otto von Bismarck.
   (E) Napoleon II.

9. Classical Economies had less influence in Germany because of the
   (A) lack of free trading unions.
   (B) lack of railroads and other industrial development.
   (C) inefficient banking system.
   (D) tradition of state-directed economic development.
   (E) bias against English systems of economic reform.

10. Writers and activists of the 1840s who rejected both industry and the domination of
    government are known as
    (A) Marxists.
    (B) Communists.
    (C) Owenists.
    (D) Anarchists.
    (E) Socialists.

Document-Based Question

On the basis of the evidence provided below, describe the experiences of women workers during the early industrial revolution. What drew women into the factories and mines of Britain?

Document A Source: Women factory workers explain their opposition to efforts to eliminate women's employment in factories, *The Examiner*.

…we have looked with no little anxiety for your opinion on the Factory Bill.…You are for doing away with our services in manufacturing altogether. So much the better, if had pointed out any other more eligible and practical employment for the surplus female labour….

We see no way of escape from starvation, but to accept the very tempting offers of the newspapers, held out as bait to us, fairly to ship ourselves off to Van Dieman's Land [Tasmania] on the very delicate errand of husband hunting, and having arrived at the "Land of Goshen" jump ashore, who a "Who wants me?"…

Document B Source: A women miner describes her life, *Parliamentary Papers*.

My cousin looks after my children in the day time . I am very tired when I get home at night. I fall asleep sometimes before I get washed. I am not so strong as I was, and cannot stand my work so well as I used to. I have drawn [filled and hauled coal baskets] till I have hathe skin off me; the belt and chain is worse when we are in the family way. My feller (husband) has beaten me many a times for not being ready. I were not used to it at first, and he had little patience.

I have known many a man beat his drawer. I have known men to take liberties with the drawers, and some of the women have bastards.

Document C Source: Women working in an early textile factory.

As textile production became increasingly automated in the nineteenth century, textile factories required fewer skilled workers and more unskilled attendants. To fill these unskilled positions, factory owners turned increasingly to unmarried women and widows, who worked for lower wages than men and were less likely to form labor organizations.   Courtesy of the Library of Congress

Document D Source: A female factory worker describes her coworkers.

I saw among my coworkers – the despised factory women -- examples of the most extraordinary sacrifices for others. If there was a special emergency in one family, then they chipped in their kreuzers to help. Even though they had worked twelve hours in the factory and many still had an hour's walk home, they mended their own clothes, without ever having been taught how. They took apart their old dresses to fashion new ones from separate pieces, which they sewed at night and on Sundays.

Free-Response Question

Describe Chartism and discuss its role in Britain in the nineteenth century.

ANSWERS AND EXPLANATIONS

Multiple-Choice Questions

☐ **1. (E) is correct.** The French practice *confection,* as used during the Industrial Revolution, refers to the production of goods in standard, rather than custom-made, sizes and styles. This practice began in many workshops as a way to compete with factories and the introduction of machine production into craft-dominated industries.

☐ **2. (C) is correct.** Police forces in the early eighteenth century were paid and professionally trained.

☐ **3. (C) is correct.** "The greatest happiness for the greatest number" is a principle of Jeremy Bentham's utilitarianism.

☐ **4. (B) is correct.** *The Condition of the Working Class in England* was written by Friedrich Engels, and it presented a devastating picture of the effects of industrial life.

☐ **5. (B) is correct.** On March 27, 1849, the parliament produced its constitution. Shortly thereafter, its delegates offered the crown of a united Germany to Frederick William IV of Prussia. He rejected the offer, asserting that kings ruled by the grace of God rather than by the permission of man-made constitutions. On his refusal, the Frankfurt Parliament began to dissolve. Not long afterward, troops drove off the remaining members.

☐ **6. (C) is correct.** After the passage of the English Factory Act in 1833, members of the working class demanded similar benefits for adult and adolescent workers as those adopted for children. Some of these reforms included a shorter workday, which would provide an opportunity for adults to spend more time with their children.

☐ **7. (D) is correct.** The largest group of employed women in France in the mid-eighteenth century worked on the land. In England, the largest group of employed women worked as domestic servants. Throughout western Europe, cottage industries employed a vast number of women. Still others were drawn to prostitution to supplement their low wages.

☐ **8. (B) is correct.** The "Second Republic" in France was headed by Louis Napoleon Bonaparte, the nephew of Emperor Napoleon Bonaparte. He was renamed Emperor Napoleon III after an empire was proclaimed in 1852.

☐ **9. (D) is correct.** Classical Economies had less influence in Germany because the tradition in that country was one dating from the enlightened absolutism of state direction of economic development.

☐ **10. (D) is correct.** Anarchists were anti-capitalist and anti-government. While they are often lumped with Socialists, anarchists are usually associated with the programs of Auguste Blanqui, who was a spokesperson for using terror to achieve political reform.

Document-Based Question

On the basis of the evidence provided below, describe the experiences of women workers during the early industrial revolution. What drew women into the factories and mines of Britain?

Convincing essays might note:

☐ The constant labor of working class women, both in and out of the home (See Documents A, B, C, and D)

☐ The vulnerability of women workers to sexual harassment (See Documents A and B)

☐ The implicit pressure for women surrender relatively high-paying factory jobs to men and prejudice against women factory workers (See Document A and D)

☐ The sense of solidarity among women factory workers (See Documents A, B, and D)

Free-Response Question

Describe Chartism and discuss its role in Britain in the nineteenth century.

Chartism was a program of political reform that grew out of the efforts of William Lovett and other radical artisans based in London. After forming the London Working Men's Association, these men issued a charter that demanded six specific reforms called the Six Points of the Charter. These reforms included universal male suffrage, the abolition of property requirements for members of the House of Commons, and annual elections for the House of Commons. Other reforms included the secret ballot and the reimbursement of salaries to members of the House of Commons and equal electoral districts.

The artisans who proposed these reforms were frustrated at their social situation and became a vocal and radical element of the working class. Increasingly, members of the British working class came to associate their economic plight with the demands and reforms sought by the Chartists.

The Chartists continued to seek these reforms in Britain, and Parliament refused to pass their Charter three times. The Chartists distributed petitions that gained millions of British signatures, but despite its efforts to make its demands known and accommodated in the British political system, it failed as a national movement—even as it made small gains on the local level.

Following the depression of the late 1830s and early 1840s, many working-class people in Britain abandoned the Chartist movement altogether. Some of the Chartists' goals were eventually enacted into law, and the movement as a whole was seen by some Continental advocates of the political mass-movement as a great achievement.

CHAPTER 22

The Age of Nation-States

The Crimean War (1853–1856)

- The Crimean War grew out of the **rivalry** between the **Ottoman Empire** and **Russia.** A war among the major European states ensued with France and Britain declaring war on Russia, and Austria and Prussia remaining neutral. Russia fell to the French and British, who settled the matter in 1856 at the **Treaty of Paris.**
- The Crimean War broke the Concert of Europe, and marked a new era in European politics.

Italian Unification

- Nationalists hoped for Italian unification, but Italian statesmen disagreed about how to accomplish it.
- Romantic republican nationalism was led by **Giuseppe Mazzini (1805–1872),** who founded the Young Italy Society to drive Austria from the peninsula. Mazzini and **Giuseppe Garibaldi (1807–1882)** led insurrections in the 1830s through the 1850s.
- Between 1852 and 1860, Italy was transformed into a nation-state governed by a constitutional monarchy. Full unification remained elusive.

German Unification

- The construction of a unified Germany was one of the most important political developments in Europe between 1848 and 1914, because it altered the international balance of power.
- In 1862, William I of Prussia turned to **Otto von Bismarck (1815–1898),** who moved against the liberal Parliament and sought support for unifying Germany through a war with Denmark.
- Bismarck supported the **duchies of Schleswig and Holstein** in their efforts to avoid getting incorporated into Denmark. Together, Prussia and Austria defeated Denmark in 1864, which elevated Bismarck's prestige and led to a conflict between the two countries in 1865.
- Bismarck then provoked war with Austria over the administration of Schleswig and Holstein. **The Seven Weeks' War** led to the defeat of Austria in 1866 and established Prussia as the only major power among the German states. In 1867, the North German Confederation formed, with Bismarck representing the King of Prussia as President. Germany had become a military monarchy, crushing Prussian liberalism.
- **The Franco-Prussian War** (1870–1871) enabled Bismarck to bring the states of southern Germany into the confederation. Bismarck orchestrated the war by provoking France against Prussia, and the southern German states joined Prussia against Napoleon III's armies. The Germans beat the French army, captured Napoleon III, besieged Paris and proclaimed the German Empire.

France: From Liberal Empire to the Third Republic

- The provinces and Paris differed on how to handle a settlement with the Prussians. The National Assembly was dominated by monarchists and led by **Adolphe Thiers,** who agreed in the Treaty of Frankfurt that France would pay an indemnity, and that Prussians would occupy France until it was paid. **Alsace** and part of **Lorraine** were granted to the Prussians.

- Parisians who had suffered under the Prussian siege rebelled against the Treaty of Frankfurt, and elected a new, short-lived municipal government on March 28, 1871, called the **Paris Commune,** that was created to administer Paris separately from the rest of France. On May 8, the National Assembly bombarded the city and broke through defenses on May 21. Troops restored order to Paris, killing 20,000 Parisians in the process and ending the Commune.
- In 1875, the National Assembly adopted a new republican political system that provided for a chamber of deputies elected by universal male suffrage, a senate chosen indirectly, and a president elected by the two legislative houses. Following the 1879 resignation of President **Marshal MacMahon,** Republicans gained control of the national government. **The Dreyfus Affair,** a case involving the trumped up case of a Jewish captain, was the major crisis.

The Habsburg Empire

- The Habsburg domains had remained primarily absolutist after the revolutions of 1848.
- In 1861, Francis Joseph issued the **February Patent,** which set up a bicameral imperial parliament or *Reichsrat,* with an upper chamber appointed by the emperor and an indirectly elected lower chamber. The Magyars refused to recognize this system, but the February Patent ruled the empire for six years. In 1867, Francis Joseph transformed the Habsburg Empire into **Austria-Hungary** to satisfy the desires of Magyars to maintain their lands separately from Austria while sharing the same monarch. The unrest of the many nationalities in the Habsburg Empire caused instability throughout Europe.

Russia: Emancipation and Revolutionary Stirrings

- **Alexander II** restructured Russian society after Russia's defeat in the Crimean War, ushering in some of the much-needed reforms, including the **abolition of serfdom** in 1861. Alexander II became known as the **Tsar Liberator,** but he was never popular with his noble subjects, who resented his control over policy.
- In the 1870s, young Russians drew on the ideas of Alexander Herzen and formed the **Populism Movement,** which sought social revolution based on the communal life of the Russian peasants.

Great Britain: Toward Democracy

- Britain took a step toward democracy in the reform bill sponsored by Benjamin Disraeli (1804–1881), a House of Commons leader, in 1867. By the time the measure had passed, the **number of voters** had been almost doubled from 1,430,000 to 2,470,000.
- William Gladstone ushered in many liberal reforms, including opening more institutions to the public and people from other classes and religious denominations. **The Education Act** of 1870 made the government responsible for administering elementary schools. Gladstone was forced to confront the **Irish question** during his administration.

For Additional Review

Consider how William Gladstone embodied British liberalism and Benjamin Disraeli embodied British Conservatism.

1. Which of the following were the opponents involved in the Crimean War?
    (A) Britain, France, and Russia against the Ottoman Empire and Austria
    (B) Britain, France, and the Ottoman Empire against Russia
    (C) Prussia and Russia against the Ottoman Empire and Britain
    (D) Russia and the Ottoman Empire against Prussia and Austria
    (E) Britain, France, and Spain against the Ottoman Empire and Russia

2. All of the following are true of the Land and Freedom Society EXCEPT
    (A) it adhered to the principles of Alexander Herzen.

    (B) it staged the assassination of Alexander II.
    (C) it was comprised of young Russians.
    (D) it was based on the Populism movement.
    (E) it split into two factions.

3. The Concert of Europe shattered as a result of
    (A) the events of the Crimean War.
    (B) Italian unification.
    (C) German unification.
    (D) the Danish War.
    (E) the Franco-Prussian War.

4. The Paris Commune emerged most directly in reaction to
    (A) the Prussian occupation.
    (B) the Treaty of Frankfurt.
    (C) Adolphe Thiers.
    (D) Battle of Sedan.
    (E) the French government's bombardment of Paris.

5. With which of the following movements is Giuseppe Garibaldi is associated?
    (A) Romantic nationalism
    (B) Communism
    (C) Socialism
    (D) Marxism
    (E) Conservatism

6. Which of the following was the central goal of Camillo Cavour's policies in Italy?
    (A) To achieve a unified state on the Italian peninsula
    (B) To serve as the monarch of a unified Italy
    (C) To repel the French from the Italian   peninsula
    (D) To assassinate Napoleon III
    (E) To make France a secret ally

7. The start of the Franco-Prussia War was skillfully manipulated by which statesmen?
   (A) Otto von Bismarck
   (B) Prince Leopold of Hohenzollern-Sigmaringen
   (C) Isabella II
   (D) Count Vincent Benedetti
   (E) William I

8. The major crisis of the Third Republic was
   (A) MacMahon's resignation.
   (B) the Dreyfus Affair.
   (C) Boulanger's challenges to the Third Republic.
   (D) unrest in the Chamber of Deputies.
   (E) lingering resentment from Paris Communards.

9. The Dual Monarchy refers to which of the following?
   (A) Austria-Hungary
   (B) Schleswig-Holstein
   (C) Hohenzollern-Habsburg
   (D) Rome-Venezia
   (E) Bourbon-Orléans

10. Alexander II instituted all of the following reforms in Russia EXCEPT
   (A) abolition of serfdom.
   (B) personal right to marry.
   (C) right to purchase and sell property.
   (D) free title to land.
   (E) freedom to pursue court actions.

Document-Based Question

Compare and contrast the three visions of nineteenth-century nationalism contained the documents below. How does each author conceive of the nation and national rights?

Document A Source: The Italian patriot Giuseppe Mazzini defines nationality, *From Absolutism to Revolution.*

The essential characteristics of a nationality are common ideas, common principles and a common purpose. A nation is an association of those who are brought together by language, by given geographical conditions or by the role assigned them by history, who acknowledge the same principles and who march together to the conquest of a single definite goal under the rule of a uniform body of law....

The people must be the basis of nationality; its logically derived and vigorously applied principles its means; the strength of all its strength; the improvement of the life of all and the happiness of the greatest possible number its results; and the accomplishment of the task assigned to it by God its goal. This is what we mean by a nationality.

Document B Source: The German historian Heinrich von Treitschke demands the annexation of Alsace and Lorraine.

In view of our obligation to secure the peace of the world, who will venture to object that the people of Alsace and Lorraine do not want to belong to us? The doctrine of the right of all the branches of the German race to decide on their own destinies, the plausible solution of demagogues without a fatherland, shiver to pieces in the presence of the sacred necessity of these great days. These territories are ours by the right of the sword, and we shall dispose of them in virtue of a higher right – the right of the German nation, which will not permit its lost children to remain strangers to the German Empire. We Germans, who know Germany and France, know better that these unfortunates what is good for the people of Alsace….Against their will we shall restore them to their true selves.

Document C Source: The English historian Lord Action condemns nationalism.

The greatest adversary of the rights of nationality is the modern theory of nationality. By making the State and the nation commensurate with each other in theory, it reduces practically to a subject condition all other nationalities that may be within the boundary….According, therefore, to the degree of humanity and civilization in that dominant body which claims all the rights of community, the inferior races are exterminated, or reduced to servitude, or outlawed, or put into a condition of dependence.

There is no principle of change, no phrase of political speculation conceivable, more comprehensive, more subversive, or more arbitrary than this [nationalism]. It is a confutation of democracy, because it sets limits to the exercise of the popular will, and substitutes for it a higher principle.

Free-Response Question

Identify the significance of the "Irish question" in Gladstone's ministries.

ANSWERS AND EXPLANATIONS

Multiple-Choice Questions

- **1. (B) is correct.** Much to Tsar Nicholas's chagrin, Austria and Prussia refused to come to Russia's aid in its conflict against the Ottoman Empire. England and France, however, rose to the occasion.
- **2. (B) is correct.** The splinter group of the Land and Freedom Society, The People's Will, carried out the assassination of Alexander II.
- **3. (A) is correct.** The Crimean War effectively signaled the end of the Concert of Europe. When Russia acted aggressively against the Ottoman Empire to extending its territory into Ottoman-controlled lands, and other European nations assisted in this effort, the Concert of Europe was overridden.

☐ **4. (B) is correct.** The Paris Commune emerged most directly in reaction to the Treaty of Frankfurt, which gave the Prussians numerous concessions without taking into account (according to Communards) the suffering of the French people. The Commune arose in response to frustration with Adolphe Thiers' settlement.

☐ **5. (A) is correct.** Giuseppe Garibaldi is associated with the Romantic nationalism movement, a kind of rabid nationalism that Garibaldi and Mazzini promoted through three decades of insurrection and guerilla warfare.

☐ **6. (A) is correct.** Cavour's policies in Italy were geared at achieving unity on the Italian peninsula; he believed that Italy's various regions could be brought together through economic and material progress, and that its enemies could be repelled though diplomacy and alliances.

☐ **7. (A) is correct.** Otto von Bismarck effectively engineered the start of the Franco-Prussian War by misrepresenting the content of a telegram from William I and creating controversy between Napoleon III and William I. This ingenious scheme helped launch France and Prussia into a pitched battle that led to French defeat.

☐ **8. (B) is correct.** The major crisis of the Third Republic was the Dreyfus Affair, which provoked widespread debate from all corners of France, and involved the Catholic church, conservatives, the army, and anti-Semitic newspapers. It divided France and put conservatives on the defensive.

☐ **9. (A) is correct.** The Dual Monarchy refers the formation of Austria-Hungary in the *Ausgleich,* or Compromise of 1867 between Francis Joseph and discontented Magyars.

☐ **10. (D) is correct.** While serfs gained much in the reforms that Alexander II instituted, they did not receive free title to their land. Instead, they had to pay their landlords over a period of forty-nine years for allotments of land that were often too small to support them and their families. Serfs were in debt to the government, and were responsible for paying additional taxes, which kept them oppressed for many years until 1905, when Russia canceled all remaining debts.

Document-Based Question

Compare and contrast the three visions of nineteenth-century nationalism contained the documents below. How does each author conceive of the nation and national rights?

Convincing essays might note:
☐ The role of race in each document (See Documents A, B, and C)
☐ The relative flexibility of Mazzini's definition of the nation in comparison to Treitschke's (See Documents A and B)
☐ Treitschke's assertion of a concept of nation that transcends the will of individuals and Lord Acton's response (See Document A and C)
☐ Lord Acton's prediction of a strong connection between nationalism and the suppression of minorities (See Document C)

Identify the significance of the "Irish question" in Gladstone's ministries.

The "Irish question" was significant during Gladstone's ministries because it threatened Great Britain's political balance. During Gladstone's first ministry, he addressed the situation in Ireland with two pieces of legislation. One involved disestablishing the Church of Ireland; this law allowed Irish Catholics not to pay money to the Irish extension of the despised Anglican Church of England. The other major issue that Gladstone sponsored in his first ministry involved a land act that compensated Irish tenants who had been evicted and helped secure loans for those who wanted to own their land.

The Irish question played a role in Gladstone's second ministry, when Irish members of the House of Commons threatened to upset the balance of power between English Liberals and English Conservatives. Charles Parnell, the leader of the Irish movement for home rule and the organizer of the Irish members in the House of Commons, tried to use this opportunity to force one of the parties to accommodate the desires of the Irish to gain home rule. Gladstone threw his support behind home rule for Ireland, and the Irish members of the House of Commons gave their votes to the formation of a Liberal ministry. Parnell's cunning attempt to achieve home rule was stymied when a faction joined with the Conservatives to defeat Gladstone's Home Rule Bill. In a new election, the Liberals were defeated by the Conservatives, and Ireland remained a part of England.

In Gladstone's third ministry, the issue of Irish home rule came up again, but it was defeated in the House of Lords. The Irish question remained a potent political issue throughout Gladstone's ministries—and it continued to be the subject of debate throughout the early twentieth century. The Third Irish Home Rule Bill passed in 1912, but the provisions of its implementation had to wait until after World War I.

CHAPTER 23

The Building of European Supremacy: Society and Politics to World War I

Population Trends and Migration

- **European** population, with respect to world population, was at its **all-time high in 1900**—one-fifth of the world was European at that time. After that time, birth and death rates leveled off in Europe and grew in other areas, which led in turn to the divide between the developed and the undeveloped world (which is still characterized by food and resource crises).
- More than 50 million Europeans migrated away from their continent between 1846 and 1932. This outflow of people relieved social and population pressures on the Continent and spread European culture throughout the world. Combined with Europe's economic and technological superiority, the migration contributed to the dominant role Europe continues to play in the world.

The Second Industrial Revolution

- **Continental industries** caught up to those of Britain toward the end of the nineteenth century, and the expansion of railroad systems on the Continent helped to spur economic growth and enable new industries to emerge. This phase of development, which concerned the production of steel, chemicals, electricity, and oil, is known as the Second Industrial Revolution.
- Several inventions were essential in this period: Henry Bessemer's process for manufacturing **steel,** the Solway process of **alkali production** enabled the recovery of more chemical by-products, the application of **electrical energy** to production and to homes and transportation, and the invention of the **internal combustion engine** (which eventually gave birth to the automobile) were the major developments during this period. Machines that required petroleum created a great need for oil.

The Middle Classes in Ascendancy

- The **middle class** was at its height in the 60 years prior to World War I: it defined consumer taste and was no longer associated with the radical revolutions of the 1840s, but with a desire to protect their assets. The middle-class grew more diverse as it came to encompass more people—some were magnates, others were entrepreneurs and professionals who had sufficient income for private homes and some basic domestic luxuries.

Late Nineteenth-Century Urban Life

- Europe became **more urbanized** as migration to the cities continued. From 1850 to 1911, urban dwellers grew from 25% to 44% of the population in France and from 30% to 60% of

the population in Germany. Rural migrants frequently lived in bad social conditions and experienced widespread discrimination.
- **Cities were redesigned** to accommodate the changes in urban living. While central urban areas had always been places for people of all social classes, urban planners transformed these areas into business and government centers, but not residential dwelling spaces.
- **Suburbs** became popular for both middle and working-classes, and improved transit eased this transformation. Sanitation improvements were made following concerns with health and housing after the cholera epidemics of the 1830s and 1840s. New water and sewer systems were constructed to improve conditions, which led to a reduction of the mortality rate.

Varieties of Late Nineteenth-Century Women's Experiences

- Women remained **second-class citizens** in the nineteenth century. Through marriage, many women lost their individual legal identities and suffered tremendous disadvantages that limited their freedom to work, to save, and to move from one location to another.
- During the Second Industrial Revolution, the **jobs available to women expanded** and more **married women withdrew from the workforce.** The jobs available to women were usually low-paying jobs that did not require training or skills. New cultural ideas that connected prosperity with women not working outside the home took root in the middle classes.

Jewish Emancipation

- Jews saw gains in **political equality** and **social status** in the nineteenth century, but changes came slowly. The conditions for Jews improved after the revolutions of 1848, especially in western Europe. Jews and Christians were granted roughly equal laws by Joseph II in 1782, and in France, the National Assembly recognized Jews as French citizens in 1789. Traditional prejudices against Jews continued in eastern Europe until World War I; in Russia, Jews were treated as foreigners and were restricted in all aspects of their daily lives.
- **Anti-Semitism** reared its head in the late nineteenth century, as critics attributed economic stagnation to Jewish bankers and financial institutions.

Labor, Socialism, and Politics to World War I

- After 1848, workers turned to new institutions and ideologies to seek change. **Trade unions** emerged in the latter part of the nineteenth century, and through them some workers attempted to gain an overall improvement of wages and working conditions. Most European workers were not represented by unions during this period, but unions did help those workers they represented bargain collectively for improvements to their employment.
- **Universal male suffrage** was extended in this era in many countries, so the voices of lower-class workers carried more political weight than they had previously. Socialist movements of many kinds emerged throughout Europe.
- **The organized political party** arose at this time. Karl Marx spoke at the First International (International Working Men's Association) of 1864, a group of radicals, Socialists, anarchists, and Polish nationalists organized by a group of British and French trade unionists.
- From the activities of the First International, **Marxism** emerged as a new kind of socialism, and it became popular in Germany. In Britain, **Fabianism** and **Early Welfare Programs** took root. French and German Socialists emerged at this time, in the **Socialist party** and the **German Social Democratic party,** respectively. In Russia, **Vladimir Lenin** emerged as a prominent Socialist, and the **Bolsheviks** seized power.

For Additional Review

Consider how the population increase in urban centers affected public health in this era.

Multiple-Choice Questions

1. By the late nineteenth century, Europe was
   (A) self-sufficient in oil production.
   (B) developing its oil reserves.
   (C) dependent on foreign oil.
   (D) exporting oil to other nations.
   (E) not yet using oil in significant quantities.

2. The typical nineteenth-century middle-class woman
   (A) enjoyed career opportunities on a peer with her male counterparts.
   (B) was restricted politically, but she found outlets for political action in universities.
   (C) enjoyed much domestic luxury, but she was limited to a life centered on home and family.
   (D) had little to do with the rearing of her children.
   (E) turned to prostitution and cottage industries to support her family.

3. Which of the following figures is most closely associated with the First International?
   (A) Vladimir Lenin
   (B) Karl Marx
   (C) Frederick Engels
   (D) Grigory Rasputin
   (E) Gregory Plekhanov

4. The development of the suburbs was a response to all of the following conditions EXCEPT
   (A) the reorganization of cities for business and governmental purposes.
   (B) the increasing congestion of urban areas.
   (C) an increasing number of slums that reduced urban property values.
   (D) improved railway systems connecting city to suburbs.
   (E) the clearing of slums.

5. What was notable about the proportion of Europeans in the world's population around 1900?
   (A) It was smaller than at any point before or since.
   (B) It was at the end of a long decline.
   (C) It was greater than at any point before or since.
   (D) It was nearly as great as it had been in the late eighteenth century.
   (E) It was about half as great as it is today.

6. Which of the following figures was responsible for the sweeping redesign of Paris in the nineteenth century?
    (A) Robert Métro
    (B) Gustave Eiffel
    (C) Georges Haussmann
    (D) Rudolf Virchow
    (E) Louis Pasteur

7. The nineteenth-century conditions for Jews improved in all of the following European countries EXCEPT
    (A) Italy.
    (B) England.
    (C) France.
    (D) Russia.
    (E) Austria.

8. The Bolshevik faction was led by
    (A) Lenin.
    (B) Marx.
    (C) Kautsky.
    (D) Bernstein.
    (E) Liebknecht.

9. The figure most responsible for Russia's industrialization was
    (A) Gregory Plekhanov.
    (B) P.A. Stolypin.
    (C) Sergei Witte.
    (D) Grigory Rasputin.
    (E) Vladimir Lenin.

10. Between 1846 and 1932, how many Europeans left their homelands?
    (A) 2,000,000
    (B) 10,000,000
    (C) 20,000,000
    (D) 35,000,000
    (E) 50,000,000

What do images below tell us about the relationship between economic change in the late nineteenth century and changes in the experiences of middle-class women? What role did women play in the exploding consumer society of late-nineteenth-century Europe?

Document A Source: Sir George Clausen's "Schoolgirls, Haverstock Hill."

Women only gradually gained access to secondary and university education during the second half of the nine-teenth century and the early twentieth century. Young women on their way to school, the subject of this 1880 English painting, would thus have been a new sight when it was painted.   Sir George Clausen (RA) (1852–1944), *Schoolgirls, Haverstock Hill*, signed and dated 1880, oil on canvas, 20 1/2 × 30 3/8 in. (52 × 77.2 cm), Yale Center for British Art/Paul Mel-lon Collection, USA/Bridgeman Art Library (B1985.10.1). Courtesy of the Estate of Sir George Clausen

Document B Source: Poster depicting women bicyclists.

The bicycle helped liberate women's lives, but as this
poster suggests, it also was associated with glamour and
fashion.   © Archivo Iconografico, S.A./CORBIS

Document C Source: Women working in the London Central Telephone Exchange.

Women working in the London Central Telephone Exchange. The invention of the telephone opened new employment
opportunities for women.   Image Works/Mary Evans Picture Library Ltd.

Department stores, such as Bon Marché in Paris, sold wide selections of consumer goods under one roof. These modern
stores increased the economic pressure on small traditional merchants who specialized in selling only one kind of good. (See
"Paris Department Stores Expand their Business," page 000.)
Image Works/Mary Evans Picture Library Ltd.

Free-Response Question

*Describe the typical lifestyles and pursuits of married middle-class women in Europe during the
Second Industrial Revolution.*

ANSWERS AND EXPLANATIONS

Multiple-Choice Questions

☐ **1. (C) is correct.** By the late nineteenth century, Europe was exceedingly dependent on
foreign oil. The automobile and industrial and chemical uses for petroleum created
significant demand for oil. Imported supplies were needed, and major oil companies like
Standard Oil, British Shell Oil, and Royal Dutch Petroleum satisfied this demand.

☐ **2. (C) is correct.** The typical nineteenth-century middle-class woman was restricted to the domestic sphere and had few opportunities to advance her career. Her responsibilities were not exclusively with her family; she was expected to be devout and to dedicate herself to charity, but her primary focus was on enriching her home.

☐ **3. (B) is correct.** Karl Marx gave the inaugural address for the First International in 1864, and is the figure associated with its efforts to reform conditions of labor within existing political and economic processes.

☐ **4. (C) is correct.** The development of the suburbs was not really a response to the increased number of slums. If anything, urban redevelopment was taking slums away from urban centers and displacing the lower-income residents who lived there.

☐ **5. (C) is correct.**

☐ **6. (C) is correct.** Georges Haussmann radically redesigned Paris, removing the small streets and replacing them with impressive boulevards and realigning the city with a grandeur that was controversial at the time.

☐ **7. (D) is correct.** Russia was a notoriously bad place for Jews in the nineteenth-century. western Europe, in general, was more friendly to Jews than eastern Europe and Russia, which strictly enforced policies of exclusion and discrimination against Jews.

☐ **8. (A) is correct.** The Bolshevik faction was led by Vladimir Lenin.

☐ **9. (C) is correct.** The figure most responsible for Russia's industrialization was Sergei Witte.

☐ **10. (E) is correct.**

Document-Based Question

What do images below tell us about the relationship between economic change in the late nineteenth century and changes in the experiences of middle-class women? What role did women play in the exploding consumer society of late-nineteenth-century Europe?

Convincing essays might note:
- The emergence of new public spaces frequented by women (See Documents A, B, C and D)
- The significance of advertising aimed directly at women (See Documents B and D)
- The connection between a changing industrial economy, women's education, and new work opportunities for women (See Document A, B, C, D)
- The increased independence offered by education and new work opportunities (See Documents A, B, and C)

Free-Response Question

Describe the typical lifestyles and pursuits of married middle-class women in Europe during the Second Industrial Revolution.

The husbands of middle-class women benefited from the improved salaries and the job opportunities of the Second Industrial Revolution, but these workplace prospects did not carry over to women. Most middle-class women adhered to the prevailing social view of the time: their place was in the home. Women's social status enabled them to participate instead in the consumerism and domestic comfort that characterized the end of the nineteenth century and the beginning of the twentieth century. Many married middle-class women devoted their attentions to the decorating, furnishing, and maintaining their homes. Some of the wealthier middle-class women could depend on a staff of servants to handle much of the food preparation and child care.

A veritable cult of domesticity arose during this era. It was a considered a mark of financial prosperity among middle-class families for women to stay at home while men worked. The roles of wife and mother became increasingly important during this time, as women were effectively limited to the domestic sphere. Many of these women set out to transform their homes into places of refuge. The home came to be seen as the center of the family and the focus of everyday life.

In the prevailing view of the era, it was expected that marriage was shortly followed by the birth of children. Of course, the rearing of children tended to fall to the woman of the house. A small family size was fairly typical for middle-class women of this era, as new contraceptive devices became available. Some middle-class women recognized that keeping family size small might help them to maintain a higher quality of life (partly through a higher level of material consumption). The small family size also enabled mothers and their children to bond more closely.

Middle-class women oversaw all domestic management and child care. In some cases, women were expected to contribute their time and efforts to charitable activities and to devote themselves to religious observance, as well.

CHAPTER 24

The Birth of Modern European Thought

The New Reading Public
- By 1900, 85% of people could read in Britain, France, Belgium, the Netherlands, Germany, and Scandinavia, thanks largely to improvements in primary education. **Improvements in literacy** led to greater secondary education opportunities in countries.
- The amount of **printed** matter available to the public increased dramatically during this time; some of the materials catered to the marginally literate or the lowest levels of public taste.
- Literacy enabled Europeans to **gain knowledge** and **improve their social situations.**

Science at Mid-century
- The **positivist philosophy** of **Auguste Comte (1798–1857)** influenced the field of science.
- **Charles Darwin's** 1859 book, ***The Origin of Species,*** formulated the principle of natural selection, which explained how species evolved over time. In his 1871 work, ***The Descent of Man,*** Darwin explored the principle of natural selection in the context of human beings, helping establish a new theory of evolutionary ethics, called *social Darwinism.*

Christianity and the Church under Siege
- Historical scholarship in the nineteenth century **attacked Christianity** on many grounds. **David Friedrich Strauss** in *The Life of Jesus* questioned the historical evidence of Jesus' existence. **Julius Wellhausen, Ernst Renan,** and **William Robertson** argued that human authors had written and edited the books of the Bible.
- The progress of science undermined the Christian underpinning of the **doctrine of Creation** by determining the actual age of the earth. Other scientists proposed that religious thought was just like any other phenomena, not spiritually inspired or revealed Truth.
- **Friedrich Nietzsche** also attacked Christianity, accusing it of promoting weakness and not glorifying strength.
- There was more conflict between church and state throughout Europe at this time. In England, there was increased hostility between Anglican Church and other Protestant denominations; in France, where the Catholic Church was frequently at odds with the Third Republic, the **Ferry Laws** (sponsored by Jules Ferry) **replaced religious instruction in the public schools with civil training.** In Germany, Bismarck removed Catholic and Protestant clergy from overseeing local education in Prussia. He instituted the **May Laws of 1873,** which demanded that priests be educated in German schools and universities and gave control of the appointment of priests to the state. This *Kulturkampf,* or "cultural struggle," failed, and Bismarck retreated from his policies.

Toward a Twentieth-Century Frame of Mind

- The scientists **Ernst Mach, Henri Poincaré** and **Hans Vaihinger** urged that scientists consider their theories hypothetical constructs of the physical world. Scientists like **Wilhelm Roentgen, Henri Becquerel, J.J. Thompson, Marie Curie,** and **Ernest Rutherford** established the important properties and uses of radioactive materials. **Albert Einstein** researched **relativity,** and **Werner Heisenberg** published his **uncertainty principle.**
- In literature, **realism and naturalism became dominant themes.** Flaubert used realism to portray life without adornment in his *Madame Bovary* and Zola set forth realism as a movement. Henrik Ibsen and George Bernard Shaw brought realism into the depiction of domestic life and romantic ideals.
- From the 1870s onward, a new movement of **modernism** was captured in works by artists trying to break away from traditional forms. Igor Stravinsky did this in his *Rite of Spring,* Pablo Picasso accomplished this in his cubist forms, and members of the Bloomsbury Group accomplished this in literature. Virginia Woolf challenged the structure of traditional literature and the assumptions of Victorian culture.
- **Marcel Proust, James Joyce, Thomas Mann,** and **T.S. Eliot** were just a few of the important literary modernists of this era.
- **Sigmund Freud (1856–1939)** introduced psychoanalysis to the modern period. He became interested in the idea that dreams expressed the repressed desires of everyday life, and he developed a theory of infantile sexuality. Freud's former student, **Carl Jung,** advanced his own ideas of collective memories constituting human souls and relied on Romanticism in his work.
- The influential **German sociologist Max Weber** advanced his belief in non-economic factors that might account for major developments in history and his faith in the role of the individual in society. Weber differed from many of his peers, who considered collective behavior more of a factor in society. These scientists included **Émile Durkheim, Georges Sorel, Gustave LeBon, Vilfredo Pareto,** and **Graham Wallas.**
- **Racial thinking** in this century supported the ideas of superior and inferior races (in Europe and beyond) and led to racist ideology. An outgrowth of this ideology was **anti-Semitism.**

Women and Modern Thought

- The **biological role of women** as mothers became more entrenched in social views of women during this century. Misogyny was not uncommon in the fiction and art of this period.
- Women were **excluded from the scientific community,** as their alleged "inferiority" made them ineligible for participation. Freud's views helped perpetuate these ideas, and he was later debunked by distinguished psychoanalysts like Melanie Klein and Karen Horney.
- **Feminists** of this era supported wider **sexual freedom for women,** and advocated **contraception.** Some women became active in Socialist groups; others sought to carve out careers for themselves in professions that had previously been unavailable to them.

For Additional Review

Consider how some of the developments in nineteenth-century science challenged Church doctrine.

1. The philosophy that human intellectual development culminates in science is called
    (A) rationalism.
    (B) empiricism.
    (C) positivism.
    (D) collectivism.
    (E) realism.

2. Which of the following figures is regarded as the father of sociology?
    (A) Sigmund Freud
    (B) Carl Jung
    (C) Auguste Comte
    (D) Charles Darwin
    (E) Thomas Henry Huxley

3. During the nineteenth century, the Church
    (A) faced renewed intellectual skepticism.
    (B) was revered as a source of morality in a changing world.
    (C) was largely abandoned by believers.
    (D) was characterized by the deterioration of the papacy.
    (E) had few conflicts with governments in Europe.

4. *Kulturkampf* was a policy promoted by
    (A) Auguste Comte.
    (B) Otto von Bismarck.
    (C) Jules Ferry.
    (D) Friedrich Nietzsche.
    (E) Carl Jung.

5. All of the following were advocates of the collective theory of behavior EXCEPT
    (A) Émile Durkheim.
    (B) Georges Sorel.
    (C) Max Weber.
    (D) Graham Wallas.
    (E) Vilfredo Pareto.

6. The Contagious Diseases Acts enforced from 1864 to 1886 required
    (A) men and women with venereal disease to undergo treatment.
    (B) women with venereal disease to do time in jail.
    (C) men with venereal disease to do time in jail.
    (D) women with venereal disease to undergo treatment.
    (E) men with venereal disease to undergo treatment.

7. Which of the following was most directly responsible for the rise in literacy in nineteenth-century Europe?
   (A) women instructors at primary schools
   (B) the growth of the suburbs
   (C) the growing prestige of the schoolteaching profession
   (D) the increased availability of state financed primary education
   (E) vastly improved textbook translations

8. The Ferry Laws passed in France between 1878 and 1886
   (A) allowed for religious instruction in public schools.
   (B) allowed members of religious orders to teach in public schools.
   (C) replaced public schools with private, parochial schools that promoted religious studies.
   (D) replaced religious instruction in public schools with civic training.
   (E) demanded that religious instructors pledge their allegiance to the state.

9. What French novelist was influential in securing Captain Dreyfus' eventual exoneration?
   (A) Gustave Flaubert.
   (B) Balthasar Simon.
   (C) George Bernard Shaw.
   (D) Émile Zola.
   (E) Honoré de Balzac.

10. Nineteenth-century racial thought was characterized by
   (A) an appreciation of the contributions made by different races to the world's civilizations.
   (B) a hierarchy of "superior" and "inferior" races.
   (C) belief in the equality of all races, based on their biological similarities.
   (D) an attention to ethnic rather than racial differences.
   (E) a lack of prejudice in racial classifications.

How did the theory of evolution influence racial thinking in the late nineteenth century?

Document A Source: Caricature of Darwin.

Document B Source: The British scientist T.H. Huxley criticizes evolutionary ethics, *Evolution and Ethic*.

As I have urged, the practice of that which is ethically best – what we call goodness or virtue – involves a course of conduct which, in all respects, is opposed to that which leads to success in the cosmic struggle for existence....

It is from neglect of these plain considerations that the fanatical individualism of our time attempts to apply the analogy of cosmic nature to society....

Let us understand, once for all, that the ethical progress of society depends, not on imitating the cosmic process, still less in running away from it, but in combating it.

Document C Source: Alexis de Tocqueville forecasts the danger of French diplomat and race theorist Count Arthur de Gatineau's racial thought, *Evolution and Ethics*.

Your doctrine is rather a sort of fatalism, of predestination, if you wish,....Whether the element of fatality should be introduced into the material order of things, or whether God willed to make different kinds of men so that He imposed special burdens of race on some, withholding from them a capacity for certain feelings, for certain thoughts, for certain habits, for certain qualities – all this has nothing to do with my own concern with the practical consequences of these philosophical doctrines. The consequence of both theories is that of a vast limitation, if not a complete abolition, of human liberty.

Document D Source: H. S. Chamberlain exalts the role of race, *Evolution and Ethics*.

Race lifts a man above himself; it endows him with extraordinary – I might say almost supernatural – powers, so entirely does it distinguish him from the chaotic jumble of peoples drawn from all parts of the world: and should this man of pure origin be perchance gifted above his fellows, then the fact of Race strengthens and elevates him on every hand, and he becomes a genius towering over the rest of mankind, not because he has been thrown upon the earth like a flaming meteor by a freak of nature, but because eh soars heavenward like some strong and stately tree – nourished by thousands of roots – no solitary individual, but the living sum of untold souls striving for the same goal.

Free-Response Question

What was Modernism, and who were some of its major pioneers?

ANSWERS AND EXPLANATIONS

Multiple-Choice Questions

- **1. (C) is correct.** Auguste Comte believed that science had entered the stage of human thought that he defined as positivism.
- **2. (C) is correct.** Auguste Comte is regarded as the father of sociology, because he argued that the positive laws of social behavior could be discovered in the same manner as laws of physical nature in the field of science.
- **3. (A) is correct**. During the nineteenth century, the Church faced numerous challenges to its authority from intellectuals who were skeptical of the historical authenticity of the Bible. Some argued that the authors of the Bible were not writing from divine inspiration, but with political agendas and other authorial motives. These issues, plus growing scientific information about the origin of the world, challenged the traditional teachings of the Church.
- **4. (B) is correct**. *Kulturkampf* was a policy promoted by Otto von Bismarck in an attempt to secularize education in Germany.
- **5. (C) is correct.** Max Weber differed from his peers in advocating theories that stressed the role of the individual in society.

☐ **6. (D) is correct.** The Contagious Diseases Acts (enforced from 1864 to 1886) demanded that women suspected of prostitution undergo medical examinations and mandatory treatment if they were found to be infected. Men were not subjected to these laws.

☐ **7. (D) is correct.** The development of state-sponsored primary schools continued during this era, spreading to other Continental countries and raising the level of literacy dramatically during this time.

☐ **8. (D) is correct.** The Ferry Laws passed in France between 1878 and 1886 replaced religious instruction in public schools with civic training. The Ferry Laws did not allow members of religious orders to teach in public schools.

☐ **9. (D) is correct.** The author responsible for Captain Dreyfus' eventual exoneration is Émile Zola, who published twenty novels that explored subjects not ordinarily treated in literature, including alcoholism, prostitution, and the problems of organizing labor.

☐ **10. (B) is correct.** Nineteenth-century racial thought was notoriously racist, as theories developed that codified a hierarchy of superior and inferior races that, inevitably, worked in the favor of the racial theorist.

Document-Based Question

How did the theory of evolution influence racial thinking in the late nineteenth century?

Convincing essays might note:
- The efforts of Huxley and de Tocqueville to separate ethics and human values from race and natural selection (See Documents A, B and C)
- Chamberlain's connection between individual accomplishment and race (See Document D)
- The potential in Chamberlain's argument for racial dictatorship (See Document B, C, and D)
- The assumption by Darwin's critics that his theory implied that all human qualities were the result of natural selection (See Document A)

Free-Response Question

What was Modernism, and who were some of its major pioneers?

Modernism was an artistic movement that germinated in the late nineteenth century and continued to develop until after the end of World War I. Modernism was taking root in all kinds of arts at this time, including literature, music, visual art, and dance. In all of these genres, it manifested itself as a concern for the aesthetic, and it was critical of middle-class society and accepted morality.

Modernists were interested in breaking traditional forms and in conveying their art in new, surprising, "modern" ways. Some of these artists shocked their contemporaries with the boldness of their "formless" works. Igor Stravinsky's *Rite of Spring* astonished listeners, who detected in it a fusion of jazz and classical music. Visual artists like Pablo Picasso and Georges Braque used cubism—a new form of assembling shapes and images using different perspectives—to startle their viewers. In literature, the spirit of modernism animated works like *To the Lighthouse* by Virginia Woolf and *Ulysses* by James Joyce, both of whom used stream-of-consciousness narrative techniques to simulate the realism of everyday life. Another feature of Modernism was its frank treatment of sexuality and its rejection of what was perceived as the antiquated and repressive sexual morality of previous generations. For instance, as James Joyce incorporated novel techniques of representation and narration in his novel *Ulysses,* he also included content that was considered sexually provocative.

Modernism is best understood in the context of the period before, during, and after World War I. As the Modernist movement developed, it offered new forms as well as new subject matter. As the Great War unfolded in Europe, people around the world were shocked and horrified at the violence wrought by new weaponry and techniques. Modernist art, with its fragmentary narratives and sense of dislocation, suddenly had become less outlandish. Now it seemed to *reflect* the real new world. In the years after the war, people were no longer shocked by the "new."

CHAPTER 25

The Age of Western Imperialism

The Close of the Age of Early Modern Colonization

■ The era of early modern European expansion that lasted from the late fifteenth to the late eighteenth centuries had witnessed the encounter, conquest, settlement, and exploitation of the American continents by the Spanish, Portuguese, French and English, the establishment of modest trading posts by European countries in Africa and Asia, Dutch dominance in the East Indies (modern Indonesia), and British domination of India. During these three centuries, the European powers had largely conducted their colonial rivalries within the context of the mercantilist economic assumptions we discussed in Chapter 16. Each empire was, at least in theory and largely in fact, closed to the commerce of other nations. Furthermore, in the Americas, from New England to the Caribbean and then throughout Latin America, slavery was a major fact of economic life with most slaves imported from Africa.

The Age of British Imperial Dominance

■ During the first half of the nineteenth century, no one doubted that Great Britain was the single power that could exert its influence virtually around the world. During this half century, Britain fostered the settlements that became the nations of Canada, Australia, and New Zealand and expanded its control of India. The early nineteenth-century British Empire also included smaller colonies and islands in the Caribbean and the Pacific and Indian Oceans. However, until the 1860s and 1870s, except in India and western Canada, Britain did not seek additional territory. Rather, it extended its influence through what historians call the **Imperialism of Free Trade**.

India—The Jewel in the Crown of the British Empire

■ Until its independence in 1947, India was the most important part of the British Empire and provided the base for British military and economic power throughout Asia. The protection of the commercial and military routes to India would be the chief concern of British imperial strategy during the nineteenth century. Other nations, particularly Russia, believed they could threaten Britain by bringing military pressure to bear on India. As we shall see later in the chapter, Britain largely became involved in Africa in the late nineteenth century to protect India.

The "New Imperialism," 1870-1914

■ In the last third of the nineteenth century, European states expanded their control over one-fifth of the world's land and one-tenth of its population. This expansion was driven by developments in science, agriculture, technology, communication, transportation, and military weapons. This movement, known as **New Imperialism,** had numerous motives.

Motives for the New Imperialism

- The many interpretations of motives for New Imperialism include an **economic theory** advanced by **J. A. Hobson** and **Lenin** that viewed imperialism as a monopolistic form of capitalism. Others argue that these undeveloped nations had **raw materials** and **provided markets,** and still others claim that imperialism was an effort to cure the **depression of 1873–1896.** None of these theories has been proven. Some view the imperialism as an effort to **extend European culture** and **Christianity** to less-industrialized regions. Some advocates of imperialism viewed these regions as inferior and "backward," and they resolved to bring them culture in the form of religion and domestic reform. Some believed that the colonies would **attract Europe's surplus population,** but in fact European emigrants preferred areas not controlled by their home countries, including North and South America.

The Partition of Africa

- For almost fifty years inter-European rivalries played out in regions far away from Europe itself and nowhere more intensely than in Africa. During the so-called "Scramble for Africa," which occurred between the late 1870s and about 1912, the European powers sought to maximize their strategic control of African territory, markets, and raw materials. Motivated by intense com- petition, the imperial powers eventually divided almost all the continent among themselves (see Map 25–2). The short- and long-term consequences were complex and in most cases devastating for the Africans. Among the long-term effects was that European control forcibly integrated largely agrarian African societies into the modern world industrial economy. In the process, new forms of agrarian production, market economies, social organizations, political structures, and religious allegiances emerged that would form the basis for the post-colonial African nations (see Map 25–3).
- The European partition of Africa was not based on a universal policy, and each power acquired and administered its new possessions in different ways. Their goals, however, were the same: to gain control, or at least dominance, through diplomacy or force and then either to place Europeans directly in charge of administering the territories or to compel local rulers to accept European "advisers" who would exercise real authority.

Russian Expansion in Mainland Asia

- The British presence in India was intimately related to Russian expansion across mainland Asia in the nineteenth century, which eventually brought huge territories and millions of people of a variety of ethnicities and religions under tsarist rule. This expansion of Russian imperialism is one of the chief sources of the ethnic tensions that exist today in the Russian Federation and in particular between that Federation and Chechnya and other parts of the Caucasus.

Western Powers in Asia

- While merchants had established the British interest in India and South Asia, French interest in Indochina arose because of the activity of Roman Catholic missionaries. The French domain in Indochina eventually consisted of Vietnam, Cambodia, and Laos.
- In 1853, a United States naval squadron under Commodore Matthew C. Perry (1794–1858) arrived in Japanese waters to open Japanese markets to American goods. In 1867, American interest in the Pacific again manifested itself when the United States bought Alaska from Russia. For the next twenty-five years, the United States assumed a fairly passive role in foreign affairs, but it had established its presence in the Pacific.

- From late 1899 through the autumn of 1901, a Chinese group called The Righteous and Harmonious Society of Fists, better known in the West as the Boxers, attempted to resist the Western incursions. The Boxers, who were supported by a faction at the Qing court, hated missionaries whom they saw as agents of the imperial powers and killed thousands of their Chinese converts.

Tools of Imperialism

- The domination that Europe and peoples of European descent came to exert over the entire globe by 1900 is extraordinary. It had not existed a century earlier and would not exist a century later. At the time many Europeans as well as Americans who worked their way across the North American continent in what many regarded as manifest destiny saw this domination as evidence of cultural or racial superiority. In fact, however, Western domination was based on distinct and temporary technological advantages, what one historian called the "tools of empire." These tools gave Westerners the capacity to conquer and dominate vast areas of the world. Steamboats, the conquest of tropical diseases, and the technological advantage of Western firearms, can all be considered "tools of imperialism."

The Missionary Factor

- The modern Western missionary movement, which continues to the present day, originated in Great Britain in the late eighteenth century as a direct outgrowth of the rise of evangelical Christianity. Evangelicalism, which influenced Protestant communities from Central Europe to the United States, emphasized the authority of the Bible, the importance of a personal conversion experience, and the duty to spread the Gospel. Many Evangelicals were also concerned to pre- pare the world for the Second Coming of Jesus by carrying the message of Christian redemption to peoples who had not heard it. British Evangelicals first looked to unchurched groups in their own nation as the primary field for bearing Christian witness, but by the close of the eighteenth century, in a largely new departure for Protestants, small groups of Evangelicals began to be active in the non-Western world. Roman Catholics later copied these early Protestant missionary efforts. The result of this widespread nineteenth-century missionary campaign was the establishment of large Christian communities in Africa and Asia, which today thrive and continue to expand.

Science and Imperialism

- The early modern European encounter with the non-Western world from the fifteenth-century voyages of discovery onward had been associated with the expansion of natural knowledge. The same would be true of Western imperialism in the nineteenth and early twentieth centuries. Commencing in 1768, Captain James Cook (1728–1779) had undertaken his famous voyages to the South Pacific under the patronage of the Royal Society of London to observe the transit of the planet Venus. Sir Joseph Banks (1744–1820), later president of the Royal Society, went with him to collect specimens of plants and animals unknown in Europe. Other British, French, and Spanish naval expeditions also carried scientists with their crews. Scientific societies often cooperated with military forces to carry out their research. For example, dozens of French scholars accompanied Napoleon's invasion of Egypt in 1798.

For Additional Review

Consider how Westerners justified imperialism.

Multiple-Choice Questions

1. Who was the person who provided the catalyst for the "scramble for Africa?"
   (A) Otto von Bismarck, chancellor of Germany.
   (B) Camillo di Cavour, premier of Italy
   (C) King Leopold II of Belgium
   (D) Queen Victoria of Great Britain
   (E) Kaiser Wilhelm II, king of Germany.

2. What was the geopolitical importance of Egypt to the British?
   (A) It was an important for protection of British interests in Latin America.
   (B) It provided a critical source of cotton fabric for sale in Asia.
   (C) It permitted the British to protect access to lucrative markets in India.
   (D) It provided a coaling station for access to the Pacific.
   (E) It gave Britain access to the Mediterranean.

3. A major commodity in Britain's exports to China was
   (A) tools
   (B) silk
   (C) tobacco.
   (D) opium
   (E) sugar

4. What country's entry into the colonial race in southern Africa threatened Britain's dominance over the Boer republics?
   (A) The Netherlands
   (B) Portugal
   (C) France
   (D) Germany
   (E) Italy

5. All of the following are explanations for the New Imperialism EXCEPT
   (A) undeveloped countries would yield higher profits, new markets and safe sources of raw materials.
   (B) 'backward' nations required the benefits of western civilization.
   (C) natives in undeveloped countries deserved to learn about Christianity.
   (D) it was politically advantageous for European powers to control colonies in undeveloped parts of the world.
   (E) African leaders had lost their authority due to a series intracontinental wars and needed help recreating their nation-states.

6. One of the most perceptive critics of imperialism was
   (A) J. A. Hobson
   (B) Charles Darwin.
   (C) Lionel Jensen
   (D) Benito Mussolini
   (E) Albert Einstein

7. The most important of England's colonies during the era of New Imperialism was
   (A) Canada.
   (B) India.
   (C) Australia.
   (D) Ireland.
   (E) Cape Colony.

8. Until 1890, who was the arbiter of European diplomacy?
   (A) Disraeli.
   (B) Bismarck.
   (C) Cavour
   (D) Gladstone
   (E) Rhodes

9. Which of the following regions was NOT part of the United States imperial network?
   (A) Panama
   (B) Africa
   (C) The Caribbean Islands
   (D) Samoa
   (E) Hawaii

10. The Boxer Rebellion was fought to:
   (A) Expel foreign missions and businesses from China
   (B) Topple the empress of China
   (C) Capture Beijing
   (D) Overturn the Open Door policy
   (E) Rid China of a Japanese presence

Document-Based Question

Discuss and analyze the factors that led to the European Imperialism of the nineteenth century.

Historical Background: During the second half of the nineteenth century, and especially after 1870, Europe exercised unprecedented influence and control over the rest of the world. North and South America, as well as Australia and New Zealand, almost became part of the European world as great streams of European immigrants populated them. Until the nineteenth century, Asia (with the significant exception of India) and most of Africa had gone their own ways, having little contact with Europe. But in the latter part of that century, almost all of Africa was divided among a number of European nations. Europe also imposed its economic and political power across Asia.

DOCUMENT 1 Source: Denis Diderot, Eighteenth-century French philosopher, Supplement au
voyage de Bougainville, 1772.

This country belongs to you. Why? Because you have set foot on it? If a Tahitian landed one day on your coast and he engraved on one of your rocks or on the bark of a tree: "This country belongs to the inhabitants of Tahiti," what would you think?

DOCUMENT 2 Source: John Ruskin, British critic, inaugural lecture, Oxford University, 1870.

There is a destiny now possible to us, the highest ever set before a nation to be accepted or refused. Will you youths of England make your country again a royal throne of kings, a sceptred isle, for all the world a source of light, a centre of peace; mistress of learning and of the Arts, faithful guardian of time-honoured principles? This is what England must do or perish: she must found colonies as fast and as far as she is able, formed of her most energetic and worthiest men; seizing every piece of fruitful waste ground she can set her feet on, and there teaching these her colonists that their chief virtue is to be fidelity to their country, and their first aim is to advance the power of England by land and sea.

DOCUMENT 3 Source: Lord Cromer, British government agent, "The Government of the Subject Races," 1882.

We need not always enquire too closely what these people, who are all, nationally speaking, more or less in *statu pupillari,* [student status] themselves think is in their own interests … it is essential that each special issue should be decided mainly with reference to what, by the light of western knowledge and experience … we conscientiously think is best for the subject race.

DOCUMENT 4 Source: Clement Hill, British Foreign Office official, Foreign Office memorandum, December 9, 1884.

The geographical position of the East coast lays it more within the general area of our foreign policy than that of the West Coast. … Our alternative route by the Cape to India may at any time make it important that we should have possession of or at least free access to good harbors. The importance is not less since the French move to Madagascar. Is it not worth considering whether in view of the European race for territories on the West Coast.… we might not confine ourselves to securing the utmost possible freedom of trade on that coast, yielding to other Powers the territorial responsibilities … and seeking compensation on the East Coast where … we are at present, but who can say for how long, without a European rival; where the political future of the country is of real importance to Indian and Imperial interests; where the climate is superior; where commerce is capable of vast extension, and where our influence could be exercised … in the extension of civilization, and the consequent extinction of the Slave Trade for which we have so long labored.

DOCUMENT 5 Source: Decree following the proclamation of a Portuguese protectorate over Dahomey, signed by Pinheiro Chagas, foreign minister, 1886.

The monarch of Dahomey, the terror of all Europeans, shows himself affable and condescending to the Portuguese alone. It was he who asked urgently that our protectorate should be established upon the coast of his kingdom. … It is he who appears disposed to accept at our hands the benefits of European civilization, and to this design he has already borne honorable witness by abolishing human sacrifices.

The Portuguese protectorate in Dahomey is the lighted pathway that links this kingdom of darkness with Europe.

DOCUMENT 6 Source: American cartoon, 1888.

DOCUMENT 7 Source: G. W. Steevens, British journalist, *Daily Mail*, June 23, 1897

Up they came, more and more, new types, new realms at every couple of yards, an anthropological museum—a living gazetteer of the British Empire. With them came their English officers, whom they obey and follow like children. And you begin to understand, as never before, what the Empire amounts to. Not only that we possess all these remote outlandish places … but also that all these people are working, not simply under us, but with us—that we send out a boy here and a boy there, and a boy takes hold of the savages of the part he comes to, and teaches them to march and shoot as he tells them, to obey him and believe in him and die for him and the Queen. … A plain, stupid, uninspired people, they call us, and yet we are doing this with every kind of savage man there is. And each one of us—you and I, and that man in his shirt-sleeves at the corner—is a working part of this world-shaping force. How small you must feel in face of this stupendous whole, and yet how great to be a unit in it.

DOCUMENT 8 Source: Rudyard Kipling, English writer, *The White Man's Burden*, poem (1899).

Take up the White Man's Burden—
Send forth the best ye breed—
Go bind your sons to exile
To serve your captives' need;
To wait in heavy harness
On fluttered folk and wild—
Your new-caught, sullen peoples,
Half devil and half child.

DOCUMENT 9 Source: Carl Peters, German author, *Die Gründung von Deutsch-Ostafrika* (*The Foundation of German East Africa*), 1906.

Manifesto of the Society for German Colonization, April 1884
In the partition of the earth, as it has proceeded from the beginning of the fifteenth century up to our times, the German nation received nothing. All the remaining European culture-bearing peoples possess areas outside our continent where their languages and customs can take firm root and flourish. The moment that the German emigrant leaves the borders of the Reich behind him, he is a stranger sojourning on foreign soil. The German Reich, great in size and strength through its bloodily achieved unity, stands in the leading position among the continental European powers: her sons abroad must adapt themselves to nations which look upon us with either indifference or even hostility. For centuries the great stream of German emigration has been plunging down into foreign races where it is lost sight of. Germandom outside Europe has been undergoing a perpetual national decline.…

The Society for German Colonization aims to undertake on its own, in a resolute and sweeping manner, carefully chosen colonization projects and thereby supplement the ranks of organizations with similar tendencies.

Its particular tasks will be:

1. to provide necessary sums of capital for colonization;
2. to seek out and lay claim to suitable districts for colonization;
3. to direct German emigrants to these regions

DOCUMENT 10 Source: Karl Pearson, English author, *National Life from the Standpoint of Science*, 1907.

History shows me one way, and one way only, in which a state of civilization has been produced, namely, the struggle of race with race, and the survival of the physically and mentally fitter race.

This dependence of progress on the survival of the fitter race, terribly black as it may seem to some of you, gives the struggle for existence its redeeming features; it is the fiery crucible out of which comes the finer metal. You may hope for a time when the sword shall be turned into the ploughshare, when American and German and English traders shall no longer compete in the markets of the world for raw materials, for their food supply, when the white man and the dark shall share the soil between them, and each till it as he lists . … The path of progress is strewn with the wreck of nations; traces are everywhere to be seen of the hecatombs of inferior races, and of victims who found not the narrow way to the greater perfection. Yet these dead peoples are, in very truth, the stepping stones on which mankind has arisen to the higher intellectual and deeper emotional life of today.

Free-Response Question

What were the "tools of imperialism?"

ANSWERS AND EXPLANATIONS

Multiple-Choice Questions

☐ **1. (C) is correct.** In the 1880s, the lands drained by the vast Congo River and its tributaries became the personal property of King Leopold II of Belgium (r. 1865–1909). As a young monarch, he had become determined that Belgium, despite its small territory, must acquire colonies. No doubt he was inspired by the great commercial wealth that the neighboring Netherlands had accumulated from its long history of trade and empire in the East Indies.

☐ **2. (C) is correct.** It prevented the Egyptians from establishing a textile industry that would compete with Britain's own mills.

☐ **3. (D) is correct.**

☐ **4. (D) is correct.**

- 5. **(E) is correct.** The question of African sovereignty was not a persuasive explanation for New Imperialism, the aims of which included acquisition of African colonies for annexation into the home country in Europe. All of the other options were explanations for the New Imperialism.

- 6. **(A) is correct.** Until the mid-twentieth century, the predominant interpretation of the motives for the New Imperialism was economic. This view originated in a book entitled Imperialism: A Study published in 1902 by the English economist and journalist J. A. Hobson (1858–1940). Hob- son had opposed Britain's conquest of the Dutch-speaking, white-ruled Afrikaner republics in South Africa during the Boer War (1899–1902), which he blamed on the influence of capitalists and bankers. He saw the same influences behind the imperialist ambitions of other European states. According to Hobson, capitalist economies overproduced, which caused manufacturers, bankers, and financiers, to press governments into imperial ventures to provide new markets for their excess goods and capital.

- 7. **(B) is correct.** The most important of England's colonies during the era of New Imperialism was India. With a population of some 300,000,000, it contained perhaps 80% of the Empire's subjects and provided much of its imperial profit.

- 8. **(B) is correct.**

- 9. **(B) is correct.**

- 10. **(A) is correct.** The Boxers attempted to resist Western incursions in China.

Document-Based Question

Discuss and analyze the factors that led to the European Imperialism of the nineteenth century.

The expansion of European influence in the nineteenth century was by no means a new development. Spain, France, Portugal, Holland, and Britain had all controlled territories overseas for centuries. But over time, Britain remained the only European power with significant overseas holdings, and by mid-century, many European countries were opposed to colonization because it entailed costly military and political entanglements far from home. These attitudes changed abruptly in the last third of the century, however, and European states rapidly spread their control over as many as 10 million square miles and 150 million people—roughly one-fifth of the world's population. Social, economic, and political factors were responsible for this movement of frantic colonization that is known as the "New Imperialism."

By the mid-nineteenth century, the fruits of the Industrial Revolution were beginning to make themselves known. Thanks to improvements in agriculture, technology, transportation, and communication, European countries had achieved tremendous economic growth. Many Europeans believed that their civilization and culture were superior to those of peoples on other continents, and they justified their imperialism as a kind of social duty. In a decree announcing the new Portuguese protectorate over Dahomey, for instance, the foreign minister Pinheiro Chagas made a self-satisfied argument in describing Dahomey's willing acceptance of all the "benefits of European civilization" (**DOCUMENT 5**). While it is certainly true that European colonization brought with it an investment of capital, a development of local infrastructure, and a transformation of the local culture and economy, these "benefits" were often was accompanied by European arrogance and attitudes of condescension toward the native inhabitants.

In the nineteenth century, many Europeans considered Africa the "Dark Continent" and believed that colonization was akin to a kind of salvation for the "savages" (**DOCUMENT 5**).

Many Christian missionaries supported imperialism because it would enable them to convert newly colonized natives to the Christian faith, enlarging the kingdom of God at the same time that they enlarged the kingdom. Rudyard Kipling, one of the most influential British writers of the era, encouraged his readers to bring civilization and culture to the unenlightened (**DOCUMENT 8**).

The view held by many Europeans that the natives of Asian and African countries were culturally "backward" was reinforced by the doctrine of "social Darwinism," a quasi-scientific application of Charles Darwin's evolutionary ideas about survival of the fittest. Karl Pearson attempts to justify imperialism on these grounds; he argues that racial struggle is a natural (and *vital*) element of human progress (**DOCUMENT 10**). Social Darwinism was quite compatible with many Europeans' patronizing view of the "inferior" cultures of conquered peoples. In this spirit, the British agent Lord Cromer argues that decisions should be made for "the subject race" because of their inability to make decisions in their own best interests without the "light of Western knowledge and experience" (**DOCUMENT 3**).

Some used economic justifications for imperialism. For instance, in his manifesto for the society for German colonization, Carl Peters expresses the theory that foreign colonies will attract a European country's excess population. One of the goals of his Society for German Colonization was directing German emigrants to the colonies (**DOCUMENT 9**). In fact, most European emigrants went to North and South America and Australia rather than colonies controlled by their countries.

Political factors were more important causes of the nineteenth century European imperialism. Leading European nations felt that colonies were essential to national security and military power. The British foreign officer Clement Hill describes the political pressure to maintain a European presence on the East Coast of Africa in **DOCUMENT 4**. When the Suez Canal was completed in 1869, it made Egypt especially important to the British, because it provided them with the shortest possible route to India, the most important colonial element in the British empire. Britain purchased a major interest in the Suez Canal in 1875, and established control over Egypt soon thereafter. This was part of the "land scramble" that is satirized in the American cartoon showing England in the form of the octopus John Bull, grabbing every bit of land within its reach (**DOCUMENT 6**).

For many European nations, the acquisition of colonies represented an opportunity to distinguish themselves in the international community. The Victorian critic John Ruskin articulates this vision of England's prestigious and superior destiny as " … a sceptred isle, for all the world a source of light, a centre of peace …" (**DOCUMENT 2**). A similar sentiment is voiced in earnest rhetorical fashion by the British journalist G.W. Steevens (**DOCUMENT 7**).

The many social, economic, and political factors responsible for the nineteenth-century phase of "New Imperialism" by European powers were complicated and different for individual powers. Nevertheless, there was undeniably a sense among the different countries that the lands they colonized were theirs for the taking. Diderot's observation that merely setting foot on foreign land seemed to justify to Europeans their right of possession is not hyperbole (**DOCUMENT 1**). Nineteenth-century European Imperialism represented human greed at its most voracious and uncontrolled.

Free-Response Question

What were the "tools of imperialism?"

The domination that Europe and peoples of European descent came to exert over the entire globe by 1900 is extraordinary. It had not existed a century earlier and would not exist a century later. At the time many Europeans as well as Americans who worked their way across the North American continent in what many regarded as manifest destiny saw this domination as evidence of cultural or racial superiority. In fact, however, Western domination was based on distinct and temporary technological advantages, what one historian called the "tools of empire." These tools gave Westerners the capacity to conquer and dominate vast areas of the world.

Steamboats, the conquest of tropical diseases, and the technological advantage of Western firearms, can all be considered "tools of imperialism."

CHAPTER 26

Alliances, War, and a Troubled Peace

Emergence of the German Empire and the Alliance Systems (1873–1890)

- In 1873, Bismarck formed the **Three Emperors' League,** which brought together Germany, Austria, and Russia. The league soon collapsed because of the Austro-Russian rivalry in the Balkans.
- The **Congress of Berlin** resulted in Russia's significant loss of territory, and a new tension arose between Germany and Russia. Germany and Austria signed the **Dual Alliance,** whereby they would protect each other if either country was attacked by Russia.
- Russia soon joined and renewed the **Three Emperors' League in 1881.** Another series of alliances between Austria, Germany, and Italy were arranged, but the rise of William II to the German throne in 1888 upset these delicate balances and led to the dismissal of Bismarck.
- New alliances and tensions led to a **Franco-Russian alliance in 1894,** and a new tension arose between Britain and Germany. Britain concluded agreements with the French in 1902 known as the *Entente Cordiale.*
- **The Triple Entente,** consisting of **Britain, France, and Russia,** was now posed against the **Triple Alliance of Germany, Austria, and Italy.** These relationships and shifting conflicts in the region pushed Europe closer to war.

World War I

- A series of **Balkan crises** precipitated war. Both Serbia and Austria-Hungary wanted to expand into the Balkans. Austria annexed Bosnia-Herzegovina in 1908, and proceeded to alienate Russia, which sided with Serbia in the crisis. Germany joined Austria's cause to keep the Russian threat in check.
- A second crisis in **Morocco** occurred in 1911, when Germany protested French occupation of the region and sent the Panther gunboat to protect German interests. This action irritated Britain, which pledged its support to France. Negotiations allowed France to establish a protectorate in Morocco and gave Germany some land in the French Congo. However, the more important outcome was **an increase of British fear and hostility toward Germany, and a closer alliance with France.**
- The June 28, 1914, **assassination of Archduke Ferdinand,** Austrian heir to the throne, by a Bosnian nationalist was the **spur to the outbreak of war.** Serbia's involvement with the plot provoked outrage in Europe. Germany agreed to support Austria in an attack on Serbia, and war was declared in July—but not begun until August. Russia was not eager for war, but Pan-Slav nationalists demanded action, and the government ordered partial mobilization. France and Britain were not eager for war, but their alliance with Russia required their assistance.

The Russian Revolution

- In March, 1917, a Russian revolution **overthrew the tsarist government of Nicholas II.** The war put too many demands on Russia's resources, and peasant discontent had plagued the country for many years. Strikes and worker demonstrations erupted, the tsar abdicated, the government fell to the members of the reconvened *Duma,* and a provisional government was formed composed of Constitutional Democrats with western sympathies. This government remained loyal to the tsarist alliances and decided to continue war against Germany.
- **The Bolshevik wing** of the Social Democratic party had been working against the provisional government. Vladimir Lenin demanded that political power go to the *soviets,* which were councils of workers and soldiers controlled by the Menshevik wing, a group of orthodox Marxists. With Lenin's help, Leon Trotsky organized a coup that concluded with the **Bolshevik rule of Russia.**

The End of World War I and the Settlement at Paris

- In March 1918, Germany agreed to accept defeat and sought peace on the basis of Woodrow Wilson's **Fourteen Points plan,** which included the creation of the **League of Nations.** The **Great War** came to an end with some 4 million dead and 8.3 million wounded among the Central Powers and 5.4 million dead and 7 million wounded among the Allies.
- The Paris settlement consisted of **five separate treaties** between victors and the defeated powers. The Soviet Union (as Russia was called after the Bolshevik victory) and Germany were not included in the peace conference. **The League of Nations** was established, and its covenant was an important part of the peace treaty. France won Alsace-Lorraine, Germany was disarmed, and the United States and Britain agreed to protect France from any future German aggression. The Austro-Hungarian Empire disappeared, giving way to five small states. Germany was required to pay $5 billion annually in reparations until 1921.

For Additional Review

Consider the international leadership of Otto von Bismarck.

Multiple-Choice Questions

1. All of the following are part of Woodrow Wilson's Fourteen Points EXCEPT
   - (A) self-determination for nationalities.
   - (B) freedom of the seas.
   - (C) disarmament.
   - (D) establishment of a League of Nations.
   - (E) aid to rebuild Germany.

2. The Dual Alliance of 1879
   - (A) was formed between Germany and Prussia.
   - (B) sought to isolate Russia.
   - (C) was formed between Bismarck and Napoleon III.
   - (D) sought Austrian neutrality if France were attacked.
   - (E) was formed between Germany and Serbia.

3. Bismarck's complicated system of secret alliances in the years prior to World War I was
   upset by
   (A)   British insistence on French neutrality.
   (B)   the accession of William II to the throne.
   (C)   his death in 1888.
   (D)   Austrian deception and rejection of the Triple Alliance.
   (E)   his increased unwillingness to keep his promises.

4. The Triple Alliance consisted of
   (A)   Britain, Germany, and France.
   (B)   Germany, Austria, and Italy.
   (C)   Russia, Britain, and France.
   (D)   Austria, Russia, and Britain.
   (E)   Italy, Russia, and France.

5. The November Revolution in Russia was
   (A)   a coup d' etat staged by General Kornilov, which then spawned the Bolshevik
          seizure of power.
   (B)   the mass uprising of the peasants that paved the way for Lenin's betrayal of both
          the peasants and the workers.
   (C)   a spontaneous street demonstration by thousands of working women that
          escalated into a full-scale insurrection that toppled General Kornilov's regime.
   (D)   a carefully planned and coordinated seizure of power by Lenin and his vanguard
          of Bolsheviks.
   (E)   a demonstration to the Russian people the effectiveness of the new government in
          dealing with the problems of food supply.

6. William II's foreign policy during the first decade of the twentieth century
   (A)   encouraged France's association with England.
   (B)   successfully isolated France.
   (C)   was patterned after that of his predecessor, Bismarck.
   (D)   isolated Germany from Italy and Austria.
   (E)   demonstrated his impressive grasp of the various existing European alliances.

7. The most important of England's colonies during the era of New Imperialism was
   (A)   Canada.
   (B)   India.
   (C)   Australia.
   (D)   Ireland.
   (E)   Cape Colony.

8. The *Entente Cordiale* was an alliance between
    (A)   France and Italy.
    (B)   France and Germany.
    (C)   France and Russia.
    (D)   France and Austria.
    (E)   France and England.

9. Which of the following events brought the United States into World War I?
    (A)   The Second Morocco Crisis
    (B)   The Bosnian Crisis
    (C)   The assassination of Archduke Ferdinand by a Bosnian nationalist
    (D)   Germany's declaration that it intended to continue submarine warfare
    (E)   Churchill's devastating failure in the Gallipoli campaign

10. The Peace at Versailles resulted in the dismantling of which nation-state?
    (A)   France
    (B)   Germany
    (C)   Italy
    (D)   Austria-Hungary
    (E)   Russia

Document-Based Question

In what ways was World War I a "new kind of war"? What role did technology play in making World War I different than previous conflicts?

Document A Source: John Singer Sargent's *Gassed*.

The use of poison gas (by both sides) during the First World War and its dreadful effects—blinding, asphyxiation, burned lungs—came to symbolize the horrors of modern war. This painting shows a group of British soldiers being guided to the rear after they were blinded by mustard gas on the Western Front. John Singer Sargent, *Gassed*, 1918–1919. Imperial War Museum, London

Document B Source: Austro-Hungarian troops.

Document C Source: British tanks moving toward the Battle of Cambrai in Flanders in 1917.

British tanks moving toward the Battle of Cambrai in Flanders late in 1917. Tanks were impervious to machine-gun fire. Had they been used in great numbers, they might have broken the stalemate in the West. Bildarchiv Preussischer Kulturbesitz

Document D Source: Siegfried Sassoon, "They,"

The Bishop tells us: "when the boys come back
They will not be the same; for they'll have fought
In a just cause: they lead the last attack
On Anti-Christ; their comrades' blood has bought
New right to breed an honorable race,
They have challenged Death and dared him face to face."

"We're none of us the same!" the boys reply,
"For George lost both his legs; and Bill's stone blind;
Poor Jim's shot through the lungs and like to die;
And Bert's gone syphilitic: you'll not find
A chap who's served that hasn't found *some* change."
And the Bishop said: "The ways of God are strange!"
October 31, 1916

Document E Source: Anna Eisenmenger describes the impact of the war on her son Karl.

Karl looked very ill. He had no underlinen or socks. His uniform was dirty and in rags. "Mother,
I am famished!" he said, and walking straight into the kitchen without waiting for me bring him
something he began to devour our rations of bread and jam. "Forgive me, Mother, but we have
got into the habit of taking what we can find." He only greeted us very casually and did not
notice until much later that Erni, who had come into welcome him on Liesbeth's arm, was
wounded. "Hullo! So it's caught you too! and then, still hurriedly chewing and swallowing:
"Well, just wait! We'll pay them out yet, the war profiteers and parasites. We've grown wiser
out there in the trenches, far wiser than we were. Everything must be changed, utterly changed."

Free-Response Question

Analyze the significance of the 1904 Entente Cordiale *between France and Britain.*

ANSWERS AND EXPLANATIONS

Multiple-Choice Questions

☐ **1. (E) is correct.** Wilson's Fourteen Points did not include any language about rebuilding
Germany; his idealistic vision for peace involved democratic reforms that were directed at
eliminating the causes of war, but it did not provide for restructuring defeated nations.

☐ **2. (B) is correct.** The Dual Alliance of 1879 was a secret agreement between Germany and
Austria that was intended for their mutual protection against the Russian threat.

☐ **3. (B) is correct.** Bismarck's complicated system of secret alliances in the years prior to
World War I was upset by the accession of William II to the throne. William eventually
forced Bismarck's resignation and proceeded to undo many of the careful balances of power
Bismarck had orchestrated.

☐ **4. (B) is correct.**

☐ **5. (D) is correct.** Lenin returned in October 1917, insisted to his doubting colleagues that the time was ripe to take power, and by the extraordinary force of his personality persuaded them to act. Trotsky organized the coup that took place on November 6 and concluded with an armed assault on the provisional government. The Bolsheviks, almost as much to their own astonishment as to that of the rest of the world, had come to rule Russia.

☐ **6. (A) is correct.** William II's foreign policy during the first decade of the twentieth century inflamed France and pushed it toward an alliance with England, which was already dissatisfied with German patterns of aggression. William II's efforts to gain Morocco in 1905 particularly angered France, which was subsequently driven closer to England in an alliance.

☐ **7. (B) is correct.** The most important of England's colonies during the era of New Imperialism was India. With a population of some 300,000,000, it contained perhaps 80% of the Empire's subjects and provided much of its imperial profit.

☐ **8. (E) is correct.** The *Entente Cordiale* was an alliance between England and France, when England abandoned its traditional antagonism toward France and concluded a series of agreements that settled outstanding differences between the two nations.

☐ **9. (D) is correct.** After the sinking of the *Lusitania,* the United States warned Germany that similar activities would result in certain retaliation. When Germany announced in 1917 that it would resume unrestricted submarine warfare, the United States decided to enter the war.

☐ **10. (D) is correct.** The Peace at Versailles resulted in the dismantling of Austria-Hungary.

Document-Based Question

In what ways was World War I a "new kind of war"? What role did technology play in making World War I different than previous conflicts?

Convincing essays might note:

☐ The stalemate on the Western Front produced by new technology (See Documents A, B and C)

☐ The nature of the changes in World War I veterans described by Sassoon and Eisenmenger (See Documents D and E)

☐ The politicization of drafted soldiers (See Document D and E)

☐ The unprecedented destructiveness of the war (See Documents A, B, C, D, and E)

☐ The impact of the war on people on the Home Front (See Documents D and E)

Free-Response Question

Analyze the significance of the 1904 Entente Cordiale *between France and Britain.*

The 1904 *Entente Cordiale* between France and Britain marked the beginning of Britain's retreat from its policy of "splendid isolation" in European affairs. It came at a time when Germany was confident that a British alliance with France or Russia was unlikely, so it upset international expectations in more ways than one.

Britain and France had a long history of antagonism and rivalry that stretched back to their countries' earliest origins. Often, they found themselves on opposite sides of disputes, such as in the case of the American colonies—which France defended and which Britain sought to defeat.

The *Entente Cordiale* was that more significant, coming after a history of frosty relations.

Though the *Entente Cordiale* was not a formal treaty and had no military provisions, it did settle all outstanding differences between France and Britain. France's existing 1894 alliance with Russia and the growing hostilities between Britain and Germany made the English-French *Entente Cordiale* even more significant, as it implied a whole new set of alliances implicit in the European community. Effectively, the *Entente Cordiale* set the stage for the Triple Entente—an informal, powerful alliance among Britain, France, and Russia, which helped to establish sides in World War I. Had Britain and France not begun to ally themselves in 1904, the makeup of the European community today could be dramatically different.

The Interwar Years: The Challenges of Dictators and Depression

After Versailles: Demands for Revision and Enforcement

- There were numerous post-war economic problems brought on partly by the many casualties of war and **Europe's loss of its financial dominance.** The reparations and debt structure of the peace made the economies of many European nations—even victorious ones—uncertain.
- **Market and trade conditions changed radically,** as much of Europe's infrastructure had been damaged or destroyed in the war. **The United States also became less dependent on European production** and was a major competitor. Slow postwar economic growth and an overall decline of economic activity lowered international demand for European goods. The prominence of labor during the war gave **unions a greater role** in national government.

Toward the Great Depression in Europe

- **Reparations** and **war debts** made international trade, capital investment, and day-to-day business difficult for European nations. After the Dawes Plan was put into effect, more American money flowed into Europe, but that changed in 1928 after the stock market crash. In 1931, President Hoover put a **year-long moratorium** on payments of international debts, which was a blow to the French economy. In 1932, the Lausanne Conference effectively ended all payment of reparations. Problems in agricultural commodities during this time also brought about a downturn in production and trade.

The Soviet Experiment

- The Bolshevik gains in Russia resulted in a **Communist party** in the Soviet Union. Communist leaders sought to spread their ideology around the world; **fear of communism** and resolve to stop its spread became a major force in Europe and the United States.
- The Bolsheviks rapidly developed authoritarian policies in response to internal and foreign military opposition. They formed the **Cheka, a new secret police,** and political and economic administration became highly centralized. Under an economic policy of *war communism,* the Bolsheviks took control of all the major industries and financial and transportation.
- After Lenin's death in 1924, two factions emerged in struggles for leadership of the party. **Leon Trotsky** and **Joseph Stalin** were on opposite sides—with Trotsky speaking for the "left wing" and urging agricultural collectivism, rapid industrialization, and new revolutions in other nations. A right-wing faction emerged with **Nikolai Bukharin** as its chief voice and Stalin manipulating the group that called for continuation of Lenin's NEP and slow industrialization. Stalin began to amass power and in the mid-1920s, he supported Bukharin and denounced Trotsky for his vision of international revolution, endorsing the doctrine of "socialism in one country." Stalin defeated Trotsky and controlled the Soviet State.

■ In 1919, the Soviet Communists founded the Third International of the European Socialist movement, known as the ***Comintern.*** In 1920, the Comintern imposed Twenty-one Conditions on any Socialist party that wanted to join it. This effort to destroy democratic socialism split every major European Socialist party, divided the political left, and created a vacuum of power for right-wing politicians, which led to the **rise of Fascists and Nazis.**

The Fascist Experiment in Italy

■ **Benito Mussolini** rose up (in response to the threat of Bolshevism) as a ***fascist,*** a term used to describe right-wing dictators that arose in Europe between the wars. These governments claimed to hold back Bolshevism and were **antidemocratic, anti-Marxist, antiparliamentary,** and often **anti-Semitic.** Fascist movements were **nationalistic.**

■ In October, 1922 Fascists marched on Rome, an event that became known as the **Black Shirt March** and that led to Mussolini's becoming Prime Minister. The Fascist party came to dominate Italy's political structure at every level.

German Democracy and Dictatorship

■ The Weimar Republic took shape in the aftermath of World War I; its constitution was written in August of 1919. While the Weimar constitution guaranteed civil liberties and provided for direct election, it had flaws that allowed its liberal institutions to be overthrown.

■ **Adolf Hitler (1889-1945)** arrived on the political scene around the time when the French occupation of the Ruhr sent inflation soaring, and unemployment had spread throughout Germany. Hitler affiliated with the Christian Social party in Vienna and absorbed much of its rabid **German nationalism** and **anti-Semitism.** He moved to Munich, and became involved with a small, nationalistic, anti-Semitic party known as the **National Socialist German Workers' party,** or the *Nazis.*

■ During the chancellorship of **Gustav Stresemann,** Germany recovered from some of its losses. Under Stresemann, a new reparations payment plan, called the **Dawes Plan,** was instituted, that gave Germany a flexible form of payment that varied according to the German economy. In 1925, the **Locarno Agreements** accepted Paris as the western frontier, Britain and Italy agreed to intervene against whichever side violated the frontier or if Germany sent troops into the Rhineland. No such agreement existed for Germany's eastern frontier. France supported Germany's membership in the League of Nations. The Locarno Treaty, which pleased all of the European powers, would not solve the tensions that continued to fester.

■ Hitler **consolidated his control** almost as soon as he took office by crushing alternative political groups, purging his rivals in the Nazi party, and capturing full legal authority of Germany. Hitler quickly outlawed all other political parties and arrested the leaders of offices, banks, and the newspapers of free trade unions. He effectively eliminated all institutions of opposition, and began moving against the governments of individual federal states in Germany. Hitler had key SA leaders murdered to gain support from the German army officer corps. After the death of Hindenburg, Hitler combined the position of chancellor and president and became head of state and head of the government.

■ Hitler oversaw the control of Germany as a **police state.** Police surveillance units, known as the SS *(Schutzstaffel),* terrorized much of Germany and focused its hatred against German Jews. The Nazis based their **anti-Semitic views** on biological racial theories rather than on religious discrimination. Jews were robbed of their citizenship, their opportunities to earn a living, and their civil liberties, and they were repeatedly persecuted and harassed. Ultimately, they were killed in Hitler's efforts to eliminate Jews in Europe. More than 6 million Jews were murdered in the Holocaust.

- Hitler effectively handled the German economic problem by subordinating all economic enterprise to the **goals of the state.** He instituted a massive program of spending and public works, many of which related to rearmament. In 1935, Hitler renounced the provisions of the Treaty of Versailles and began open rearmament to prepare for his next aggression.

Trials of the Successor States in Eastern Europe

- The **"successor states"** was the name given to the lands that emerged after the breakup of the German, Austro-Hungarian, and Russian empires. Many of the post-war states (Czechoslovakia, Poland, Germany, Austria) faced major economic difficulties; except for Czechoslovakia, all of them depended on foreign loans to finance their economic rebuilding. The collapse of the old empires allowed ethnic groups to pursue nationalistic goals.

For Additional Review

Define some of the major terms of this period: *kulaks, Comintern, syndicate, collectivize, corporation.*

Multiple-Choice Questions

1. The leader of the Popular Front was
   (A) Édouard Daladier.
   (B) Léon Blum.
   (C) Jean Jaures.
   (D) Andre Citroen.
   (E) Fritz von Papen.

2. Which of the following characterizes Mussolini's economic policies?
   (A) rearmament given first priority in industry
   (B) a planned economy organized into syndicates of labor and management
   (C) agricultural collectivization and rapid industrialization
   (D) the state annexed the means of production outright
   (E) a *laissez-faire* policy

3. The Hoover moratorium on payment of international debts was
   (A) intended to give the United States time get out of a deficit.
   (B) designed to give Germany an opportunity to recover from its financial tailspin.
   (C) created to boost France's economy.
   (D) an effort to sabotage the 1929 Young Plan.
   (E) only a brief pause in reparations payments.

4. Britain's National Government was all of the following EXCEPT
    (A) a coalition ministry.
    (B) composed of Labour, Conservative, and Liberal ministers.
    (C) formed by Ramsay MacDonald.
    (D) a source of frustration to the Labour party.
    (E) succeeded in eliminating the unemployment problem.

5. The Stavisky Affair of 1934
    (A) involved a secret bond scheme between France and Poland.
    (B) resulted in the ousting of the coalition government.
    (C) resulted in a riot between left-wing and right-wing leagues.
    (D) helped Édouard Daladier rise to power.
    (E) resulted in the physical destruction of building that housed the Chamber of Deputies.

6. All of the following are true of the SS EXCEPT
    (A) it consisted of Nazi security units commanded by Heinrich Himmler.
    (B) its members were also known as "storm troopers."
    (C) it was called the *Schutzstaffel,* or "protective force."
    (D) it became an elite paramilitary organization under Hitler.
    (E) it originated as a bodyguard for Hitler.

7. Stalin's policy in postwar Russia is best characterized as
    (A) rapid industrialization and agricultural collectivism.
    (B) rearmament was given first priority in industry.
    (C) a planned economy organized into syndicates of labor and management.
    (D) the state annexed the means of production outright.
    (E) a *laissez-faire* policy.

8. The Great Purges were a feature of which leader's rule
    (A) Benito Mussolini.
    (B) Adolph Hitler.
    (C) Joseph Stalin.
    (D) Léon Blum.
    (E) Ramsay MacDonald.

9. Immediately after his appointment as chancellor, Adolf Hitler
    (A) moved to consolidate his iron control over the government.
    (B) oversaw the assassination of President Hindenburg.
    (C) staged an attack on the building of the Reichstag.
    (D) ruled by decree.
    (E) outlawed other German political parties.

10. Nazis grounded their discriminatory policies toward Jews in
    (A) contempt for Jewish religious beliefs.
    (B) racial theories of Jewish inferiority.
    (C) anxiety about Jewish intellectual superiority.
    (D) jealousy concerning Jewish financial holdings.
    (E) longstanding land disputes with the Jewish community.

Document-Based Question

What were the most important themes of Nazi propaganda? Why did so many Germans find the Nazi message so appealing?

Document A Source: Joseph Goebbels outlines the key tenets of the Nazis, "Nationalists, Socialists, and Jews."

WHY ARE WE NATIONALISTS?

We are NATIONALISTS because we see in the NATION the only possibility for the protection of the people and the furtherance of our existence….

WE ARE NATIONALISTS BECAUSE WE, AS GERMANS, LOVE GERMANY. And because we love Germany, we demand the protection of the national spirit and we battle against its destroyers.

WHY ARE WE SOCIALISTS?
We are SOCIALISTS because we see in SOCIALISM the only possibility for maintaining our racial existence and through it the reconquest of our political freedom and the rebirth of the German state.

WHY DO WE OPPOSE THE JEWS?

We are ENEMIES OF THE JEWS, because we are fighters for the freedom of the German people. THE JEW IS THE CAUSE AND THE BENEFICIARY OF OUR MISERY.

Document B Source: A Nazi propaganda message, "Free Germany!"

HITLER is the password of all who believe in Germany's resurrection.
HITLER is the last hope of those who were deprived of everything….
HITLER is the word of deliverance for millions….
HITLER was bequeathed the legacy of two million dead comrades of the World War….
HITLER is the man of the people hated by the enemy because he understands the people and fights for the people.
HITLER is the furious will of Germany's youth….Hence Hitler is the password and the flaming signal of all who wish for a German future.

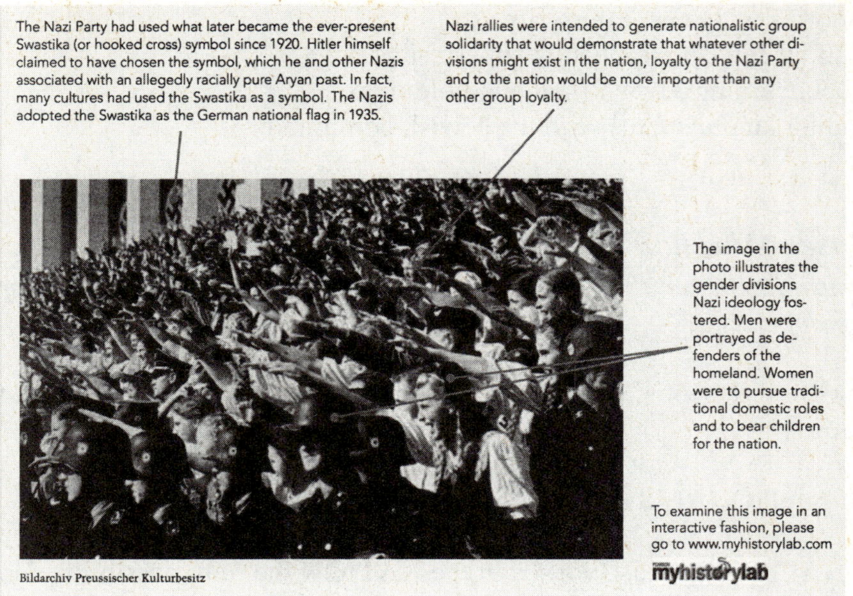

Document D Source: Nazi harassment of German Jewish businesses.

Soon after seizing power, the Nazi government began harassing German Jewish businesses. Non-Jewish German citizens were urged not to buy merchandise from shops owned by Jews. Art Resource/Bildarchiv Preussischer Kulturbesitz

What were some of Stalin's major policies for organizing the Russian economy?

ANSWERS AND EXPLANATIONS

Multiple-Choice Questions

1. (B) is correct. The leader of the Popular Front was Léon Blum.

2. (B) is correct. Mussolini's economic policies were known as corporatism, and they revolved around a planned economy that was linked to the private ownership of capital and to government arbitration of labor disputes. Major industries were organized into syndicates representing labor and management.

3. (B) is correct. The Hoover moratorium on payment of international debts was intended to aid Germany, which had a stagnant economy that did not permit them to keep up with their reparation payments according to the Young Plan. This moratorium hurt France's economy.

4. (E) is correct. Britain's National Government did not succeed in eliminating the problem of unemployment. By 1937, the number of jobless had fallen to 1.5 million, still a significant number in a small country.

5. (C) is correct. The Stavisky Affair of 1934 resulted in an ugly riot between left-wing and right-wing groups. Fourteen demonstrators were killed, and many others were injured.

6. (B) is correct. The SS *(Schutzstaffel)* was distinct from the SA *(Sturmabteilung),* also known as the storm troopers. The SA were organized under Ernst Roehm, and was a paramilitary organization used by the Nazis to intimidate prior to the party's control of the German government. The SS was founded after Hitler took control, and originated as a bodyguard for Hitler.

7. (A) is correct. Stalin's policy in postwar Russia is best characterized as rapid industrialization and agricultural collectivism. These policies resulted in the deaths of millions of workers and peasants.

8. (C) is correct. The Great Purges were a feature of Joseph Stalin's rule.

9. (A) is correct. Immediately after his January, 1933 appointment as chancellor, Adolf Hitler moved to consolidate his control of the government. He strove to capture full legal authority, to crush alternative political groups, and to purge rivals in the Nazi party, but he did not outlaw other German parties until the end of 1933, and he was not able to rule by decree until March of 1933, when an Enabling Act gave him permission to do so. He did not stage an attack on the Reichstag building or assassinate President Hindenburg.

10. (B) is correct. Nazis persecution of Jews was couched in the rhetoric of Jewish racial inferiority rather than German contempt for Judaism itself.

Document-Based Question

What were the most important themes of Nazi propaganda? Why did so many Germans find the Nazi message so appealing?

Convincing essays might note:
- The assertion that national survival was at stake (See Documents A and B)
- The connection between love of country, the Nazi program, and anti-Semitism (See Documents A, B, and D)
- The promise of belonging to a cohesive, purposeful group and the identification of an enemy of the group (See Document A, B, C, and D)
- The identification of the Nazis, in general, and Hitler, specifically, as the solution to Germany's problems (See Documents A and B)

Free-Response Question

What were some of Stalin's major policies for organizing the Russian economy?

In order to organize the Russian economy at a time when industrial growth in Russia had slowed, Joseph Stalin decided to push for rapid industrialization in 1927. This departure from Lenin's policies was dramatic, and it represented a major element of Stalin's plan for "Socialism in One Country." Through this rapid industrialization, Stalin hoped to overpower the productive abilities of capitalistic rivals. The plan required the rapid establishment of major industries that would facilitate the production of iron and steel, as well as the generation of electricity. This process was extremely complicated and was overseen by various centralized agencies or ministries.

The expansion of a vast industrial base created Russia's first factory-oriented labor force. Workers were recruited from rural districts to take positions in new work districts in the cities. The government used propaganda to convince people to displace themselves and join the factory industries that would dominate the Russian economy.

In addition to his plan for rapid industrialization, Joseph Stalin began a new phase of collectivizing agriculture. Stalin decided that government control of agriculture would standardize the Russian system and prevent farmers from profiting at the expense of the rest of Russia's citizenry. Stalin ordered party agents to confiscate lands. If farmers (known as *kulaks)* refused, they faced death at the hands of the government. Stalin's forces killed thousands of resisting peasants in the process of forcing the nation to undergo collectivization. Ironically, this program did not improve the Russian economy, as the newly collectivized farms still did not manage to produce enough grain to feed the Russian population.

CHAPTER 28

World War II

Again the Road to War (1933–1939)

- Hitler envisioned **enlarging Germany beyond its 1914 borders,** and wanted to bring the entire German people, the *Volk,* into one nation. Hitler hoped to extinguish Jews from his new Germany, to reunite the German people of the old Habsburg Empire, and to seize land from neighboring countries—beginning with Poland and Ukraine.
- In 1935, **Mussolini attacked Ethiopia,** which engendered anger in the international community. Britain and France did not want to alienate Mussolini, but in the end he turned to Germany and in 1936 the **"Rome-Berlin Axis"** was born. Hitler marched into the demilitarized Rhineland in 1936 and seized control, registering only weak protests in the form of a policy of appeasement from Britain and France.
- Hitler and Mussolini supported Francisco Franco in his bid to take control of Spain. Hundreds of thousands of Spaniards died in the Spanish Civil War. **Japan joined the Axis Powers.**
- Germany and Austria entered into an *Anschluss,* or union, that had profound implications for Czechoslovakia, which was surrounded by Germany. The Czechs appealed to France, England, and Russia for aid, but the British prime minister, *Neville Chamberlain,* was committed to the **policy of appeasement** and did not want Britain in another war.
- In 1939, Hitler invaded Prague, putting an end to the Czech state. Hitler began aggressive acts in Poland, and England and France considered allying with the Russians to prevent him. But in 1939, a **Nazi-Soviet nonaggression pact** was revealed. This pact divided Poland between the two nations and allowed Russia to occupy the Baltic states. This pact effectively led to the French and English commitment to go to war.

World War II (1939–1945)

- Germany's attack on Poland was swift—a *Blitzkrieg*—or "lightning warfare."
- Hitler invaded Denmark and Norway in 1940, and a month later, he attacked Belgium, the Netherlands, and Luxembourg. British and French armies in Belgium fled to the English Channel and escaped from the **beaches of Dunkirk,** saving thousands of lives. The **Maginot Line,** an imaginary line that ran from Switzerland to the Belgian frontier, was exposed on its left flank after Hitler remilitarized the Rhineland, and Hitler's advance through Belgium avoided French defense. Mussolini staged an invasion of southern France, and less than a week later, France, led by Marshal Pétain, asked for an armistice.
- Britain was isolated after the fall of France, but the rise to power of **Prime Minister Winston Churchill** ended the government's days of **appeasement.** Churchill established a connection with President Franklin D. Roosevelt, and the United States aided the British before it entered the war
- **Hitler invaded Britain** in 1940, bombing London and destroying much of the city. British morale grew during this time and united the nation against Hitler.

- War was thrust on the Americans in 1941 when Japan, an Axis member, launched an attack on the U.S. naval base at **Pearl Harbor,** in Hawaii. The next day, the U.S. and Britain declared war on Japan; three days later, Germany and Italy declared war on the United States. In 1942, the Allies gained control of the Mediterranean Sea, and in 1943 they conquered German-controlled Italy, gaining the new leader of the government as an ally against Germany. In the Battle of Stalingrad in 1942, the Russians lost more soldiers than the U.S. lost in combat in the entire war, but they prevailed against Germany, and Hitler's army was destroyed.
- In 1943, the American and British began a series of day and night bombings of German cities. On June 6, 1944, **"D-Day,"** American, British, and Canadian troops landed on the coast of Normandy, France, and penetrated the German defense. France was liberated by September. The **Battle of the Bulge** in December of 1944 resulted in heavy Allied losses, but the Allies pushed on and crushed German resistance. By May 1, 1945, the German resistance was completely defeated and Berlin was occupied. Japan refused to surrender, and in 1945, American warplanes dropped an atomic bomb on the city of **Hiroshima,** killing a third of its residents. Two days later, another atomic bomb was dropped on **Nagasaki.** The Japanese government under Emperor Hirohito surrendered on August 14, 1945.

The Domestic Fronts

- In Germany, the economy remained buoyant until the army's failure to overwhelm the Russians, after which time a wartime economy took over. Germany suffered severe food shortages and demanded major sacrifices from its people. The manufacture of armaments replaced the production of consumer goods, and food rationing began in 1942. Women, teenagers, and retired men were required to work in factories, and thousands of people from conquered lands were forced to labor in Germany. Political propaganda intensified in Germany, and the role of women became important to the German ideology.
- In France, the **Vichy government** that followed Germany's aggression was a source of national controversy. It encouraged an intense nationalism that fostered **anti-Semitism.** Internal resistance to the Vichy government developed in 1942, but a large-scale movement did not arise until 1944, when **General Charles de Gaulle,** who had fled to Britain, urged the French people to resist their conquerors and to support the **French National Committee of Liberation.** In 1945, France voted to end the Third Republic, and the Fourth Republic was formed with a new constitution.

For Additional Review

Consider how the Big Three established the peace.

Multiple-Choice Questions

1. Who comprised the Big Three by the time of the Potsdam summit in July of 1945?
   (A) Clement Attlee, Harry Truman, and Joseph Stalin
   (B) Franklin D. Roosevelt, Winston Churchill, and Joseph Stalin
   (C) Winston Churchill, Harry Truman, and Joseph Stalin
   (D) Clement Attlee, Franklin D. Roosevelt, and Joseph Stalin
   (E) Winston Churchill, Benito Mussolini, and Joseph Stalin

2. The surrender of the Japanese government in 1945 was forced by
   (A) a policy of sanctions and withdrawal of military and domestic support.
   (B) Emperor Hirohito.
   (C) the bombing of Hiroshima and Nagasaki.
   (D) Harry Truman, who promised continued atomic attacks.
   (E) Joseph Stalin, who declared war on Japan and invaded Manchuria.

3. A *Blitzkrieg* is
   (A) a massive atomic bomb.
   (B) fast-moving, massed armored columns supported by air power.
   (C) an attack on a fortified city.
   (D) a brutal form of torture used by the Germans in their attacks on Jews.
   (E) a German-made machine gun.

4. Hitler's success in Czechoslovakia was facilitated in part by
   (A) Neville Chamberlain's policy of appeasement.
   (B) the Germans in Sudetenland who supported Hitler's efforts to reclaim Czechoslovakia.
   (C) his persuasive manner in dealing with Czech leaders.
   (D) his willingness to sign a non-aggression arrangement with the Czech government.
   (E) his commitment to keeping Czechoslovakia democratic.

5. The United States entered into World War II as a result of
   (A) the Japanese alliance with Germany and Italy.
   (B) the Japanese treaty of neutrality with the Soviet Union.
   (C) the Japanese conquest of Indochina, following France's defeat by Germany.
   (D) the Japanese surprise attack on Pearl Harbor.
   (E) the Japanese plan to gain control of Malaya and the East Indies.

6. The Spanish Civil War
   (A) brought Italy and Germany together into the Rome-Berlin Axis Pact of 1936.
   (B) isolated Spain from European affairs.
   (C) represented a victory of liberal government over fascist regimes.
   (D) destroyed the political career of General Francisco Franco.
   (E) had little or no effect on world politics because of its internal nature.

7. Hitler's conduct of the war in the Soviet Union differed from the war in the West in that
   (A) Hitler viewed the war in the East as a "holy war"; hence, the Nazi troops were
       encouraged to commit the worst atrocities against people in the East.
   (B) the Nazis felt less was at stake in this theater of the war; hence, it was not as harshly
       fought.
   (C) the West represented all that was decadent to Hitler, while the Russians were considered
       more like the German Aryans.
   (D) the conflict was more crucial to Nazi victory because the Japanese were invading the
       Soviet Union from the south and Hitler wanted to link with them.
   (E) Hitler believed the Soviets represented less of a threat to the German Wehrmacht.

8. "D-Day"
   (A) represented a major defeat for the Allies.
   (B) involved a massive loss of life for the Axis powers.
   (C) was an amphibious assault that led to the liberation of France.
   (D) represented the single largest loss of Allied lives during the war.
   (E) involved French and British troops liberating Belgium.

9. The French Vichy government
   (A) rebelled against German authority.
   (B) collaborated with the Germans to preserve as much autonomy as possible.
   (C) was friendly to non-French and Jews who had been oppressed in Germany.
   (D) was led by General Charles de Gaulle.
   (E) was popular with liberals in France, who saw it as an opportunity to reshape French national character.

10. The Atlantic Charter was
   (A) an agreement between the Big Three that they would defeat Germany.
   (B) an agreement between Churchill and Roosevelt that invoked the spirit of Wilson's Fourteen Points.
   (C) Germany's secret plan to spread their influence to the United States.
   (D) an agreement among Canada, the United States, and Britain to rescue the French.
   (E) the name of the British plan of appeasement of Hitler.

Document-Based Question

To what extent was Italy's aggression in Ethiopia significant in the outbreak of World War II?

Historical Background: In October, 1935, Benito Mussolini ordered his Italian forces to invade Ethiopia, using a petty border incident as a justification for his offensive. This attack shocked the League of Nations, which was designed to protect acts of unwarranted aggression between countries. It also came at a time when Adolph Hitler was consolidating his power in Germany, and it was a real threat to European stability.

DOCUMENT 1 Source: *Corriere alla Sera,* Italian newspaper, February 13, 1935.

"The cause of Italy is that of civilization."

DOCUMENT 2 Source: *Libro e Moschetto,* Italian newspaper, on news of the Italian-Ethiopian
conflict, February 16, 1935.

"Italy: a population without land. Africa: a land without population."

DOCUMENT 3 Source: Sir Robert Vansittart, permanent under-secretary in British Foreign Office, letter to Foreign Secretary Sir Anthony Eden, June 8, 1935.

Italy will have to be bought off—let us use and face ugly words—in some form or other, or Abyssinia [Ethiopia] will eventually perish. That might in itself matter less if it did not mean that the League would also perish (and that Italy would simultaneously perform another volte face [about-face] into the arms of Germany.)

DOCUMENT 4 Source: Marxist, anti-fascist pamphlet, referring to Ethiopian-Italian conflict, February 1935.

Not one man, not one cent for the African adventure of capitalism!

DOCUMENT 5 Source: *The Times* (London), on Ethiopian-Italian conflict, April 8, 1936.

If there are degrees of turpitude in the willful destruction of agreements, zero in the scale has been reached when a Power claiming the characteristics of civilization takes to the indiscriminate employment of gas against a primitive people who neither possess nor can acquire the means of defense against it.

DOCUMENT 6 Source: Benito Mussolini, Italian Fascist dictator, speech from balcony of Palazzo Venezia, May 5, 1936.

I announce to the Italian people and to the world that the war is finished. I announce to the Italian people and to the world that peace is re-established … Ethiopia is Italian … the diverse races of the Lion of Judah have shown by the clearest signs that they wish to live tranquilly in the shadow of the Italian tricolor. We are ready to defend our resplendent victory with the same intrepid and incontestable determination as that with which we have won it.

DOCUMENT 7 Source: Haile Selassie, emperor of Ethiopia, speech to League of Nations, June 30, 1936.

The Wal-Wal incident, in December, 1934, came as a thunderbolt to me. The Italian provocation was obvious and I did not hesitate to appeal to the League of Nations. I invoked the provisions of the treaty of 1928, the principles of the Covenant; I urged the procedure of conciliation and arbitration. Unhappily for Ethiopia this was the time when a certain Government considered that the European situation made it imperative at all costs to obtain the friendship of Italy. The price paid was the abandonment of Ethiopian independence to the greed of the Italian Government. This secret agreement, contrary to the obligations of the Covenant, has exerted a great influence over the course of events. Ethiopia and the whole world have suffered and are still suffering today its disastrous consequences. This first violation of the Covenant was followed by many others. Feeling itself encouraged in its policy against Ethiopia, the Rome Government feverishly made war preparations, thinking that the concerted pressure which was beginning to be exerted on the Ethiopian Government, might perhaps not overcome the resistance of my people to Italian domination …

DOCUMENT 8 Source: Benito Mussolini, speech to constituents, detailing week-old German-Italian alliance, November 1, 1936.

This Berlin-Rome vertical line is not an obstacle but rather an axis around which can revolve all those European states with a will to collaboration and peace.

DOCUMENT 9 Source: Father Messineo, Italian Jesuit, *Necessità di vita e diritto di espansione,* (Necessities of Life and the Law of Expansion), 1936.

We may now legitimately conclude that a state, under the pressure of vital necessity because of the narrowness of its own territories and the deficiency of the means indispensable to individual and collective life, has the faculty of appropriating a part of the earth possessed by others, in the measure required by its necessity. This power becomes even more evident if the material means necessary for freeing oneself from these straits lie inactive, in the possession of a people that does not use them, exploit them, and increase their value, whether because the extent of its territory is greater than it needs, or because of the scarcity of man power, or else because of a backwardness of its economic system. The order of nature cannot require that immense riches of the soil remain inert … while another nation overflows with population that it cannot nourish because of the absolute insufficiency of public and private means … Vital necessity can legitimize the occupation of a part of colonial territory, in order to satisfy the needs of individual and social life.

DOCUMENT 10 Source: British Prime Minister Neville Chamberlain, letter to Benito Mussolini, July 27, 1937.

Dear Signor Mussolini,
… Since I became Prime Minister, I have been distressed to find that the relations between Italy and Great Britain are still far from that old feeling of mutual confidence and affection which lasted for so many years. In spite of the bitterness which rose out of the Abyssinian [Ethiopian] affair I believe it possible for those old feelings to be restored, if we can only clear away some of the misunderstandings and unfounded suspicions which cloud our trust in one another …

Free-Response Question

Assess the significance of the Nazi-Soviet pact of 1939.

ANSWERS AND EXPLANATIONS

Multiple-Choice Questions

■ **1. (A) is correct.** The Big Three by the time of the Potsdam summit were Clement Attlee, Harry Truman, and Joseph Stalin. Harry Truman replaced President Roosevelt after his death, and Clement Attlee's Labour party had defeated Churchill's Conservative party in a general election.

- **2. (B) is correct.** The surrender of the Japanese government in 1945 was forced by Emperor Hirohito. The Japanese government was not willing to surrender after the bombings of Hiroshima and Nagasaki, but Hirohito intervened.
- **3. (B) is correct.** A *Blitzkrieg* is a fast-moving "lightning strike" against an enemy using armed forces and air power.
- **4. (A) is correct.** Hitler's success in Czechoslovakia was facilitated in part by Neville Chamberlain's policy of appeasement, whereby he chose to avoid Britain's involvement in a war and gave Hitler numerous concessions.
- **5. (D) is correct.** The United States entered into World War II as a result of the bombing of Pearl Harbor. The United States declared war on Japan just three days after the attack.
- **6. (A) is correct.** The Spanish Civil War made possible the Rome-Berlin Axis Pact of 1936, as Germany and Italy threw their collective support behind the efforts of General Francisco Franco, a fellow fascist and right-wing dictator.
- **7. (A) is correct.** Hitler's regime was probably unmatched in history for carefully planned terror and inhumanity. His plan of giving *Lebensraum* to the Germans was to be accomplished at the expense of people he deemed to be inferior. Hitler established colonies of Germans in parts of Poland, driving the local people from their land and employing them as cheap, virtually slave labor. He had similar plans on an even greater scale for Russia. The Russians would be driven back to Central Asia and Siberia. Frontier colonies of German war veterans would keep them in check while Germans settled European Russia.
- **8. (C) is correct.** "D-Day" was a major event in World War II, because it enabled France to gain its liberation. Britain, Canada, and the United States staged a surprise assault on the French coast at Normandy and penetrated the German defense.
- **9. (B) is correct.** The French Vichy government worked with the German government more than it worked against it. Conservatives and right-wing French believed that the Vichy government represented an opportunity to rid France of some of what they perceived as decadent liberalism that had characterized France previously.
- **10. (B) is correct.** The Atlantic Charter was set in place by Churchill and Roosevelt in 1941, before the United States had entered the war. It invoked the spirit of Wilson's Fourteen Points and provided a theoretical basis for peace.

Document-Based Question

To what extent was Italy's aggression in Ethiopia significant in the outbreak of World War II?

The Italian aggression in Ethiopia played an important role in the outbreak of World War II. Prior to this act, Italy had been a relatively neutral party in European affairs, despite its Fascist government under Benito Mussolini. Italy's invasion of Ethiopia and the subsequent uproar by western European nations effectively pushed the alienated Mussolini into the waiting arms of Hitler, who had long hoped for an alliance that would increase his power against the rest of western Europe.

Mussolini's agenda in Ethiopia was purely one of conquest. For years, Italy had aspired to gain colonial areas in Africa. Italy had small colonial outposts in Somaliland and Eritrea in East Africa and Libya in North Africa. In 1896, Italy had been repulsed by the Ethiopians at Adowa when it attempted to invade and conquer the country. In 1935, Mussolini used a small border incident at Wal-Wal to provoke an invasion in Ethiopia that shocked the rest of Europe. For some time, Mussolini had been advocating the spread of Italy's civilization to other areas. He encouraged women to bear more children to spread Italy's population across the globe. An Italian newspaper noted that "the cause of Italy is that of civilization" (**DOCUMENT 1**), but more accurately the cause of Italy was that of *Italian* civilization. Mussolini was not interested in preserving Ethiopian liberties or culture; he intended to wipe them out in order to spread Italian culture.

Other supportive interpretations of Mussolini's actions in Ethiopia in 1936 ranged from the argument that Ethiopian land was needed for the growing Italian population, as voiced in *Libro e Moschetto* (**DOCUMENT 2**) to Father Messineo's willingness to overlook the vital necessities of the Ethiopian people as he asserted that "vital necessity can legitimize the occupation of a part of colonial territory, in order to satisfy the needs of individual and social life" (**DOCUMENT 9**). Essentially, Mussolini's agenda was one of greed, and any number of apologists were willing to argue other motives for the Italian conquest of Ethiopia. There were anti-Fascist Italian dissenters to Mussolini's policies who expressed their displeasure with "the African adventure of capitalism," but these were largely shouted down by Mussolini and supporters (**DOCUMENT 4**).

Italy's invasion of Ethiopia was significant to the outbreak of World War II because England and France did not want to engage in a war with Italy at a time when Hitler was conquering the rest of Europe. And so a policy of appeasement began that effectively enabled Mussolini to carry on with his acquisition of Ethiopia. Sir Robert Vansittart of the British Foreign Office acknowledges this policy of appeasement directly in saying that "Italy will have to be bought off" in order to prevent the League of Nations from collapsing and Mussolini from allying with Germany (**DOCUMENT 3**). The League of Nations condemned the Italian aggression and voted economic sanctions against Italy, but—as Haile Selassie, then Emperor of Ethiopia, indicated in his address to the League of Nations, Great Britain deemed it "imperative at all costs to obtain the friendship of Italy" (**DOCUMENT 7**). This friendship is further confirmed in the 1937 letter from British Prime Minister Neville Chamberlain to Benito Mussolini in which he expresses a desire for "old feelings" between the two countries to "be restored" (**DOCUMENT 10**).

Italy's invasion of Ethiopia rightly shocked the world, but it occurred at a time when the League of Nations was relatively powerless because it did not want to alienate Mussolini. The *Times* of London condemned in strong words the brutal attack against the Ethiopians, arguing that the Italian gassing of the defenseless Ethiopian people amounted to pure evil (**DOCUMENT 5**). In his balcony speech, Mussolini couched the victorious conquest of Ethiopia in the rhetoric of peace ("… the diverse races of the Lion of Judah … wish to live tranquilly in the shadow of the Italian tricolor"). Eventually, with the League of Nations and Italy in a hostile situation, Mussolini turned to Hitler and made a pact that he referred to as the Berlin-Rome "axis around which can revolve all those European states with a will to collaboration and peace" (**DOCUMENT 8**).

The Italian invasion of Ethiopia effectively demonstrated the weakness of the League of Nations in the face of the threat of Adolph Hitler. It also illustrated the dangers of appeasement, an issue that was central to the developments of World War II. Further, it pushed Hitler and Mussolini into an alliance that would dictate the conflict to come between the Allies and the Axis powers. Though the Ethiopian invasion is not usually remembered in the countdown of aggressive acts that led to World War II, it was decisive in aligning European powers against each other.

Reader's Comments on Sample Student DBQ Essay
- The essay has a clear, well-developed thesis that is reinforced by the use of the documents
- The student makes excellent use of all of the documents
- The essay recognizes authorial bias and groups documents appropriately
- The extensive use of outside information gives the essay an overall coherence
- The essay offers a fairly nuanced consideration of the different elements involved in the invasion of Ethiopia and connects it consistently to events that led up to World War II

Possible student score: 8-9

Free-Response Question

Assess the significance of the Nazi-Soviet pact of 1939.

The Nazi-Soviet pact came as a blow to western Europe. Poland was a target of German expansion in 1939. France and England hoped to help the Poles, and toward that end, British Prime Minister Neville Chamberlain in 1939 announced a joint Franco-British guarantee of Polish independence. Adolf Hitler did not take this guarantee seriously. Of course, France and Britain had no real way to defend Poland against Germany, because of their own political situations. That is, the only way to protect Poland would be to ally with Russia—an untenable solution because of prevailing French and British hostility toward the programs and policies of Joseph Stalin.

For their part, the Russians were still bitter about having been left out of the Munich Agreement. They were also conscious of the fact that western Europe might expect Russia to bear the military burdens of a war with Germany. Germany and Russia began negotiating, and in 1939, they established a German-Russian non-aggression pact that shocked the rest of Europe.

The Nazi-Soviet non-aggression pact had major ramifications for the rest of Europe. It allied two of the most powerful and dangerous forces in Europe—the Nazi regime and the Stalinist Communist state. It meant that hundreds of thousands of lives in central Europe were to be divided up between two military giants. The pact not only sealed the fate of Poland, but also it effectively pushed the French and the British into World War II.

CHAPTER 29

The Cold War Era and the Emergence of the New Europe

The Emergence of the Cold War

- The Soviet Union and the United States entered into a tense relationship at the end of World War II. The U.S. pursued a policy of **containment** to prevent Soviet expansion into eastern Europe.
- In 1947, President Truman set forth what has been called the **Truman Doctrine,** and Americans also devised the **Marshall Plan**—a program that restored prosperity to Western Europe by providing broad economic aid to European states working together for their mutual benefit.
- In 1949, the Western nations formed the **North Atlantic Treaty Organization in 1949,** which was a commitment to mutual assistance in the event of an attack.
- The **state of Israel** was created in 1948, and the Arab-Israeli conflict over this disputed territory involved Europe and the United States. The Soviet Union became an ally of Arab states, and the United States continued to support Israel, further intensifying existing tensions.
- The **Korean conflict in 1950** brought the United States and the Soviet Union on opposite sides of yet another international dilemma.

The Three Crises of 1956

- **The Suez Intervention,** which involved French and British intervention in the war between Egypt and Israel, proved that without U.S. support, nations of Western Europe could not use military force to impose their will on the rest of the world.
- Poland's efforts toward independence temporarily caused a crisis of **Soviet troop movements** in the region, but the country managed to be led by a Communist figure, Wladyslaw Gomulka, who was approved by the Soviet Communist party.
- After the rise to power of Imre Nagy in **Hungary,** Soviet troops invaded the country and deposed Nagy. The United States did not liberate Hungary as they had promised in the Truman Doctrine.

Later Cold War Confrontations

- The **1960 Paris Summit talks** (intended to promote the peaceful coexistence of the Soviet Union and the United States) collapsed. The aborted conference produced the most difficult period of the Cold War, as the East Germans closed the wall along the border between East and West Berlin, shutting the two parts of the city off from each other.
- The **Cuban Missile Crisis,** which followed in 1962, tested John F. Kennedy's presidency. The threat of a Soviet ally just 100 miles from the United States was ratcheted up when it was discovered that the Soviet Union was storing nuclear

weapons in Cuba. After a standoff between the U.S. and U.S.S.R., the Soviets backed down after a week of tense negotiations. In 1963, the Soviet Union and the United States **concluded a nuclear test ban treaty** that marked the beginning of reduced tensions.
- In 1968, Leonid Brezhnev declared the right of the Soviet Union to interfere in the domestic policies of other Communist countries, after the Soviet Union sent troops into Czechoslovakia to repress a more liberal form of communism. This ***Brezhnev Doctrine*** sought to sustain the Communist governments of Eastern Europe and to prevent liberalization.

The European Retreat from Empire
- Many European empires broke away from their colonies after World War II, in a mass act of **decolonization** that was as much a result of war as it was a response to the nationalist movements in Africa, Asia, and the Middle East. The one exception to this rule was the Soviet Union. Many of the states that became newly independent were called the **Third World,** because they were aligned neither with the United States nor with the Soviet Union.

France, the United States, and Vietnam
- France's decolonization became an important part of the Cold War, as the United States became involved in the war in **Vietnam**.

Toward Western European Unification
- Much of Western Europe's political power has come from its **postwar cooperation.** In 1957, the members of this group agreed to form a new organization, called the **European Economic Community (EEC),** or ***Common Market.*** This group hoped to achieve the elimination of tariffs, a free flow of capital and labor, and similar benefits in their countries.
- In 1988, the leaders of the EEC had decided that by 1992 the EEC was to be a free-trade zone with no trade barriers or restrictive trade policies. In 1991, the Treaty of Maastricht proposed a series of steps leading to a unified European currency (the Euro) and a strong central bank. In 1993, the EEC was renamed the **European Union.** The **euro** was launched in 1999.

The Collapse of European Communism
- Communism collapsed in Europe in part because of changing Soviet Union policy advanced by **Mikhail Gorbachev.** Gorbachev wanted to revive the Russian economy. Under the policy of ***perestroika,*** he proposed major reforms the centralized economic ministries. He also **abandoned traditional Marxist ideology** by advocating private ownership of property and moving toward free market ideology. When these policies did not achieve all the economic gains Gorbachev desired, he pursued bold political reform, such as his policy of ***glasnost,*** or "openness."
- Throughout 1989, one after another Eastern European country moved toward independence. The Berlin Wall fell in 1989, as well, and in the coming months and years, communism and the Soviet Union crumbled. Gorbachev was unseated by a coup in 1991.

Europe at the Opening of the Global Century

■ The **collapse of communism** and the emergence of the European Union fundamentally altered the political, social, and economic landscape of contemporary Europe, and Europe today faces renewed challenges to its role in the world. The **globalization of the world economy** has made Europe increasingly dependent on other nations, including many of its former colonies and the United States, for its continued prosperity and peace.

For Additional Review

Analyze the effects of *glasnost* and *perestroika* during Mikhail Gorbachev's presidency in the Soviet Union.

Multiple-Choice Questions

1. Margaret Thatcher is affiliated with which of the following political parties?
   (A) Tory
   (B) Labour
   (C) Liberal
   (D) Green
   (E) Reform

2. Under Leonid Brezhnev, Soviet government policy was
   (A) more liberal.
   (B) more repressive.
   (C) more open to foreign diplomacy.
   (D) more inclusive of younger persons in the administration.
   (E) characterized by a reduction of olice surveillance.

3. All of the following are true of the Soviet invasion of Afghanistan in 1979 EXCEPT
   (A) the invasion depleted Soviet military and financial resources.
   (B) the C.I.A. became involved in the conflict.
   (C) China favored the invasion.
   (D) it led to the U.S. boycott of the 1980 Olympic Games in Moscow.
   (E) the Afghans killed approximately 2,000 Soviet troops a year.

4. The departure of European imperial powers from their former colonies is known by the term
   (A) exit strategy.
   (B) decolonization.
   (C) repatriation.
   (D) expatriation.
   (E) détente.

5. The Cuban Missile Crisis occurred during which American presidency?
    (A) John F. Kennedy
    (B) Dwight D. Eisenhower
    (C) Harry S. Truman
    (D) Lyndon Johnson
    (E) Jimmy Carter

6. All of the following powers were incorporated in the 1957 organization of the EEC,
    or Common Market, EXCEPT
    (A) Great Britain.
    (B) France.
    (C) Italy.
    (D) West Germany.
    (E) Belgium.

7. According to the Geneva Accords of 1954,
    (A) France agreed to depart from South Vietnam.
    (B) Vietnam was permanently divided into two countries.
    (C) elections were to be held within two years to revive Vietnam.
    (D) an armistice line was drawn at the 38th parallel.
    (E) the Communists were granted control over all of Vietnam.

8. All of the following countries invaded Israel in the early days after it declared its
    independence EXCEPT
    (A) Iraq.
    (B) Syria.
    (C) Lebanon.
    (D) Egypt.
    (E) Kuwait.

9. The American policy of containment
    (A) was devised in the 1960s.
    (B) was effectively a kind of Soviet appeasement.
    (C) did not reflect a major departure in American foreign policy.
    (D) did not affect the international situation in the second half of the twentieth
        century.
    (E) resisted Soviet expansion in hopes that the Soviet Union would eventually
        collapse.

10. The collapse of communism and the Soviet Union occurred under which Soviet
    leader?
    (A) Brezhnev
    (B) Gorbachev
    (C) Andropov
    (D) Yeltsin
    (E) Chernenko

Document-Based Question

What common ideals inspired anti-colonialists in the years immediately following World War II? To what extent were anti-colonialists inspired by Western notions of freedom and independence?

Document A Source: Decolonization since World War II.

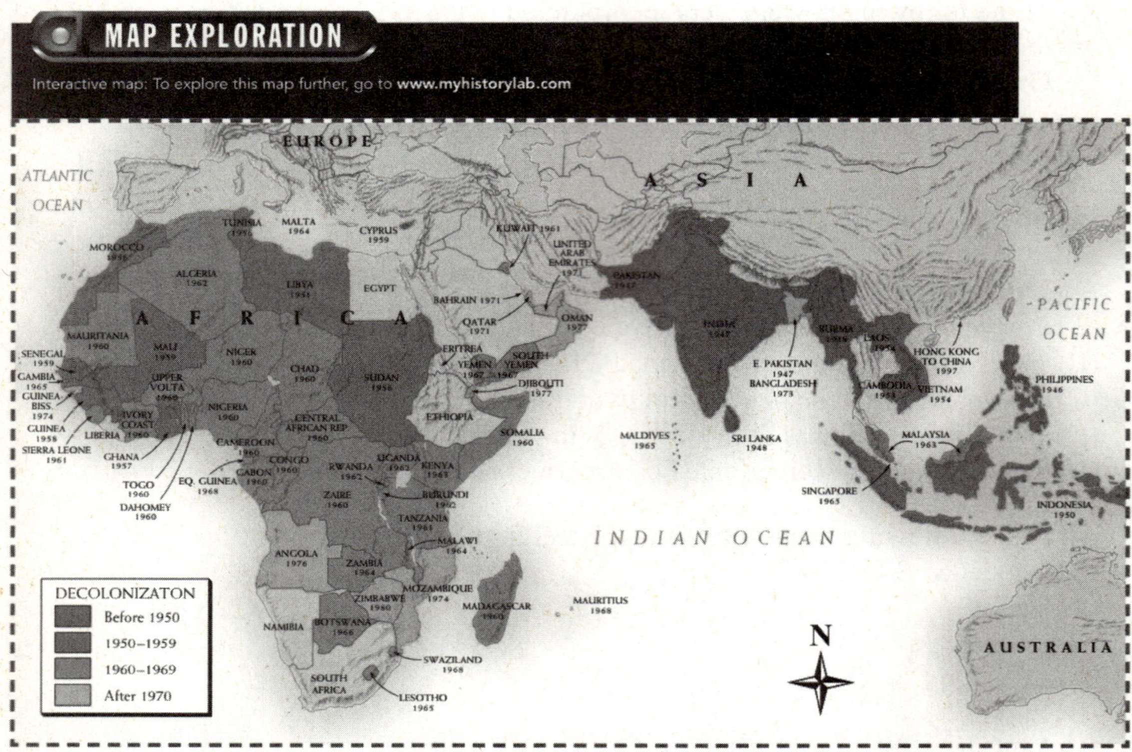

Map 29–6 **DECOLONIZATION SINCE WORLD WAR II** The Western powers' rapid retreat from imperialism after World War II is graphically shown on this outline map covering half the globe—from West Africa to the southwest Pacific.

Document B Source: Ho Chi Minh, "Determined to Fight to the Bitter End."

"All men are created equal. They are endowed by their Creator with certain unalienable Rights; among these are Life, Liberty, and the pursuit of Happiness"….

The Declaration of the French Revolution made in 1791 on the Rights of man and the Citizen also states: "All men are born free and with equal rights, and must always remain free and have equal rights."

Those are undeniable truths.

Nevertheless, for more than eighty years, the French imperialists, abusing the standard of Liberty, Equality, and Fraternity, have violated our Fatherland and oppressed our fellow citizens. They have acted contrary to the ideals of humanity and justice….

For these reasons, we solemnly declare to the world that Vietnam has a right to be a free and independent country – and in fact is so already. The entire Vietnamese people are determined to mobilize all their physical and mental strength, to sacrifice their lives and property in order to safeguard their independence and liberty.

Document C Source: Gamal Abdel Nasser responds to the Suez Crisis, "Those Who Attack Egypt Will Never Leave Egypt Alive."

In these decisive days in the history of mankind, these days in which truth struggles to have itself recognized in international chaos where powers of evil domination and imperialism have prevailed, Egypt stands firmly to preserve her sovereignty. Your country stands solidly and staunchly to preserve her dignity against imperialistic schemes of a number of nations who have uncovered their desires for domination and supremacy….

We shall defend our freedom and independence to the last drop of our blood. This is the staunch feeling of every Egyptian. The whole Arab nation will stand by us in our common fight against aggression and domination. Free peoples, too, people who are really free will stand by us and support us against the forces of tyranny.

Document D Source: India's first prime minister, Jawaharlal Nehru explains the ideas that underlay the non-aligned movement.

I speak of India because it is my country, and I have some right to speak for her. But many other countries in Asia tell the same story, for Asia today is resurgent, and these countries, which long lay under foreign yoke, have won back their independence and are fired by a new spirit and strive toward new ideals. To them, as to us, independence is as vital as the breath they take to sustain life, and colonialism in any form, or anywhere, is abhorrent….

The preservation of peace forms the central aim of India's policy. It is in the pursuit of this policy that we have chosen the path of non-alignment in any military or like pact or alliance….

Through the centuries, India has preached and practiced toleration and understanding….During these millennia of history, India has experienced both good and ill but, throughout her chequered history, she has remembered the message of peace and toleration.

Free-Response Question

To what extent did the Solidarity movement in Poland help bring about the fall of communism and of the Soviet Union?

ANSWERS AND EXPLANATIONS

Multiple-Choice Questions

☐ **1. (A) is correct.** Margaret Thatcher is affiliated with the Tory Party. Thatcher was the first woman prime minister to take office in Great Britain in 1979. Under her leadership, Britain pursued a free market economy.

☐ **2. (B) is correct.** Under Leonid Brezhnev, Soviet government policy became more repressive. Police surveillance was stepped up, dissidents like Aleksandr Solzhenitsyn, who protested Soviet policies, were expelled, and Jewish citizens experienced increased harassment.

☐ **3. (C) is correct.** The Chinese were not in favor of the 1979 invasion of Afghanistan by the Soviet Union. The Chinese government gave material assistance to Afghani rebels who were trying to prevent the Soviet Union from successfully overtaking their country.

☐ **4. (B) is correct.** The departure of European imperial powers from their former colonies is known by the term decolonization. Decolonization was not a systematic process. In the years after World War II, it evolved as indigenous nationalist movements expanded in colonial countries.

☐ **5. (A) is correct.** The Cuban Missile Crisis occurred during the presidency of John F. Kennedy. The Soviet Union's positioning of nuclear missiles in Cuba, a country near enough to the United States to cause concern, resulted in a stalemate between the United States and the Soviet Union that was resolved by the Soviet Union's willingness to back down and remove their nuclear installations.

☐ **6. (A) is correct.** All of the following powers were incorporated in the 1957 organization of the EEC, or Common Market, EXCEPT Great Britain, because EEC members felt that Britain was too closely tied to the United States to support the EEC fully.

☐ **7. (C) is correct.** According to the Geneva Accords of 1954, elections were to be held in 1956 to reunify the Vietnam. In addition, the country was divided at the 17th parallel, with the Viet Minh in control of the north and the French in control of the south.

☐ **8. (E) is correct.** Kuwait did not participate in the invasion of Israel just a few days after it had declared its independence. Egypt, Lebanon, Iraq, and Saudi Arabia were the principal participants in the invasion, which was thwarted by the Israeli forces and their allies.

☐ **9. (E) is correct.** The American policy of containment was an attempt to prevent the Soviet Union from expanding into Eastern Europe. It was promulgated on the idea that if the Soviet Union were kept within its boundaries, it would eventually weaken and become less of an international threat.

☐ **10. (B) is correct.** The collapse of Communism and the Soviet Union occurred under Mikhail Gorbachev, whose radical policies of perestroika and glasnost exposed the vast Communist regime to new challenges from its provinces and to the possibility of internal criticism.

Document-Based Question

What common ideals inspired anti-colonialists in the years immediately following World War II? To what extent were anti-colonialists inspired by Western notions of freedom and independence?

Convincing essays might note:
- The emphasis on independence in each document (See Documents A, B, C, and D)
- The assertion of common interests and experiences among former colonies (See Documents B, C, and D)
- The evocation of European models of freedom and independence (See Document B)
- Nehru's insistence that India's foreign policy was rooted in Indian history (See Document D)
- The compressed timeframe in which decolonization took place around the world (See Documents A, B, C, and D).

Free-Response Question

To what extent did the Solidarity movement in Poland help bring about the fall of Communism and of the Soviet Union?

The Solidarity movement first challenged the Soviet government in 1980 with a strike at the Gdansk shipping yard, setting off a series of strikes at factories and facilities affiliated with the shipbuilding industry. The strikers were unwilling to negotiate through government channels and were eventually recognized as an independent union. In 1981, the Solidarity movement's gains were suppressed by General Jaruzelski, who imposed martial law in Poland. This action effectively silenced Solidarity, as it resulted in the imprisonment of several of the movement's leaders.

The Polish government's relaxation of martial law enabled Solidarity to rise to the forefront of Polish politics again in 1988. Solidarity prisoners were released, and the group staged powerful new strikes that prevented the Communist government from maintaining control over the situation. Lech Walesa, a leader of Solidarity, took control of the strikes and demanded that the Polish government and General Jaruzelski sought to accommodate. With the consent of the Soviet Union, Jaruzelski offered political reforms in Poland, including free elections to a parliament with increased powers. Solidarity candidates won overwhelmingly in the next election, and a non-Communist prime minister was appointed in 1989.

This incredibly significant event—which occurred because of a loosening of some Communist policies—was the first in a series of collapses of Soviet-controlled states in eastern Europe. The Solidarity movement demonstrated to other European nations that it was possible to achieve more democratic government through effective resistance to the Communist party. In a sense, the Solidarity movement is responsible for setting off the wave of independence that followed in eastern Europe. Of course, this event would have been impossible without some bending on the part of Communist leaders, who recognized, perhaps, that eventually something would have to give.

CHAPTER 30

The West at the Dawn of the Twenty-First Century

The Twentieth-Century Movement of Peoples
■ World War II created a terrible **refugee problem** as millions of people were displaced from their homes. Between 1945 and 1960, half a million Europeans left Europe each year.

The Welfare State
■ The emergence of a modern European **welfare state** evolved after the economic dislocation, unemployment, rise of authoritarian states, and the devastating effects of World War II. After World War II, the concept that **social insurance against risks** should be available to all citizens came into being. Britain created the first welfare state, with universal health coverage for all citizens. Western European attitudes toward **providing social security** and coverage to their citizens grew in response to **Communist promises** (largely unfounded) of the same.

New Patterns in the Work and Expectations of Women
■ Women in the years since World War II have made important gains in the workplace. More women are in managerial positions and have better opportunities, but gender inequality remains a problem.

Transformations in Knowledge and Culture
■ Many intellectuals in the 1930s viewed communism as a vehicle for protecting **humane values.** Some did not know of Stalin's terror; others simply ignored it or defended it. Four events that were crucial to the transformation of intellectual thought with regard to communism: **the Spanish Civil War, the great public purge trials of the 1930s, the Nazi-Soviet pact,** and **the Soviet invasion of Hungary in 1956.**
■ Many **intellectuals remained fans of Marxism,** which they distinguished from the agenda of the Communist party. Another powerful intellectual trend during this time was **existentialism,** which had its roots in the thinking of Søren Kierkegaard and Frederick Nietzsche.
■ The **university populations in Europe expanded** in the post-war years, with higher education available to women throughout Europe.
■ In the postwar years, the American military presence in Europe, tourism, and student exchanges have all led to the **Americanization of Europe.**

The Christian Heritage
■ Christianity continues to struggle against the **forces of secularization** in contemporary society. Strands of neo-orthodoxy and liberalism are evident in contemporary Christianity.

Late Twentieth-Century Technology: The Arrival of the Computer

■ The importance of the computer in the twentieth century cannot be underestimated. It altered forever the way business was done, and it effectively brought the world closer together, with new means of technological communication like email and the Internet.

For Additional Review

Compare and contrast neo-orthodox and liberal theologies.

Multiple-Choice Questions

1. All of the following are late-twentieth century technological developments that have revolutionized communication EXCEPT
   (A) the development of the World Wide Web.
   (B) the development of the personal computer.
   (C) the development of calculating machinery.
   (D) the development of the microchip.
   (E) the development of the mouse.

2. All of the following are true of women in Mussolini's Italy EXCEPT
   (A) they were urged to have more children.
   (B) they were not allowed to join the work force.
   (C) they were discouraged from participating in the work force.
   (D) they were given subsidies if they had large families.
   (E) they were discouraged from using contraception.

3. Which of the following issues is connected to the political emergence of the Greens?
   (A) The Americanization of Europe
   (B) The Jewish community in Palestine
   (C) Environmentalism
   (D) The Marshall Plan
   (E) Feminism

4. Neo-orthodoxy is associated with which of the following figures?
   (A) Paul Tillich
   (B) Karl Barth
   (C) Søren Kierkegaard
   (D) Pope John XXIII
   (E) Jean-Paul Sartre

5. The Jewish community in Poland
   (A) was virtually eradicated as a result of the Holocaust.
   (B) fared better than other Jewish communi ties during the Nazi regime.
   (C) was not dramatically affected by Nazi methods of racial discrimination.
   (D) emigrated *en masse* to Palestine during the Nazi era.
   (E) experienced financial prosperity in the twentieth century.

6. Which of the following was the first European nation to create a welfare state?
   (A) France
   (B) Germany
   (C) Spain
   (D) England
   (E) Ireland

7. The *Americanization* of Europe refers to all of the following EXCEPT
   (A) America's economic influence.
   (B) the military influence of America.
   (C) the pervasive presence of American culture.
   (D) the omnipresence and influence of American entertainment.
   (E) the threat of American aggression on Europe.

8. Which of the following is an existential work?
   (A) *Being and Nothingness*
   (B) *The Second Sex*
   (C) *The Screwtape Letters*
   (D) *Mein Kampf*
   (E) *Darkness at Noon*

9. All of the following were true of the period between 1945 and 1960 EXCEPT
   (A) Europe experienced its largest outward migration since the 1920s.
   (B) many European colonials returned to Europe from overseas.
   (C) many non-European colonials migrated to Europe.
   (D) European governments discouraged migration immediately after World War II.
   (E) emigrants from Europe included both rural and city dwellers.

10. All of the following were results of Soviet collectivization EXCEPT
    (A) a widespread famine in 1932 and 1933.
    (B) an increase in education in the countryside.
    (C) a rise in rural literacy.
    (D) peasant flight from the land to the cities.
    (E) a surplus of urban housing.

Does the movement toward European unification represent a fundamental break with Europe's past? What new challenges to unification have emerged since 1990?

Document A Source: Members of the European Union in 2005.

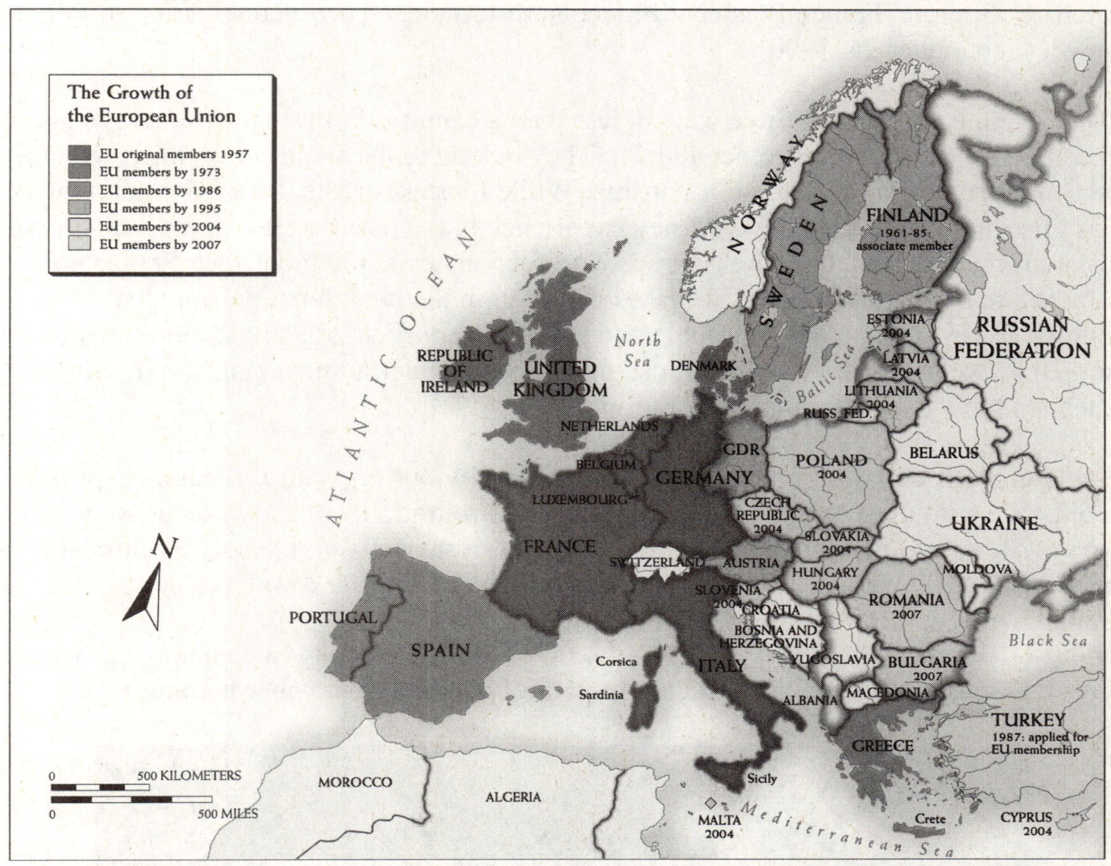

Map 30–1 **THE GROWTH OF THE EUROPEAN UNION**   This map traces the growth of membership in the European Union from its founding in 1957 through the introduction of its newest members in 2007. Note that Turkey, though having applied for membership, has not yet been admitted.

Document B Source: German Chancellor Helmut Khol, "A United Germany in a United Europe," (June 5, 1990).

We Germans are not oblivious of the fact that here and in other countries we are being asked questions as we head for unity:
--What kind of Germany will emerge?
--What will German unity mean for peace and security in the heart of Europe?
--Will this Germany revert to old patterns of behavior; or has it learned the lessons of history?...

A future Germany…will from the very beginning be a member of the European Community. A united Germany will take part in 1992 when the large single market with 336 million people is completed. A united Germany will, together with France, be a driving force behind European unification…

A future united Germany as a member of the Western defense alliance will increase the security of everyone concerned and thus become a cornerstone of a stable, peaceful, order in Europe.

Document C Source: French President François Mitterrand, "The Reconciliation of France and Germany," (September 24, 1990).

After destroying each other in three wars in less than a century, France and Germany have sealed their reconciliation, a rare occurrence indeed: They belong to the same community, they meet together, they are forging a genuine friendship. While I speak, on the eve of German unity, instead of harping on the tragic events they experience in the past because of each other, our two peoples are turned toward the same future….The deep understanding between France and Germany is a reality. As you know, it makes itself felt in the twelve-nation European Community. Can you imagine the trouble and strife, the conflicts of age-old ambitions that were overcome forty years ago by a bold, almost unbelievable undertaking engaged in by first six, nine, then ten, now twelve countries of Europe?...

At the beginning of this century and at the end of the previous one, our forbearers expressed their dream of peace with these three words: disarmament, arbitration, collective security. Theirs came to be an era of unrest, dictatorship and war. Let us act in such a way, I beseech you, that through the United Nations, law, solidarity, and peace may finally rule over a new era.

Document D Source: On January 1, 1999 the European Community launched the Euro, a single monetary unit that replaced the national currencies of most of its member nations.

Describe the Existentialist philosophy and the ideas of some of its thinkers.

ANSWERS AND EXPLANATIONS

Multiple-Choice Questions

1. **(C) is correct.** The need for calculating machinery arose at the beginning of the late-nineteenth century, as governments increasingly required devices that would enable them to administer data efficiently. The manufacturing of such machinery did not occur until the late 1920s.

2. **(B) is correct.** Women were allowed to participate in the workforce. In fact, some 25% of the Italian work force consisted of women. They were subtly discouraged from joining the workforce, which was seen as taking them away from their most important task—bearing children.

3. **(C) is correct.** The Greens developed in response to some of the ethical issues brought about by rapid post-war expansion. Concerns about pollution and environmental contamination were some of the major interests of the Greens.

4. **(B) is correct.** Neo-orthodoxy is associated with Karl Barth, the Swiss pastor whose 1919 work *A Commentary on the Epistle to the Romans* stressed the transcendence of the divine and the dependence of human beings on God.

5. **(A) is correct.** The Polish Jewish Community was nearly obliterated by the Holocaust. Under Hitler's regime of systematic elimination of Jews from Poland, some 90 percent of the pre-1939 population of Jews in Poland was displaced and/or died in concentration camps and massacres.

6. **(D) is correct.** Great Britain was the first European nation to create a welfare state. It did so under the 1945-1951 Labour Party Ministry of Clement Attlee. Under Attlee, the National Health Service was established, which granted universal health care to all citizens.

7. **(E) is correct.** The *Americanization* of Europe refers to the domination of American ways of thought and American popular culture, but it does not refer to a threat of American aggression on Europe. The Americanization of Europe was made possible in part by the friendly relationship between the two continents.

8. **(A) is correct.** *Being and Nothingness* (1943) by Jean-Paul Sartre is a classic work of existentialism that examines the randomness inherent in the human experience on Earth.

9. **(D) is correct.** Between 1945 and 1960, approximately 500,000 Europeans left the farms and cities of the Continent each year. Their reasons for leaving varied, but some immigrants were encouraged by European governments that felt that their economies could not support their populations. Colonials returned from overseas to Great Britain, France, and the Netherlands. Non-European colonials migrated to Europe from the Caribbean, India, Pakistan, and Africa.

10. **(E) is correct.** Soviet collectivization was a brutal process that resulted in massive changes for peasants, including widespread famine and peasant flight from the rural areas to the cities. This influx of peasants in urban areas led to dramatic shortages in urban housing for displaced peasants.

Document-Based Question

Does the movement toward European unification represent a fundamental break with Europe's past? What new challenges to unification have emerged since 1990?

Convincing essays might note:
- Kohl and Mitterrand's acknowledgement of past conflict (See Documents A, B, C, and D)
- The close political and economic ties that have developed in Europe since World War II (See Documents A, B, C, and D)
- The rapid expansion of the European Union since 1990 (See Document A)
- The political and economic implications of monetary union (See Document D)

Free-Response Question

Describe the Existentialist philosophy and the ideas of some of its thinkers.

Existentialism was an intellectual movement that drew some of its energy from the mood of mid-twentieth century postwar culture. The uncertainty of this period was captured in works by existentialists. Many of these thinkers disagreed with each other on major issues, but the movement as a whole continued a revolt against reason that had begun in the nineteenth century.

Two of the major thinkers of this era were Kierkegaard and Nietzsche. Kierkegaard maintained that the truth of Christianity could be understood only by those who had experienced extreme situations. Nietzsche's critique of reason was also a popular subject of the Existentialist study and discussion. As World War I caused many people to doubt whether human beings were in charge of their own destinies, the existentialist philosophy of Nietzsche (which challenged the role of the Church and the role of human reason) became increasingly popular.

Others who questioned the role of rationalism at this time included Jean-Paul Sartre, whose books *Nausea* and *No Exit* seemed to sum up the sensibility of many Europeans in the postwar period. Authors like Albert Camus stressed the anguish and distress of human beings in extreme conditions. Existentialism in literature tended to treat the notion that human beings must arrive at their own system of ethics instead of depending on traditional structures to impose morality or guidance. Many existentialists wrote in reaction to a world in which technology and traditional modes of thought had brought about death, war, and genocide. Existentialists stimulated and fostered intellectual and ethical debates provoked by the drastic conditions of the times.

PART III

SAMPLE TESTS WITH ANSWERS AND EXPLANATIONS

On the following pages are two sample exams. They mirror the actual AP* exam in format and question types. Set aside a time to take these exams, timing yourself as you will be timed when you take the real test, to prepare you for your actual test-taking experience.

AP* European History

Sample Practice Test 1

European History
Section I

Time: 55 minutes 80 Questions

Directions: Each of the questions or incomplete statements below is followed by five suggested answers or completions. Select the one that is best in each case and then fill in the corresponding oval on the answer sheet.

1. The scholarly renaissance in Italy in the fifteenth and sixteenth centuries can be attributed to all of the following EXCEPT
   (A) the spread of humanism.
   (B) the rise of the use of the vernacular in literary and political communications.
   (C) the invention of movable type.
   (D) the recovery of classical knowledge and languages.
   (E) the end of mercantilism.

2. Based on the map above, where would you say the empire of Charles V was based?
   (A) Rome
   (B) England
   (C) Franche-Comté
   (D) France
   (E) Castile

3. All of the following are considered major factors that fostered the ideals of the Enlightenment EXCEPT
   (A) the colonial worldview.
   (B) the stability and commercial prosperity of Great Britain after 1688.
   (C) the Newtonian worldview.
   (D) the need for administrative and economic reform in France after the wars of Louis XIV.
   (E) the consolidation of a print culture.

4. Which of the following pairs of historical figures helped to shape and implement Philip II's policy toward the Netherlands?
   (A) Henry of Navarre and Don Carlos
   (B) The Count of Egmont and the Duke of Alba
   (C) Cardinal Granvelle and the Duke of Alba
   (D) The Count of Egmont and William of Nassau
   (E) Louis of Nassau and William of Nassau

5. The Girondists who participated in the French Revolution are best characterized as
   (A) a radical group of Jacobins.
   (B) religious conservatives opposed to violent revolution.
   (C) secret supporters of the *émigrés*.
   (D) secret sympathizers with Austria.
   (E) monarchists.

"The great questions of the day will not be decided by speeches and majority decision—that was the mistake of 1848–1849—but by iron and blood.'

6. The quotation above was said by which of the following?
   (A) Camillo Cavour
   (B) Giuseppe Garibaldi
   (C) Kaiser William I
   (D) Giuseppe Mazzini
   (E) Otto von Bismarck

7. The idea that society should let strong men dominate and not protect the weak is most closely associated with the work of
   (A) Thomas Henry Huxley.
   (B) Herbert Spencer.
   (C) Jules Ferry.
   (D) David Friedrich Strauss.
   (E) William Paley.

"Men have less hesitation in offending a man who is loved than one who is feared, for love is held by a bond of obligation which, as men are wicked, is broken whenever personal advantage suggests it, but fear is accompanied by the dread of punishment which never relaxes."

8. The quotation above is from a work by which of the following?
   (A) Michelangelo
   (B) Cosimo dé Medici
   (C) Baldessare Castiglione
   (D) Niccolò Machiavelli
   (E) Desiderius Erasmus

9. In what way was political life in the Netherlands unique in Europe in the seventeenth and eighteenth centuries?
   (A) The Netherlands was a republic with a decentralized government.
   (B) The Netherlands enjoyed a strongly centralized government.
   (C) The Netherlands was ruled by a powerful monarchy.
   (D) The Netherlands established the first parliamentary system of government.
   (E) Political life in the Netherlands was dictated by the rules of a strict theocracy.

10. Elizabeth I's religious settlement is best described as
   (A) an Episcopal system with broadly defined Catholic doctrine and traditional Protestant ritual.
   (B) an Episcopal system with broadly defined Protestant doctrine and traditional Catholic ritual.
   (C) moderate Catholicism with toleration of Protestants assured.
   (D) a Catholic system with broadly defined Protestant doctrine and traditional Catholic ritual.
   (E) an Episcopal system with broadly defined Calvinist doctrine and traditional Catholic ritual.

11. The phrase "Crush the Infamous Thing" is associated with
   (A) Louis XVI's view of the Paris Commune.
   (B) Rousseau's attitude toward thedistribution of property.
   (C) Voltaire's attitude toward the Catholic Church.
   (D) Joseph II's attitude toward the Catholic Church.
   (E) Spinoza's views of God and nature.

12. The "September Massacres" involved
   (A) the assassination of the Jacobins.
   (B) murders of members of the Legislative Assembly by the *sans-culottes*.
   (C) the execution of prisoners in city jails believed to be counterrevolutionaries.
   (D) riots in Versailles in September 1792 that resulted in the deaths of over 1,200 aristocrats.
   (E) the putting to death of Louis XVI and his family for treason against the state.

13. All of the following are true of the Austro-Prussian War of 1866 EXCEPT
    (A) it resulted in the permanent exclusion of the Habsburgs from German affairs.
    (B) it led to Italy's gaining control of Venetia.
    (C) it came about as a result of tension over administration of Schleswig and Holstein.
    (D) it was provoked by Denmark, which wanted to annex Schleswig and Holstein.
    (E) it established Prussia as the only major power among the German states.

14. Nietzsche's main problem with Christianity was that
    (A) it glorified weakness rather than strength.
    (B) it had been disproved by modern science.
    (C) it promoted intolerance of other faiths.
    (D) it was monotheistic.
    (E) it demanded self-sacrifice and required strict adherence to doctrine.

15. Northern humanists differed from their Italian Renaissance counterparts in all of the following ways EXCEPT
    (A) they were more willing to write for lay audiences.
    (B) they were more willing to write for an elite intelligentsia.
    (C) they were less devoted to religious reforms.
    (D) they were influenced by the Brothers of the Common Life.
    (E) they came from more diverse social backgrounds.

16. Which of the following factors best explains why Puritans fled to America from England?
    (A) They were protesting English intolerance.
    (B) They failed to obtain exemption from Catholic services.
    (C) James I became determined to uphold and develop the Anglican episcopy.
    (D) James I decided to punish dissenters.
    (E) Mary I became determined to maintain and enhance militant Catholicism.

17. The British political system in the age of Walpole was
    (A) dominated by a large standing army.
    (B) characterized by little or no dissent.
    (C) generally more responsive to public opinion than Continental governments were.
    (D) characterized by a lack of free speech and association.
    (E) immune to popular political pressure.

18. All of the following are valid explanations for the rise of Enlightenment political thought in France EXCEPT
    (A) the corruption of the royal court.
    (B) the blundering of the administrative bureaucracy.
    (C) the less-than-glorious mid-century wars.
    (D) the power of the church.
    (E) the freedom of speech, worship, and literary expression under Louis XIV.

19. All of the following are true of Maximilien Robespierre EXCEPT
    (A) he opposed the war in 1792.
    (B) he gained considerable support from the *sans-culottes* faction.
    (C) he favored the de-Christianization of France.
    (D) he served as the chief figure of the Committee of Public Safety.
    (E) he managed the Terror against republican political figures.

20. The long-term goal of the Paris Commune was the
    (A) creation of a workers' republic.
    (B) creation of Paris as an autonomous commune separate from France.
    (C) destruction of the National Assembly.
    (D) institution of a Marxist state.
    (E) institution of a new National Assembly for France.

21. Which of the following best characterizes women in the new service work force of the late
    nineteenth century?
    (A) They were unmarried and young.
    (B) They were young, married, and middle-class.
    (C) They were young, married, and mothers of children.
    (D) They were middle-aged.
    (E) They were independently wealthy.

22. Bismarck's attitude toward the German Social Democratic Party (SPD) and its policies is
    best characterized as
    (A) a continuum of hostility and antisocialist legislation.
    (B) total approval of the policies of the SPD.
    (C) sudden acceptance of socialist reforms.
    (D) an anti-SPD perspective that modulated into gradual acceptance of some socialist
        policies.
    (E) an indifference to the efforts of the SPD.

23. In *A Room of One's Own,* Virginia Woolf took the position that women
    (A) should be apolitical.
    (B) should not attempt to compete with men.
    (C) should not merely imitate men.
    (D) should refuse to acknowledge their gender differences with men.
    (E) should shed all of their attachments to men in order to pursue their goals.

24. As a result of the Napoleonic code of 1804,
    (A) all privileges based on birth were abolished.
    (B) the laws of primogeniture were renewed.
    (C) salaried officials were paid in accordance with their land inheritances.
    (D) women gained social and political equality with men.
    (E) divorce became easier for women to obtain than in the past.

25. Which of the following was a distinctive feature of Romanticism?
    (A) a belief that love could conquer all political differences
    (B) a focus on religious values and principles
    (C) the glorification of individuality
    (D) the cult of the courtier and worship of the lady
    (E) an abrupt end to nationalism

26. Which of the following is famous for his newspaper article *"J'accuse"* in support of Alfred Dreyfus?
    (A) Adolphe Thiers
    (B) Marshal MacMahon
    (C) Émile Zola
    (D) Pierre Joseph Proudhon
    (E) George Boulanger

27. Nineteenth-century Russian populism
    (A) was an agricultural reform movement that sought the improvement of harvests through modern technology.
    (B) was a social revolutionary movement based on the ideas of Karl Marx.
    (C) was a political movement that sought to celebrate Tsar Alexander II as a liberator.
    (D) reflected an easing of relations between peasants and the tsar.
    (E) was intended to appeal to peasants who were distrustful of its student revolutionary founders.

28. The Nazis sought to attract
    (A) big business and corporate interests.
    (B) social and political groups experiencing economic instability and displacement.
    (C) labor unions.
    (D) religious minorities.
    (E) land speculators.

29. Which of the following was NOT something President Ronald Reagan did during an intensification of Cold War rhetoric?
    (A) describe the Soviet Union as an "evil empire"
    (B) increase military spending
    (C) slow arms limitation negotiations
    (D) propose the Strategic Defense Initiative, involving high-tech space-based defense against nuclear attack
    (E) deploy a major new missile system in Asia

30. Which of the following factors led most directly to Martin Luther's posting of his "Ninety-five Theses" on the door of Castle Church in Wittenberg?
    (A) Pope Leo X's revival of a plenary Jubilee Indulgence to rebuild St. Peter's Basilica in Rome
    (B) John Tetzel's claim that indulgences remitted sins and released the dead from punishment in purgatory
    (C) the election of Charles I of Spain as Emperor Charles V
    (D) the Diet of Worms in 1521
    (E) the death of Emperor Maximilian I and the subsequent search for a new emperor

31. Which of the following contributed most dramatically to Polish instability in the late-seventeenth and early eighteenth centuries?
    (A) political divisions among the Polish nobility
    (B) the incompetence of King John III Sobieski
    (C) pervasive military incompetence
    (D) a series of border wars with neighboring countries that depleted the Polish economy
    (E) an uprising within the legislative body that led to the ouster of King John III Sobieski

"I … will venture to assert, that till women are more rationally educated, the progress of human virtue and improvement in knowledge must receive continual checks.…

"The mother, who wishes to give true dignity of character to her daughter, must, regardless of the sneers of ignorance, proceed on a plan diametrically opposite to that which Rousseau has recommended with all the deluding charms of eloquence and philosophical sophistry…"

32. The quotation above best illustrates the ideology of
    (A) Marie-Thèrese Geoffrin (1699–1777).
    (B) Julie de Lespinasse (1733–1776).
    (C) Claudine de Tencin (1689–1749).
    (D) Mary Wollstonecraft (1759–1797).
    (E) Catherine the Great (r. 1762–1796).

33. All of the following are true of the steam engine EXCEPT
    (A) it enabled industrialization to grow and expand into different areas of production.
    (B) its use spread slowly because James Watt retained exclusive patent rights until 1800.
    (C) it provided the first steady and virtually unlimited source of inanimate power.
    (D) it differed from other contemporary engines in that it was powered by burning coal.
    (E) it was invented by James Watt in 1769.

34. Which country's government most aggressively and thoroughly restricted the freedom of Jews during the second half of the nineteenth century?
    (A) France
    (B) Germany
    (C) Austria-Hungary
    (D) Italy
    (E) Russia

35. Which of the following best characterizes the aims of Bismarck's diplomacy after 1871?
   (A) achieving territorial gains
   (B) encouraging an alliance with France, Austria, and Russia
   (C) a broad policy of expansion in the Ottoman Empire
   (D) improving Germany's position of inter national dominance and security
   (E) conquering Russia

36. *Perestroika* refers to
   (A) restructuring the Soviet economy and bureaucracy.
   (B) openness.
   (C) cooperation of hard-line conservatives and moderates in the Soviet Communist party.
   (D) a rapid build-up of weapons of mass destruction.
   (E) the isolationist nature of Soviet foreign policy.

37. The concept of the "elect" is associated with which Protestant reformer?
   (A) Martin Luther
   (B) Ulrich Zwingli
   (C) John Calvin
   (D) Martin Bucer
   (E) Conrad Grebel

38. Peter the Great made all of the following advancements in his reorganization of the Russian army EXCEPT
   (A) conscripting 300,000 total troops by the end of his reign.
   (B) adopting policies of military discipline patterned on western European forces.
   (C) founding a College of War in 1718–1719 to administer the army.
   (D) adopting special policies for the officer corps.
   (E) designating his son, Alexis, as commander of the military.

39. The group known as the Roundheads in the English Civil War referred to
   (A) supporters of Charles I.
   (B) supporters of Parliament.
   (C) peasantry that supported Charles I.
   (D) Catholics that supported Charles I.
   (E) supporters in the northwest half of England.

40. The Peterloo Massacre of 1819
   (A) resulted in the banning of large unauthorized public meetings in Britain in the *Six Acts*.
   (B) involved the killing of thousands of protestors in Manchester.
   (C) was a plot by a figure named Thistlewood to blow up the British cabinet.
   (D) resulted in the British government's consultation with radical leaders to improve
       legislation on protest gatherings.
   (E) was the act of the Liverpool ministry.

41. Which doctrine was promoted by the First International?
    (A) Fabianism
    (B) Anarchism
    (C) Marxism
    (D) Liberalism
    (E) Social conservatism

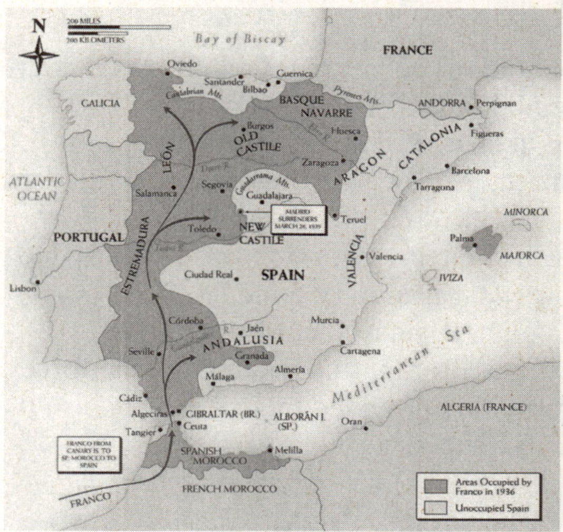

42. According to the map above, all of the following are true EXCEPT
    (A) Franco entered Spain from the south.
    (B) eastern Spain remained unoccupied longer than other regions of Spain.
    (C) Franco controlled lands bordering Portugal and France.
    (D) Madrid was one of the first Spanish cities occupied by Franco's army.
    (E) Franco occupied western Spain during the first year of the Spanish Civil War.

43. An important reason for the collapse of the Soviet Union was Gorbachev's
    (A) support of the conservative military leadership.
    (B) failure to negotiate new arrangements between the republics and the central government.
    (C) failure to deal with the growing threat from China.
    (D) inability to make use of the strong executive powers afforded him in the Soviet
        constitution.
    (E) refusal to strike a balance between support for a new diplomatic relationship with the
        United States and rapid build-up of the Soviet military.

44. Peasants tended to support the Reformation because
    (A) it appeared to promise improved financial conditions.
    (B) it would lead to the end of feudalism and initiate independent ownership of land.
    (C) it seemed to promise political liberation and greater social opportunities.
    (D) it guaranteed social enfranchisement for all.
    (E) it would mean an end to monarchy.

45. Which of the following was a result of the 1598 Edict of Nantes?
    (A) an end to hostilities between France and Spain
    (B) a lasting friendship between Catholics and Protestants in France
    (C) an end to Protestant freedom of public worship
    (D) an end to Protestant fortification of their towns
    (E) a recognition of the Protestant minority's religious rights

46. Which of the following is the best definition of *ancien régime?*
    (A) French royalty
    (B) Nobles who did not hold office or favor with the royal court at Versailles
    (C) Social, economic, and political conditions prior to 1789
    (D) The elder statesmen in charge of the government prior to 1789
    (E) Nobles who held office or favor with the royal court at Versailles

47. The Russian success against the invasion of Napoleon was due in part to
    (A) the small size of Napoleon's military force.
    (B) a "scorched-earth" policy against Napoleon's troops.
    (C) Russia's refusal to retreat from the advancing French forces.
    (D) the intelligence information provided by Russian spies in the French military forces.
    (E) Russian superiority in weaponry.

48. All of the following are true of the Bolsheviks EXCEPT
    (A) they represented Lenin's faction of the Russian Social Democratic Party.
    (B) their name meant "majority."
    (C) they seized power in 1917.
    (D) they were generally supportive of western European socialist parties that sought to work
        within their nation's existing political structures.
    (E) they succeeded in part because of weakened support for the tsar after World War I.

49. Which of the following statements would Karl Barth probably have found most acceptable?
    (A) Religion is a human rather than a divine phenomenon.
    (B) Humankind is transcended by God and depends on His grace.
    (C) Man must trust and depend on himself.
    (D) Reason and science are the sources of truth.
    (E) God condemns our sins and is a vengeful God.

50. A historian would be most likely to cite the portrait that follows as emblematic of
    (A) Elizabeth I's use of the prospect of marriage to her diplomatic advantage.
    (B) the cultivation of Elizabeth I as "supreme governor" and English sovereign.
    (C) Elizabeth I's elegant bearing and disciplined manner.
    (D) Elizabeth I's subordination of religious unity to political unity.
    (E) the political importance of Elizabeth I's status as "Virgin Queen."

51. Which of the following was a new artistic technique developed by artists during the Renaissance?
    (A) Drafting
    (B) Chiaroscuro
    (C) Surrealism
    (D) Expressionism
    (E) Realism

52. All of the following were aspects of nineteenth-century prison reform EXCEPT
    (A) grouping men, women, and children together in "family" units.
    (B) the complete separation of prisoners at all times.
    (C) the separation of prisoners during the night.
    (D) an individual cell for each prisoner.
    (E) long periods of silence among prisoners.

53. Which of the following is the best definition of an early-twentieth-century *soviet?*
    (A) a revolutionary organization in tsarist Russia
    (B) a council of workers and soldiers
    (C) a Russian tsar
    (D) a Russian university
    (E) an impoverished Russian peasant

54. The U-2 incident of 1960 involved
    (A) the shooting down of an American spyaircraft over the Soviet Union.
    (B) the American ejection of Soviet diplomatic personnel.
    (C) the nuclear armament of Cuba.
    (D) a Soviet spy ring in the U.S. Department of Defense.
    (E) the shooting down of a Soviet aircraft on a U.S. reconnaissance mission.

55. During the presidency of Richard Nixon, the United States
(A) sought to close the U.S.S.R. out of world markets.
(B) worked for *détente* with the Soviet Union.
(C) retreated into relative isolation.
(D) sought measures for the respect of human rights throughout the world.
(E) recognized the Soviet sphere of influence in eastern Europe in the Helsinki Accords.

56. Which of the following best describes Luther's doctrine of "justification by faith alone"?
(A) Christians are entitled to political advantages not afforded non-believers.
(B) Belief in Christ is sufficient justification for receiving God's grace.
(C) Christians should abandon their jobs and social responsibilities in order to adhere to the rules of the faith.
(D) Christians should not depend on their faith alone to understand social ills.
(E) Good works must be performed to achieve perfection in God's sight.

57. The Scientific Revolution of the sixteenth and seventeenth centuries was characterized by all of the following EXCEPT
(A) a rejection of the tenets of western scholasticism.
(B) a rational approach to understanding the physical world.
(C) a newly mechanistic view of nature.
(D) an emphasis on empirical research.
(E) a reliance on an all-powerful monarch to interpret natural phenomena.

58. Which of the following was the primary goal that led to the passage of the Sugar Act in 1764?
(A) to produce more revenue by taxing British farmers who grew sugar cane
(B) to produce more revenue by taxing imports into the colonies
(C) to produce more revenue by taxing legal documents and items such as newspapers
(D) to produce more revenue by enforcing a restrictive harvest of sugar cane in the colonies, thus forcing them to import more sugar from Britain
(E) to produce more revenue by taxing the profits of colonial sugar harvesters

59. The eighteenth-century House of Commons was
(A) an unrepresentative body dominated by landowners and the wealthy.
(B) a national legislature split between parties of different political philosophies.
(C) a representative and democratic institution.
(D) a representative body dominated by local merchants and middle-class workers.
(E) an egalitarian body of British, Irish, and Scottish citizens.

60. International reaction to British policy during the Boer War is best characterized as
(A) indifference.
(B) hostility.
(C) approval.
(D) voluntary offers of assistance.
(E) unified resistance.

61. The Berlin blockade of 1948–1949
    (A) forced the Russians to back down and reopen access to Berlin.
    (B) lowered Cold War tensions.
    (C) reunited East and West Germany.
    (D) failed to prevent the Soviets from moving into West Germany.
    (E) weakened the resolve of the United States to help the Germans.

62. In 1956, the real motive behind British and French intervention in the war between Egypt and Israel was to
    (A) separate the combatants.
    (B) seize the Egyptian oil fields.
    (C) seize the Suez Canal.
    (D) ensure Palestinian independence.
    (E) prevent the financially-strapped international peacekeeping forces from having to resolve the conflict

63. Which of the following best explains reasons for the growing tension between the aristocracy and the middle class in Europe in the eighteenth century?
    (A) The middle class sympathized with impoverished peasants.
    (B) The middle class generally lived in urban areas; the aristocracy flourished along the rivers.
    (C) The aristocracy refused to share its power and access to political influence.
    (D) The middle class had little opportunity for social mobility or change in lifestyle.
    (E) The middle class and aristocracy practiced different faiths.

64. The 1779 cartoon "The Horse America Throwing his Master" might best be described as a
    (A) commentary on the American colonies' inability to govern themselves.
    (B) satire of the uselessness of American colonists' efforts to defend themselves.
    (C) satire of George III's vulnerability in the face of the American colonies' rebellion.
    (D) commentary on the American colonies' penchant for violence.
    (E) satire on the cruelty toward animals displayed by early American colonists.

65. Not long after the 1851 plebiscite that elected Louis Napoleon,
    (A) Louis Napoleon executed the 600,000 people who had voted against him.
    (B) an empire was proclaimed with Louis Napoleon named as Emperor Napoleon III.
    (C) France ratified its desire to become a true republic.
    (D) France rejected the action to make Louis Napoleon Emperor Napoleon III.
    (E) dissenters in France sought to overturn the election results.

66. During the Holocaust, Jewish women
    (A) were protected from harm by virtue of their gender.
    (B) were systematically raped by Germans who sought a new German race.
    (C) were singled out for death to prevent them from bearing future Jews.
    (D) were usually sterilized instead of being killed.
    (E) were usually imprisoned with their husbands if they were married.

67. Which of the following is true of the late Middle Ages?
    (A) kingship was despotic
    (B) monarchs and clergy used parliaments and council to limit the power of the pope
    (C) democracy became a cornerstone of several European governments
    (D) feudal relationships became less important
    (E) monarchy was not yet in place; loose "governments" were run by nobles

68. Which of the following statements best characterizes France in the 1660s under Louis XIV?
    (A) France was superior to any other European nation in administrative bureaucracy, armed
        forces, and national unity.
    (B) France was weakened by a diminished army and economic shortfalls.
    (C) France was no longer a major international commercial power.
    (D) France demonstrated economic strength akin to that of a modern industrial economy.
    (E) France was tolerant of minority religious groups like the Jansenists.

69. Which of the following was the most significant problem faced by the French monarchy
    immediately prior to the start of the French Revolution?
    (A) the loss of the Seven Years' War to Spain
    (B) its poor handling of finances
    (C) continuous religious conflict with the pope
    (D) a hostile relationship with the American colonies
    (E) an insurmountable national debt

70. All of the following are true of France's occupation of the Ruhr EXCEPT
    (A) the occupation raised French inflation.
    (B) the occupation raised German inflation.
    (C) the occupation alienated the English.
    (D) the occupation weakened the League of Nations.
    (E) the occupation led to a cancellation of German reparations.

71. The *Cheka* was a name for the Russian
   (A) ministry.
   (B) secret police.
   (C) army.
   (D) assembly.
   (E) Bolshevik opposition party.

72. All of the following conditions led to Great Britain's preeminence as an industrial leader in the eighteenth century EXCEPT
   (A) a thriving newspaper industry regularly publicized consumer goods.
   (B) the economy benefited from consumer demand from the North American colonies.
   (C) the country's social structure encouraged lower classes to imitate the lifestyles of their social superiors.
   (D) its lack of free trade kept supply low, which in turn increased consumer demand.
   (E) the bustling city of London exposed large numbers to the latest in fashions and style.

73. The "Great Patriotic War" was a phrase used by
   (A) the BBC (British Broadcasting Company) to encourage the British people to make personal sacrifices during the war.
   (B) Nazi propagandists to stiffen German resolve against Allied bombing.
   (C) Winston Churchill in his speeches to the British people.
   (D) America to recruit soldiers for the war effort against Japan.
   (E) Soviet leadership to resist German aggression.

74. England became a fully Protestant country during the reign of which of the following?
   (A) Henry VIII
   (B) Mary I
   (C) Edward VI
   (D) Richard III
   (E) Elizabeth II

75. Which of the following ways of thinking developed out of the work of Isaac Newton?
   (A) religion must be rejected because it is inherently false.
   (B) Scientific discovery reveals Biblical truths.
   (C) Science and religious faith are compatible and mutually sustaining.
   (D) God does not exist.
   (E) Science and religious faith cannot be reconciled because they are inherently contradictory.

76. By about 1875, many of the liberal issues and proposals that formed the basis for the revolutions of 1848
   (A) had disappeared completely from the political landscape.
   (B) saw a resurgence among liberal leaders determined to make some gains for their constituents.
   (C) had been adopted by conservative leaders in control of European governments.
   (D) had been instituted with liberal states men in control of European governments.
   (E) were rejected outright by the liberals who had originally espoused them.

77. Which of the following was NOT a justification for the nineteenth-century land grab in Africa and Asia?
    (A) Imperialism was a tool of social policy.
    (B) Imperialism was a way to bring Christianity and "civilization" to foreign peoples.
    (C) Imperialism would serve as a source of economic security and would finance a program of domestic reform and welfare.
    (D) Imperialism would help cure the depression of 1873–1896
    (E) Imperialism would help to increase the diminishing European population.

78. The transfer of the Spanish throne from Habsburg to Bourbon resulted in
    (A) an administrative emphasis on councils rather than royal ministers.
    (B) the decline of the Spanish domestic economy.
    (C) the end of Spanish trade with the United States.
    (D) a stimulation of the Spanish role in European affairs.
    (E) an abrupt end to the Spanish role in European affairs.

79. In the last years of his reign, Charles II
    (A) was extremely suspicious of Parliament.
    (B) had a cooperative relationship with Parliament.
    (C) exiled his traitorous brother, James.
    (D) watched his enemies get elected to Parliament.
    (E) exonerated many of his political enemies.

80. Which group had the greatest influence on the thought of Blaise Pascal?
    (A) Atheists
    (B) Deists
    (C) Jansenists
    (D) Skeptics
    (E) Jesuits

European History
Section II Part A

Suggested writing time: 45 minutes
Percent of Section II score: 45

Directions: The following question is based on the accompanying Documents 1–10. (Some of the documents have been edited for the purpose of this exercise.) Write your answer on the pages of the essay booklet.

This question is designed to test your ability to work with historical documents. As you analyze the documents, take into account both the sources of the document and the author's points of view. Write an essay on the following topic that integrates your analysis of the documents. **Do not simply summarize the documents individually.** You may refer to relevant historical facts and developments not mentioned in the documents.

1. *What advantages and disadvantages did female workers experience during the Industrial Revolution?*

Historial Background: As European societies moved toward an increasingly industrial economy, major changes occurred in the workplace and labor force. With these shifts came population growth and significant migration from the countryside to urban areas. The advent of the factory transformed the working experiences of men and women alike, giving them less individual control over means of production but yielding a more regular and predictable product. The factory system altered European family structures during the Industrial Revolution, as women and children were often put to work doing unskilled labor. While these new industrial occupations offered significant employment advantages for women, often these jobs took place under conditions that were exhausting at best—and exploitative or dangerous at worst.

DOCUMENT 1 Source: Anonymous, "Observations… on the Loss of Woollen Spinning," article, 1794
These Machines then once set up, and the expense of them does not appear very great, 20 Girls do the work of 2,000 Women and Children, and when these Girls are of age to go into a Farmer's Service, how can they endure the fatigue and exposure to weather, necessary to their situation. Numbers confined together in one room cannot make them so hardy and strong, as running at the wheel in a cold cottage, and frequently at the outside of their door in the open air. If they marry, they can neither teach their children to work, or spin, or bring in any earnings to maintain them. Who then shall patch the clothes, mend the shoes, and economize their little store?

DOCUMENT 2 Source: Richard Guest, English historian, *Compendious History of the Cotton Manufacture,* 1823
A Steam Loom factory containing two hundred Looms, with the assistance of one hundred persons under twenty years of age, and of twenty-five men will weave seven hundred pieces per week, of the length and quality before described. To manufacture one hundred similar pieces per week by the hand, it would be necessary to employ at least one hundred and twenty-five Looms,

because many of the Weavers are females, and have cooking, washing, cleaning and various other duties to perform; others of them are children and, consequently, unable to weave as much as the men.

DOCUMENT 3 Source: Anonymous, drawing, ca. 1830

DOCUMENT 4 Source: Anonymous English factory worker(s), letter to the editor, *The Examiner,* February 26, 1832

…In this neighborhood, hand-loom has been almost totally superseded by power-loom weaving, and no inconsiderable number of females, who must depend on their own exertions, or their parishes for support, have been forced, of necessity into the manufactories, from their total inability to earn a livelihood at home. It is a lamentable fact, that, in these parts of the country, there is scarcely any other mode of employment for female industry, if we except servitude and dressmaking.…

DOCUMENT 5 Source: Sarah Gooder, 8-year-old English mine worker, testimony gathered in 1842 by Ashley's Mines Commission, published in British *Parliamentary Papers,* 1842

I'm a trapper in the Gawber pit. It does not tire me, but I have to trap without a light and I'm scared. I go at four and sometimes half past three in the morning, and come out at five and half past. I never go to sleep. Sometimes I sing when I've light, but not in the dark; I dare not sing then. I don't like being in the pit. I am very sleepy when I go sometimes in the morning. I go to Sunday-schools and read Reading made Easy… They teach me to pray.… I have heard tell of Jesus many a time. I don't know why he came on earth, I'm sure, and I don't know why he died, but he had stones for his head to rest on. I would like to be at school far better than in the pit.

DOCUMENT 6 Source: Louise Aston, German political radical, poem, 1844

The factory owner has come,
And he says to me: "My darling child,
I know your people
Are living in misery and sorrow;
So if you want to lie with me
For three or four nights,
See this shiny gold coin!
It's yours immediately."

DOCUMENT 7 Source: Charles Dickens, English author, "A Walk in a Workhouse," article,
25 May 1850

We have come to this absurd, this dangerous, this monstrous pass, that the dishonest felon is, in respect of cleanliness, order, diet, and accommodation, better provided for, and taken care of, than the honest pauper.

DOCUMENT 8 Source: Statistics compiled in British *Parliamentary Papers,* 1852–3, 1863, 1873

Occupation	1851	1861	1871
Agricultural laborer	1,460,896	1,188,789	980,178
Warehouse man/woman	17,861	21,798	44,013
Domestic servant	1,038,791	1,106,974	1,237,149

DOCUMENT 9 Source: Eliza Lynn Linton, English novelist, "On the Side of the Maids,"article, *The Cornhill Magazine,* 1874

Remains of the absolutism of slavery still linger in the conventional arrangements of domestic service. Only in quite exceptional houses are servants held to have any rights beyond the elemental ones of food, lodging, and wages…. Let us consider for a moment what the life of a servant is, forgetting all that we have been taught of the sacredness of present conditions. She lives under ground or just below the roof. Damp, drains, want of efficient ventilation, with the constant presence of draughts, surround her in winter; in summer these are supplemented by a furious fire for many hours in the day.

DOCUMENT 10 Source: Anonymous (possibly Eliza Lynn Linton), "On the Side of the Mistresses," article, *The Cornhill Magazine,* 1874

It must be remembered, too, what are the homes from which these miserable maids first come; what are the rooms in which they have been used to live ever since they were born…. When we contrast the condition of our maids with some ideal state, in which every detail of life shall be regulated by the dictates of an elevated humanity, we must not forget the details of that domestic life from which our servants emerge, or that in every possible respect, except that of freedom (which they are paid to give up), their personal comforts are greater than they have been accustomed to from their childhood.

European History
Section II Part B

Suggested planning and writing time: 70 minutes
Percent of Section II score: 55

Directions: You are to answer TWO questions, one from each group of three questions below. Make your selections carefully, choosing the questions that you are best prepared to answer thoroughly in the time permitted. You should spend 5 minutes organizing or outlining each essay. In writing your essays, *use specific examples to support your answer.* Write your answers to the questions on the lined pages of the essay booklet. If time permits when you finish writing, check your work. Be certain to number your answers as the questions are numbered below.

Group 1

Choose ONE question from this group. The suggested writing time for this question is 30 minutes. *You are advised to spend 5 minutes planning your answer.*

2. *In what sense was the Reformation either the culmination of the medieval experience or the beginning of the modern age? Defend your position with specific examples.*

3. *Compare the importance of the imagination in the works of Romantic writers and the importance of reason in the works of Enlightenment writers. Illustrate your answer with references to specific individuals and their works.*

4. *Analyze the causes of the collapse of communism in Eastern Europe and the Soviet Union.*

Group 2

Choose ONE question from this group. The suggested writing time for this question is 30 minutes. *You are advised to spend 5 minutes planning your answer.*

5. *Discuss several of the advances made during the Agricultural Revolution.*

6. *Discuss the Nazi regime's view of women and of their place in German society.*

7. *Discuss the transformation from the Second Empire of Napoleon III to the establishment of the Third Republic in France.*

ANSWERS AND EXPLANATIONS

Sample Test 1

Section I: Multiple Choice

■ **1. (E) is correct.** Mercantilism, the name given to the efforts by European governments to regulate trade and commerce to increase national wealth, was just beginning at this time, and its impact on scholarship in Italy is arguable. The spread of humanism, the rise of the vernacular, the invention of movable type, and the recovery of classical knowledge and languages all advanced the scholarly renaissance considerably.

■ **2. (E) is correct.** Only nineteen years old, Charles I became Emperor Charles V, and his empire was based in modern-day Spain in land composed of the kingdoms of Castile, Aragon, and Navarre.

■ **3. (A) is correct.** The colonial worldview was not a major factor in the development of Enlightenment ideals. The calls for reform in Europe and the ideas of the Enlightenment were fostered by the economic security and high level of prosperity in Great Britain after 1688, which provided Europe with a blueprint for a successful society in which enlightened reforms appeared to benefit all. In France, Louis XIV's legacy of absolute monarchy, a large standing army, heavy taxation, religious persecution, and few liberties or personal freedoms spurred the need for administrative and economic reform. Newton's achievements in physics inspired philosophers like John Locke to explain human psychology in terms of experience, which in turn encouraged a reformist approach to society. The emergence of a print culture revolutionized Europe as the printed word came to be the chief vehicle for the communication of ideas.

■ **4. (C) is correct.** The resistance of the Netherlands to Philip II's attempts to impose his will proved especially troublesome to the Spaniard's dreams of empire. He recruited Cardinal Granvelle to break down the local economy of the Netherlands and to establish a centralized government based in Madrid. In 1561, Granvelle proceeded with an ecclesiastical reorganization of the Netherlands. The Count of Egmont and William of Nassau had Granvelle ousted. Philip dispatched the duke of Alba to make an example of the Protestant rebels organized by Louis of Nassau (brother of William of Nassau). The duke of Alba executed several thousand suspected heretics on a campaign known as the Council of Blood. Alba ruled over the Netherlands for six years, incurring the hatred of its people.

■ **5. (A) is correct.** The Girondists were a radical group of Jacobins in the Legislative Assembly opposed to counterrevolutionary forces. (They are also frequently called the Brissotins after Jacques-Pierre Brissot, their chief spokesperson in early 1792.) They were infuriated by *émigrés,* and sought to punish their betrayal by seizing their property. In 1792, the Girondists urged the Legislative Assembly to declare war on Austria, believing that the pursuit of war would safeguard the revolution against domestic enemies.

■ **6. (E) is correct.** Otto von Bismarck (1815–1898) was a political pragmatist who put more faith in control and deeds than in ideas. He made this declaration in his first speech as prime minister.

■ **7. (B) is correct.** Herbert Spencer was a famous advocate of evolutionary ethics and a philosopher who believed that human society progressed through competition. One of the chief opponents to such thinking was Thomas Henry Huxley, who argued that the cosmic process of evolution was at odds with human ethical development. Jules Ferry was responsible for a series of education laws passed between 1878 and 1886 by the French government, which replaced religious instruction in schools with civic training. David Friedrich Strauss published *The Life of Jesus,* in which he questioned the Bible proof of Jesus' existence. William Paley's *Natural Theology* popularized the belief that the scientific examination of nature supported Christianity.

■ **8. (D) is correct.** The humanist Niccolò Machiavelli believed that an important personality trait of a successful ruler was an ability to instill fear in his subjects. In *The Prince,* the work from which this quotation comes, Machiavelli advised rulers to discover the advantages of fraud and brutality as a temporary means to the higher goal of a unified Italy.

■ **9. (A) is correct.** In the seventeenth and eighteenth centuries, much of Europe pursued paths toward strong central government, generally through monarchies, as in France, or in the case of England, under a strong parliamentary system. By contrast, the Netherlands was formally a republic. Each of the provinces retained considerable authority, even as they ceded some control to central government in the Hague. Extensive religious toleration marked Dutch religious life.

■ **10. (B) is correct**. Between 1559 and 1563, Elizabeth and her adviser, Sir William Cecil, guided a religious settlement through Parliament that prevented England from being splintered by religious differences. Elizabeth fused a centralized Episcopal system, which was fully in her control, with broadly defined Protestant doctrine and traditional Catholic ritual. In the resulting Anglican church, inflexible religious extremes were not permitted.

■ **11. (C) is correct**. Many of the *philosophes* attacked churches and the clergy with a great vehemence. Voltaire constantly scorned the truthfulness of priests and the morality of the Bible. His cry, "Crush the Infamous Thing" summed up the attitude of a number of *philosophes* toward the Church and Christianity, particularly the Catholic church.

■ **12. (C) is correct.** The "September Massacres" refer to the murders that took place in first week of September 1792, when the Paris Commune summarily executed roughly 1,200 people who were imprisoned in the city jails and suspected of being counterrevolutionaries. Some of these people were aristocrats or priests, but most were common criminals.

■ **13. (D) is correct.** Prior to the Austro-Prussian War of 1866, the Danish Parliament sought in 1863 to incorporate Schleswig and Holstein into its territory. Smaller states of the German Confederation protested this move and sought an all-German war to protest the acts of the Danes. As allies, Prussia and Austria defeated Denmark in 1864.

■ **14. (A) is correct.** During the last quarter of the century, Friedrich Nietzsche attacked the Church's morals. He claimed that Christianity lauded weakness rather than encouraging human beings to courageous acts and heroic living

■ **15. (C) is correct.** Northern humanists tended to be more devoted to religious reforms than their Italian counterparts. Northern humanism was stimulated by the importation of Italian learning through students, merchants, and the Brothers of Common Life, an influential lay religious movement that began in the Netherlands.

■ **16. (C) is correct.** Some religious dissenters began to leave England during the reign of James I. James angered the Puritans by declaring his intention to maintain and even enhance the Anglican episcopacy. In 1620, Puritan separatists founded Plymouth Colony in North America. Later that decade a larger, better financed group of Puritans left England to found the Massachusetts Bay Colony.

■ **17. (C) is correct.** In the age of Walpole, British political life was generally freer than that on the Continent. There were definite limits on Walpole's power, even though he exercised a great deal of authority. Parliament had to address popular political pressure, and many members of Parliament maintained views independent to Walpole. Newspapers and public debate flourished, and there was no large standing army.

■ **18. (E) is correct.** Under Louis XIV's iron-fisted monarchical reign, freedom of speech, worship, and expression were strongly curtailed. Many *philosophes* were discontented with certain political features of their countries, but most especially in France. There the pervasive corruption of the royal court, numerous mistakes made by the administration, the overwhelming power of the Church, and the disappointing legacy of mid-century wars led to feelings of disgust.

■ **19. (C) is correct.** Robespierre was against the de-Christianization of France, because he believed it was an enormous political mistake. He is best known as a shrewd politician whose supporters, the *sans-culottes,* eventually turned against him after he executed some of the more extreme *sans-culottes* in the Terror.

■ **20. (B) is correct.** In 1871, Parisians elected a new municipal government, formally proclaimed the Paris Commune, that was intended to administer Paris separately from the rest of France. The National Guard of Paris sought to organize the city as an autonomous commune, an effort that was ultimately crushed by the National Assembly under Adolphe Thiers.

■ **21. (A) is correct.** Young and unmarried women were the employees of choice in most of the new service positions. Upon marriage, or after the birth of children, most women withdrew from the labor force. Employers preferred young, unmarried women whose family responsibilities would not interfere with their work. In the decades of the Second Industrial Revolution, a significant withdrawal of married women from the workplace occurred.

■ **22. (D) is correct.** Bismarck was relentlessly antisocialist in his policies and attitude toward the SPD, suppressing their party in every possible way. Eventually he undertook his own conservative alternatives to socialism, but he never embraced the socialist movement espoused by the SPD, and this stance ultimately led to his forced resignation.

■ **23. (C) is correct.** Virginia Woolf's *A Room of One's Own* challenged the idea that women should blindly imitate men and posed the idea that women should bring to all of their activities qualities of experience that they possessed by virtue of their gender.

■ **24. (A) is correct.** All the privileges based on birth that had marked the Old Regime and that had been overthrown during the revolution were officially abolished in the Napoleonic Code of 1804. In addition, laws of primogeniture were abolished, salaried officials were employed based on merit, men were granted increased control over their children (and husbands over their wives), and divorce remained difficult for women.

■ **25. (C) is correct.** In addition to their belief in the imagination as an example of God at work in the mind of man, the Romantics emphasized the individuality and worth of each separate people and culture. Romanticism was a move away from a rational approach to the world and a focus on absolute values. Instead, it recognized the supremacy of the individual's experience and imagination.

■ **26. (C) is correct.** Émile Zola wrote the newspaper article *"J'accuse"* ("I accuse") in reaction to the events of the so-called Dreyfus Affair. Zola argued that the army had convicted Captain Alfred Dreyfus on trumped-up charges and had plotted to forge evidence.

■ **27. (E) is correct.** Russian students and intellectuals disenchanted with the reforms of Alexander II drew on the ideas of Herzen and other radicals and formed a revolutionary movement known as populism. They sought a social revolution based on the communal life of the Russian peasants, but the peasants were distrustful of their agenda and turned them in to the Russian police.

■ **28. (B) is correct.** The Nazis focused their party efforts to convert groups experiencing pressure and economic uncertainty. They tailored their messages to appeal to the particular local problems that these groups confronted throughout Germany.

■ **29. (E) is correct.** In the course of intensifying the Cold War rhetoric, Ronald Reagan did not deploy a missile system in Asia, but he did do so in Europe.

■ **30. (B) is correct.** Martin Luther's "Ninety-five Theses" protested the impression created by indulgence preachers like John Tetzel that indulgences actually remitted sins and exculpated the dead from eternal punishment. Luther and his followers contended that this practice had no scriptural authority. Pope Leo X's revival of a plenary Jubilee indulgence spawned the activities of the indulgence preachers that Luther found so reprehensible. The Diet of Worms of 1521 was the forum in which Luther refused to recant his views on indulgences.

31. (A) is correct. Poland in the late-seventeenth century was characterized by an extremely strong aristocratic presence. The nobility in Poland became the single most powerful political factor in the country, but it refused to submit to authority. Deep distrust and divisions among the nobility prevented the election of a leader from among themselves, and so there was no effective central authority in the form of either a king or Parliament, with the exception of King John III Sobieski, who ruled from 1674-1696. As a result of these divisions, Poland had no way to collect enough taxes to build up an army.

32. (D) is correct. A "feminist" before the term existed, Mary Wollstonecraft was opposed to certain policies of the French Revolution that were unfavorable to women and had been espoused by Jean-Jacques Rousseau in his novel *Émile*. In *A Vindication of the Rights of Women,* Wollstonecraft exposed aspects of Rousseau's arguments that limited women's experience and independence. She argued that to confine women to the domestic sphere because of their supposed limitations of their physical nature was to condemn them to slavery. Marie-Thèrese Geoffrin, Julie de Lespinasse, and Claudine de Tencin were patrons who held salons that helped promote the careers of the *philosophes* by giving them social and political access and a receptive environment in which to circulate their ideas. Catherine the Great was the shrewd ruler of Russia who was familiar with the ideals of the Enlightenment, but who never completely abandoned a policy of absolutism during her rule.

33. (E) is correct. James Watt did not invent the steam engine, but he improved on an existing invention by Thomas Newcomen, who had developed the first practical steam engine early in the eighteenth century. Newcomen's invention was cumbersome and inefficient, but it was used by English operators in coal and tin mines. James Watt did not experiment with Newcomen's steam engine until the 1760s, when he developed an improved version that was more energy efficient and that eventually came into popular use.

34. (E) is correct. In Russia, and in Poland under Russian rule, prejudice and discrimination against Jews was severe. Under Russian rule, Jews were treated as foreigners and all aspects of community life were suppressed. After the revolutions of 1848, European Jews experienced improvements in their situation that lasted for several decades in Germany, Italy, the Netherlands, Scandinavia, Great Britain, and Austria-Hungary.

35. (D) is correct. After 1871, Bismarck sought to avoid any entanglements that might do away with his achievement of a large, powerful German empire.

36. (A) is correct. *Perestroika* was a policy instituted by Mikhail Gorbachev in the Soviet Union that meant "restructuring." Under the policy of *perestroika,* the Soviet Union proposed major economic and political reforms of the various centralized economic ministries, which were reduced in size and importance.

37. (C) is correct. John Calvin believed in predestination and the individual's responsibility to reorder society according to God's plan. According to John Calvin, "the elect" should live in a way that was pleasing to God.

38. (E) is correct. Peter the Great had a turbulent relationship with his only son, Alexis, who he believed was not prepared to inherit the throne because he refused to take military matters seriously. Jealous of his son and fearing that he might attempt to overthrow him, Peter had Alexis imprisoned in 1718, and during that time Alexis died under mysterious circumstances. Peter claimed his right to name a successor but never designated one, and when he died in 1725, there was no firm policy on succession to the throne.

- **39. (B) is correct.** Charles's supporters, also known as Cavaliers, lived primarily in the northwestern half of England. Parliamentary opposition, known as Roundheads because of their close-cropped hair, was based in the southeastern regions of the country. Supporters of both sides comprised a diverse demographic group, but Puritans tended to favor Parliament.
- **40. (A) is correct.** The aftermath of the "Peterloo Massacre" was the passage of a series of laws, called the *Six Acts.* These new laws cracked down on protest gatherings and—among other things—forbade unauthorized large groups from assembling in public.
- **41. (C) is correct.** The First International is associated with Karl Marx, who delivered its inaugural address in 1864. Though the First International counted among its members socialists, anarchists, Polish nationalists, and other political radicals, it enabled Marxism to emerge as the dominant socialist theory.
- **42. (D) is correct.** Franco entered Spain from Spanish Morocco to the south, and his armies gradually marched northward during 1936. Western cities such as Seville, Córdoba, Toledo, and Salamanca were occupied in this first year of the war, whereas Madrid was not occupied until March 1939.
- **43. (B) is correct.** Throughout 1990 and 1991, Gorbachev sought to negotiate new constitutional arrangements between the republics and the Soviet central government. His failure to effect such arrangements caused great discontent in Azerbaijan and Tajikistan, and Lithuania declared its independence.
- **44. (C) is correct.** Peasant leaders saw Martin Luther as a sympathetic figure, thanks in part to Luther's teaching about Christian freedom and his open criticism of monastic landowners. They sought Luther's support in their revolutionary attempts to abolish serfdom.
- **45. (E) is correct.** The 1598 Edict of Nantes was a confirmation of the promise Henry IV had made in 1591 to give Huguenots qualified religious freedoms. It recognized minority religious rights in an officially Catholic country and granted Huguenots freedom of public worship, the right of assembly, admission to public offices and universities, and permission to maintain fortified towns, but it did not improve the distrust between French Protestants and Catholics.
- **46. (C) is correct.** The term *ancien régime* refers to the conditions and institutions of pre-revolutionary Europe. Tradition, hierarchy, privilege, and an outmoded economy were some of the chief social characteristics of the *ancien régime.*
- **47. (B) is correct.** Facing the enormous advancing forces of Napoleon's army, the Russians followed a "scorched earth" policy, destroying all food and supplies as they retreated. The Russians' retreat disappointed Napoleon, who had hoped for a crucial battle that would enable his forces to demonstrate their superiority. Napoleon's army could not survive the severe food shortages, and extreme weather conditions ultimately eroded the morale of the French army, leading to Russian success.
- **48. (D) is correct.** The Bolsheviks, who had historically been political outsiders in European socialism, tended to treat with contempt other western European socialist parties that sought accommodation within their nations' political systems.
- **49. (B) is correct.** Karl Barth was a Swiss pastor who published *A Commentary on the Epistle to the Romans,* which re-emphasized the transcendence of God and the dependence of humankind on the divine. Barth portrayed God as wholly other than, and different from, humankind.
- **50. (B) is correct.** The portrait displays Elizabeth I in her most grand and imposing regalia. Her extremely elaborate clothing and regal bearing serve to underscore her role as ruler over

her countrymen. By portraying her standing on a map of England, the artist uses the painting as a metaphor for Elizabeth's domestic control over England.

■ **51. (B) is correct.** Chiaroscuro was a technique perfected during the Renaissance that involved using effects of light (chiaro) and dark (oscuro) in a painting to enhance naturalness and achieve a sense of modeling in figures. Drafting had existed prior to the Renaissance. Realism, surrealism, and expressionism were defined in later eras.

■ **52. (A) is correct.** The grouping of men, women, and children together occurred in European prisons prior to the nineteenth-century reforms, which tended to involve greater isolation and separation of prisoners.

■ **53. (B) is correct.** A *soviet* was a revolutionary council of workers and soldiers in tsarist Russia. Leon Trotsky led the powerful Petrograd *soviet*. The Bolsheviks demanded that all political power go to *soviets,* which they controlled.

■ **54. (A) is correct.** The U-2 incident of 1960 involved the Soviet Union shooting down an American U-2 aircraft that was flying reconnaissance over Soviet territory. Khrushchev demanded an apology from Eisenhower for this air surveillance. Eisenhower accepted full responsibility for the surveillance policy, but refused to apologize publicly.

■ **55. (B) is correct.** Under President Richard Nixon, the United States began a policy of *détente* with the Soviet Union, and the two countries concluded agreements on trade and on reducing strategic arms.

■ **56. (B) is correct.** The medieval theology that taught that God required perfect righteousness for salvation frustrated Martin Luther (who was well aware of his own sinful condition). Luther came to believe that man was justified in the eyes of God by his unswerving faith and nothing else. Rejecting the arguments made by the Church that God was satisfied by man's good works and that salvation was possible through indulgences, Luther articulated his theory of "justification by faith alone."

■ **57. (E) is correct.** The Scientific Revolution was influenced by many of the scientists and philosophers of the era: Galileo Galilei popularized the Copernican system of planetary motion and articulated the concept of a universe subject to mathematical laws; Isaac Newton discovered the laws of gravitation and upheld the importance of empirical data and observation; Francis Bacon dissented from the reliance on antiquity and Western scholasticism to understand contemporary phenomena and argued the importance of empirical evidence; René Descartes concluded that human reason could comprehend the world. All of these thinkers viewed nature with a growing scientific awareness, one based on the idea of *mechanism.* Nature understood as machinery removed much of the divine mystery of the world—these thinkers now looked to nature for utility, whereas they had previously looked to nature for symbolic or sacramental meaning.

■ **58. (B) is correct.** The Sugar Act was passed by Parliament in 1764 in response to a growing British sentiment that the American colonies should bear some of the cost of their protection and administration. The measure was designed to generate more revenue from imports into the colonies by the scrupulous collection of a tax. The Stamp Act was designed to increase revenue by taxing legal documents and items such as newspapers.

■ **59. (A) is correct.** The structure of Parliament and the election of the House of Commons gave owners of property and wealthy nobles dominance in the government of England. Because their positions in the House of Commons were not dependent on the will of the people, these leaders showed little interest in representing districts or being responsive to public opinion. These landowners were suspicious of the crown's role in government and sought to diminish royal influence by serving as local government administrators, judges, militia commanders, and tax collectors.

- **60. (B) is correct.** Most countries were appalled by the British Boer War against ill-prepared South African farmers. The general reaction of world opinion was one of hostility. Some countries, like Germany, openly sympathized with the Boers.
- **61. (A) is correct.** Western powers responded to the Berlin blockade by airlifting supplies into the city for almost a year. In May of 1949, the Russians had to back down and reopen access to Berlin, but the incident effectively accelerated the division of Berlin into eastern and western regions.
- **62. (C) is correct.** In July 1956, Egypt's President Gamal Abdel Nasser (1918–1970) nationalized the Suez Canal (it had been controlled previously by British and French interests). Egyptian control of the canal threatened British and French access to Persian Gulf oil supplies, which were essential to European industrial economies. When war broke out between Egypt and Israel in October 1956, Britain and France intervened to regain control of the canal.
- **63. (C) is correct.** During the eighteenth century, tensions arose between the nobles and the middle class involving issues of power sharing or access to political influence, rather than clashes over values or goals associated with class. Wealthy members of the middle class tended to imitate the lifestyle of the nobility by purchasing large estates, but these attempts at social mobility conflicted with the determination on the part of the nobles to maintain their own privileges and protect their own wealth.
- **64. (C) is correct.** This eighteenth-century cartoon mocks George III about the rebellion of the American colonies. The American colonies are depicted as a wild, ungovernable, willful horse throwing its rider—embodied in the caricature of George III. The cartoon makes fun of George III's futile attempts to impose his tyranny and control on the American colonies.
- **65. (B) is correct.** In the plebiscite of 1851, more than 7.5 million voters voted for Louis Napoleon and approved a new constitution that consolidated his power. In 1852, Louis Napoleon was made Emperor Napoleon III of the French Empire.
- **66. (C) is correct.** Nazi racial ideology focused on women as the bearers of both the desired and undesired races. Government policy rigorously attempted to eradicate the latter. During the Holocaust, this policy was used to target Jewish women for death, in part to prevent them from giving birth to a new generation of Jews.
- **67. (B) is correct.** In the late Middle Ages, kings worked through parliaments and the clergy worked through councils to place lasting limits on the pope's temporal power. The notion, derived from Roman law, that a secular ruler is accountable to the body of which he or she is head had already found expression in documents like the Magna Carta. True, unfettered democracy was not yet in place at this time; transfers of power could often throw countries into turmoil and war. Late medieval rulers depended on carefully negotiated alliances with lesser powers, relying on feudal relationships that stressed loyalty to a leader.
- **68. (A) is correct.** French national unity was strong in 1660 and by then, Louis XIV had sufficient resources to raise and maintain a powerful army and secure international boundaries for France in the north and south. His controller general of finances, Jean-Baptiste Colbert, had simplified the administrative bureaucracy and exerted careful control over the economy, transforming France into a major commercial power that was strong—but not yet a modern industrial economy.

69. (B) is correct. On the eve of the French Revolution, the interest and payments on the royal debt were equal to just over half of the national budget, an amount that was proportionate to the debts of other European powers. The government failed to utilize the wealth of the French nation to repay its debt.

70. (E) is correct. German reparations were not cancelled after the French invasion of the Ruhr; the invasion was an attempt to force Germany to comply with the reparations stipulations of the Versailles treaty. The English were alienated by the French heavy-handedness, took no part in the occupation, and became more suspicious of France and more sympathetic to Germany. The cost of the Ruhr occupation vastly increased French (as well as German) inflation and hurt the French economy.

71. (B) is correct. The Cheka was a secret military police that emerged shortly after the Bolshevik revolution.

72. (D) is correct. England was the single largest free-trade area in Europe. Its many newspapers advertised available consumer goods, and its economy was aided by demand from colonists in North America. The social structure encouraged a kind of class envy, whereby members of lower classes aspired to fashion themselves after their upper-class counterparts. London was the largest city in Europe and many thousands of British citizens and tourists were exposed to consumer products on visits there.

73. (E) is correct. During World War II, Soviet propaganda emphasized Russian patriotism rather than traditional Marxist themes that stressed class conflict. The struggle against the Germans was called "The Great Patriotic War."

74. (C) is correct. Edward VI was the monarch responsible for England's becoming a Protestant country. He was aligned with Calvin and the Protestant Reformation. In 1549, the Act of Uniformity imposed Thomas Cranmer's *Book of Common Prayer* on all English churches. Images and altars were removed from churches in 1550. Edward enacted the Second Act of Uniformity in 1552, which imposed a revised edition of the *Book of Common Prayer* on all English churches. A 42-article confession of faith was adopted, setting forth a moderate Protestant doctrine that taught justification by faith and the supremacy of the holy scripture.

75. (C) is correct. Newton's scientific research focused on the natural universe as a realm of law and regularity. The scientific study of nature permitted people to arrive at a closer understanding of the Creator of nature. Science and religious faith were not at odds with each other; rather, they reinforced each other. The religious thought associated with deducing of religious conclusions from nature became known as *physico-theology*.

76. (C) is correct. After the unsuccessful revolutions of 1848, conservative regimes made gains across the Continent. By the 1870s, many of the goals of the early-nineteenth-century liberals and nationalists had been accomplished and embraced under the auspices of conservative governments.

77. (E) is correct. Many European nations hoped that the colonies might attract their surplus population—not increase their populations in Europe. Imperialism was justified by politicians variously as a form of social policy, a way to bring culture to the unenlightened masses, a form of bolstering economies, and an antidote to the great depression of 1873–1896.

78. (D) is correct. The War of the Spanish Succession (1701–1714) and the Treaty of Utrecht (1713) replaced the Spanish Habsburgs with the Bourbons of France on the Spanish throne. Philip V (r. 1700–1746) and his successors tried to use French administrative skills to reassert the imperial trade monopoly, which had declined under the last Spanish Habsburgs.

In this way, they attempted to improve the domestic economy and revive Spanish power in European affairs. Trade expanded and became more varied, but economic life was still organized to benefit Spain's economy.

- **79. (A) is correct.** After the Popish Plot, Charles II was more suspicious than ever of Parliament, and he sought increased customs duties and the assistance of Louis XIV for additional income. He ruled from 1681–1685 without recalling Parliament, and he suppressed much of his opposition—by bullying local groups into electing members of Parliament who were obsequious, and by driving his enemies into exile. When he died in 1895, he left James a Parliament filled with monarchist supporters.
- **80. (C) is** correct. Blaise Pascal was a French mathematician and physical scientist who strove to pursue an austere, self-disciplined life. He allied himself with the Jansenists, Catholic adversaries of the Jesuits, who believed as Calvin did in the total sinfulness of human beings, predestination, and justification by faith.

Section II Part A

1. What advantages and disadvantages did female workers experience during the Industrial Revolution?

This DBQ requires you to *explain* and *consider* the experiences of women during the Industrial Revolution, and to respond in your answer to both the advantages and disadvantages that came about as a result of shifts in technology and the workforce. You might break the question down into:

WHO: women workers **WHAT:** advantages and disadvantages **WHEN:** the Industrial Revolution (1830–1860, roughly)

You do not need to limit your area of response to a particular country, but rather to a specific gender and subset (working women) and a social movement (Industrial Revolution) in your response.

As you read through the documents, pay close attention to the point of view (and potential bias) of each author or source. **DOCUMENT 3** contains an image of women working in an industrial setting. You can glean from the depiction that most of the people working in the factory are women engaged with large textile machinery. The artist represents the scene in what seems to be a neutral, documentary style. The image may prompt you to recall that most women who worked in factories during the Industrial Revolution were young unmarried women and widows who were willing to work for lower wages than men—and who frequently were given "unskilled" jobs that required the performance of certain repetitive tasks.

The source for **DOCUMENT 5**, the testimony of an 8-year-old mine worker delivered to Ashley's Mines Commission in 1842 (and published that year in the British *Parliamentary Papers*) suggests that a government body of some kind collected first-hand accounts of contemporary labor conditions. In this case, Sarah Gooder's impressions convey vividly her anxiety about the work she does—going into a dark "pit" for some kind of mining. Gooder's guileless, forthright descriptions are driven by personal—not political—concerns. This document may trigger your recollection of information about children who sometimes found themselves exploited for labor in the Industrial Revolution. For instance, you might recall that the English Factory Act of 1833, which forbade the employment of children under age nine, limited the workday of children older than nine and mandated daily education at the expense of the factory owner.

DOCUMENTS 9 and **10** may have been written by the same person, an English novelist named Eliza Lynn Linton—despite the fact that the views they express are in stark opposition. In **DOCUMENT 9**, Linton identifies with the situation of domestic servants by focusing on the discomfort and isolation of their living conditions in the houses of their employers. By contrast, the author of **DOCUMENT 10** contends that the lives of servants are vastly and instantly improved the moment they ascend from their own poverty-filled homes into the more comfortable rooms of their employers. Clearly these documents need to be paired in your response. The raw statistics complied by the British government and published in the *Parliamentary Papers* (**DOCUMENT 8**) show how the number of warehouse workers (both men and women) more than doubled in twenty years; they show also a decline in the number of agricultural workers. Both of these conditions were brought on in part by the Industrial Revolution. The statistics regarding domestic servants could perhaps reinforce your analysis of **DOCUMENTS 9** and **10.**

DOCUMENT 7 is a short excerpt from an article by the celebrated English novelist Charles Dickens. Though this document does not comment exclusively on women, it does make a claim that prisoners live in better conditions than the poor. Dickens's language ("monstrous pass," "dishonest felon," "honest pauper") give a clear indication of his bias: he champions the poor, the powerless, and the downtrodden. This document might be useful in a discussion about the poverty endured by women in the new workforce. Any knowledge you have about Dickens's tendency toward social commentary—such as can be found in novels such as *Hard Times, Oliver Twist,* and *Great Expectations*—will support your analysis of Dickens as sympathetic to various underclasses.

The source listing for **DOCUMENT 6** identifies the bias implicit in the lyrics of the poem or song. A contemporary German radical presents two persons—a factory owner and a female worker—in a situation that has both personal and political overtones. Though the factory owner seems to use a polite tone of voice as he addresses the worker, he is in fact exercising his economic power over her in order to exploit her sexually. Aston places herself in the role of the powerless worker, and we understand that her condemnation of such workplace oppressors is not only harsh but general. As a radical, she is interested in making a universal criticism of the unfair (even brutal) treatment of women workers by the lords of industry.

You might wish to group **DOCUMENTS 1**, **2**, and **4**, as all of them treat the effects of new machines on traditional weavers. Words such as *forced* and *lamentable* should help you recognize the bias implicit in the author(s) of **DOCUMENT 4**: The advent of power-looms made it difficult (if not impossible) for women to earn a living by weaving at home, and so they were forced to take factory jobs. Moreover, the fact that the text of **DOCUMENT 4** was written and printed as a letter to the editor indicates its intended purpose—to persuade others to recognize the difficult situation of female workers in the wake of the Industrial Revolution. **DOCUMENT 2**, from a contemporary history of cotton manufacture, considers how looms have improved the productivity of weaving, and compares that productivity to that which women could accomplish weaving at home. Overall, the historian seems to view industrialization favorably, as he emphasizes process and product over the ramifications for human laborers. **DOCUMENT 1** laments the possibility that textile factories will make it impossible for women to do weaving at home. Using powerful rhetorical questions, the author conveys his displeasure with the prospect of factory work weakening women and leaving them ill-prepared to do the work that would be required of them as farmer's wives.

Clearly the author prefers that women remain in the home, and he believes there is a danger of women losing the ability to perform domestic tasks—patching clothes, spinning, rearing children, and running a household—that are valuable to the fabric of contemporary society.

As you prepare your thesis, you should remember to consider both the advantages and disadvantages experienced by women in the workforce during the Industrial Revolution. One possible way of accommodating these competing ideas would to be to acknowledge both in your thesis, an example of which follows:

Although working women in the Industrial Revolution were exposed to new kinds of labor and machinery, for many women these technological advances were accompanied by discrimination and exploitation at the hands of their employers.

An excellent essay might group the documents as follows. After an introductory paragraph that incorporates a thesis, a subsequent paragraph would sketch a broad overview of some of the challenges facing working women during the Industrial Revolution. The responsibilities of family and work should be addressed, as some women did not have the option to remain home with their families in lieu of working. The Industrial Revolution brought with it a host of new social assumptions—for instance, that men should work outside the home and that women should be completely domestic and tend to home and family. Women who did work in the labor force tended to work at spinning and weaving. Introducing the conflicting sentiments in **DOCUMENTS 1**, **2**, and **4** would work well in an early discussion of some of the advantages and disadvantages women experienced during this time period.

A second paragraph might talk about the changing demographics of the workplace, and how young, unmarried women were preferable to married women as factory employees. The image in **DOCUMENT 3** and the chart in **DOCUMENT 8** would enable you to discuss how more young women (and, in the case of **DOCUMENT 5**, children) found themselves working no longer as agricultural laborers, but instead as weavers, miners, and textile workers.

A third paragraph could develop the idea that the Industrial Revolution pushed more women into cottage industries or into domestic servitude of the kind described in **DOCUMENTS 9** and **10** (and alluded to in the chart in **DOCUMENT 8**). Analyzing **DOCUMENT 10** would allow you to develop the idea that some of these domestic servants were living in better conditions than they might do otherwise—yet you should consider also that the same contemporary magazine (if not the same author) advocated the opposite position (**DOCUMENT 9**).

In discussing the advantages experienced by women, you might consider that they were able to earn an income to help themselves and their families, and that they could gain some satisfaction from their work. However, these gains were offset by the risk of exploitation, such as the kind described in **DOCUMENT 6**. You could also discuss the fact that many women were paid less than their male counterparts, a situation that led to a kind of endemic poverty among female factory laborers. This line of argument might allow you to incorporate Charles Dickens' comment about paupers in **DOCUMENT 7**.

By incorporating all of the documents, addressing the bias inherent in the sources, and introducing any outside information you may have on this subject, you should be able to construct an essay that reflects your ability to analyze and discuss this time period with tremendous ease and intellectual depth.

Sample Student Responses

2. *In what sense was the Reformation either the culmination of the medieval experience or the beginning of the modern age? Defend your position with specific examples.*

The Reformation caused a radical break in the Christian church, and this rupture anticipated the beginning of pluralism in western religious life. While it sprang from the discontent with some medieval traditions and aspects of medieval daily life, the Reformation represented the beginning of a new era in religious culture and European society.

The Reformation was a broad revolution against the practices and traditions of the medieval church. In 1517, when Martin Luther posted his "Ninety-five Theses" on the Castle Church at Wittenberg, he questioned and condemned the selling of indulgences and the traditional sacrament of penance that lay behind them. In addition, Luther and his followers protested the inattention of some members of the clergy, lapses in clerical celibacy and morality, and the *benefice* system which permitted clergy members to abandon their local congregations and live in Rome. The Lutheran protest came at a time of tremendous political and social discontent with the church. Many laypeople resented traditional clerical rights and privileges, like clerical exemptions from secular laws and taxes. Spiritual and secular protest combined to make the Protestant Reformation a successful assault on the old church. In town after town and region after region within Protestant lands, the major institutions and practices of traditional piety were significantly transformed.

While it is certainly true that the Reformation also challenged aspects of the Renaissance, including its glorification of human over divine nature, Protestant Reformation leaders tended to embrace aspects of the Renaissance that involved reform—including the area of education reform and the Renaissance humanists' return to ancient languages. For Protestant reformers, the study of Greek and Hebrew scripture enabled them to ground their refutations of traditional medieval institutions in biblical authority.

Luther's posting of his theses effectively divided western Christendom into Protestant and Catholic camps. While other reformers like Ulrich Zwingli, John Calvin, and the Anabaptists, Spiritualists, and Antitrinitarians would also emerge in this climate of Protestant reform, the single most important division occurred between Catholics and Protestants, two groups that would always remain apart as a result of this development. As a result of the Reformation, the pluralism that defines contemporary religious culture was born.

3. *Compare the importance of the imagination in the works of Romantic writers and the importance of reason in the works of Enlightenment writers. Illustrate your answer with references to specific individuals and their works.*

During the eighteenth century, leading Enlightenment figures challenged the intellectual authority of tradition and the Christian past, spurred on by their faith in the power of rational criticism and their confidence in the human mind and human enterprise. The writers and critics who forged the attitudes of the Enlightenment, called *philosophes,* sought to apply the rules of reason and common sense to nearly all major institutions and practices of the day. The *philosophes* believed that reason and rationality enabled all kinds of social reforms.

The rationality of the physical universe became a standard against which the customs and traditions of society could be measured and criticized. The chief bond among the *philosophes* was their common desire to reform thought, society, and government for the sake of human liberty. Many were influenced by the work of Isaac Newton, whose gravitational theory convinced them that nature was rational, that the God who had created nature *must* be rational, and that the religion through which God was worshiped *should* be rational. This led to the rise of deism, a faith that promoted religion as natural and rational rather than supernatural and mystical.

The Enlightenment period is most closely associated with Diderot and d'Alembert's publication of *The Encyclopedia* in 1772. This monumental book was a collective plea for freedom of expression, and it included the most advanced critical ideas of the time on religion, government, and philosophy. Some *philosophes,* such as Voltaire, felt that Church hindered pursuit of a rational life and the scientific study of humanity and nature. For the Enlightenment *philosophes,* reason and the rational life represented all of the best advances of their society.

Romanticism was a reaction against much of Enlightenment thought. It is helpful to consider imagination and reason as radically opposed in the minds of Romantic and Enlightenment thinkers. Imagination represented something almost spiritual, a kind of divine inspiration to Romantics, whereas reason referred to the empirical justification for drawing conclusions to Enlightenment *philosophes*. Romantic writers accused the *philosophes* of demeaning feelings and imagination to geometrical and scientific models. Romantic thinkers were interested in understanding physical nature and human society in organic (rather than rational) terms and categories. Unlike the *philosophes,* the Romantics celebrated all things medieval. They were fascinated by folklore, folk songs, and fairy tales. The Romantics were also interested in dreams, hallucinations, sleepwalking, and any phenomena that alluded to the existence of a world beyond the rational one. Many of these writers urged a revival of Christianity, such as had permeated Europe during the Middle Ages.

Immanuel Kant was a leading philosopher of the Romantic era, and his best-known work, *A Critique of Pure Reason,* refuted much of the rationality of the Enlightenment. The Romantics believed in the presence of a special power in the human mind that could transcend the limits of passive human understanding set forth by Enlightenment thinkers like Locke, Hobbes, and Hume. Many Romantics believed that poets and artists possessed this "intuition" or "imagination" in abundance. In his novel, *Émile,* Jean-Jacques Rousseau articulated a concept of human development that emphasized rearing children with maximum individual freedoms. To Romantic writers, this concept of human development promoted the rights of nature over those of (artificial) rational society. In their groundbreaking *Lyrical Ballads,* the English Romantics Wordsworth and Coleridge delivered a manifesto of a new poetry that rejected the rules of eighteenth-century criticism. Poems like "Ode on Intimations of Immortality" by Wordsworth addressed the question of poetic vision, which Wordsworth believed was influenced by the closeness to spiritual reality experienced by children. For Wordsworth and Coleridge and other Romantics, imagination represented the highest, most intuitive level of understanding possible for human beings.

4. *Analyze the causes of the collapse of communism in Eastern Europe and the Soviet Union.*

The collapse of the Soviet Union is unique in history, because the nation basically imploded from within and divided into separate successor states. No foreign invasion, military defeat, or internal revolution caused its collapse. While many of the factors leading to the Soviet collapse remain unknown, a relatively clear case can be made for the known factors that contributed to its fall.

Mikhail Gorbachev's rise to power in 1985 was a significant factor in the collapse of the Soviet Union. He introduced reforms that radically altered the country and ended both Communist rule and the Soviet Union itself as it had existed since 1917. Policies such as *perestroika* ("restructuring") and *glasnost* ("openness") dramatically altered the Soviet landscape. Gorbachev challenged the Communist party with his radical policies, but many of these policies did not achieve all that he had hoped they would. For instance, the Soviet economy remained stagnated, and shortages of food and housing became chronic.

Gorbachev's policies in the Soviet Union had deleterious effects on the army, an institution that traditionally had enjoyed enormous prestige and public support. Gorbachev made funding decisions regarding the military that lowered morale; a series of clashes between the military and minority ethnic groups challenging the government led to further loss of morale in the military ranks. Spending cuts led to the further disintegration of the Soviet armed forces. In 1990, Gorbachev proposed that the Soviet Communist party abandon its position as the lone legal party. This action followed similar actions by several of the Communist parties in Eastern Europe.

In 1989, Poland appointed a non-Communist prime minister, and Gorbachev approved the appointment. A series of Soviet-dominated states in Eastern Europe moved toward independence and splintered away from the communism of the Soviet Union. The Hungarian government opened its border with Austria; thousands of East Germans moved into Austria through Hungary, and then into West Germany. The East German government resigned, enabling the rise to power of a younger generation of Communist leaders who remained in office for just a few weeks. In November 1989, the government of East Germany opened the Berlin Wall, inaugurating free travel between East and West Germany. By 1990, Germany underwent a full reunification. Revolution in Czechoslovakia led to the election of Vaclav Havel, a former prisoner of the Communist government, as president. These revolutions could not have occurred if the Soviet Union had intervened militarily. Gorbachev's policy enabled thousands of citizens to denounce Communist party domination and to express their desire for democracy.

By 1990, Gorbachev faced challenges from three major political forces. Conservative members appointed by Gorbachev in late 1990 and early 1991 wanted to preserve the influence of the Communist party and the Soviet army. A second group, headed by Boris Yeltsin, wanted more extensive and rapid change, and this group was critical of Gorbachev's authority. The third force was regional unrest in the Soviet republics of Latvia, Estonia, and Lithuania. Gorbachev used military force to resist the efforts of these Baltic republics to gain their independence from the Soviet Union. Riots broke out in Azerbaijan and Tajikistan, where the army was used against Soviet citizens. Gorbachev failed to negotiate new constitutional arrangements with these republics, and this failure may have been the single most important reason for the collapse of the Soviet Union.

The conservatives staged a coup in 1991, but the coup collapsed after two days. Yeltsin became a dominant political figure, and in the months immediately afterward, the Communist party—compromised by its participation in the coup—collapsed as a political force.

5. *Discuss several of the advances made during the Agricultural Revolution.*

The Agricultural Revolution occurred around the time that the European population was growing and contributing to a steady rate of inflation. This inflation included rising prices for grain, which benefited landowners and aristocrats. Landowners could improve their incomes and overall lifestyle by selling grain at a profit. In order to do so, landowners introduced a series of innovations in farm production known today as the Agricultural Revolution.

Landowners and farmers began to improve agricultural production in the Netherlands in the sixteenth and seventeenth centuries, using new techniques of draining and fortifying land to protect it from the elements and erosion. In addition, they experimented with new crops that were less damaging to the soil. English landlords and innovators implemented numerous agricultural improvements in the eighteenth century. They borrowed heavily from the successes of the Dutch, incorporating many of the concepts popularized in the Netherlands. The landowner Jethro Tull experimented and helped finance the experiments of others. Tull instituted the use of an iron plow to till the earth more deeply. He also developed the technique of planting wheat with a drill rather than by casting seeds. Tull did not advocate the use of manure as fertilizer—an oversight that would be corrected in later generations. As a result of his experiments, land was able to be cultivated for longer periods before it had to be left fallow.

Another important innovator was Charles "Turnip" Townsend, who gained knowledge from the Dutch agricultural *avant-garde*. Townsend instituted crop rotation and alternated crops in fields to help restore essential nutrients to the soil. Townsend also learned how to cultivate sandy soil with fertilizers. Townsend's advances enabled the growth of more livestock, because of his supply of additional animal fodder from crops. As a result, more food existed for humans and animals. Finally, Robert Bakewell pioneered new methods in animal husbandry that helped produce healthier animals and more animals, and milk and meat of improved quality. All of these advances contributed significantly to the successes of the Agricultural Revolution.

6. *Discuss the Nazi regime's view of women and of their place in German society.*

Women in the Nazi regime were most strongly identified with their traditional roles as wives and mothers. Hitler and his Nazi followers believed that women's place was in the domestic sphere and that men belonged in the active sphere. Women who sought liberation and who adopted traditionally masculine roles were social pariahs in the Nazi regime. When women's employment was encouraged in Germany during the Depression of the 1930s, women were urged to pursue employment that was suitable for their sex, including agricultural labor, teaching, nursing, social service, and domestic service. Women were expected to transmit the cultural and national values of the German society to their children—that is, to teach them how to cook, dress, and behave, and to instill in them a respect for their country's traditions.

A vocal minority of Nazi feminists urged greater equality among men and women, but they did not succeed in influencing the policies of the party. Adolph Hitler dismissed this desire for the emancipation of women, calling it an invention of Jewish intellectuals. He characterized the German program for women in society as focused entirely on women's roles as mothers and wives.

The Nazis were obsessed with the notion that women must help to perpetuate the racial purity of the German people. Women were to breed offspring for the German nation. Women giving birth were compared to men engaged in battle—each gender serving the state in its particular ways. Nazi racial ideology focused on women as the carriers and bearers of both desired and undesired races. During the Holocaust, Jewish women were specifically targeted for death, in part to prevent them from bearing a new generation of German Jews.

To support motherhood among those women they wanted to perpetuate the purified German race, the Nazis provided loans to encourage early marriage, gave tax cuts for families with children, and also provided child allowances. Of course, the Nazis sent these subsidies and payments to husbands rather than to wives, further emphasizing how German women needed to tether themselves to a husband and family in order to stay afloat financially.

7. *Discuss the transformation from the Second Empire of Napoleon III to the establishment of the Third Republic in France.*

The Second Empire effectively fell when Napoleon III became involved in the Franco-Prussian War. The war of 1870 against Prussia had been the French government's attempt to support its foreign policy and secure domestic popularity. Napoleon III was captured after the Battle of Sedan in 1870, imprisoned, and exiled to Britain. Shortly after news of the battle reached Paris, a republic was proclaimed and a government of national defense was established. The Prussian conflict moved into the capital at this point, with Paris surrendering in January 1871.

A National Assembly was elected in February 1871, but division between the provinces and Paris intensified. The National Assembly gave power to Adolphe Thiers, an avowed monarchist, who negotiated a settlement with Prussia that involved the continued military occupation of Paris until an indemnity was paid. Many Parisians were unhappy with the monarchist tendencies of the National Assembly, and they elected a new municipal government, which they named the Paris Commune, in March 1871. The Paris Commune was designed to administer Paris separately from France, and it especially appealed to radicals and socialists.

In response to the threat to its authority, the National Assembly surrounded Paris with an army that bombarded the city (killing about 20,000 inhabitants) and restored order. Though Karl Marx and Vladimir Lenin would later claim the Paris Commune as a major victory for international socialism, the socialism of the Commune had its roots in Blanqui's and Proudhon's anarchism rather than in Marx's concept of class conflict. The goal of the Paris Commune was a nation composed of relatively independent, radically democratic cooperatives. Its suppression represented the defeat of an alternative political group by a centralized nation-state.

The National Assembly and Adolphe Thiers soon began promoting a republican form of government that did not appeal to the monarchists. The monarchists ousted Thiers from office and elected Marshal MacMahon, who was expected to prepare for a monarchist restoration. In 1875, the National Assembly decided to standardize the political system of enfranchisement, adopting a law that provided for a Chamber of Deputies elected by universal male suffrage, a Senate chosen indirectly, and a president elected by the two legislative houses.

MacMahon resigned in 1879, and dedicated republicans generally controlled the national government. The Third Republic was a strong political structure that survived challenges to its leadership from General Georges Boulanger and several internal scandals involving corruption. It also endured the "Dreyfus affair," the controversial (and fraudulent) case against a Jewish member of the military.

AP EUROPEAN HISTORY

SAMPLE PRACTICE TEST 2

European History
Section I

Time: 55 minutes 80 Questions

Directions: Each of the questions or incomplete statements below is followed by five suggested answers or completions. Select the one that is best in each case and then fill in the corresponding oval on the answer sheet.

1. In the late fifteenth century, taxation and enforcement of the laws were assumed by
   (A) monarchs.
   (B) feudal warlords.
   (C) nobles.
   (D) representative legislatures.
   (E) semi-autonomous vassals.

2. The 1628 Petition of Right issued by Parliament to Charles I was all of the following EXCEPT
   (A) a declaration of constitutional freedom.
   (B) an expression of resentment.
   (C) an expression of resistance to the monarchy's power at the local level.
   (D) a demand that no loans or taxation could be made without Parliamentary consent.
   (E) a demand that King Charles I abdicate his throne.

3. The Game Laws exemplified what aspect of eighteenth-century social life in Britain?
   (A) a governmental willingness to overlook gambling
   (B) a nascent environmentalism
   (C) preferential treatment for aristocrats
   (D) fair policies for British landowners and city-dwellers alike
   (E) restrictive policies on aristocratic privilege

4. The famous "Tennis Court Oath" of 1789 resulted in
   (A) a commitment by the National Assembly to write a new French constitution.
   (B) the start of the French Revolution.
   (C) Louis XVI's abdication.
   (D) rioting in Paris.
   (E) a permanent rift between the Third and First estates.

5. The 1819 suppression of the *Burschenschaften* was accomplished by which European
    monarch?
    (A) Prince Klemens von Metternich of Austria (1773–1859)
    (B) Viscount Castlereagh (1769–1822)
    (C) Lord Liverpool (1770–1828)
    (D) Louis XVIII (r. 1814–1824)
    (E) Tsar Alexander I (r. 1801–1825)

6. The years after the Crimean War were characterized by
    (A) instability in European affairs.
    (B) Prussian aggression being held in check by the Concert of Europe..
    (C) France and Austria holding the Concert of Europe together in the face of Italian and
        German unification.
    (D) British maintenance of military forces on the Continent to preserve the Concert of
        Europe.
    (E) a stable and uninterrupted peace among nations.

7. The cartoon above, which represents Bismarck and Pope Pius IX seeking to outmaneuver
    each other in a game of chess, parodies what aspect of *Kulturkampf?*
    (A) the German effort to incorporate cultural activities into the Catholic education system
    (B) the Catholic hierarchy's desire to engage the German government and improve their
        relations
    (C) the hostility between Bismarck and the Catholic church
    (D) Pope Pius's light-hearted attitude about religious observance
    (E) the rampant opportunities for graft in dealings between Bismarck and the Catholic
        Church

8. Slavery in Italy during the Renaissance
    (A) disappeared.
    (B) decreased from its ancient-world numbers.
    (C) was thriving and widespread.
    (D) stagnated as a result of the Plague.
    (E) involved African slaves exclusively.

9. Why was Parliament victorious in the English Civil War?
   (A) The king had no support from the English people.
   (B) The king was supported mainly by lower-middle-class subjects.
   (C) Parliament was able to bar Presbyterians from attendance in 1648.
   (D) Cromwell reorganized the army, and Parliament accepted the Solemn League and
       Covenant with Scotland.
   (E) John Milton's defense of Parliament roused the English people to rebel against the king.

10. Which of the following best describes the trading relationship between India and Britain and
    between India and France during the eighteenth century?
    (A) Piracy was endemic to overseas trade.
    (B) India's products were not desired by Europeans.
    (C) Each country traded through a chartered company that enjoyed a legal monopoly.
    (D) Europeans were unable to establish trading posts in these regions.
    (E) Asians were not interested in setting up trade markets with Europeans.

11. All of the following are true of the French war against Austria in 1792 EXCEPT
    (A) Louis XVI favored it in the hopes that it would restore the *ancien régime*.
    (B) it led to a second revolution that overthrew the monarchy and established a republic.
    (C) it radicalized the revolution.
    (D) the Girondists believed that it would preserve the revolution from domestic enemies.
    (E) it strengthened domestic support for Louis XVI.

12. Which of the following best characterizes the aims of the Concert of Europe?
    (A) It sought to prevent nations from gaining colonial empires.
    (B) It sought to prevent member nations from entering into non-aggression treaties with other
        member nations.
    (C) It sought to maintain international peace and prevent member nations from taking major
        actions in international affairs without member assent.
    (D) It sought to extend principles of conservative government throughout Europe.
    (E) It sought to hold member nations financially responsible for damages incurred in
        international conflicts.

13. German unification in the second half of the nineteenth century was dramatically
    strengthened by
    (A) the liberal Prussian Parliament.
    (B) the conservative policies of Otto von Bismarck.
    (C) the acquisition of Schleswig from Denmark.
    (D) the *Zollverein* (tariff union).
    (E) heavy taxes approved by the Prussian Parliament.

14. All of the following were elements of Leo XIII's 1891 encyclical *Rerum Novarum* EXCEPT
    (A) a defense of private property, religious education, and religious control of marriage laws.
    (B) a defense of the right of employees to be paid properly and treated fairly by their
        employers.
    (C) an opposition to labor unions.
    (D) a condemnation of Marxism and socialism.
    (E) a desire to reorganize society according to Christian corporate groups.

15. Historians would be most likely to cite this famous title page illustration for Hobbes's
    Leviathan as an example of
    (A) the distance of the ruler from the desires and needs of the people over which he rules.
    (B) the insecurity and fear of destruction and death that constantly haunted human beings.
    (C) the generosity and goodwill of the sovereign.
    (D) the dangers of tyrannical rule and unchecked power of political and governmental
        leaders.
    (E) rulers as absolute lords over their lands, incorporating in their persons the individual wills
        of all their people.

16. Which phrase best sums up the spirit of Louis XIV's government?
    (A) "Traditional liberties"
    (B) "I am the state."
    (C) "The Sufferer"
    (D) "Thorough"
    (E) "King of straw"

17. Sixteenth-century European slave traders
    (A) were universally reviled by African societies.
    (B) sometimes acquired slaves from Africans selling other Africans.
    (C) were typically English.
    (D) brought the slave trade to Africa.
    (E) were typically Dutch

18. The success of the French Revolution
   (A) enabled France to make an alliance with its former rival, Great Britain.
   (B) intensified existing reform movements throughout Europe.
   (C) had little effect on reform movements elsewhere in Europe.
   (D) made the French increasingly isolationist and wary of foreign entanglements.
   (E) brought other reform movements in Europe to a rapid close.

19. Brazilian independence in 1822
   (A) came about as the result of a series of bloody battles.
   (B) was resisted by Dom Pedro and his Portuguese army.
   (C) came about thanks to the support of Dom Pedro.
   (D) was forged by a coalition government of Creoles, Portuguese, and Mestizos.
   (E) was delayed by Brazil's wars with local Indians.

20. After 1860, Napoleon III became increasingly liberal in his domestic policies in response to
   (A) rioting in Paris by radicals.
   (B) the stable French economy.
   (C) a more conservative French bureaucracy.
   (D) severe problems in the French economy.
   (E) his unsuccessful foreign policy.

21. In Sigmund Freud's most important book, *The Interpretation of Dreams,* he argues that
   (A) unconscious drives and desires contribute to conscious behavior.
   (B) there is no mediation between the id and the ego.
   (C) the content of dreams have no reason able scientific explanation.
   (D) sexuality can be determined during infancy.
   (E) dreams contain little or no valuable information about a person's psyche.

22. Scientific experimentation and investigation during the sixteenth and seventeenth centuries was
   (A) largely an informal endeavor.
   (B) funded exclusively by universities.
   (C) condemned by the Church.
   (D) discouraged by the monarchy.
   (E) embraced by the Church.

23. The chief difference between the Whigs and the Tories after the Hanoverian succession in 1714 was that
   (A) the Tories were more oriented toward social reform than were the Whigs.
   (B) the Whigs had access to public office and royal patronage, whereas the Tories did not.
   (C) the Whigs represented the views of the lower classes, whereas the Tories represented the ideology of the upper classes.
   (D) the Tories were organized like a modern political party, and the Whigs were organized according to local connections and economic influence.
   (E) the Whigs were organized like a modern political party, and the Tories were organized according to local connections and economic influence.

24. Which of the following was NOT an outcome of the terms of the Treaty of Paris of 1763?
    (A) Britain received all of Canada, the Ohio River Valley, and the eastern half of the Mississippi River Valley.
    (B) Britain surrendered conquests in India the French.
    (C) France received Guadeloupe.
    (D) France received Martinique.
    (E) Britain surrendered Canada to the French.

25. The Thermidorian Reaction of 1794 consisted of all of the following EXCEPT
    (A) the executions of some former terrorists.
    (B) the establishment of the Directory.
    (C) the destruction of the machinery of terror.
    (D) the institution of a constitutional regime.
    (E) amnesty for Jacobins.

26. Russian government from 1801 to 1855, during the reigns of Alexander I and Nicholas I, is best characterized as
    (A) open to limited democratic reforms.
    (B) extremely autocratic.
    (C) republican.
    (D) socialist.
    (E) violently opposed to the role of the Russian Orthodox Church.

27. The March Laws passed by the Hungarian diet and approved by Emperor Ferdinand in 1848 ensured all of the following EXCEPT
    (A) equality of religion.
    (B) a relatively free press.
    (C) payment of taxes by the nobility.
    (D) jury trials.
    (E) the establishment of a separate Hungarian state within the Habsburg domains.

28. The *benefice* system
    (A) was a reform that Martin Luther fervently advocated in his "Ninetyfive Theses."
    (B) facilitated increased interaction between parishes and priests.
    (C) allowed ecclesiastical positions to be auctioned off to the highest bidder.
    (D) secured parishioners a place in the afterworld.
    (E) met the need for a more personal piety and a more informed religious life.

29. Cardinal Richelieu sought
    (A) support for Catholicism abroad, but not in France.
    (B) decentralization of the French government.
    (C) oppression of Catholicism in France and abroad.
    (D) the revocation of the Edict of Nantes.
    (E) support for the Catholic cause at home, and support for the Protestant cause abroad.

30. In pre-industrial Europe, "servant" referred to someone
    (A) who ministered to the needs of the affluent.
    (B) who received room, board, and wages in exchange for household responsibilities.
    (C) with the social status of a serf.
    (D) who served as an artisan or craftsperson.
    (E) who tended to be married, elderly, and employed as a "jack-of-all trades" by more than one family at a time.

31. Which of the following was the group of writers and critics who fostered reformist attitudes during the Enlightenment?
    (A) Utilitarians
    (B) Professors
    (C) Enlightened despots
    (D) *Philosophes*
    (E) Courtiers

	POPULATION (TOTAL)	SOLDIERS POTENTIALLY AVAILABLE	MILITARY EXPENDITURES (1913–1914)	BATTLESHIPS IN SERVICE OR BEING BUILT	CRUISERS	SUBMARINES	MERCHANT SHIPS (TONS)
GREAT BRITAIN	45,000,000 (Overseas Emp. 390 Million)	711,000	250,000,000	64	121	64	20,000,000
FRANCE	40,000,000 (Overseas Emp. 58 Million)	1,250,000	185,000,000	28	34	73	2,000,000
ITALY	35,000,000 (Overseas Emp. 2 Million)	750,000	50,000,000	14	22	12	1,750,000
RUSSIA	164,000,000	1,200,000	335,000,000	16	14	29	750,000
BELGIUM	7,500,000	180,000	13,750,000				
ROMANIA	7,500,000	420,000	15,000,000				
GREECE	5,000,000	120,000	3,750,000				
SERBIA	5,000,000	195,000	5,250,000				
MONTENEGRO	500,000						
UNITED STATES	92,000,000	150,000	150,000,000	37	35	25	4,500,000
GERMANY	65,000,000	2,200,000	300,000,000	40	57	23	5,000,000
AUSTRIA-HUNGARY	50,000,000	810,000	110,000,000	16	12	6	1,000,000
OTTOMAN EMPIRE	20,000,000	360,000	40,000,000				
BULGARIA	4,500,000	340,000	5,500,000				

32. All of the following statements about the combatants in World War I can be deduced from the chart above EXCEPT
    (A) England and France had a strategic advantage over Germany in terms of their submarine power.
    (B) Russia's population exceeded the com bined population of France and Great Britain(excluding their overseas empires).
    (C) the number of soldiers potentially available in Belgium was about half of the number available in the Ottoman Empire.
    (D) France had about 50,000 more soldiers available than did Russia.
    (E) the combined military expenditures of the Ottoman Empire and Austria-Hungary were less than the military expenditures of the United States.

33. Mikhail Gorbachev's *glasnost* policy included all of the following EXCEPT
   (A) release of dissidents from prison.
   (B) allowance of criticism of the government.
   (C) allowance of national minority demonstrations.
   (D) the end of the Cold War.
   (E) freedom of expression.

34. The *Marburg Colloquy* resulted in
   (A) the Swiss Civil Wars.
   (B) a newfound respect between Zwingli and Calvin.
   (C) divisions between members of the Reformation movement.
   (D) Luther's excommunication
   (E) a compromise between the Tetrapolitan and Augsburg confessions.

35. Which was the source of many of the agricultural reforms later adopted and expanded upon
   in Britain during the Agricultural Revolution?
   (A) Spain
   (B) Germany
   (C) France
   (D) Poland
   (E) The Low Countries

36. All of the following were reforms demanded by the program of Chartism EXCEPT
   (A) payment of salaries to members of the House of Commons.
   (B) universal manhood suffrage.
   (C) the secret ballot.
   (D) annual elections in the House of Commons.
   (E) the maintenance of the property requirement for members of the House of Commons.

37. By the terms of the *Entente Cordiale* of 1902,
   (A) Britain was obliged to aid Russia in the event of a German invasion.
   (B) Britain was obliged to aid France in the event of an invasion.
   (C) Britain and France patched up colonial differences without making a formal alliance.
   (D) France and Spain became allies.
   (E) Britain and France made a formal alliance against Japan.

38. During the Great Depression,
   (A) the numbers of employed always well exceeded the numbers of those without work.
   (B) the majority of Europeans were without a job.
   (C) product quality declined.
   (D) government regulation of industry decreased.
   (E) a business-as-usual attitude prevailed.

39. Which of the following best describes the changing attitudes of western Europeans in the fifteenth century, on the eve of the Reformation?
    (A) Growing interest in eastern religions
    (B) Desire for global expansion
    (C) Renewed interest in medieval art
    (D) Fear of the printed word
    (E) Disdain for the institution of slavery

40. The map above shows
    (A) the slow, gradual erosion of the Royalist position in 1645.
    (B) the decline of Parliamentarian power in 1645.
    (C) the rapid deterioration of the Royalist position in 1645.
    (D) the importance of the Battle of Turnham Green.
    (E) the reasons for Oliver Cromwell's invasion of Ireland.

41. As a result of revolutionary activity in France, the largest new propertied group to emerge was
    (A) the peasants.
    (B) the *sans-culottes*.
    (C) the Church.
    (D) the nobility.
    (E) the bourgeoisie.

42. Nineteenth-century proletarianization was characterized by
    (A) patronage of workers by the owner of a factory.
    (B) the gradual control of workers in setting the wages and working conditions for a factory.
    (C) the gradual loss of workers' ownership of the means of production and of control over their own trades.
    (D) the gradual lowering of the cultural level of society due to the influx of the poor into urban areas.
    (E) the use of local artisans in factories to restore craftsmanship to the engines of mass production.

43. The Eiffel Tower was built in 1889
    (A) as the major entrance to the city of Paris.
    (B) as a symbol of French cultural superiority.
    (C) as a temporary structure for the international trade exposition.
    (D) as a radio tower that would enable France to conduct espionage on its neighbors.
    (E) from funds collected from schoolchildren.

44. Nineteenth-century British imperialism was centered in which area of Africa?
    (A) Egypt and southern Africa
    (B) East Africa
    (C) West Africa
    (D) Senegal
    (E) Algeria

45. The first Labour ministry in British history under Ramsay MacDonald
    (A) sought to institute public seizure of industry.
    (B) established Labour as a viable governing power, and effectively ended the Liberal party.
    (C) reduced British unemployment significantly.
    (D) returned the country to the gold standard.
    (E) radically transformed the British political landscape.

46. Stalin's power and influence lay in his
    (A) oratorical abilities.
    (B) brilliant writings and theories.
    (C) mastery of the crucial details of the party structure.
    (D) military abilities.
    (E) diplomatic finesse.

47. The "Black Legend" was
    (A) an untrue story of an Indian leader who massacred Spanish missionaries.
    (B) the Native American origin myth shared with Spanish conquerors.
    (C) the true story of an Indian leader who massacred Spanish missionaries.
    (D) an encyclopedic book written about victims of the Black Death.
    (E) an account of Spanish mistreatment of the Indians.

48. Which of the following events helped bring about the 1572 Saint Bartholomew's Day
massacre?
   (A) Catherine de Médicis's support for a radical Catholic faction
   (B) Catherine de Médicis's insinuation that a Huguenot coup was about to occur
   (C) The assassination attempt against Catherine de Médicis by Gaspard de Coligny
   (D) A coup led by Gaspard de Coligny to wrest the crown from Catherine de Médicis
   (E) Henry of Navarre's divorce from Marguerite of Valois

49. All of the following are true of Louis XV EXCEPT
   (A) his uncle, the duke of Orléans, served as regent and weakened the power of the
       monarchy.
   (B) Cardinal Fleury served as his chief adviser.
   (C) he was not an effective monarch.
   (D) his personal life generated considerable court gossip and scandal.
   (E) despite his shortcomings, his political leadership inspired the French people.

50. Which of the following Romantic figures is renowned for his philosophical theory of the
evolutionary development of ideas?
   (A) Hegel
   (B) Kant
   (C) Rousseau
   (D) Herder
   (E) Goethe

51. By the 1830s, which social group took the lead in formulating protections for their political
and economic interests?
   (A) factory workers
   (B) workshop masters
   (C) displaced farmers
   (D) teachers
   (E) urban artisans

52. All of the following were major developments in Europe between 1860 and 1914 EXCEPT
   (A) centralized bureaucracies decreased in importance
   (B) socialism became a major political force
   (C) increasing numbers of white-collar workers appeared
   (D) the labor force became organized into unions
   (E) urban life came to dominate society

53. Which of the following best characterizes the impact of World War I on the trend of modernism in literature?
   (A) Modernism did not exist prior to World War I.
   (B) Modernism flourished after World War I, nourished by the turmoil and social dislocation it created.
   (C) World War I effectively ratified old political structures and social expectations and did not dramatically affect modernism.
   (D) Readers were more shocked by the upheavals in literary forms brought on by modernism after World War I than they had been previously.
   (E) Modernism did not change dramatically after World War I.

54. At various points in time, William of Orange professed which of the following religious ideologies?
   (A) Catholicism, Lutheranism, Calvinism
   (B) Catholicism, Lutheranism, Anabaptistism
   (C) Lutheranism, Calvinism, Anabaptistism
   (D) Lutheranism, Catholicism, Antitrinitarianism
   (E) Calvinism, Lutheranism, Antitrinitarianism

55. All of the following conditions enabled the British economy to survive the "Continental System" of Napoleon EXCEPT
   (A) Britain still controlled the seas.
   (B) Britain had access to the markets of North and South America.
   (C) Britain had access to the markets of the eastern Mediterranean.
   (D) Continental members were resentful of the economic advantages of the system for France, and they engaged in smuggling whenever possible.
   (E) Britain brokered separate deals with Spain and Portugal that enabled them to trade.

56. The theory that the human population grows geometrically while the food supply can expand only arithmetically is most commonly associated with which of the following thinkers?
   (A) Saint-Simon
   (B) Robert Owen
   (C) Thomas Malthus
   (D) Charles Fourier
   (E) Louis Blanc

57. The most dynamic force for change in the revolutions of 1848 originated with which of the following groups?
   (A) Political liberals
   (B) Working classes
   (C) Disgruntled military personnel
   (D) Middle classes
   (E) Political elites

58. The most significant late-nineteenth-century industrial development was the
    (A) perfection of the steam engine.
    (B) application of electrical energy to production.
    (C) use of gas lighting in factories.
    (D) development of hydraulic lifts.
    (E) introduction of women into the workplace.

59. The demands of the Nazi platform of 1920 included all of the following EXCEPT
    (A) repudiation of the Versailles treaty.
    (B) unification of Austria and Germany.
    (C) agrarian reform.
    (D) anti-Semitic public policy.
    (E) the replacement of small retail shops with large department stores.

60. The "Little Entente" formed in 1920–1921 consisted of
    (A) France and England.
    (B) Czechoslovakia, Romania, and Yugoslavia.
    (C) Hungary, Russia, and Poland.
    (D) Germany, Poland, and Hungary.
    (E) Czechoslovakia, Russia, and Poland.

61. All of the following were gains made by Maria Theresa as a result of the War of the Austrian
    Succession (1740–1748) EXCEPT
    (A) the re-conquest of Silesia.
    (B) keeping her domain largely intact.
    (C) gaining loyalty from her subjects, especially the nobility.
    (D) preserving the Habsburg state.
    (E) recognizing Hungary as the most important of her crowns.

62. Trade between Britain and America after the Revolutionary War
    (A) increased.
    (B) decreased.
    (C) remained the same.
    (D) decreased, then increased quickly.
    (E) effectively stopped until the nineteenth century.

63. The nineteenth-century attempts to create new police forces and reform prisons are reflective
    of which growing political sentiment?
    (A) reactionary conservatism
    (B) a need to impose order on a growing and migrating population
    (C) the end of Enlightenment influence
    (D) an intolerance of the lower classes
    (E) new attitudes of social benevolence and welfare

64. Which of the following was a result of the expansion of literacy in the late nineteenth century?
   (A) A decline in the production of visual art
   (B) A strengthened love of democracy among most literary activists
   (C) An explosion in the number of cheap newspapers published
   (D) A weakened spirit of nationalism
   (E) An instant improvement in the overall quality of literature available

65. The "Scramble for Africa" was precipitated by which of the following events?
   (A) The completion of the Suez Canal
   (B) France's prevention of Italy from annexing Tunisia
   (C) Britain's expansion into presentday Zimbabwe
   (D) Bismarck's annexations of southwest Africa, Togoland, the Cameroons, and East Africa
   (E) Britain's advance into the Sudan

66. Which of the following ideas was endorsed in Montesquieu's *Spirit of the Laws* (1748) as a prescription for regulating the power of government?
   (A) A republic
   (B) A benevolent but absolute monarchy
   (C) A monarchy tempered by a reformed aristocracy
   (D) Unrestricted democracy
   (E) The division of powers among different government branches

Growth of Major European Cities		
(FIGURES IN THOUSANDS)		
	1850	1880	1910
Berlin	419	1,122	2,071
Birmingham	233	437	840
Frankfurt	65	137	415
London	2,685	4,470	7,256
Madrid	281	398	600
Moscow	365	748	1,533
Paris	1,053	2,269	2,888
Rome	175	300	542
St. Petersburg	485	877	1,962
Vienna	444	1,104	2,031
Warsaw	160	339	872

67. According to the chart above, all of the following are true statements about European city
populations from 1850 to 1910 EXCEPT
(A) all of these European cities experienced a population increase from 1850 to 1910.
(B) all of these European cities more than doubled their population from 1850 to 1910.
(C) Warsaw's population in 1910 was closer to St. Petersburg's population in 1880 than it
was to Birmingham's population in 1910.
(D) the city that experienced the least population growth by 1910 in proportion to its
population in 1850 was Frankfurt.
(E) Berlin's population in 1880 was closer to Vienna's population in 1880 than it was to any
other city on the chart.

68. The 1914 assassination of Archduke Ferdinand
(A) led Austria into war with Serbia.
(B) was welcomed by William II of Germany.
(C) resulted in the disintegration of the German and Austro-Hungarian alliance.
(D) resulted in Germany's assisting Serbia in a war against Austria.
(E) resulted in swift military retaliation by Austria.

69. The mixed economies that developed across Europe in the 1930s
(A) involved governments becoming directly involved in economic decisions.
(B) incorporated elements of capitalism and socialism.
(C) incorporated elements of socialism and communism.
(D) were dependent upon income derived from a nation's colonies.
(E) tended to benefit the elite over the middle and lower classes.

70. The First, Second, and Third estates organized French society into which of the following
political groups, respectively?
(A) clergy; peasantry, middle class and artisans; nobility
(B) nobility; peasantry, middle class and artisans; clergy
(C) clergy; nobility; peasantry, middle class and artisans
(D) peasantry, middle class and artisans; clergy; nobility
(E) nobility; clergy; peasantry, middle class and artisans

71. Jean-Jacques Rousseau's *Émile* or *On Education* (1762) promoted
(A) the idea of public funding of elementary education.
(B) the idea that university education is essential to intellectual development.
(C) the idea of giving children maximum freedom in their development.
(D) the idea that rearing children requires strict discipline and inculcation of morality.
(E) the idea of sending children away from the home for formal schooling.

72. Which best explains Hindenburg's decision to appoint Hitler as chancellor in 1933?
(A) Hindenburg was a dedicated Nazi.
(B) The Nazis won a majority of the popular vote in the previous election.
(C) Big business firmly supported the Nazis.
(D) The alternative was a coalition including groups from the political left.
(E) Franz von Papen had been ousted by Hitler, and there was public support for Hitler's

succession to the role of chancellor.

73. Which of the following statements best represents the existentialist philosophy of Jean-Paul Sartre?
    (A) God does not exist, therefore man is doomed to despair.
    (B) God exists, and man depends on his grace.
    (C) Whether God exists or not is irrelevant, for man must define his own values.
    (D) God does not exist, and man should rely on reason alone.
    (E) God exists, and man must seek his presence in all things

74. The Berlin Wall was erected
    (A) to halt the stream of refugees from East Berlin into West Berlin.
    (B) as a symbol to the West of the closed nature of Communist society.
    (C) in response to the Cuban missile crisis.
    (D) under the presidency of Lyndon Johnson.
    (E) to demonstrate the superiority of Russian and East German workmanship.

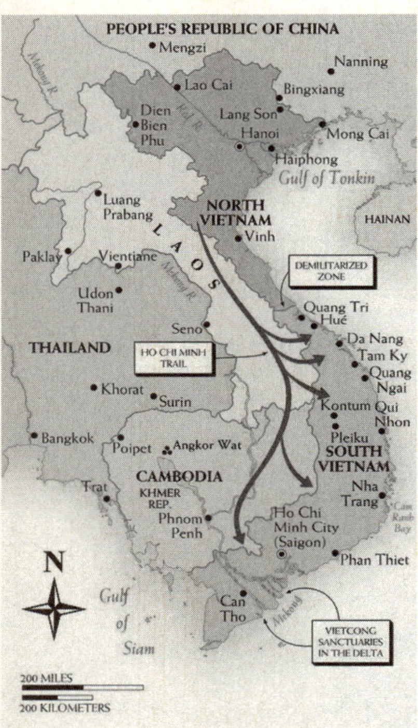

75. The map above illustrates all of the following EXCEPT
    (A) the territory occupied by France between 1857 and 1893.
    (B) how Vietnam was divided into North Vietnam and South Vietnam.
    (C) how the Ho Chi Minh Trail was used by North Vietnam to infiltrate troops and supplies in South Vietnam.
    (D) the placement of the demilitarized zone.
    (E) the reason for the American bombing of North Vietnam in August 1964.

76. Which of the following contributed most significantly to France's becoming the major
    gathering place for Enlightenment thought?
    (A) The strict control of politics, religion, and society imposed by Louis XIV and his
        successors
    (B) Its history of rights for women and religious minorities
    (C) Its long history of peaceful political and social movements
    (D) The highly literate populace
    (E) The generally liberal political attitudes of French politicians and citizens

77. The Paris Commune is best characterized as a
    (A) socialist experiment in communal living.
    (B) radical reaction against the National Assembly of the New French Republic.
    (C) successful municipal division of the Third French Republic.
    (D) genuine proletariat government suppressed by the French bourgeoisie.
    (E) worker's republic.

78. Unlike Darwin's evolutionary theory, which was generally accepted among scientists, his
    mechanism of natural selection
    (A) never really received support within the scientific community
    (B) was accepted only later with the corrob orating evidence of modern genetics
    (C) was seriously flawed
    (D) infuriated evolutionary biologists
    (E) conflicted with the prevailing genetic trends

79. All of the following are true about the Easter Monday uprising of Irish nationalists in 1916
    EXCEPT
    (A) it was suppressed in less than a week.
    (B) its leaders were executed by the British government.
    (C) it led to the unraveling of Sinn Fein.
    (D) it led to a dramatic shift in the leadership of the nationalist cause toward extremism.
    (E) its victims became national martyrs.

80. All of the following are criticisms that can be made of the Treaty of Versailles EXCEPT
    (A) the peace was disastrous economically
    (B) no satisfactory machinery for enforcing the peace was established
    (C) the peace was a Carthaginian peace
    (D) the peace rested on a victory that Germany did not admit
    (E the peace was a peace without victors

European History
Section II Part A

Suggested writing time: 45 minutes
Percent of Section II score: 45

Directions: The following question is based on the accompanying Documents 1–10. (Some of the documents have been edited for the purpose of this exercise.) Write your answer on the pages of the essay booklet.

This question is designed to test your ability to work with historical documents. As you analyze the documents, take into account both the sources of the document and the authors' points of view. Write an essay on the following topic that integrates your analysis of the documents. **Do not simply summarize the documents individually.** You may refer to relevant historical facts and developments not mentioned in the documents.

1. *Assess the validity of this statement: The events that led Europe into World War II were precipitated by Germany's dissatisfaction with the terms of the Versailles treaty of World War I.*

Historical Background: The Versailles treaty of 1919–1920 was organized by representatives of the victorious states; defeated nations were not allowed to participate in treaty decision-making, but were obligated to assent to its terms without the opportunity for negotiation. France demanded a physical barrier between its territory and Germany. The Austro-Hungarian Empire was divided up into five small successor states, with most of its German-speaking population in the Republic of Austria, separated from Germans in Bohemia and forbidden to join the rest of Germany. German reparations included an annual payment of $5 billion until 1921, at which time a final figure would be determined that the Germans would have to pay in thirty years.

DOCUMENT 1 Source: The Treaty of Versailles, June 28, 1919
Article 27
The boundaries of Germany will be as follows:
5. With Poland
From the point defined above to a point to be fixed on the ground about 2 kilometres east of Lorzendorf: the frontier as it will be fixed in accordance with Article 88 of the present Treaty; thence in a northerly direction to the point where the administrative boundary of Posnania crosses the river Bartsch: a line to be fixed on the ground leaving the following places in Poland: Skorischau, Reichthal, Trembatschau, Kunzendorf, Schleise, Gross Koscl, Schreibersdorf, Rippin, Furstlich-Niefken, Pawelau, Tscheschen, Konradau, Johallnisdorf, Modzenowe, Bogdaj, and in Germany: Lorzendorf, Kaulwitz, Glausche, Dalbersdorf, Reesewitz, Stradam, Gross Wartenberg, Kraschen, Neu Mittelwalde, Domaslawitz, Wedelsdorf, Tscheschen Hammer....

DOCUMENT 2 Source: German children playing with paper money that became worthless as a
result of post-war inflation, photograph, 1923

DOCUMENT 3 Source: Munich Pact (excerpt) between Germany, Great Britain, France, and
Italy, providing for the annexation of Sudetenland by the German government,
September 30, 1938

Germany, the United Kingdom, France and Italy, taking into consideration the agreement, which
has been already reached in principle for the cession to Germany of the Sudeten German
territory, have agreed on the following terms and conditions governing the said cession and the
measures consequent thereon, and by this agreement they each hold themselves responsible for
the steps necessary to secure its fulfillment…

DOCUMENT 4 Source: Winston Churchill, member of British Parliament, speech, in response
to the conclusion of the Munich Pact, September 30, 1938

All is over. Silent, mournful, abandoned, broken, Czechoslovakia recedes into the darkness.
She has suffered in every respect by her association with the Western democracies and with the
League of Nations, of which she has always been an obedient servant.…

DOCUMENT 5 Source: Map of Europe, showing partitions of Poland and Czechoslovakia, 1938–1939

DOCUMENT 6 Source: Neville Chamberlain, British prime minister, speech in the House of Commons, September 1, 1939

We have no quarrel with the German people, except that they allow themselves to be governed by a Nazi Government. As long as that Government exists and pursues the methods it has so persistently followed during the last two years, there will be no peace in Europe. We shall merely pass from one crisis to another, and see one country after another attacked by methods which have now become familiar to us in their sickening technique. We are resolved that these methods must come to an end.

DOCUMENT 7 Source: Robert Coulondre (French ambassador to Germany) relating an exchange with Joachim von Ribbentrop (German minister of foreign affairs), telephone conversation with Georges Bonnet (French minister of foreign affairs), September 3, 1939

[Coulondre]: "'I have the painful duty to notify you that as from today, September 3, at 5 P.M., the French government will find itself obliged to fulfill the obligations that France has contracted towards Poland, and which are known to the German government.'

"'Well,' Herr von Ribbentrop remarked, 'it will be France who is the aggressor.'

"I replied to him that history would judge of that."

DOCUMENT 8 Source: Official communication from the German government to the British government, September 3, 1939

Since the time when the Versailles Treaty first tore Germany to pieces, all and every peaceful settlement was refused to all German Governments. The National Socialist Government also has since the year 1933 tried again and again to remove by peaceful negotiations the worst rapes and breaches of justice of this treaty. The British Government have been among those who, by their intransigent attitude, took the chief part in frustrating every practical revision. Without the intervention of the British Government—of this the German Government and German people are fully conscious—a reasonable solution doing justice to both sides would certainly have been found between Germany and Poland.

DOCUMENT 9 Source: Adolf Hitler, German chancellor of the Reich, proclamation to the German people, September 3, 1939

I am more firmly determined than ever to beat back this attack. Germany shall not again capitulate. There is no sense in sacrificing one life after another and submitting to an even worse Versailles Diktat *[harsh settlement or decree imposed unilaterally, especially on a defeated nation]*. We have never been a nation of slaves and will not be one in the future. Whatever Germans in the past had to sacrifice for the existence of our realm, they shall not be greater than those which we are to-day prepared to make.

DOCUMENT 10 Source: Atlantic Charter (excerpt), August 14, 1941

The President of the United States of America and the Prime Minister, Mr. Churchill, representing His Majesty's Government in the United Kingdom, being met together, deem it right to make known certain common principles in the national policies of their respective countries on which they base their hopes for a better future for the world.

First, their countries seek no aggrandizement, territorial or other;

Second, they desire to see no territorial changes that do not accord with the freely expressed wishes of the peoples concerned;

Third, they respect the right of all peoples to choose the form of government under which they will live; and they wish to see sovereign rights and self government restored to those who have been forcibly deprived of them…

European History
Section II Part B

Suggested planning and writing time: 70 minutes
Percent of Section II score: 55

Directions: You are to answer TWO questions, one from each group of three questions below. Make your selections carefully, choosing the questions that you are best prepared to answer thoroughly in the time permitted. You should spend 5 minutes organizing or outlining each essay. In writing your essays, *use specific examples to support your answer.* Write your answers to the questions on the lined pages of the essay booklet. If time permits when you finish writing, check your work. Be certain to number your answers as the questions are numbered below.

Group I
Choose ONE question from this group. The suggested writing time for this question is 30 minutes. *You are advised to spend 5 minutes planning your answer.*
2. *Compare the "right-wing" fascism of Mussolini with the "right-wing" communism of Stalin.*
3. *How did the French Revolution support as well as violate the motto "liberty, equality, and fraternity"?*
4. *Discuss the parallels between England's relationship with Ireland and the nationality problem of the Austrian empire under Metternich*

Group 2
Choose ONE question from this group. The suggested writing time for this question is 30 minutes. *You are advised to spend 5 minutes planning your answer.*
5. *Assess the validity of this statement: Religious institutions impeded the development of "new science" in the sixteenth and seventeenth centuries.*
6. *To what extent was Peter the Great successful in his efforts to modernize Russia?*
7. *Compare and contrast the ideas and policies affecting women under Soviet communism and Italian fascism.*

ANSWERS AND EXPLANATIONS

Sample Test 2

Section I: Multiple Choice
- **1. (A) is correct.** In the late fifteenth century, towns began to ally with monarchs rather than with feudal vassals. This new alliance between king and town led to the advent of sovereign states, in which the powers of taxation, war-making, and law enforcement were no longer handled by vassals, but concentrated in the monarch and exercised by his or her chosen agents.
- **2. (E) is correct.** The Petition of Right did not demand Charles's abdication, but it did signal the fury of the Parliament in other important ways. The Petition of Right was an important

assertion of constitutional freedom that curtailed forced loans or taxation without consent of Parliament, forbade the imprisonment of freemen without due cause, and forbade the quartering of troops in private homes.

- **3. (C) is correct.** Between 1671 and 1831, English landowners had the exclusive legal right to hunt game animals, including hares, partridges, pheasants, and moor fowl. The poor and those without property were forbidden from hunting on these lands. These various game laws upheld the superior status of the aristocracy and the landed gentry.

- **4. (A) is correct**. Just three days after the Third Estate and a handful of clergy and nobles declared itself the National Assembly, the group met at a tennis court (because their other meeting place was locked) and took an oath to continue to sit until they had given France a constitution.

- **5. (A) is correct.** Prince Klemens von Metternich of Austria suppressed the *Burschenschaften* by using the Carlsbad Decrees, which cracked down on free expression and freedom of the press. This act was consistent with Metternich's conservatism and his refusal to recognize the rights of nationalist organizations.

- **6. (A) is correct.** For about twenty-five years after the Crimean War, European affairs were unstable, producing a period of uninhibited speculation in foreign policy and annexations. Without the restraining influence of the Concert of Europe, each nation believed that only the limits of its military power and its diplomatic influence should constrain its international ambitions.

- **7. (C) is correct.** This cartoon parodies *Kulturkampf* or "cultural struggle," which was Bismarck's failed policy against the German Catholic church. The cartoon particularly makes fun of the intense hostility that existed between Bismarck and the Catholic church by depicting him playing a chess match with the pope.

- **8. (C) is correct.** Throughout Renaissance Italy, slavery thrived. After the Black Death (1348–1350) reduced the supply of laborers throughout Europe, the demand for slaves soared. By the end of the fourteenth century, many affluent homes included slaves.

- **9. (D) is correct.** The two factors that led to Parliament's victory were the alliance with Scotland (consummated in 1643 when John Pym persuaded Parliament to accept the terms of the Solemn League and Covenant) and the coordination of the Parliamentary army under Oliver Cromwell. Charles had support from the Cavaliers, who were a demographically diverse group located in the northwestern half of England. The poet John Milton was decidedly pro-Parliament and pro-Cromwell in his political sentiments, but he did not dramatically affect the victory.

- **10. (C) is correct.** Britain and France traded through chartered companies that enjoyed a legal monopoly in India. The British East India Company and the French *Compagnie des Indes* were trading rivals in India.

- **11. (E) is correct.** The war against Austria radicalized the revolutionaries and led to what is usually called the second revolution, which led to the overthrow of the constitutional monarchy and the establishment of a republic. On August 10, 1792, a Parisian mob invaded the Tuileries and forced Louis XVI and Marie Antoinette to take refuge in the Legislative Assembly. Subsequently the king was not allowed to perform any of his official duties.

- **12. (C) is correct.** This Concert of Europe was designed as a way for different nations to resolve mutual foreign policy issues. It was effectively an alliance that prevented extreme or radical political decisions that would adversely affect the international community.

■ **13. (B) is correct.** Bismarck was the driving force behind the German unification that occurred in the second half of the nineteenth century. His conservative policies were focused on bringing Prussia and Germany into a confederation with a strong industrial base, and he pursued a series of skirmishes that would enable Prussia/Germany to gain land and territory that would facilitate unification.

■ **14. (C) is correct.** Among other things in the *Rerum Novarum,* which was a decidedly pro-laborer encyclical, Leo specifically sought the right for laborers to organize in labor unions.

■ **15. (E) is correct.** In this title page illustration for Hobbes's *Leviathan,* the ruler is imagined as absolute lord of his lands. The mass of individuals that make up his "corporate body" have their interests served by their willing consent to accept him and to cooperate with him. Hobbes believed that absolute authority might be lodged in either a monarch or a legislative body and that rulers should be absolute in their power.

■ **16. (B) is correct.** Louis XIV allegedly uttered the declaration, *"L'état, c'est moi."* The divine right that justified Louis XIV's position of authority over his subjects was championed repeatedly during his rule, most powerfully by the political theorist and Louis's tutor, Bishop Jacques-Bénigne Bossuet. Louis's royal predecessors had laid the institutional foundations for absolute monarchy, but Bossuet and other advisers emphasized Louis's God-given right to rule over the French.

■ **17. (B) is correct.** The African slave trade was active before Europeans began trading for slaves. Many African nations were willing to sell their slaves to Europeans. Africans selling and acquiring other Africans as slaves was not uncommon during this time.

■ **18. (E) is correct.** European monarchs perceived the inflammatory nature of the ideas expressed in the Rights of Man and Citizen and the aggression of revolutionary France. Reacting to this threat, many European governments turned to repressive domestic policies as a way to avoid similar revolutions in their own countries.

■ **19. (C) is correct.** Brazilian independence came about relatively simply and peacefully when Don Pedro, the son of the prince regent João who had improved conditions in Brazil and helped it win autonomy, embraced the movement for independence from Portugal and gained domestic support for his position.

■ **20. (E) is correct.** Napoleon III's liberal concessions were last-ditch efforts to recover from embarrassments in foreign policy that tainted him with failure and unpopularity. His diplomatic failures in the Italian unification and his foolhardy expedition against Mexico were cast against the success of Prussia and Germany, and he sought to distract the French people from his errors.

■ **21. (A) is correct.** In *The Interpretation of Dreams,* Freud argued that dreams enabled the unconscious drives and desires of people to be played out in the safe context of the unconscious mind. He also contended that these suppressed drives and desires affected conscious behavior.

■ **22. (A) is correct.** Science and the study of natural philosophy was not a formal pursuit in the sixteenth and early seventeenth centuries. By the mid-seventeenth centuries, this situation had changed somewhat, with new societies and academies invested in the pursuit of natural philosophy. For the most part during this period, scientific research was carried out by individuals unaffiliated with each other, and possibly, but not exclusively, funded by royal courts or a university.

- **23. (B) is correct.** George I clearly favored the Whigs. After the Hanoverian accession and the eventual Whig success in achieving the full confidence of George I, the chief difference between the Whigs and the Tories was that one group had access to patronage and the other did not.

- **24. (E) is correct.** Britain did not surrender Canada to the French in the Treaty of Paris of 1763, but the treaty did reflect somewhat less of a victory than Britain had won on the battlefield. Britain received all of Canada, the Ohio River valley, and the eastern half of the Mississippi River valley. Britain returned Pondicherry and Chandernagore in India and the West Indian sugar islands of Martinique and Guadeloupe to the French.

- **25. (E) is correct.** The Thermidorian Reaction, which began in July 1794 and consisted of the destruction of the machinery of terror and the institution of a new constitutional regime, did not overlook the culpability of the Jacobins. The Paris Jacobin Club was closed, and Jacobin clubs in the provinces were forbidden to correspond with one another. The executions of former terrorists marked the beginning of "the white terror." Throughout the country, Jacobins were summarily executed.

- **26. (D) is correct.** Tsar Alexander I and his successor, Nicholas I, were notorious in their efforts to suppress liberalism and nationalism. Their absolute monarchies were extremely repressive and devoid of social reforms, and they continued the brutality of serfdom in Russia.

- **27. (E) is correct.** The March Laws did not include the establishment of a separate Hungarian state, though the Magyars hoped to establish a separate Hungarian state within the Habsburg domains and sought to do so. Eventually, the Austrian government and some of the ethnic groups in regions that the Magyars sought to annex went to war against the Hungarians to prevent the formation of a separate Magyar state.

- **28. (C) is correct.** The *benefice* system of the medieval church permitted important ecclesiastical posts to be sold to the highest bidders and left residency requirements in parishes unenforced. Luther objected to the effects of this system on congregations that had little or no interaction with their local clergy.

- **29. (E) is correct.** Cardinal Richelieu was a shrewd leader who used the politics of religion to his advantage. In 1631, Richelieu pledged funds to the Protestant army of Gustavus Adolphus, the king of Sweden, while also insisting that Catholic Bavaria be spared from attack and that Catholics in conquered countries be permitted to practice their religion. Richelieu was rabidly anti-Protestant in his domestic policies and began the anti-Huguenot campaign.

- **30. (B) is correct.** In pre-industrial Europe, a servant was a person—either male or female—who was hired, sometimes under contract, to work in a household in exchange for room, board, and wages. Servants tended to be young but were not always the socially inferiors of their employers.

- **31. (D) is correct.** The reformists favorable to change in the eighteenth century who flourished in the emerging print culture were known as the *philosophes*. Not philosophers in a formal sense, they sought to apply the rules of reason to the major social practices of the era. The most famous of their number included Voltaire, Montesquieu, Diderot, D'Alembert, Rousseau, Hume, Gibbon, Smith, Lessing, and Kant.

- **32. (E) is correct.** The chart indicates that the combined military expenditures of the Ottoman Empire and Austria-Hungary total $150,000,000. The military expenditures of the United States were also $150,000,000. All of the other choices can be inferred from the chart.

■ **33. (D) is correct.** *Glasnost,* or openness, was a policy that Gorbachev introduced during his direction of the Soviet Union. Although *glasnost* as a policy did not specifically aim to end the Cold War, it allowed for levels of criticism and freedom of speech that came at a time when other conditions were facilitating the fall of the Soviet Union and the end of the Cold War.

■ **34. (C) is correct.** The Marburg Colloquy, Landgrave Philip of Hesse's effort to unite Swiss and German Protestants in a mutual defense pact, resulted in a further division between Zwingli and Luther. The two Protestant reformers refused to compromise on the question of Christ's presence in the Eucharist.

■ **35. (E) is correct.** The drive to improve agricultural production began during the sixteenth and seventeenth centuries in the Low Countries. There the unique pressures of the growing population and the shortage of land required a revolution in cultivation to improve conditions and food supply.

■ **36. (E) is correct.** Among the many reforms demanded by Chartists was the idea that property qualifications for members of the House of Commons be abolished, in order to open up government to citizens who owned no land.

■ **37. (C) is correct.** Britain and France abandoned their traditional antagonism in 1904 in the series of informal agreements known as the *Entente Cordiale.* Although it was not a formal treaty and had no specific military provisions, the *Entente* settled all outstanding colonial differences between the two nations.

■ **38. (A) is correct.** Despite its devastating effect on the world's population, the Great Depression did not mean absolute economic decline. People with work always outnumbered those without work, and not everyone was out of a job.

■ **39. (B) is correct.** On the eve of the Reformation, the geographical as well as the intellectual horizons of western Europeans were changing. The fifteenth century saw the beginning of western Europe's global expansion. The Portuguese, the Spanish, and other Europeans sponsored exploration of the African coast, of South and North America, as well as of India and southeast Asia.

■ **40. (C) is correct.** The map underscores the rapid success of the Parliamentarians in southwestern England and Wales in 1645. By then, the Royalists were rapidly losing ground to Parliamentary forces.

■ **41. (A) is correct.** The French Revolution has often been considered a victory of the bourgeoisie, or middle class. The largest new propertied class to emerge from the revolutionary tumult was actually the peasantry, who owned their land free and clear as a result of the destruction of aristocratic privilege.

■ **42. (C) is correct.** During the nineteenth century, artisans and factory workers underwent a process of proletarianization, whereby they entered into a wage economy and gradually lost individual ownership of the means of production and lost control over the conduct of their own trades. The process occurred rapidly whenever factories took root, as overseers replaced the formerly independent craftsmen and artisans.

■ **43. (C) is correct.** In 1889 the Eiffel Tower was originally built as a temporary structure for the international trade exposition of that year.

■ **44. (A) is correct.** Britain was focused primarily on Egypt and on the region that would later be conquered by them during the Boer War in present-day South Africa. France controlled Algeria and Senegal. Just a few years later, Britain expanded its holdings into the areas surrounding these original outposts, and into Nigeria and British East Africa.

- **45. (B) is correct.** Ramsey MacDonald's program consisted of plans for extensive social reform rather than for the nationalization or public seizure of industry. The establishment of Labour as a viable governing party signaled the permanent demise of the Liberal party, as the bulk of its voters began to drift into either the Conservative or the Labour parties.
- **46. (C) is correct.** As the Party general secretary, a post that Party intellectuals disdained as merely clerical, Stalin amassed tremendous power through his command of the bureaucracy and administration of the Party. His familiarity with this arena of the Party made him more popular with lower-level Communists.
- **47. (E) is correct.** The "Black Legend" was a work that portrayed all Spanish treatment of Indians as unprincipled and inhumane. It grew out of the writings of people who were inspired by the ideas of the Dominican friar, Bartolomé de Las Casas, who believed that conquest was not necessary for conversion.
- **48. (B) is correct.** Catherine persuaded Charles IX that a Huguenot coup was underway, inspired by her enemy Coligny, and that rapid execution of Protestant leaders was the only guaranteed way to preserve the crown from Protestant insurgents. Catherine misled Charles IX to cover up her own part in the failed assassination attempt against Coligny.
- **49. (E) is correct.** Louis XV possessed no strong political leadership, and he was a mediocre king who made few important changes during his reign. Cardinal Fleury, his chief adviser, was unsuccessful in his attempts to prepare Louis XV for the challenges and demands on him. As a result, France remained disorganized and uninspired as a nation.
- **50. (A) is correct.** Hegel believed that ideas develop in an evolutionary fashion that involves conflict. At any given time, a predominant set of ideas, which he termed the *thesis,* predominates. The thesis is challenged by other conflicting ideas, which Hegel termed the *antithesis.* As these patterns of thought clash, a *synthesis* emerges that eventually becomes the new thesis. Then the process begins all over again. Periods of world history receive their character from the patterns of thoughts predominating during them.
- **51. (E) is correct.** By the middle of the nineteenth century, artisans, proud of their skills and frustrated by their social limitations, became the most radical political element in the European working class. From at least the 1830s onward, artisans all over Europe began defending their social and economic interests.
- **52. (D) is correct.** From 1860 to 1914, centralized bureaucracies became even more important to the everyday administration of government. It was during this period that many current institutions took shape. The centralization of bureaucracy was a key to the success of these governments.
- **53. (B) is correct.** Modernism in literature existed before World War I and continued to thrive after the war—stimulated in part by many of the social issues that emerged from the conflict. The extremely violent war made readers and writers alike more open to upheavals in literary form and moral content.
- **54. (A) is correct.** Like other successful rulers in his era, William of Orange chose to embrace different creeds according to the political advantages of each. In 1561, he married Anne of Saxony, the daughter of the Lutheran elector Maurice and the granddaughter of the late Landgrave Philip of Hesse. He remained Catholic until 1567, when he converted Lutheranism. In response to the Saint Bartholomew's Day Massacre, he became an avowed Calvinist.
- **55. (E) is correct.** As a means of surviving the Continental System of Napoleon, Britain did not broker separate deals with Portugal *and* Spain. Although Portugal assisted Britain, Spain

did not. Napoleon sent troops into Spain in 1807 after the king of Spain agreed to aid France *against* Portugal.

■ **56. (C) is correct.** In his 1798 *Essay on the Principle of Population,* Thomas Malthus contended that population must eventually outstrip the food supply. Although the human population grows geometrically, the food supply can expand only arithmetically. Malthus articulated his belief that there was little hope of averting a disaster of enormous proportions.

■ **57. (A) is correct.** The dynamic force for change in 1848 originated with political liberals who were generally drawn from the middle classes. Throughout the Continent, liberals sought a program of more representative government, civil liberty, and unregulated economic life.

■ **58. (B) is correct.** The most significant change in the nineteenth century for industry (and eventually for everyday life) involved the application of electrical energy to production. Electricity was the most versatile and transportable source of power ever discovered.

■ **59. (E) is correct.** The National Socialist German Worker's Party was opposed to large department stores and urged their replacement with small retail shops in their 1920 platform. The party also called for the repudiation of the Versailles treaty, the unification of Austria and Germany, the exclusion of Jews from German citizenship, agrarian reform, the prohibition of land speculation, the confiscation of war profits, and state administration of giant cartels.

■ **60. (B) is correct.** In 1920 and 1921, Czechoslovakia, Romania, and Yugoslavia formed the Little Entente as a way of safeguarding their independence in the face of possible revisions of the Versailles treaty.

■ **61. (B) is correct.** Maria Theresa never succeeded in reacquiring Silesia, which had been wrested from her in 1740 by the Prussians. However, she did manage to keep most of her territory together, despite numerous challenges to her authority.

■ **62. (A) is correct.** After their defeat in the Revolutionary War, the British came to terms with losing the American colonies. Economically this loss did not prove disastrous. In fact, British trade with America after the war actually increased.

■ **63. (B) is correct.** The various efforts to create a reliable police force and to reform prisons are suggestive of the post-revolution concern in France about maintaining order and stability in society. With the shifts in population, this desire for order became increasingly elusive, so certain civil reforms were put into effect as a means of eliminating some of the more dangerous or uncertain elements of society.

■ **64. (C) is correct.** The expanding literate population created a vast market for new reading material. Printed matter of every variety proliferated as technological advances in printing and paper technology lowered production costs. Cheap mass-circulation newspapers were especially popular.

■ **65. (D) is correct.** Managing fewer colonies than its European peers, Germany began a frantic effort to annex land in the African continent. In a very short period of time, Germany controlled Southwest Africa, Togoland, the Cameroons, and East Africa, which led to a wild scramble by other European powers to divide up what land remained.

■ **66. (C) is correct.** In his *Spirit of the Laws,* Montesquieu concluded that there could be no single set of political laws that applied to all peoples at all times and in all places. He believed in the importance of a division of powers, using the structure of the government of Great Britain as his model.

■ **67. (D) is correct.** The city that experienced the least population growth in 1910 in proportion to its population in 1850 was Madrid. Frankfurt increased more than six-fold. Madrid did little more than double its population.

■ **68. (A) is correct.** The assassination of Archduke Ferdinand (heir to Austria) by a Bosnian nationalist effectively led Austria into war with Serbia—and subsequently led the rest of the world into World War I. Though Germany offered its support to Austria, it was frustrated by the pace of the Austrian war and uncertain at the start that the war was a just and necessary retribution.

■ **69. (A) is correct.** A mixed economy is one in which government—alongside business and labor—is directly involved in economic decisions. As the economies of governments declined in the 1930s, this development was an attempt to make economic progress in individual countries.

■ **70. (C) is correct.** The First Estate was represented by the clergy; the Second Estate constituted the nobility; and the Third Estate technically encompassed everyone else—even though its representatives were primarily from wealthy members of the commercial and professional middle classes. All the representatives in the Estates General were men.

■ **71. (C) is correct.** Rousseau set forth his view on the individual's development toward the good and happy life in his novel, *Émile*. He stressed the difference between children and adults, distinguished the stages of human development, and urged that children be raised with maximum individual freedom.

■ **72. (D) is correct.** In November of 1932, Franz von Papen resigned as chancellor of Germany. General Kurt von Schleicher became chancellor. Fear of civil war between the left and right mounted. Schleicher tried to build a broad-based coalition of conservative groups and trade unionists. The prospect of such a coalition including groups from the political left concerned the German government even more than the prospect of Hitler, and so von Schleicher was appointed chancellor.

■ **73. (C) is correct.** According to the existentialists, human beings are compelled to formulate their own ethical values and cannot depend on traditional religion, rational philosophy, intuition, or social customs for ethical guidance.

■ **74. (A) is correct.** Throughout 1961, thousands of refugees from East Germany crossed the border into West Berlin. The western sector of the city was the single point in Eastern Europe where persons living under Soviet dominance might escape to a free political culture. This outflow of people embarrassed East Germany and hurt its economy. The Berlin Wall was constructed in August of 1961 by the East Germans—with the support of the Soviet Union—to halt the flow of refugees.

■ **75. (E) is correct.** Between 1857 and 1893, the French occupied the territory containing Laos, Cambodia, and Vietnam. In 1954, the Geneva conference created the division of North Vietnam and South Vietnam. The Ho Chi Minh Trail was a system of paths and roads through mountains and jungles that were used by the North Vietnamese to aid attacks on South Vietnamese forces. American involvement in the Vietnam War escalated dramatically (beginning with the bombing of North Vietnam) after an attack on an American ship in the Gulf of Tonkin.

- **76. (A) is correct.** France's legacy from Louis XIV was absolute monarchy, a large standing army, heavy taxation, and religious persecution of Protestants and dissident Roman Catholic Jansenists. This lack of political and religious liberty, coupled with strict restrictions on freedom of expression, filled many French people with a desire for change that came to be embodied in many of the liberal values of the Enlightenment.
- **77. (B) is correct.** The Paris Commune was effectively a reaction against the National Assembly of the French Republic, which basically ignored the horrible conditions suffered by Parisians during the Prussian siege and alienated many Parisians so much that a new municipal government in Paris seemed preferable.
- **78. (B) is correct.** Darwin's theory of evolution by natural selection was controversial and garnered criticism from religious and scientific communities. The acceptance of the theory occurred in the scientific community in the 1920s and 1930s, when Darwin's theory was combined with the insights of modern genetics.
- **79. (C) is correct.** After the Easter Monday rebellion, the extremist Sinn Fein movement replaced the Irish Party in Parliament as the leadership of the Irish nationalist cause.
- **80. (E) is correct.** The Treaty of Versailles did not create (as some claimed) a peace without victors, but it did come under bitter criticism as soon as it had been inked. Although it did not effectively put an end to imperialism, the treaty distinguished between winning and losing nations and attempted to promote the national interests of the winning nations.

Section II Part A

1. Assess the validity of this statement: The events that led Europe into World War II were precipitated by Germany's dissatisfaction with the terms of the Versailles treaty of World War I.

This DBQ question requires you to *evaluate the accuracy* of the statement presented. As there is no right or wrong answer, you should choose to support the position that you can argue most strongly from the documents provided and from your outside knowledge of the subject matter.

    WHO: Europe / Germany

    WHAT: events preceding World War II / dissatisfaction with the Versailles treaty

    WHEN: World War II / World War I

It is important to note that this question demands your familiarity with two phases of history—the period immediately after World War I (when the Versailles treaty was issued, requiring Germany's cooperation) and the months and events prior to the start of World War II, during which Germany's behavior instigated the start of another world war that would involve all of Europe.

    As you begin to consider the documents, pay close attention to those that refer to World War I and those that refer to World War II. **DOCUMENT 2** shows a photograph of German children playing with valueless paper money in 1923. This document represents a post-World War I experience among Germans of skyrocketing inflation and extreme budget deficits. You should remember that one of the most contested aspects of the Treaty of Versailles was war reparations that Germany was required to pay for its role in World War I. These became increasingly difficult for Germany to complete, as its economy became weaker and weaker in the 1920s and early 1930s. This document should remind you of the economic instability faced by Germany after World War I.

DOCUMENT 1 is a fairly straightforward account of some of the boundaries between Germany and Poland specified in the Versailles treaty. Don't focus too much on the content of this document, which is fairly impenetrable unless you are an expert in German and Polish geography. If you recall, World War II began when France and England protested German incursions into Poland. This document illustrates some of the restrictions that had been placed on Germany as a result of the Versailles treaty, and it should help you recall that Germany violated these conditions in the months and years prior to the start of World War II.

DOCUMENTS 7, **8**, and **9** involve communications on September 3, 1939, among the governments of Germany, Britain, and France just prior to the declaration of World War II. **DOCUMENT 7**, from the French ambassador to Germany in 1939, expresses the idea that the French government has obligations to Poland, and that it will not renege on those promises. It also suggests the irony of Germany calling France the "aggressor." In **DOCUMENT 8**, the German government specifically refers to the Versailles treaty as the source of all of Germany's woes, and it accuses the British government of having been responsible for the worst conditions of the treaty. This document should be the centerpiece of your response to the question, as it addresses German dissatisfaction with the Versailles treaty on the eve of World War II. **DOCUMENT 9** is a speech from Adolph Hitler, leader of the National Socialist (Nazi) government, in which he declares that Germany will not "capitulate" and will not submit to "an even worse Versailles Diktat." Hitler, a notorious anti-Semite and rabid nationalist, voices his aims using the rhetoric of a nation that has suffered under an oppressor and will not consent to be a nation of "slaves." **DOCUMENT 6** could also be grouped with these documents. The author, British Prime Minister Neville Chamberlain, addresses the reason for British frustration with the activities of Germans— chiefly their attack of one country after another. This document is dated just two days prior to **DOCUMENTS 7**, **8**, and **9**.

DOCUMENTS 3, **4**, and **6** date from a year earlier than the documents immediately prior to World War II, and they describe the German annexation of the Sudetenland in Czechoslovakia. This conflict preceded World War II and bore similarities to the territorial acquisition of Poland by Germany. In **DOCUMENT 3**, the Munich Pact notes the agreements and stipulations of the pact between Germany and other European powers. In **DOCUMENT 4**, Winston Churchill (not yet prime minister) expresses his regret at the loss of the Sudetenland to Germany. You may recall that this conflict was precipitated by the presence of numerous German speakers in the Sudetenland; however, the region was also part of a border area between Germany and Czechoslovakia, and the annexation opened Czechoslovakia to a total takeover by Germany. **DOCUMENT 5**, a map of Europe in 1938– 1939, shows the Germans' access to and annexation of Poland and Czechoslovakia.

DOCUMENT 10 is an excerpt from the Atlantic Charter, the document that effectively led to the entrance of the United States into World War II. You should note that the right of people to choose their own government and the restoration of sovereignty are among the goals expressed—aims that are directly in contrast with the behavior of Germany in the Sudetenland and Poland in 1938 and 1939, respectively.

As you prepare your thesis, you should take these documents into account along with the outside knowledge you may have on this subject. One possible way to incorporate your knowledge of the Versailles treaty and of German dissatisfaction and pre–World War II aggression would be in thesis like the following:

The nationalist aims of the National Socialist party led to a policy of annexing regions of strategic importance (such as the Sudetenland and Poland) that was in direct conflict with the restrictions that had been imposed on Germany as a result of the Versailles treaty—the terms of which were unacceptable to many Germans. This unlawful annexation ultimately led to Europe's immersion in World War II.

Given that this essay requires your knowledge of more than one period of time, you might wish to structure your essay chronologically. By considering the Versailles treaty (**DOCUMENT 1**) and German inflation (**DOCUMENT 2**) in the first part of your response; the German acquisition of the Sudetenland (**DOCUMENTS 3** and **4**) in a second part; and the German aggression in Poland (**DOCUMENTS 6**, **7**, **8**, and **9**), the map of the region (**DOCUMENT 5**) and the Atlantic Charter (**DOCUMENT 10**) in a third part, you will have constructed a useful structure on which to build your argument.

In your essay, you must remember to address the *validity* of the statement. The sample thesis asserts that it was the Nazi party's nationalist aims, not its dissatisfaction with the Versailles treaty, that led to World War II. In this case, the writer claims that the statement is partly true—that is, German dissatisfaction with the Versailles treaty played a role in the start of World War II, but German nationalist aims and annexations played a greater role in the start of the war.

An excellent answer would analyze the various documents and group them according to their relevance to each other. Any excellent response will focus on **DOCUMENTS 8** and **9**, which address German sentiment about the Versailles treaty. These documents should be interpreted in light of their bias—that is, in light of the fact that they might be used as justifications for the land grab that was going on in eastern Europe at the time. Certainly, in the case of Hitler's account in **DOCUMENT 9**, this is the case.

Section II PART B

Sample Student Responses

2. *Compare the "right-wing" fascism of Mussolini with the "right-wing" communism of Stalin.*

    In many ways, "right-wing" dictators in Russia and Italy in the 1920s were quite similar. Stalin and Mussolini both instituted repressive policies that limited the power of individuals. Both leaders focused on expanding their own domains at the expense of the quality of life of their citizens. Their governments were characterized by intolerance for minorities, and their political agendas tended to involve widespread destruction of particular ethnic groups and societies. In addition, both dictators made excellent use of propaganda to bolster their individual popularity.

    Joseph Stalin represented the "right-wing" politics of Communist Russia. Contrary to Trotsky, the "left-wing" leader who preceded him, Stalin urged that socialism could be achieved in Russia alone, and its success did not depend on the fate of revolutions elsewhere. Stalin nationalized the previous international scope of the Marxist revolution, and he enforced some of the most brutal aspects of Trotsky's agricultural collectivization, forcing the *kulaks* (farming class) off their land and confiscating their crops. Stalin was a ruthless dictator who used propaganda to terrific effect and who ordered the murders of thousands of his countrymen.

Mussolini's "right-wing" Fascist government was anti-democratic, anti-Marxist, anti-parliamentary, and anti-Semitic. His government's nationalism was partly a response to the fears of the expansionism of communism. The politics of the Italian Fascists disregarded the liberal belief in the rule of law and the consent of the governed. Mussolini headed an attack on Ethiopia that was a clear violation of international law. Fascists were put in charge of the police force, and terrorist squads became a government militia. The party used propaganda to great effect. By the late 1920s, the Grand Council of the party, which Mussolini controlled, had become an organ of the state.

Though Mussolini's "right-wing" Fascist dictatorship did not exactly echo Stalin's "right-wing" Communist rule, these two leaders shared a similar approach to terrorizing their citizens into doing exactly as they demanded.

3. *How did the French Revolution support as well as violate the motto "liberty, equality, and fraternity"?*

The French Revolution involved a growing distrust between the aristocracy and the more radical middle-class leaders. The calling of the Estates General by Louis XVI led to a major reorganization of the French government that supported the motto "liberty, equality, and fraternity," in the sense that it resulted in the restructuring of the Estates General in a manner that was more egalitarian and in the sense that it gave the Third Estate equal voice with the First and Second estates. This movement—whereby the National Assembly (renamed the National Constituent Assembly) embraced all of the members of the Estates General and granted them equal power, was the beginning of the end of government by the privileged.

Louis XVI's attempts to undermine the new Assembly deviated from the motto of "liberty, equality, and fraternity." Louis's plot to overthrow the liberal government and regain power, his refusal to grant the Assembly a form of constitutional monarchy, and his affiliation with the conservative aristocracy were decisive steps toward autocratic government and away from the "liberty" of the motto.

The storming of the Bastille on July 14, 1789, was an unqualified political disaster for Louis XVI and for the throngs who sought to release prisoners. While the crowd sought weapons to defend themselves against Louis XVI's forces, their behavior was driven less by the idea of "liberty" than by a desire for their own protection and defense.

As the "Great Fear" spread through the French countryside, liberal nobles renounced their special privileges in an attempt to stop the growing disorder and destruction. This effort to equalize life for all French citizens, while reflecting the "liberty, equality, and fraternity" of the motto, subjected all French citizens to the same laws, a development that made possible later reforms in the reconstruction of France. The Declaration of Rights of Man, which was drawn up in 1789, further reflected the motto in its proclamation of all men as "free and equal in rights," but it denied these rights to women—as if interpreting "fraternity" in the limited sense of pertaining only to men.

4. *Discuss the parallels between England's relationship with Ireland and the nationality problem of the Austrian empire under Metternich*

England's relationship to its Irish citizens was similar to that of Austria's relationship to the Poles, Czechs, Slovaks, Slovenes, and other ethnic groups that populated its empire. As a result of legislation passed by William Pitt the Younger, Ireland and England had passed an Act of Union, which entitled Ireland to send 100 members to the House of Commons—although it forbade the country from sending Irish Catholics. Irish nationalists began to agitate for Catholic nationalism in the 1820s. When Daniel O'Connell, a Catholic, was elected to Parliament but was not permitted to serve because of his religious faith, the English government began to get nervous about the possibility of a civil war. Britain passed an act that allowed for Catholic emancipation essentially in order to keep the peace in Ireland. Great Britain moved slowly toward a more liberal position toward Ireland, but it did not grant Catholic Ireland its full independence until 1949.

In Metternich's Austria, conservatism reigned. The Austrian government could not contemplate the forces of liberalism and nationalism that were burgeoning in other European countries at this time because of its own complex relationship with the ethnic groups living in its borders—that is, Poles, Czechs, Slovaks, Slovenes, and others on the Italian peninsula. Unlike England, which eventually had to grant Catholic Ireland political recognition in the form of emancipation, Austria held to a policy of dynastic integrity that did not permit any acknowledgment of the various needs and aspirations of ethnic and national groups in its empire. Metternich moved to prevent the formation of a German national state, and he rejected the movement for independent constitutions in the Austrian states.

Metternich maintained repressive policies throughout his rule, clamping down on—and ultimately dissolving—the student associations *(Burschenschaften)* in three southern German states. While England sought to placate the Irish by granting limited liberties to Irish Catholics, Metternich refused outright to grant ethnic groups rights or constitutional autonomy.

5. *Assess the validity of this statement: Religious institutions impeded the development of "new science" in the sixteenth and seventeenth centuries.*

"New science" posed a threat to religious institutions in the sixteenth and seventeenth centuries, because it challenged biblical authority and gave new explanations for phenomena that had been understood in religious terms for centuries. Some religious organizations sought to compel scientists to renounce their views.

Some of the important discoveries in astronomy called into question the Bible's account of God's creation of heaven and earth. The most famous example of this occurred in the case of Galileo Galilei, who published his own account of how religious faith could be accommodated in light of scientific discoveries. Galileo's faith in the Copernican theory of the solar system put him squarely against the religious leaders of his time. In 1616, the Roman Catholic church censured the Copernican theory and condemned those who believed in it. Galileo, with permission granted by Pope Urban VIII of Florence, developed the Copernican idea at length in a series of dialogues that made those who didn't believe in Copernicanism look like fools. Pope Urban ordered a trial, and Galileo was ultimately forced into house arrest for the last decade of his life. The Catholic church aligned itself fairly early on with a repressive attitude toward any scientific theories or discoveries that challenged its authority and power.

Many scientists of this era sought to reconcile their discoveries with their religion. One of these figures was Blaise Pascal, a mathematician and physical scientist who was also a Jansenist. Pascal sought to strengthen traditional religious belief, and in his famous wager, he was willing to stake everything on the existence of God. He believed that some of the rationalism of new science led to a kind of false optimism that should not be allowed to stray far from faith in God.

After Newton's seventeenth-century discovery of the laws of gravitation, more scientists were able to reconcile their faith in God with the rationality of the universe. These thinkers believed that God must be rational in order to create a universe that abided by the laws of reason. A new form of religious thought developed out of this concept of religion and science being mutually supportive; it was known as physico-theology. This merging of science and faith enabled new science to spread more rapidly, because physico-theology did not challenge the authority of the Church, but rather acknowledged God's role in the creation of all rational and observable scientific phenomena.

While some religious issues arose during the sixteenth and seventeenth centuries that stood in the way of scientists (such as in the case of Galileo), not all religious developments at this time were opposed to the tremendous discoveries taking place in the universities and laboratories throughout Europe. On the contrary, as this period progressed, the Church became more and more comfortable with the idea that scientists were uncovering truths that God intended them to uncover. This outlook enabled religion and science to coexist more peacefully; a situation that continued into future centuries.

6. *To what extent was Peter the Great successful in his efforts to modernize Russia?*

Peter the Great began his rule inauspiciously in 1682, as a ten-year-old boy who ascended the throne with his sickly half-brother. He didn't rule personally until 1689, when his *streltsy* followers helped overthrow Peter's sister, Sophia. Peter recognized that he needed to accomplish two things during his rule: make secure the role of the Russian tsar, and help shore up Russia's military.

Peter made a reconnaissance mission to Europe to gain an understanding of the resources of powerful maritime powers. On this trip, he learned a great deal and formed impressions of western European militaries that he transplanted to his native Russia. Peter recognized that power in warfare could help Russia rise in importance, and to this end he sought to build a major army and navy for Russia. Peter oversaw the construction of ships to protect his Black Sea interests. He sought to secure a warm-water port that would enable Russia's trade with the west and bolster its international influence; this was not achieved ultimately, and the quest led Russia into a series of battles with the Turks. Peter adopted policies for his military that vastly improved and reorganized the army. He required greater military discipline and founded the "college of war" to administer the army.

In addition to the reforms Peter made in the Russian military, also he seized secular control of the church, forcing that institution to accept westernization and change. Peter also reorganized his domestic administration into a series of "colleges" modeled after the Swedish bureaucracy. This organization improved Russia's administration significantly. Another reform that Peter achieved was making Russia into one of the greatest iron producers in Europe. While this industry did not flourish for long, it enabled Russia to make its mark in western Europe as an economic power to be reckoned with.

One of Peter's greatest accomplishments was forcing the *boyars* (old nobility) into state service. He shaved the long beards of court *boyars* personally, forcing them to dress and groom themselves in a more modern fashion. Peter instituted "A Table of Ranks" in 1722 that ranked people according to their place in the bureaucracy or military rather than by traditional hierarchies. Peter did not fare as well in reforming the *streltsy;* he brutally suppressed a revolt by the *streltsy,* demonstrating that his military was created to uphold the tsar.

Peter's reforms ushered Russia into a modern age. Though all of his efforts were not unqualified successes (for instance, he did not improve the situation of Russian peasants), he did enable the country to make significant advances.

7. *Compare and contrast the ideas and policies affecting women under Soviet communism and Italian fascism.*

The policies women experienced under Soviet communism and Italian fascism were similar in the sense that these policies tended to promote political repression and paternalistic attitudes about marriage and childbearing.

In the Soviet Union, women were encouraged to embody the goal of the "Soviet Woman"—a counterpart to the "Soviet Man," newly conceived human beings that would populate the Communist party. The Bolsheviks made it easier for women to obtain divorces, legalized abortion in 1920, and removed religious sanction as a requirement for marriage. Women were encouraged to work and given some protections in the workplace. Consequently, women advanced in the Communist party, though they were rarely given the same opportunities for promotion and impact as men. In the 1930s, the Soviet government reversed many of its policies regarding women and families. Suddenly women experienced greater repression and government control over policies pertaining to marriage, childbearing, and sexuality. Abortion became illegal, and divorce became more difficult for women. Some educational opportunities for women remained. However, primarily women were responsible for raising their families—and for coping with the failing economy of the Soviet Union, which made it difficult to find food to put on the table.

Under the Fascist regime of Mussolini, women were not allowed to use contraception or to seek out abortions. In fact, women were seen simply as child bearers, and one of the most important elements of Mussolini's governmental policy was increasing the Italian population for the good of the Italian state. Fascism promoted the idea that women's responsibility was to rear and raise children to support the state. As in the case of the Soviet Union, women were not prohibited from working, and in fact a significant number of women did continue to work. However, the Fascist government passed laws that discouraged women's success in the workplace and effectively kept them in lower-level jobs. Over time, the representation of women in the workplace in Italy declined dramatically, and women became increasingly linked to their responsibilities in the home.

The policies regarding women and family that were developed initially by the Soviet government stand in marked contrast to later Soviet policies. However, these later policies (in effect during the 1930s) were notably similar to those put forth by Italian Fascists during the same era. In both the Communist and the Fascist society, women faced not only paternalistic ideas about marriage, childbearing, child rearing, and family, but also widespread political repression.